The German Historical School and European Economic Thought

T0270836

The financial crisis of 2008 has revived interest in economic scholarship from a historical perspective. The most in-depth studies of the relationship between economics and history can be found in the work of the so-called German Historical School (GHS). The influence of the GHS in the US and Britain has been well documented, but far less has been written on the rest of Europe.

This volume studies the interconnection between economic thought and economic policy from the mid-nineteenth century to the interwar period. It examines how the school's ideas spread and were interpreted in different European countries between 1850 and 1930, analyzing its legacies in these countries. In doing so, the book is able to trace the interconnection between economic thought and economic policy, adding new voices to the debate on the diffusion of ideas and flow of knowledge. This book identifies issues related to topics such as nationalism and cosmopolitanism in the history of ideas and clarifies themes in policy making that are still currently debated. These include monetary policy and benefits of free trade for all parties involved in international exchanges.

This book will be of great interest to those who study history of economic thought, economic theory and political economy.

José Luís Cardoso is a research professor at the Institute of Social Sciences, University of Lisbon, Portugal.

Michalis Psalidopoulos is a professor at the Department of Economics, University of Athens, and chairman of the Board and scientific director of the Centre for Planning and Economic Research, Athens, Greece.

Routledge Studies in the History of Economics

The German Historical School and European Economic Thought

Edited by
José Luís Cardoso and
Michalis Psalidopoulos

Routledge
Taylor & Francis Group

LONDON AND NEW YORK

First published 2016 by Routledge

2 Park Square, Milton Park, Abingdon, Oxfordshire OX14 4RN
52 Vanderbilt Avenue, New York, NY 10017

*Routledge is an imprint of the Taylor & Francis Group,
an informa business*

First issued in paperback 2019

British Library Cataloguing in Publication Data
A catalogue record for this book is available from the British Library.

Library of Congress Cataloging-in-Publication Data
The German historical school and European economic thought /
   edited by José Luís Cardoso and Michalis Psalidopoulos.
      pages cm
   1. Historical school of economics. 2. Economics—Europe—
History. I. Cardoso, José Luís, editor. II. Psalidopoulos,
M. (Michales), editor.
   HB97.G475 2015
   330.15′42—dc23
   2015022106

ISBN: 978-1-138-94050-5 (hbk)
ISBN: 978-0-367-87462-9 (pbk)

Typeset in Times New Roman
by Apex CoVantage, LLC

Contents

Contributors

António Almodovar is a full professor at the Faculdade de Economia, Universidade do Porto, and head of Cef.up, a research unit on economics and finance. Recent publications include a chapter for the *Oxford Handbook of Christianity and Economics* (edited by Paul Oslington) and a forthcoming paper in the *European Journal for the History of Economic Thought* on political economy and the modern view as reflected in the history of economic thought.

Jesús Astigarraga is a full professor at the Department of Structure and Economic History of the University of Zaragoza. His research interest has focused on the history of Spanish and European economic thought, with particular emphasis on the eighteenth century. He is author of a wide number of articles in the leading journals of the history of economic thought and modern history as well as author of monographs, among which are *Luces y republicanismo: Economía y Política en las "Apuntaciones a Genovesi" de Ramón de Salas* (Centro de Estudios Constitucionales, 2011), *L'Économie Politique et la sphère publique dans le débat des Lumières* (Collection de la Casa de Velázquez, 2013) or *The Spanish Enlightenment Revisited* (Voltaire Foundation, 2015).

Vladimir Avtonomov is a professor and scientific supervisor of the Faculty of Economic Sciences (National Research University Higher School of Economics in Moscow) and a section head of the Institute of World Economy and International Relations of the Russian Academy of Sciences. He is a corresponding member of the Russian Academy of Sciences. His research interests include problems of economic methodology, such as models of man and the role of abstraction in economic science, and the history of Western and Russian economics. He translated and edited Russian editions of many classical works, including Schumpeter's *Theory of Economic Development, Capitalism, Socialism, and Democracy, History of Economic Analysis* and *Ten Great Economists*, and works of Eucken, Blaug and others. He is the editor of one of the best-known Russian textbooks on the history of economic thought, the periodic almanac "Istoki" (The Sources), devoted to economic history and the history and methodology of economics.

José Luís Cardoso is a research professor and director of the Institute of Social Sciences of the University of Lisbon. He is author and editor of several books on the Portuguese history of economic thought from a comparative perspective, with special emphasis on the study of the processes of diffusion and assimilation of economic ideas. He has published articles in the main international journals on the history of economic thought. His research interests also include economic history and methodology of economics. He is the general editor of the series Classics of Portuguese Economic Thought (30 volumes), cofounder of the *European Journal of the History of Economic Thought* and coeditor of the e-journal *Portuguese History*.

Benny Carlson is a professor of economic history at the School of Economics and Management, Lund University. He has published a number of books and articles on the history of economic ideas, on economic, monetary and social policies and on the economic integration of immigrants. Some of these writings have focused on the spread of ideas between Germany, the US and Sweden, some have focused on the US (welfare capitalism, social engineering, institutionalism, deregulation, welfare reform) and some, of course, on Sweden.

Günther K. Chaloupek, Dr. iur., MA, was director of the economic research department of the Austrian Chamber of Labour from 1986 to 2013; member of the Advisory Council for Economic and Social Affairs; vice president of the Government Debt Committee, retired December 2013; and the author/editor of books on economic policy, history and theory, including *Die Ökonomik der Arbeiterbewegung zwischen den Weltkriegen* (6 vols., 2006–2011). He wrote many articles (in German and in English) in journals and contributions to books in the field of history of economic theory and economic policy.

Guido Erreygers (1959) is a professor of economics at the University of Antwerp. He obtained his PhD from the University of Paris X – Nanterre. In recent years, his main fields of research have been the history of economic thought, linear production models and measurement of socioeconomic inequality of health. He has published widely in international journals. He has edited or coedited seven books, including *The Origins of Universal Grants: An Anthology of Historical Writings on Basic Capital and Basic Income* (with John Cunliffe; Palgrave Macmillan, 2004), *The Analysis of Linear Economic Systems: Father Maurice Potron's Pioneering Works* (with Christian Bidard; Routledge, 2010) and *Inherited Wealth, Justice and Equality* (with John Cunliffe; Routledge, 2013).

Vitantonio Gioia is a full professor of history of economic thought (University of Salento), former dean at the Faculty of Political Sciences (University of Macerata) and coordinator of the International Doctorate "The European Tradition in Economic Thought", University of Macerata (2003–2010), and now director of the Department of History, Society and Human Studies (University of Salento). His main research topics are Marxian and classical economics, the

German Historical School of economics, history of Italian economics, utopian thought and political economy and business cycle theories.

Georgy Gloveli is a professor of the National Research University Higher School of Economics in Moscow. He is the author of several books and articles on the history of Russian economic and social thought from a comparative perspective, with special emphasis on such aspects as the distinguishing features of reception of Western economic schools in Russia, Russian conceptions of economic evolution and the elements of geopolitics and geoeconomics in Russian political economy. His research interests include reinterpretation of Russian economic history and revaluation of economic schools in a context of the world-system approach. He is the author-compiler of the anthology *Russian Writers on the Economy* (Moscow, 2013) and author of a new Russian textbook on economic history (Moscow, 2014).

Harald Hagemann is a professor of economic theory at the University of Hohenheim, Stuttgart, Germany. He is also a life member of Clare Hall, University of Cambridge. In 1999/2000 he was Theodor Heuss Professor at the Graduate Faculty of Political and Social Sciences at the New School for Social Research in New York. He formerly taught at the Universities of Bremen and Kiel, the Free University of Berlin, and as visiting professor at the Universities of Bologna, Graz, Linz, Lyon 2, Nice, Paris I Pantheon-Sorbonne, Strasbourg and Sydney. His main research covers growth and structural change, technological change and employment, business cycle theory and the emigration of German-speaking economists in the Nazi period. He was president of the European Society for the History of Economic Thought during 2010–2012. Since 2013 he has been the chairman of the Keynes-Gesellschaft.

Nikolay Nenovsky is a professor at the University of Picardie, Amiens. Previously he was a professor at the University of Orleans and University of World and National Economy in Sofia, and served as a member of Bulgarian Central Bank Governing Council. His area of research is monetary theory and policy, monetary history and history of monetary theories, as well as history of economic thought in general. He is the author of books on money (in Bulgarian) and articles in reputable international journals. He is a founder of South-East European Monetary History Network.

Eyüp Özveren is a professor in the Department of Economics of the Middle East Technical University in Ankara, Turkey. He teaches history of economic thought, institutional economics and economic history. He has widely published in English as well as Turkish on the history of Ottoman and Turkish economic thought. He is particularly specialized in nineteenth- and twentieth-century economic thought. He is interested in the dissemination of economic ideas in general and in the Mediterranean world in particular. He is among the founding members of the Initiative for Economic Thought network in Turkey, which organizes annual workshops and puts out a book series. His recent work explores the structural affinities between economics and literature as well delineating economic ideas embedded in literature.

Pencho D. Penchev is an associate professor at the University of National and World Economy, Sofia. He is the author of several books on the Bulgarian economic history and papers on the history of Bulgarian economic thought, with special emphasis on the study of the processes of diffusion and assimilation of economic ideas. He is also the editor of a textbook, *Introduction to Economic History* (in Bulgarian).

Jean-Pierre Potier is an emeritus professor of economics at the University Lumière-Lyon 2 and a member of the CNRS research staff *Triangle – Action, discours, pensée politique et économique*. He is the author of numerous essays concerning French and Italian economic thought in the nineteenth and twentieth century. He is one of the editors of the *Oeuvres économiques complètes* of Auguste and Léon Walras (14 volumes) and of the *Oeuvres complètes* of Jean-Baptiste Say (four volumes).

Michalis Psalidopoulos is a professor of the history of economic thought in the Department of Economics, University of Athens, and, since June 2015, Alternate Executive Director at the International Monetary Fund, Washington D. C. He was a Fulbright fellow at Duke, a Stanley J. Seeger fellow at Princeton, a visiting research professor at King's College, London, and Constantine G. Karamanlis Professor at the Fletcher School of Law and Diplomacy, Tufts University. His research focuses on national traditions in the history of economics and the relation between economic thought and economic policy. His latest book is *The History of the Bank of Greece, 1928–2008* (Athens, 2014) (in Greek). He has also published articles in *History of Political Economy*, *The European Journal for the History of Economic Thought* and *History of Economic Ideas*.

Evert Schoorl was the director of graduate studies at the University of Groningen. His research interests are classical political economy and the history of Dutch economic thought. He wrote his dissertation on the economics of J. B. Say (1980) and published a biography of the latter (Routledge, 2013). He was the researcher/editor of the autobiography of the former OECD secretary-general Emile van Lennep (1991, English translation 1998).

Yorgos Stassinopoulos is an assistant professor of economics at Panteion University of Athens, Department of International European and Area Studies. His earlier research includes economic policy, monetary economics and history of economic thought; his current research interests focus on the postwar economic policy in Greece, European political economy and international political economy. He published *Monetary Theory and Policy in 19th-Century Greece* and *The Rhetoric of Development: Economic Ideas and Economic Policy in Greece during the Reconstruction Period, 1944–1952* (both in Greek and published by Gutenberg). He is currently working on a monograph on the economic policy of the European Union.

Bert Tieben is head of the unit for competition and regulation policy at SEO Economic Research (University of Amsterdam). He also teaches economic thought in historical perspective at Amsterdam University College. His dissertation is entitled *The Concept of Equilibrium in Different Economic Traditions* (Edward Elgar, 2012). He specializes in the history of economic regulation and the dynamics of conflict and cooperation between schools of thought in economics. He is coeditor of the Dutch e-journal for political economy, *TPEdigitaal*.

Maarten Van Dijck (1975) studied history and international politics at the University of Leuven. His PhD was on the influence of classical political economy on Belgian economic policy between 1830 and 1884. His research interests are the public role of economists in nineteenth-century Belgium, the influence of economic ideas in public discourse and politics, the popularization of economic science and the Belgian economist Gustave de Molinari. He is currently a researcher at the Flemish Heritage Agency.

Juan Zabalza is an associate professor at the Faculty of Economics of the University of Alicante, where he teaches history of economic thought, economic history and international economics. His research in the field of the history of economic thought gives particular emphasis to the international spread of economic ideas, the popularization of political economy and the institutionalization of economics, topics on which he has published monographs and articles in reputed Spanish and international journals.

Introduction

José Luís Cardoso and Michalis Psalidopoulos

Purpose

The financial crisis of 2008 has revived interest in economic scholarship from a historical perspective. Having laid for a long while emphasis on model building and general equilibrium approaches as tools to explain the workings of the economic system, economists are increasingly aware of the historical and evolutionary explanations of the workings of complex processes as economic meltdowns, economic policy making, the power of vested interests in the economy, the aims of political elites and the formation of institutions and public opinion (out of many examples, see Acemoglou & Robinson, 2012; Reinhart & Rogoff, 2009). Indeed, the historical approach to economic problems has yielded important insights, enriching knowledge and challenging perceived wisdom (see, among others, Burgin, 2012; Gorton, 2012; James, 2012; Reinert, 2011).

For historians of economics the need to study economics as a social science, to use the history of their subject as a tool is a self-evident truth, their daily interest and preoccupation. This occurs despite the fact that the history of economic thought has long ceased to be of interest in the mainstream study of economics, as has economic history, with the possible exception of cliometrics and the "new institutionalism". The interplay between economics and history has been discussed in many writings of economists. It is found in Adam Smith's *Wealth of Nations*, but mostly in the work of German economists from the mid-nineteenth century up to World War I (see Brandt, 1992; Winkel, 1977), the members of the so-called German Historical School (GHS), whose influence in the US (Bateman, 2011; Dorfman, 1955; Herbst, 1965; Myles, 1959) and in Britain (Koot, 1980, 2008) has already been documented, whereas for Japan and the rest of Europe, despite scattered references (see, e.g., Heinonen, 2002), there remains a void for a detailed study that waits to be filled.

The purpose of the present volume is to address the question of the diffusion of ideas and teachings related to the GHS in a series of European countries and to search for the legacy of the GHS in these countries. In other words we aim to study the interconnection between economic thought and economic policy from the mid-nineteenth century to the interwar, with the aim to trace the influence of the GHS in a series of European countries that were not the focus of scholarly attention until now. We aim to identify issues related to topics such as nationalism and cosmopolitanism in the history of ideas and clarify themes in policy making that are still currently debated, such as monetary policy and benefits of free trade for all parties involved in international exchanges. We will refer to major texts that influenced European economic thinking greatly, but we will not insist on textual exegesis and interpretation of theoretical transfers between Germany and the rest of Europe. Instead we will focus on processes of dissemination of economic ideas and circumstances advocating the adoption of certain economic paradigms. By using a comparative approach we hope to arrive at a new and fresh approach to debates about the flow of economic ideas and channels of dissemination as translations and the diffusion, the appropriation and the emulation of knowledge.

Our approach presupposes familiarity with the study of liberalism in Europe in the nineteenth century (De Ruggiero, 1959) and the efforts of many European economists to blend their own version of liberalism with ideas related with protectionism, social reform, nation building and growth enhancing policies and so forth (see the papers in Psalidopoulos & Mata, 2002). The present introduction sets the stage of our project and is structured as follows. We first introduce our initial motivation and continue with a chapter on the clash between the GHS and classical political economy. We continue with a section on the relevance of our investigation for present-day historiography. In a further step we discuss recent debates about the GHS in literature. Finally we reflect on the dissemination of economic ideas and introduce our questions and the individual chapters of the book.

Relevance

German economists of the early nineteenth century espoused initially with enthusiasm Adam Smith's teachings. When, however, the classical system was codified by Ricardo and his followers, dissent among the advocates of the cameralist and administrative tradition in Germany started getting articulated. This gave rise to the historical approach in economic reasoning, an approach related to German "Staatskunst", the art of conducting the business of the state. The main objection of German authors to classicism was the dismissal of ethical judgments and values for the benefit of an analysis that narrowed down economic action to selfishness and egoism. Furthermore the fact that Germany became a customs union in 1834 and reached political unification under Prussia in 1871 encouraged until then disunity and particularism among German economists. The latter focused on the national past, through the study of the evolution of law at first, with the creation of a historical school of law as an outcome, and then through the push for empirical research that distinguished German research from the classical one as it offered empiricism and induction in place of deduction. This led to the formation of a distinct GHS in economics.

The German economists of the late nineteenth century rejected in their majority the existence of universal laws in economics and accused the classical approach of misusing abstract reasoning, and of promoting an inadequate psychological foundation of economic action. They were in favor of social reforms and accepted state intervention to a far larger extent than the classicals did. Finally they were in their vast majority not committed free traders. One can argue that for those economists who formed the core of the GHS, empirical investigations and economic history were more important than theoretical work and the promotion of economic analysis.

Of course, the historical approach was not an entirely German phenomenon. Advocates of historical analysis, dissenters of the classical political economy tradition existed all over Europe. They also existed in Britain, but could not, however, reverse the dominance of classical and later neoclassical economics in academia and in public discourse there, whereas in Germany the historical approach remained dominant until 1914.

Many studies have been published concerning the GHS as a whole or its individual authors, on its discourse and influence (out of many, see Backhaus, 1993; Balabkins, 1988; Grimmer-Solem, 2003; Hagemann, 2012a; Nau & Schefold, 2002; Shionoya, 2001, 2005). On the other hand these studies paid little attention to the interconnection between professionalization processes, public policy agendas and the institutional framework of the wide impact the GHS was able to create for many decades in countries outside Germany. Newborn countries that became independent in the nineteenth century in Northern as well as in Southern Europe, countries that needed economic theory and economic policy arguments that would assist them in their efforts to grow and prosper, showed sympathy with the German paradigm, and the aforementioned studies have not focused on these latecomer nations. They also tend to neglect the nowadays very relevant issue of European cultural identity, stemming among other things from a common approach in the history of ideas, a topic that has been very little scrutinized in current historical studies.

Perceived wisdom in the history of economics says that the GHS had its distant roots in the work of Friedrich List and was dominant in academia and in public administration in Germany from the mid-nineteenth century to the immediate post–World War I period (Eisermann, 1956; Schumpeter, 1954; Screpanti & Zamagni, 1993; Spiegel, 1991). Although some interpreters have expressed reservations about a chronological distinction within the school (see Lindenfeld, 1993), there is a tacit agreement on the differentiation between two generations of the GHS, the "older" and the "younger". Both personified the mainstream opposition to the British classical political economy and, later, to the neoclassical school, by taking the view that history was the key source of knowledge about human actions and on economic matters. Even Marxism, another opposing view to the classical paradigm, practiced "historical materialism" and shared with the GHS, despite major differences, a propensity to use history as the ultimate test of any economic theory.

Historicism was a mental attitude in Europe, closely connected with growing nationalisms in many countries that put history at the center of a combination of all forms of intellectual life. According to this approach, classical economics was considered responsible for many social evils in Britain, such as pauperism, poverty and inhuman working conditions. These evils should not occur in other countries. The point of economists pursuing a historical inquiry in their investigations was not to take the situation that sprang out of the industrial revolution as natural and given, but to try to shape it. Economics had according to the critics of the abstract, classical method to be closer to existing realities and provide advice on how to change things. Economic man with his profit-maximizing behavior did not account for law, tradition, habits and national moods of thought. Therefore distance from abstract theory and an inclination towards empirical research that started mainly in Germany were welcome. Economic processes were studied here from an evolutionist perspective. State action was for this approach not an unwelcome evil but a must. In place of egoism, utilitarianism and causality, German economists took an ethical stance towards all things economic (Tribe, 1995).

Indeed, the GHS was a resort of anticlassical economists of the period after 1850. If we look at this period in context we find John Stuart Mill recanting the wages fund theory in 1868, leaving his followers in limbo. Two years later, in 1870, in a famous lecture before the British Academy, William Stanley Jevons lamented the disarray of British economic science. In 1871 Prussia won the war against France and emerged as a major economic power in continental Europe. Its economic success was attributed to the qualities of its educational system with the result of an influx of foreign students in the country to study, among other sciences, economics. Then followed, in 1873, the Vienna crisis, the first global financial crisis, a crisis with contagious effects, for which the disintegrating classical school had no clear-cut explanation (Lindenfeld, 1997).

In this climate of the rejection of the old and in the search for new principles, the first neoclassical treatises were written. But views espousing the historical method were also circulated and in fact won at that juncture hearts and minds of most European intellectuals for the following twenty years (Takebayashi, 2003), anticipating debates on the "soul of economics" that would become more accurate throughout the interwar period (see Yonay, 1998). The GHS pioneered social policy, as this particular policy concern gained international attention due to the emergence of universal male voting and of the growing presence of labor/ socialist parties in European parliaments. Its members founded a professional scientific association to discuss economic policy issues and to influence public opinion (out of the many existing histories see Hagemann, 2001). It is therefore fair to say that the GHS constituted an alternative for economic research, due to its openness in research and in policy advice. Furthermore, latecomers in development could find in the GHS a different agenda for research and economic reforms, different than the one based on the allegedly universal principles of classical political economy; these included, as is well-known, a condition known as the stationary state, an uninspiring vision for the less developed European economies.

In short, the GHS espoused the view that history was the key source of knowledge about human actions and economic matters. It offered an alternative to the existing classical doctrine on many fronts: on method, on the necessity of social reform and on the need of promoting economic growth and development. Fiscal, monetary and commercial policies were, for historical economists, instruments for the promotion of government aims and targets. GHS economists pioneered empirical work in economics and studied the business cycle. They also stressed the importance of statistics and conducted empirical economic investigations. They were hostile to Marxism, the other emerging economic doctrine of the period after 1883, and tended to underestimate from a scientific point of view what neoclassicism was about. Alfred Marshall on the opposing side rightly saw the GHS as an enemy for his "economics" and undermined it in Britain (Maloney, 1999).

It is also worth mentioning the proximity of the GHS with economists belonging to the institutionalist tradition, especially as regards the awareness of the centrality of law and normative rules explaining the functioning of human societies and their political organization. In this sense, they contributed to building up a new approach to the legal environment and political context associated with the diversity of economic action (Pearson, 1997).

Finally the GHS was open to social engineering for fast growth. It introduced for emerging economies a stages of development theory, an ideology of nation building and growth, addressing itself to the nation and to all social classes. It did not employ the analytical device of three antagonistic social classes in society. In this context protectionism was not simply a departure from free trade. It was in line with liberal principles of governance and a tool to shape society by fostering its developmental potential.

Reaction to classical economics

The reaction against political economy in the three last decades of the nineteenth century cannot be dissociated from the historical national contexts that did not favor the acceptance of its main tenets and the rigidity of its assumptions.

Furthermore, the intellectual milieu was favorable to the acceptance of a historical approach to economic phenomena, which was not in itself an exclusive prerogative of the German school. When using or quoting German authors in support of their arguments, European political economists were merely using rhetoric devices to make their proposals sound and acceptable.

Three main lines of argument proved useful, as Bob Coats summed up for the English case:

> They [the historists] questioned the scientific status of political economy and the purpose of the subject; they protested against the narrowness of its scope; and they complained of the excessive reliance on the abstract-deductive method of reasoning, and the dogmatic application of conclusions to policy.
>
> (Coats, 1954: 221; see also Coats, 1993)

The questioning of the scientific status of political economy was largely motivated by the political implications of a laissez-faire program and strong individualistic beliefs that could not be welcome as proper science. Indeed, "the privileged standing of political economy was comprehensively called into doubt in the 1870s and 80s as a result of several intellectual as well as practical developments" (Collini, 1983: 249). The benefits of a closer relationship with other scientific disciplines were due to the very nature of economic phenomena that required for many authors a variety of angles and approaches, including non-economic ones.

As regards the underlying method of economic science, the criticism put forward was based on the refusal to accept that a same general theory and a same set of rigid conceptual categories could be applicable to different concrete situations, in terms of both time and place. Therefore, methodological disputes indicated that more attention should be given to the observation of facts and to the method of induction in order to conclude on the existence (or not) of regularities in economic and social life (Blaug, 1992).

According to the defenders of the historical approach, political economy could not survive as confined to a logical, formal deductive enterprise with no relations with the actual facts of real economic life and with no concern with the discussion of current affairs. It had to be based on empirical data and subject to the examination of statistical regularities. By doing it, through attention given to both the historical background and the policy implications of facts observed, political economy was gaining a historical mood that invited an innovative approach to social phenomena. Political economy was making the best efforts to become "historical economics" (Tribe, 1995), or "historical political economy" (Grimmer-Solem & Romani, 1999).

The comparative approach to societies that find themselves in different stages of development was a precondition for the application of any basic principles whose validity was taken for granted by the practitioners of economic science. Through that type of approach it would be possible to emphasize how different historical situations could call for diversified application of, allegedly, universal laws. The acceptance of economic doctrines and principles as appropriate to the historical conditions of a certain time should not mean that they kept being adequate and applicable to new circumstances and different kinds of practical problems.

The fact that different critics shared a common ground as opponents to orthodox political economy did not mean that they were able to build together a new alternative scientific discipline, or a new and universal set of economic principles (cf. Koot, 1980). Though the outcome of the historicist approach did not result in a substantial change of the construction of mainstream economics, it gave stimulus to autonomous advances in economic history and in a global science of society grounded on positivist sociology. Economics did not become a historical science, but the historical school made important contributions to the understanding of the problems dealt with by politicians and economists (cf. Kadish, 1989).

One of the key issues at stake was to understand how the existing economic system, capitalism, that had created progress and contributed to economic welfare for the middle classes, could not spread out its beneficial effects to society as a whole and could not extend similar positive effects to other countries. Therefore, critics of cosmopolitan political economy were also defenders of a new approach to economic reforms and state intervention, considering that markets acting by themselves could not provide alone the riches needed to sustain basic equilibria in society (Beiser, 2012).

The social question was obviously a key issue for the authors associated with the GHS, concerned as they were with the potential disruptive consequences of the rapid developments of industrial society and the radical changes at the work-place. Thus, the convergence of opinions of authors belonging to different doctrinal families or schools of thought was a consequence of the common problems serving as a starting point to justify the need of social and political reform in the national organization of economic life. The national element was only a part of a wider concern with the social question (cf. Nau, 2000). The same global convergence occurred with the interpretation of the enlarged functions of the state as the main provider and regulator of public policies aiming at social justice and a better distribution of wealth.

Dissemination of economics through German economics textbooks

The presence of German authors in European economic literature was made possible by different cultural vehicles – namely, those fostered by the strong influence of the German literature on history and law (cf. Hagemann & Rösch, 2012; Tribe, 1995). It is also worth referring to the diffusion and acceptance of the standard economic textbooks produced in Germany throughout the period 1825–1875 – namely, those by Karl Rau (1832), Wilhelm Roscher (1843) and Albert Schäffle (1867). The French translations of Rau and Roscher were widespread in various European countries and proved essential for the institutionalization of the teaching of political economy, especially in law faculties. Theory, policy and public finance were the pillars of teaching economics as a social science.

The key notions transmitted by these German textbooks were essential to build up a theoretical critique of traditional classical-Ricardian political economy, since they offered arguments to show that it was possible to harmonize the classical theory of production and growth with a theory of value and distribution explained by individual demand and utility. Furthermore, it was precisely this attention paid to subjective motivations that is at the heart of the development of political economy in Germany by the mid-nineteenth century. As well summed up by Keith Tribe,

> This conception of economic action arising from the process by which humans satisfy their wants and needs, and in so doing constitute a realm of goods

out of a world of objects, is continuous with the standard definition of economic action that had emerged at the turn of the century in Germany.

(Tribe, 1995: 70)

Even though all European readers of Rau, Roscher and other members of the historical school may not have grasped the essential message that was well captured by Carl Menger and Alfred Marshall – as pointed out by Erich Streissler (1990), who labeled this influence as "the German protoneoclassical mood" – it is nevertheless clear that it was not necessary to fully adhere to the coherent program of the GHS in order to emphasize the weaknesses of classical political economy demonstrated by German authors at large.

In this context, the scattered, circumstantial or even loose references in European economic literature to German schools and traditions – being those in history, law or economics – gain a stronger meaning, as they serve to demonstrate that there was a common concern with a multiplicity of practical problems that justify the development of new theoretical and methodological approaches. The GHS may have existed in its full strength only in Germany. But it served as a mirror where the same critical points could be addressed and reflected. It served as a landmark for the development of political economy in different European national contexts as documented in the essays that make up the present volume. Many scholars, attracted by German economics textbooks, made the decision to visit Germany for graduate studies in person. Thus they formed in their majority an "army" of sympathizers of induction and of government regulation in the economy.

Historiographical dialogues and relevant questions

Although these issues underline the relevance of the GHS for current scholarship, there are further reasons to revisit the subject. Despite the fact that textbooks on the history of economics (Backhouse, 1985; Screpanti & Zamagni, 1993; Spiegel, 1991) have chapters of various lengths on the GHS, the standard things referred to by many scholars are grossly misleading. One example is the standard reference to GHS economists as "Kathedersozialisten", socialists of the chair. This associates German economists with socialism, an economic doctrine they didn't believe in; they simply sought a middle ground between pecuniary business interests demanding a laissez faire economic environment and Marxian revolutionary socialism. Another one is their identification with protectionism. But this is again very ambiguous, too. Whereas some of the GHS economists became protectionists and approved relevant legislation, having initially in their careers espoused free trade, others (e.g., Lujo Brentano) did not. It is therefore misleading and an oversimplification to label all German economists and the GHS as protectionist. Finally, and for reasons of taxonomic convenience, it is repeated that the GHS was important and dominant in Germany until 1933, whereas it had actually declined after 1918.

A fresh look at the GHS influence in Europe is needed in order to analyze its legacy from a contemporary perspective and to contribute to a better understanding of its relevance for policy making in various national contexts in the continent. This need stems out of contemporary debates surrounding the GHS. Erik Grimmer-Solem and Roberto Romani (1999) have argued, for instance, that there was no "school" based on German economic thinking, due to the diversity of approaches and the simultaneous existence of economists using history as an analytical tool of analysis in various non-German-speaking European countries. Similarly Heith Pearson (1999) dismissed the very idea of a GHS, on the basis of the lack of coherence and any spirit of community between German economists of the particular period. However, as it has been pointed out by Bruce Caldwell (2001) and others, certain schools in economics, like the mercantilists or the classical school of political economy, were not "schools" in the sense of closed "towers of faith" either. Were the Salamanca scholastics members of a school? What about the diversity and the difference between the members of the first neoclassical "school"? The fact that physiocracy may have been a school in the sense described earlier, with individual members promoting the same economic principles and promoting the same beliefs and values, can be attributed to the special cultural circumstances prevailing in prerevolutionary France at the time. These also explain the withering away of physiocracy after 1789.

We side with Keith Tribe in his view that the GHS has multiple meanings stemming out of differences registered in economic thinking, when we consider the spread of the school outside Germany (Tribe, 2000). Historicism was a brand of economic study that was imitated in different national settings. In the following chapters we start by considering the notion of a GHS as a heuristic device for taxonomic purposes, and we aim to clearly define what the GHS was about in different European countries. By focusing on economic policy we attempt to shed new light on a series of open questions in the literature. For us the GHS did exist, but it was not a closed shop with committed members and a "faith" in all things economic; it was about a belief in the historical method and the possibility of extracting developmental laws from historical experience. We will, therefore, contribute with the present volume to a refinement of the definition about the existence of a "GHS" in the history of economics.

Europe in the late nineteenth century was in a stage of continuous transformation. Great empires, such as the Russian, the Habsburg and the Ottoman, were trying to cope with the economic consequences of the expansion of the world capitalist system. Other countries had engaged in nation building, such as Greece after 1830, Italy after 1861 and Bulgaria after 1878. The diversity of country experiences and case studies makes it impossible to follow a rigid approach throughout the present volume. A not exhaustive list of variations of this broad theme, to be addressed in the individual chapters that follow, includes:

- Through which channels did the process of dissemination from Germany to other places in Europe occur?
- What was disseminated? The method, the rationale, the policy message, aspects of certain policy endorsements?

- Who were the main characters involved in the receiving side, what did they write and how did they disseminate historicism? Were they academics, intellectuals, publicists?
- How long did the influence of the GHS remain strong? How did it come to dominate, if it did, and when did it start to decline?
- What were the main economic policy issues in the countries where the tradition of the GHS got hold? Was legislation in these countries influenced by the teaching of the GHS?
- Are there particular authors in each of the countries deserving special attention for the innovative character of their contributions to spreading the message of the GHS?
- How can the legacy of the GHS in Europe be best defined?

Our case studies

Throughout the second half of the nineteenth century and the early decades of the twentieth century, European countries were facing new economic problems whose resolution implied the challenge of the usual way of dealing with social realities. The references to historical and cultural backgrounds to understand economic reality, as well as to address policy responses to economic and financial problems, were taken as a condition to improve the knowledge of changing societies. The richness of debates and fights among historians, economists and sociologists alike was not only a proof of intellectual vitality. It was also the revelation of the need to definitely include a new dimension in the study of economic phenomena, one that could not avoid the mention of culture and history as a means to capture the essence of economic behavior at both the individual and the institutional levels (cf. Bruhns, 2004). The dialogue on values and traditions was a common feature of the development of economic reasoning in the countries considered in this volume.

The book begins with *Austria*, more precisely the German-speaking parts of the Austrian monarchy, the closest German neighbor, where, despite Schumpeter's claim to the contrary, a significant influence of the GHS can be said to have existed. As Günther Chaloupek explains, Catholicism, realism and logical positivism were the currents of thought, when academics as Karl-Theodor von Inama-Sternegg and Carl Grünberg plowed the seeds of historical-empirical inquiry. The study of economic history was promoted not least by well-known later liberal economists, such as Karl Pribram. Even Carl Menger was not hostile to economic history. As Chaloupek argues, it was Schmoller's "extremism" in Menger's eyes that he found worth fighting against, whereas Schumpeter was the great Austrian economist who managed to bridge economic history with economic theory in a way that led to the diminishing of any Austrian historical school of economics.

The chapter on *France*, authored by Jean-Pierre Potier, shows that though not well grounded in methodological terms, the influence of the GHS was more relevant than traditionally admitted. In fact, the alleged hostility of French liberal economists towards nationalist and protectionist ideas did not prevent a critical assimilation of economic policy orientations – namely, concerning labor legislation. The appeal to develop statistical, empirical elements supporting economic analysis should also be taken as one of the features developed by French economists in convergence with the efforts of the German school. The frequency of quotations and the high number of translations of canonical GHS texts prove at least that the French environment was receptive to the circulation of German economic literature.

The intellectual milieu in *Belgium* was naturally open and favorable to the assimilation of political economy texts produced by French authors. It is therefore remarkable, as stressed by Guido Erreygers and Maarten Van Dijck, that Belgian economists took the GHS teachings as a main source for the development of economic analysis in their country throughout the period 1870–1914. The interest in empirical research using historical data and statistical tools was one of the features that Belgian economists and historians learned during their frequent stays at German universities. The inspiration for the development of an institutional framework with capacity to promote innovative research and policy orientations is also worth referring to as one of the most enduring legacies of the GHS in Belgium.

The *Netherlands* provides another example of a country that due to Schumpeter's far-reaching statement is supposed to have been immune to historical economics. As Bert Tieben and Evert Schoorl, however, convincingly show, Protestant social thought and the debate on poor relief elevated Professor H.P.G. Quack to the status of the first historical Dutch economist, almost before the historical school debate started up. Posts at the state universities remained in the hands of followers of the classical paradigm, because of the centralized appointing system. Historical economics was popular in public opinion and political debates. Tieben and Schoorl follow the debate between orthodox and historical economists as it evolved from its beginnings to its intensification and to a rift that was impossible to reconcile despite the efforts of academics, such as, among others, H.B. Greven in Leyden. In the political arena things were more pronounced: the younger liberal MP Sam van Houten, a follower of the historical school (and a rejected candidate for the Leyden chair), initiated the first bill regulating child labor. Economists like Nicolaas G. Pierson and C. A. Verrijn and the Protestant political leader Abraham Kuyper left their mark in heated debates around social reform and its necessity for Dutch society. Only after 1900, in the two Amsterdam universities (the one municipal, the other Protestant) followers of the historical school were appointed to economics chairs. A final stage of symbiosis set in, with historical economics losing ground to the rigid neoclassicism dominant at the university level in the interwar period.

In *Italy*, important economists such as Ferrara, Pantaleoni and Pareto championed a militant opposition against the antitheoretical and antiliberal features of the GHS. However, there were also strong reasons to emulate the German model of economic growth and to develop new fields of economic inquiry. The new methodological and empirical tools were also acclaimed, as Vitantonio Gioia points out in the chapter on the Italian case. But maybe the main reason to explain a somehow reduced adherence to the GHS was the propensity offered by the Italian cultural and political environment to accept the role of historical and empirical facts to explain the real economy and the inadequacy of preconceived abstract models. The acknowledgment of the role of the state and the relevance of economic policies to foster economic growth complete the global framework to explain the assimilation of the GHS in Italy.

Political motivation is a strong factor explaining also the reception of German authors in *Spain*. In their contribution to this volume Jesús Astigarraga and Juan Zabalza give particular emphasis to the roots of this influence going back to the success of the cameralist influence in Spain in the late eighteenth century. It is likely that this powerful influence is at the origin of a long-lasting presence of German influences in the discussion of public administration and public finance issues. But it was above all the influence of national political economy in the Listian vein that paved the way to the scattered, though meaningful, presence of the successive generations of the GHS in Spain, especially in Catalonia, and particularly in relation to the design of protectionist economic policies. Another intellectual condition explaining the spread of German traditions was the extraordinary impact that Karl Krause's ethical critique of classical political economy had on Spanish authors of the second half of the nineteenth century.

A similar process of adherence through a variety of German sources is to be found in *Portugal*, as explained by António Almodovar and José Luís Cardoso. German historicist and law traditions were particularly active at the University of Coimbra, where the main supporters of the GHS are to be found throughout the second half of the nineteenth century. The proximity of policy orientations shared by both historicists and supporters of Katheder socialism serves to explain the instrumental nature of influences that were operated to criticize the universal dogmas of classical political economy and the need to rely on history to understand the opportunities of economic development with strong state intervention. Here again, we find that the main motivation to accept some of the tenets of the GHS had a political nature.

To complete the picture of the reception of GHS in Southern European countries, *Greece* offers another example of the use of economic doctrines for catching up and promoting economic modernization, especially during the first decades of the twentieth century. Michalis Psalidopoulos and Yorgos Stassinopoulos emphasize the role of German influences in the shaping of a national strategy of economic development put forward by Greek authors who had learned their economics at German universities. The influence of these economists was long-lived as they dominated economic discourse in the country until the mid-1960s, whereas the historical method was seen as an important tool of analysis even by liberal economists, such as Andreas Andréadès and Xenophon Zolotas. The attention paid to historical factors, such as the warlike conditions in the 1910s, and to practical problems to be solved, such as the refugee problem after 1922, was, of course, another sign of sharing common concerns. But the use of German references of authority served the basic purpose of gradually escaping from liberal doctrines of the nineteenth century and smoothly moving to the defense of protectionism and state intervention as the chief conditions to promote economic sustainability and social tranquility in the long run.

In the case of *Turkey*, as Eyüp Özveren demonstrates, historicism entered the scene through the intermediation of Russia and in direct relation to the national economy approach espoused by the father of Turkish nationalism Ziya Gökalp. The case of the journal *Kadro* in the 1920s and various authors therein is discussed, as is their affiliation with Istanbul University, which assisted them in attacking from an authority perspective the more liberal academics of schools for public servants. Then in 1933 German émigré economists, such as Fritz Neumark, Wilhelm Röpke, Alexander Rüstow and others, brought into the country their own versions of historicism and liberalism, interacting with Turkish economists in the search for industrialization plans for their country. Özveren discusses the legacy of these German refugees in Turkey with detailed reference of various existing sources. Their bottom line is a relativist plea for understanding processes of dissemination of economic ideas.

When moving towards Northern European countries, one faces a comparable absence of a genuine school of thought faithful to the original precepts of the GHS. In the case of *Sweden*, presented in this volume by Benny Carlson, it is nevertheless clear that the permanence of Swedish authors in German universities, under the supervision of GHS disciples, was of an utmost importance to the development of new economic approaches during the three last decades of the nineteenth century. Not all of the Swedish authors of the period were thrilled by the advantages of the historical method. The fields of enquiry where they proved more receptive to the GHS lessons were those associated with the improvement of economic and social policies claiming for a stronger state intervention. The political message was a parallel motivation that could accommodate the conventional obedience to universally accepted principles of political economy.

The chapter on *Russia* by Vladimir Avtonomov and Georgy Gloveli follows the import of political economy since the times of the older GHS when Ivan Babst and Alexander Korsak adopted evolutionary and historical patterns of economic reasoning. At the peak of fame for the younger GHS Alexander Chuprov and Ivan Yanzul undertook together with other younger economists the task of continuing and modernizing the historist tradition in Russia. Avtonomov and Gloveli turn then their attention to Russian ministers of finance and to social policy makers as they espoused a similar approach in their everyday decisions. They also discuss Russian Marxism as well as two authors at the dawn of the twentieth century, Iosif Kulisher, an industrial, and Nikolay Oganovsky, an agricultural expert on Russian development, and their respective contributions.

Finally Nikolay Nenovsky and Pencho Penchev present the evolution of the GHS in *Bulgaria*. From independence to the end of World War I the most prominent Bulgarian economists were French-trained Grigor Nachovich, English-trained Ivan Geshov and German-trained Georgi Danailov, who brought in the country various strands of thought and a concern for the development and welfare of the Bulgarian people. World War I and its devastating effects for the country brought pluralism in economic approaches to the forefront for ultraliberals and Marxists. The careers and publications of Konstantin Bobchev, Alexander Tsankov and Ivan Kinkel are discussed and their work put into perspective as it marks the heyday of the influence of the GHS in the country.

Conclusions

The study of the dissemination and transmission of economic ideas is a complex issue (Cardoso, 2003; Goodwin & Holley, 1968; Spengler, 1970). Ideas are not commodities to be sold and bought for the purposes of trade, and their emergence does not simulate market processes where "[n]ew ideas are sold very much the way new automobiles are sold: by exaggerating their superiority over the older models" (Stigler, 1969: 222). Moreover, the logic of the history of ideas cannot entirely unfold by analyzing their meanings solely from a historical perspective (Bevir, 1999), since ideas are not only means for the comprehension and appreciation of reality founded on facts but also instruments and occasionally fighting devices against false perceptions of "reality", for the interpretation and arrangement of socioeconomic and political conditions, acting hence as normative guiding rules for the preservation or the transformation of the real world. Furthermore, the international diffusion of theories requires a complex historical and doctrinal approach that focuses more on which ideas dominate the intellectual field and their effects on social and political processes "underlying the transmission of ideas from culture to culture and from nation to nation" (Spengler, 1970: 133).

The foregoing reservations do not imply the impossibility of getting any historical meaning out of the emergence and propagation of ideas, but intend to demonstrate the limitations of the rationalist approaches that seek to reconstruct the birth and dissemination of historical objects and their true meaning on the basis of the available historical material, disregarding the inherent constraints that mine the field and make "any easy generalization difficult, even impossible" (Kurz, Nishizawa & Tribe, 2011: 3). The chapters in this volume, adopting a relativist stance, demonstrate that contrary to some existing sources, the GHS was quite influential even in countries that had a long academic tradition in abstract economic reasoning. Harald Hagemann's final chapter reflects on this topic and provides an overall assessment of this set of contributions.

As economic conditions prevailing in most less developed European countries were changing, it seems that the more in need of catching up, the more the historical method was put to use to work out strategies of deliberate industrialization and development in various countries. In the long run, however, neoclassicism prevailed, both on method and on the question of a value-free economics. This state of affairs was to be challenged after the Great Depression by Keynesianism. This is, however, a different chapter in the history of economic ideas and their diffusion.

References

Acemoglu, D. & Robinson J.A. (2012). *Why nations fail: The origins of power, prosperity, and poverty*. New York: Crown Business.

Backhaus, J. G. (ed.) (1993). *Gustav von Schmoller und die Probleme von heute*. Berlin: Duncker & Humblot.

Backhouse, R. (1985). *A history of modern economic analysis*. Oxford: Blackwell.

Balabkins, N.W. (1988). *Not by theory alone: The economics of Gustav von Schmoller and its legacy to America*. Berlin: Duncker & Hublot.

Bateman, B.W. (2011). German influences in the making of American economists 1885–1935, in H. D. Kurz, T. Nishizawa & K. Tribe (eds.), *The dissemination of economic ideas*. Cheltenham: Edward Elgar, 108–124.

Beiser, F. (2012*). The German historicist tradition*. Oxford: Oxford University Press.

Bevir, M. (1999). *The logic of the history of ideas*. Cambridge: Cambridge University Press.

Blaug, M. (1992). *The methodology of economics, or how economists explain*. Cambridge: Cambridge University Press.

Brandt, K. (1992). *Geschichte der deutschen Volkswirtschaftslehre*. Freiburg in Breisgau: Haufe.

Bruhns, H. (ed.) (2004). *Histoire et économie politique en Allemagne de Gustav Schmoller à Max Weber*. Paris: Editions de la Maison des sciences de l'homme.

Burgin, A. (2012). *The great persuasion: Reinventing free markets since the depression*. Cambridge, MA: Harvard University Press.

Caldwell, B. (2001). There really *was* a German Historical School of economics. *History of Political Economy*, 33(3), 649–654.

Cardoso, J.L. (2003). The international diffusion of economic thought, in W. Samuels, J. Biddle & J. Davis (eds.), *A companion to the history of economic thought*. Oxford: Blackwell, 622–633.

Coats, A.W. Bob (1954) [1992]. The historist reaction in English political economy, 1870–90. *Economica* (May). Reprinted in A. W. Coats, *On the history of economic thought: British & American economic essays*. London: Routledge, Volume 1, 220–230.

Coats, A.W. Bob (1993). Sociological aspects of British economic thought (ca. 1880–1930). *The sociology and professionalization of economics: British and American economic essays*, London: Routledge, Volume 2, 105–133.

Collini, S. (1983). Particular polities: Political economy and the historical method, in S. Collini, D. Winch & J. Burrow (eds.), *That noble science of politics: A study in nineteenth-century intellectual history*. Cambridge: Cambridge University Press, 247–275.

De Ruggiero, G. (1959). *The history of European liberalism*. Beacon Hill: Beacon Press.

Dorfman, J. (1955). The role of the German Historical School in American economic thought. *American Economic Review, Papers and Proceedings*, 45(2): 17–28.

Eisermann, G. (1956). *Die Grundlagen des Historismus in der deutschen Nationalökonomie*. Stuttgart: Enke.

Goodwin, C.D.W. & I.B. Holley Jr. (eds.) (1968). *The transfer of ideas: Historical essays*. Durham, NC: Duke University Press.

Gorton, G.B. (2012). *Misunderstanding financial crises: Why we don't see them coming*. Oxford: Oxford University Press.

Grimmer-Solem, E. (2003). *The rise of historical economics and social reform in Germany: 1864–1894*. Oxford: Oxford University Press.

Grimmer-Solem, E. & Romani, R. (1999). In search of full empirical reality: Historical political economy, 1870–1900. *European Journal of the History of Economic Thought*, 6(3): 333–364.

Hagemann, H. (2001). The Verein für Sozialpolitik from its foundation (1872) until World War I, in M. M. Augello & M.E.L. Guidi (eds.), *The spread of political economy and the professionalisation of economists: Economic societies in Europe, America and Japan in the nineteenth century*. London: Routledge, 152–175.

Hagemann, H. (2012). Heinrich Herkner: Inequality of income distribution, overcapitalization and underconsumption, in D. Besomi (ed.), *Crises and cycles in economic dictionaries and encyclopaedias*. London: Routledge, 361–373.

Hagemann, H. & Rösch, M. (2012). Economic textbooks in the German language area, in M. M. Augello & M.E.L. Guidi (eds.), *The economic reader: Textbooks, manuals and the dissemination of the economic sciences during the nineteenth and early twentieth centuries*. London: Routledge, 96–123.

Heinonen, V. (2002). The influence of the German Historical School in Finnish economic thought around the turn of the century, in M. Psalidopoulos & M. E. Mata (eds.), *Economic thought and policy in less developed Europe: The nineteenth century*. London: Routledge, 55–73.

Herbst, J. (1965). *The German Historical School in American scholarship: A study in the transfer of culture*. Ithaca, NY: Cornell University Press.

James, H. (2012). *Making the European monetary union*. Frankfurt: ECB and BIS.

Kadish, A. (1989). *Historians, economists and economic history*. London: Routledge.

Koot, G. M. (1980). English historical economics and the emergence of economic history in England. *History of Political Economy*, 12(2): 174–205.

Koot, G. M. (2008). *English historical economics, 1870–1926*. Cambridge: Cambridge University Press.

Kurz, H. D., Nishizawa, T. & Tribe, K. (eds.) (2011). *The dissemination of economic ideas*. Cheltenham: Edward Elgar.

Lindenfeld, D. F. (1993). The myth of the older historical school of German economics. *Central European History*, 26(4): 405–416.

Lindenfeld, D. F. (1997). *The practical imagination: The German sciences of state in the nineteenth century*. Chicago: University of Chicago Press.

Maloney, J. (1999). *The professionalization of economics: A. Marshall and the dominance of orthodoxy*. London: Transaction.

Myles, J. (1959). *German historicism and American economics*. Princeton, NJ: Princeton University Press.

Nau, H. H. (2000). Gustav Schmoller's historico-ethical political economy: Ethics, politics and economics in the younger German Historical School, 1860–1917. *European Journal of the History of Economic Thought*, 7(4): 507–531.

Nau, H. H. & Schefold, B. (eds.) (2002). *The historicity of economics*. Berlin: Springer.

Pearson, H. (1997). *Origins of law and economics: The economists' new science of law, 1830–1930*. Cambridge: Cambridge University Press.

Pearson, H. (1999). Was there really a German Historical School of economics?, *History of Political Economy*, 31(3): 547–562.

Psalidopoulos, M. & Mata, M.E. (eds.) (2002). *Economic thought and policy in less developed Europe: The nineteenth century*. London: Routledge.

Rau, K. H. (1832). *Lehrbuch der politischen Oekonomie*. Heidelberg: Winter.

Reinert, S.A. (2011). *Translating empire: Emulation and the origins of political economy*. Cambridge, MA: Harvard University Press.

Reinhart, C. M. & Rogoff, K. (2009). *This time is different: Eight centuries of financial folly*. Princeton, NJ: Princeton University Press.

Roscher, W. (1843). *Grundriss zu Vorlesungen über die Staatswirthschaft, nach geschichtlicher Methode*. Göttingen: Dieter.

Schäffle, A. (1867). *Die nationalökonomische Theorie der ausschliessenden Absazver-hältnisse*. Tübingen: Lauppsche Buchhandlung.

Schumpeter, J.A. (1954). *History of economic analysis*, ed. E. Boody-Schumpeter. New York: Oxford University Press.

Screpanti, E. & Zamagni, S. (1993). *An outline of the history of economic thought*. Oxford: Clarendon Press.

Shionoya Y. (ed.) (2001). *The German Historical School: The historical and ethical approach to economics*. London: Routledge.

Shionoya Y. (2005). *The soul of the German Historical School: Methodological essays on Schmoller, Weber and Schumpeter*. New York: Springer.

Spengler, J.J. (1970). Notes on the international transmission of economic ideas. *History of Political Economy*, 2(1): 133–151.

Spiegel, H.W. (1991). *The growth of economic thought*, 3rd ed. Durham: Duke University Press.

Stigler, G.J. (1969). Does economics have a useful past?, *History of Political Economy*, 1(2): 217–230.

Streissler, E.W. (1990). The influence of German economics on the work of Menger and Marshall, in B.J. Caldwell (ed.), *Carl Menger and his legacy in economics*. Durham: Duke University Press, 31–68. [Annual supplement to *HOPE*, volume 22]

Takebayashi, H. (2003). *Die Entstehung der Kapitalismustheorie in der Gruendungsphase der deutschen Soziologie*. Berlin: Duncker and Humblot.

Tribe, K. (1995). *Strategies of economic order: German economic discourse, 1750–1950*. Cambridge: Cambridge University Press.

Tribe, K. (2000). The historizisation of political economy?, in B. Stuchtey & P. Wende (eds.), *British and German historiography 1750–1950*. Oxford: Oxford University Press, 211–228.

Winkel, H. (1977). *Die deutsche Nationaloekonomie im 19. Jahrhundert*. Darmstadt: Wissenschaftliche Buchgesellschaft.

Yonay, Y.P. (1998). *The struggle over the soul of economics: Institutionalist and neoclassical economists in America between the wars*. Princeton, NJ: Princeton University Press.

1 The impact of the German Historical School on the evolution of economic thought in Austria

Günther Chaloupek

Economic and state sciences in Austria in the first half of the nineteenth century

Economic and state sciences had a promising start in Austria in the seventeenth and eighteenth centuries. Being the largest and most powerful territorial state of the German *Reich*, the Habsburg monarchy was an attractive workplace for mercantilist economists from other parts of the *Reich* (Becher, Schröder, Hörnigk, Justi). In 1763 Joseph von Sonnenfels, author of the textbook *Grundsätze der Polizey, Handlung und Finanz* (3 vols., 1765–1776), was appointed to the newly established chair for administrative and cameral sciences at the University of Vienna. With strict state control over university teaching before 1848, reception of classical economics was delayed considerably, so that Austrian participation in the lively development of economics in Germany[1] in the first half of the nineteenth century was rather weak and belated.

Austria took a route different from Germany in the human sciences, not only in economics but also in philosophy and history. Whereas for many decades during the nineteenth century, German philosophy was dominated by Hegel's idealism and historicism, and later by the anti-Hegelian reaction, in Austria Catholicism, realism and logical positivism were the prevailing currents of thought. In the same vein, Austria lacked anything comparable to the broad-based movement of *Historismus* that dominated human sciences in Germany in general (law – Savigny, history – Niebuhr, Ranke, Droysen) from the early 1800s.[2]

If the origins of the German Historical School (GHS) date back to the middle of the century, at that time in Austria the state of economics was clearly under-developed. The universities' teaching staff consisted mostly of rather obscure scholars, except for Lorenz von Stein, who had been appointed to the chair at the University of Vienna (previously held by Sonnenfels and Josef Kudler) in 1855. Hence, there is no parallel movement to the older, so-called first-generation historical school (Roscher, Knies, Hildebrand) in Austria. After the appointment of Albert Schäffle (1868) and of Carl Menger (1871) at the University of Vienna, the historical school (HS) had a late start in Austria in 1868 with the call of Theodor Inama von Sternegg to the University of Innsbruck. Thereafter, the HS established itself and gained strength in the academic as well as in the political sphere under the influence of two leading figures: Karl Theodor von Inama-Sternegg and Carl Grünberg.

The leading scholars: Inama-Sternegg and Grünberg

Inama-Sternegg[3]

In 1868, Karl Theodor von Inama-Sternegg was appointed to the chair of state science at the University of Innsbruck. Born 1843 in Augsburg, Bavaria, he had studied law and state sciences at the University of Munich, where he was habilitated in 1868. Descended from an old South Tyrolian family, he followed the call from his home country. At the University of Innsbruck the preferred subject of Inama's economic studies was history of the medieval economy. His studies on the formation of manorial estates and its system of administration in the early Middle Ages (Inama-Sternegg 1872, 1878) were widely quoted and discussed in the economic history literature.[4] Of Inama's most encompassing work, *Deutsche Wirtschaftsgeschichte*, which covers the economic development of Germany during the Middle Ages, only the first volume was completed when he left Innsbruck; Volumes 2 and 3 were published in 1891 and 1901, respectively. He is credited for having coined the term *Wirtschaftsgeschichte*. From Innsbruck Inama moved to the more prestigious University of Prague in 1880. In 1881, Inama-Sternegg left his academic post and became director of the Bureau for Administrative Statistics. In 1884 he was elevated to the prestigious position of president of the Austrian Central Statistical Commission. At the same time he was honorary professor and director of statistical studies at the University of Vienna. In addition, he lectured on administrative sciences (*Verwaltungslehre*) after Lorenz von Stein's retirement (1885). Without establishing a "school" of his own, Inama trained his students primarily for service in the statistical office, from which many advanced to important positions in the administration and in the universities. Inama retired from his post as president of the Statistical Commission in 1905 and died in 1908, just after having completed a revision of Volume 1 of his *Deutsche Wirtschaftsgeschichte*.

As economist and statistician Inama represented the kind of unity of theory and practice which was so important to the German "socialists of the chair" (*Kathedersozialisten*). He acquired considerable reputation as the organizer of a modern statistical system in Austria. He was equally concerned with issues of social policy and engaged himself actively in the organization of poor relief by serving as president of an association against poverty and begging.[5] Inama became an active politician when he was appointed member of the upper chamber of the Austrian parliament by the emperor in 1891, where he supported social reforms and the introduction of general franchise (for men) in 1907.

For his general approach, Inama aimed at a synthesis between historical-empirical investigation and classical – that is the Smithian type of economic theory. He followed Lorenz von Stein[6] in his high appreciation of Adam Smith's achievements in the "investigation of the fundamental relationships in the world of goods (*Güterwelt*)" as a lasting contribution to economics as a social science. Like Stein, Inama accepted "self-interest as the guide for the best use of labour and capital." However, Smith's view of the economy suffered from a principal deficiency. If there are general economic laws rooted in the "immutable relationship between man and nature", their effects vary according to changing social, institutional, legal and political circumstances. In his *Wealth of Nations*, Smith pays insufficient attention to the changeability of conditions under which goods production takes place. More importantly, he does not provide a viable starting point for analyzing what can be attributed to the nature of man or to human nature's concrete manifestations under specific historically given conditions (Inama-Sternegg 1876: 13ff.). The HS deserves credit for correcting this one-sidedness of classical economic theory.

Inama is in agreement with Schmoller, who rightly demonstrates "the aberrations of the individualistic economic theory" – that is the Austrian Schools paradigm, which Schumpeter called "methodological individualism" (Inama-Sternegg 1908: 107). As "collective phenomena" economic facts and processes have a logic of their own, they are not "mere aggregates of individual actions" (ibidem: 97). Yet, in Inama's view Schmoller goes too far in his attempt to demonstrate the social determinedness of man's economic actions. In his endeavour to trace economic behaviour to varying psychological, biological, racial, ethnical, geographical and educational conditions, Schmoller puts too great a strain on economics, with the unsatisfactory result that he produces "only fragments of a general theory of society which are often superficial explanations of an immature sociology", which tend to spoil the achievements of Schmoller's *Grundrisse* (ibidem: 109). Instead, Inama pleads for sticking to the existing specialization among the social sciences. Whereas for Schmoller progress of economic knowledge is the product of detailed historical studies of concrete subjects, Inama points to the merits of the "method of isolation" – that is the formulation of abstract hypotheses, which has a major share in the achievements of economics as a social science (Inama-Sternegg 1876: 28). If, therefore, Inama's understanding of economic method is different from Schmoller's extreme inductivism, his views somehow anticipate the modification which Sombart and the members of the third generation of the GHS considered necessary for an appropriate application of the historical method.

But with these qualifications, Inama thought that sound economic knowledge must be based on detailed historical research and the gathering of statistical data, in order to support hypothetical judgments based on scattered observations. In addition, "descriptive economics" is an important source of knowledge where representation in quantitative terms is impossible (Inama-Sternegg 1908: 105). As president of Austria's statistical office, Inama emphasized that working with original historical data should meet the same technical and professional standards which apply to current statistics (Inama-Sternegg 1903: 275). As far as capacities permitted, he supported such efforts from members of the staff who published a large number of historical statistics in the official media of the Central Commission as well as in personal publications.

Inama had only limited ambitions in economic theorizing. As a consequence of his interest in the "Social Question" and his favourable attitude towards social policies, his main interest lay in the theory of rent formation.[7] On the basis of the theoretical approaches of Ricardo and Schmoller, he extended the concept of rent beyond land to goods production, national and international trade and even to national economies, which he saw as collective economic entities competing with each other. He was also interested in monopoly theory and in the organization of markets, and in tendencies and determinants of long-term economic development. He used rather simple analytical concepts taken from classical economics, without being interested in subjecting them to critical discussion. Inama published two volumes of collected essays at the end of his career. He did not write a general tract containing his theoretical views in a systematized form.

Inama's duties as president of the statistical office did not permit him to write longer studies in economic history apart from the time-consuming completion of his work on the German economy during the Middle Ages. His statistical publications include studies on the possession of real property and on wages of workers in agriculture.

Carl Grünberg[8]

By his date of birth Grünberg belongs to the age group of the authors of the third generation of the GHS. Born 1861 in a Jewish family in Focsany, Rumania, Grünberg moved to Austria. After having completed the gymnasium in Czernowitz, he studied law and state sciences under Lorenz von Stein and Anton Menger at the University of Vienna. Under the influence of Anton Menger Grünberg had come to sympathize with socialist ideas. While working in a private law firm, Grünberg started with extensive studies in agricultural history at the University of Strasbourg under the tutorship of G. F. Knapp. He was habilitated in Strasbourg in 1893. His appointment to extraordinary professor at the University of Vienna in 1899 was supported by Eugen von Philipovich, one of the few *Kathedersozialisten* among the Austrian School. A joint motion of Philipovich, Friedrich Wieser and Heinrich Lammasch to promote Grünberg to ordinary professor was turned down twice by the majority of the law faculty, but was finally accepted in 1909. Thus, Grünberg was the first avowed Marxist who obtained a full professorship at a university in Austria and Germany.

Similar to Inama's, Grünberg's first subject of research was in agricultural history. In the tradition of the GHS, in particular of Knapp's work on peasant emancipation and land reform in Prussia, he wrote a voluminous study on peasant emancipation and the dissolution of hereditary subjection in the Austrian crownlands Bohemia, Moravia and Silesia (Grünberg 1894). Grünberg's continued interest in the process of peasant emancipation resulted in a variety of publications (see especially Grünberg 1899, 1922) in which he carefully described and analyzed the different forms of land tenure and the successive legislative steps that gave peasants full ownership of their property and changed their status from personal subjection to citizenship.

Going beyond Menger's "lawyers' socialism" ("*Juristensozialismus*") he created a distinctive version of Marxian historical materialism which, in its methodological orientation, adopts a teleological view of history, like the younger GHS. Grünberg defined himself as "Marxist", yet he did not accept the truth of Marxist economic and social doctrines for deductive reasons, but emphasized the necessity of subjecting them to empirical validation. He was rightly characterized as "*Kathedermarxist*" (Marxist of the chair), as opposed to the Kathedersocialists, who rejected both Marxism and the socialist movement. Grünberg applied his historicist approach to socialism and the labour movement. In 1910 he founded the famous "*Archiv für die Geschichte des Sozialismus und der Arbeiterbewegung*", to which he contributed many articles. The programmatic orientation of the journal was to encourage research that "enhances pragmatic knowledge" of the evolution of socialist thought and the labour movement, "its positive and negative influence on economic theory and policy, on the philosophy of law and state science, and the other way round" – that is the influence of the latter on socialism (Grünberg 1910: 11). Among Grünberg's students are the most important representatives of Austro-Marxism (Karl Renner, Otto Bauer, Rudolf Hilferding, Max Adler, Friedrich Adler). He entertained a close relationship to Social Democratic Party and its leader Victor Adler, but he became a member only in 1919. In cooperation with Victor Adler and professors of the University of Vienna (among them Philippovich and the historian Ludo Hartmann) Grünberg founded the nonpartisan "*Sozialwissenschaftlicher Bildungsverein*", in order to bridge the gap between the academic institutions and the labour movement. Grünberg also actively engaged himself in the formation of community colleges (*Volkshochschulen*) to improve levels of knowledge and education of the working population.

After the war, Grünberg's venia was augmented to include economic policy. He was appointed to director of the university's institute for state sciences by the short-term social democratic minister of education Otto Glöckel. When Grünberg's project to establish a "social museum" in combination with an institute for social research failed, he left Vienna in 1924, accepting a call from Frankfurt to become director of the newly established *Institut für Sozialforschung*, a position combined with a chair at the University of Frankfurt. He was forced to retire after a stroke in 1930, from which he never recovered. Grünberg died in 1940. Max Horkheimer became Grünberg's successor as director of the Frankfurt institute, while Adolph Löwe took Grünberg's chair at the university.

Grünberg's most visible impact in Austria stems from his role as mentor[9] of the authors of the essential works of Austro-Marxist literature. But of the large number of studies of Grünberg's students, many were written in the true spirit of the HS without being committed to Marxism.[10]

Studies in economic history

Monographs and sectoral studies

Initiated mostly by Inama and later by Grünberg, an increasing number of studies in economic history were published starting in the 1880s, with the main body of this research coming forward after the turn of the century. There were two series which served the publication of these studies: the *Wiener Staatswissenschaftliche Studien*, starting in 1898, edited by Philippovich and the legal scholar Edmund Bernatzik, and the *Studien zur Sozial-, Wirtschafts- und Verwaltungsgeschichte*, starting in 1905, edited by Carl Grünberg. Besides that, there was the *Zeitschrift für Volkswirtschaft, Sozialpolitik und Verwaltung* (1892–1918), and after World War I *Zeitschrift für Volkswirtschaft und Sozialpolitik* (1921–1927), which was open for contributions from economists of various theoretical orientations. The special studies of the Austrian historicist economists were primarily devoted to subjects of Austria's economic development during the eras of mercantilism and industrialization in the nineteenth century. Generally, economic modernization was considered a crucial prerequisite if the Habsburg monarchy wanted to solve the problems resulting from pronounced diversity and heterogeneity of its provinces, and to preserve its status as a major European power. Besides that, issues of social policy were favourite subjects of research.

Compared to Western European countries, the Habsburg monarchy was a latecomer in economic development. Of the crownlands, Bohemia and Lower Austria (including the city of Vienna) were industrialized at the end of the nineteenth century, while agriculture was still dominant, especially in the eastern part of the empire. Progress in industrial development was the most important subject of the studies in economic history. Studies on commercial and industrial policies, like Max Adler's[11] (1903) book on the beginnings of mercantilist commercial policy before Empress Maria Theresia, show the efforts of the government to promote new industries and to remove the obstacles with which they were confronted, especially from traditional craft gilds. Helene Landau's (1906) monograph, written under Grünberg's supervision, describes and analyzes the policies aimed at creating a unified market within the Austrian part of the monarchy in order to facilitate the sale of industrial products across all provinces[12] written under Grünberg's supervision. Other studies focused on particular projects, such as Hans J. Hatschek's (1886) monograph on Johann Joachim Becher's Viennese manufacturing plant, and the monograph on the development of the silk industry in Vienna, Bohemia and in the southern provinces by Helene Deutsch (1909). Henryk Grossmann[13] (1916) analyzes the development of population structure and the state of manufacturing in the light of early population and industrial surveys in the eighteenth century. Explicitly or implicitly, the authors of these studies take a positive attitude towards policies that promote protoindustrial enterprises and strengthen their competitive position vis á vis the craft gilds.

The authors of the HS in Austria do not share the predilection of part of the GHS for medieval craft gilds and the economy of medieval towns as objects of research, nor their concern with the survival of the small crafts (*Handwerk*) in an industrializing economy. The reason behind this difference is that cities in the Habsburg crownlands were under the jurisdiction of the prince, without the independence of German *Reichsstädte* like Nürnberg or Hamburg. In his study on the situation of the crafts in Austria Emanuel Adler (1898) does not support the demands of the crafts' movement (*Handwerkerbewegung*) to reintroduce restrictions for competition which had been abolished by the liberal *Gewerbeordnung* (small businesses act) of 1859. Instead, he suggests the crafts should improve their competitive position through the foundation of cooperatives to facilitate credit and cheaper purchase of materials. Rudolf Klimburg's (1900) monograph on the development of vocational education demonstrates the important contribution of various forms of vocational schools at the secondary level for Austria's industrial development.

Studies in the agricultural economy are almost solely focused on the efforts to reform the system of land tenure, with the final step towards peasant emancipation and exoneration of their land from duties and obligation in 1848. Both the final law and its execution, which was a demanding exercise for the bureaucracy, were praised as successful operations by Grünberg (1899). In addition to the aforementioned studies by Grünberg and Inama, there is the massive study by Walther Schiff[14] (1898) and the monograph on land tenure and peasant emancipation in Galicia by Ludwig von Mises (1902).

In his memoirs Mises remarks that he has tried to not to follow Grünberg (1894), whose concentration on the legal side of peasant emancipation Mises considered too narrow (Mises 1978: 6–7). He says that in his essay on the early Austrian factory laws (Mises 1905) genuine economic history is still coming up short against administrative history. Remarkably, yet, in the latter essay Mises took a very favourable attitude towards social policy measures. In particular, he praised an edict of Emperor Joseph II of 1786 which imposed heavy requirements on child labour as a unique act, as it was enacted 16 years ahead of the Morals and Health Act in England (Mises 1905: 231). Schiff wrote historical studies on child labour (1913) and accident insurance. He was appointed director of the staff of the newly established office of labour statistics (*Arbeitsstatistisches Amt*) in 1908. There he prepared and executed the first consumption survey, which served as a basis for automatic wage adjustments during the postwar inflation period in Austria. Grünberg's advice is respectfully recognized by the author of the first comprehensive history of the trade union movement in Austria, Julius Deutsch (1908). If Deutsch was a functionary of the Social Democratic Party, his book also breathes the spirit of historicist economics.

Karl Pribram[15]

The most important monograph is Karl Pribram's impressive *Geschichte der österreichischen Gewerbepolitik 1740–1798* (1907), written under the supervision of Carl Grünberg. The book goes far beyond the description and analysis of commercial policy measures during the reign of Empress Maria Theresia and her successors. Pribram starts with a presentation of economic concepts that underlie the political strategies during the various phases of development. In dealing with the changing ideas upon which policies were built, Pribram discusses the teachings and recommendations not only of major mercantilist economists, like J.H.G. Justi and J. von Sonnenfels, but also of forgotten authors who introduced Adam Smith's economic liberalism into the debate that took place among Austrian bureaucrats and businessmen. Based on meticulous archival studies, Pribram gives an account of the political endeavours of the administration to create an economic base capable of sustaining the aspirations of the Habsburg monarchy as a European imperial power. Pribram is always careful to give a balanced judgment when he evaluates successes and failures of approaches and measures, which oscillated between tight interventionism and more reliance on market forces.

Pribram did not follow his original intention to write a second part covering the remaining period until 1860. At least partially Johann Slokar's[16] voluminous *Geschichte der österreichischen Industrie und ihrer Förderung unter Kaiser Franz I* is a continuation of Pribram's work (until 1835). The book was commissioned by a group of Austrian industrialists with the intention to demonstrate Austria's industrial traditions and capacities in historical perspective. Slokar's book does not have the wide scope and multidimensional approach of Pribram's, concentrating primarily on detailed sectoral developments and concrete policy measures.

Karl Pribram's later work is divided between social policy, statistics, history of economic theory and social philosophy. In his brochure on the origins of the individualistic social philosophy (Pribram 1912) he juxtaposed nominalism and universalism as basic paradigms not only in epistemology but also for political theory, with nominalism corresponding to liberalism, and universalism corresponding to collectivism and organicism. Thus, in the debate between Menger and Schmoller, Pribram stands firmly on the side of the Austrian School, rejecting Schmoller's inductivism as well as his emphasis on an "organic" relationship between economic and social phenomena (Pribram 1983: 220). And yet, Pribram had a higher appreciation of the significance of historical and empirical work for economic theory than Menger and his followers. By this, he developed his own synthesis between historicism and economics of the Austrian School. As director of the legislative division of the Austrian ministry for social affairs, Pribram played an important role in the wave of social policy legislation after World War I (Pribram 1921).

Studies in the history of economic theory

Most studies on economic development of the Habsburg monarchy in the seventeenth and eighteenth centuries contain parts on the concepts of mercantilist authors which they proposed to the Austrian authorities. Except for Sonnenfels, they came from other states of the German empire, eager to see their ideas implemented in the greatest territorial state of the *Reich.*

Encouraged by Grünberg, Louise Sommer (1920, 1925) wrote a comprehensive study about the work of mercantilist (cameralist) economists in their service to the Habsburg monarchy in the seventeenth and eighteenth centuries. In the style of Karl Pribram's historicism, Sommer presents and discusses the economic, social and political theories of Becher, Schröder, Hörnigk, Justi and Sonnenfels, as well as some of their detailed policy concepts and recommendations. She concludes that their influence on the conduct of policies was substantial by stimulating and initiating reforms not only in the economic sphere but also in the methods of governance and administration. Sommer argues that Wilhelm Roscher's *Geschichte der National-Ökonomik in Deutschland* fails to capture the essence of mercantilism by focusing too narrowly on its economic elements (Sommer 1925: 460–461).

In her extensive contribution to the *Festschrift für Carl Grünberg* Sommer (1932: 486–496) put the *Methodenstreit* between Schmoller and Menger in the wider context of evolution of philosophical fundamentals of economic theorizing. If the debate between Schmoller and Menger had come to be seen primarily as a question of "induction versus deduction", the other dimension of the controversy which consisted in the different modes of conceptualization had got lost. The concepts used by historically oriented economists follow "principles of styliza- tion" (of fact) which are different from those of theoretical economists.[17] Historical economics does not put much effort into formation of precise concepts; it is more interested in understanding life in its totality, and hence rejects drawing sharp lines between the different disciplines of human sciences, such as psychol- ogy, politics, sociology, anthropology and so forth.

Views on economic and social policies – *Kathedersozialismus* in Austria

With respect to economic and social policies, Inama thought that Lorenz von Stein's approach of public administration science (*Verwaltungslehre*) was a neces- sary corrective to a predominantly economic perspective: "A one-sided emphasis on economic motives leads to one-sided judgements and decisions" (Inama- Sternegg 1903: 75). Inama conceived of politics as "applied social ethics" which should aim at "strengthening social values among the population" (ibidem: 28). Inama followed Stein's juxtaposition of society and the state. If society is charac- terized by a multitude of different interests of the various groups of the population, it is the task of the state "to combine their powers into a higher unity" (ibidem: 21). For that purpose it would be counterproductive to suppress the articulation of partial interest. Instead, the state should promote the formal organization of interests through private associations (*Vereinsbildung*), cartels and trade unions. To strengthen social responsibility of interest associations, they should be autono- mous self-governing bodies (*Selbstverwaltung*), subject only to some loose form of state supervision (ibidem: 29–30). This contrasts with the position taken by Schmoller, who opposed unconditional freedom of association for workers and was an enemy of the Social Democratic Party (Schüller 1899).

In the same vein, Inama thought that credit cooperatives could be an effective instrument to give the "poor man" access to credit, which hitherto had been mainly an instrument for the rich to add to their wealth (Inama-Sternegg 1903: 120ff.). On this issue, there is a remarkable accordance with Friedrich von Wieser, who also gave intellectual support to the cooperative movement (Chaloupek 2006).

In the spirit of ethical politics, Inama referred to the problem of "*justum pretium*", which had been unjustly neglected by classical economics. To its great merit, the HS had brought back this issue into discussion, thereby "opening up a way for its solution through perfection of the organization of the market" (Inama-Sternegg 1908: 120). He devoted special attention to rent prices for urban housing, where he vigorously pleaded for a variety of measures against "undeserved capital gains through socially harmful practices of construction" (ibidem: 175).

There was, however, serious disagreement between Inama and Schmoller on the issue of international trade policy. Whereas Schmoller supported the policy of strategic protectionism of Germany, Inama (1908: 16ff.) had a clear preference for free trade in the liberal spirit of Smithian classical economics. Inama considered international division of labour between countries indispensable as a source of augmentation of national income and wealth. He disliked that the system of mutually granted most-favoured-nation status had been replaced by autonomous customs tariffs in the second half of the nineteenth century, with the introduction of schemes for subsidization of exports and protective tariffs for agricultural and industrial products. If certain branches of production had been able to increase their profit rates, the other parts of the economy had to bear the costs. Inama expressed sympathies for the decision of the British parliament in 1906 which had turned down an initiative to established a protectionist trade regime for the British Empire, and thus had opened new avenues for a return to a free trade system in the world economy (ibidem: 47).

In Vienna the most active socialists of the chair were not attached to the HS. Undoubtedly, Anton Menger[18] was the most radical representative of non-Marxist socialist thinking in Austria. He developed his socialist ideas from a legal science perspective. Menger criticized civil law codes for their failure to protect the interests of the propertyless classes. He called for peaceful transformation of the "individualistic power state" into a "popular worker's state" by transferring the law of property rights and contract law from the sphere of civil law to public law, in order to model the legal order according to the needs of the majority of the population. Among professors of political economy, Eugen von Philippovich,[19] whose widely used textbook *Grundriß der Politischen Ökonomie* was in its theoretical parts based on the teachings of the Austrian School, was the most prominent socialist of the chair. Against the socialists, he thought that the economic order should in principle be based on private property. Social policy measures should contribute to improvement of living conditions of the propertyless classes and provide for basic needs, and also support cooperative organizations and interest associations (Philippovich 1910: 142–143). He was among the founders of the

Viennese Fabian Society and also of the *Sozialpolitische Partei* (Party for Social Policy), which fought for social and economic reform measures, such as shortening of the work week, old age insurance, control of cartels and so forth, in parliament (Fuchs 1984: 141–142). Grünberg was one of the founders of the social democratic *Sozialwissenschaftlicher Bildungsverein*, which cooperated with Philippovich's Fabian Society (Nenning 1966: 152ff.).

Quarrels with the Austrian School of economics

There is an important and lasting impact of the GHS on economics in Austria, partly of an indirect, negative kind. The debate about economic method – *Methodenstreit* – that followed the reaction from the side of the GHS to Menger's *Untersuchungen über die Methode der Sozialwissenschaften und der politischen Ökonomie insbesondere* (1883) contributed to the sharpening of the profiles of both, the GHS and the Austrian School. The Austrian School was pushed further into overemphasizing its method of abstract reasoning by deductive arguments, which found its extreme expression in Ludwig Mises's outright rejection of empiricism. In Germany, Schmoller's dominant influence on appointments for university chairs for political economy and state sciences considerably delayed the spread of marginalism in Germany, thereby reducing the contribution of German scholars to what became standard economic theory in the twentieth century.

   In his "Investigation into the Method of the Social Sciences with Special Reference to Economics" Menger had not denied the relevance of historical research for economic theory – to the contrary, he thought that "we cannot imagine a highly developed theory of economic phenomena without the study of the history of economy." What he denied was that "from the study of history in general and of economy in particular, insight may be gained into the general nature and the general connection of the phenomena of human economy in general. . . . For along with the historical . . . basis for theoretical research, the experience of everyday life is indispensable" (Menger 1883/1985: 117). "The history of economy does not give us insights into actions of the individual (*individualwirthschaftliche Vorgänge*)." If "history does not speak by itself" (Menger 1884: 49), it is necessary to "reduce human phenomena to their most original and simplest constitutive factors . . . and finally try to investigate the laws by which more complicated human phenomena are formed from those simplest elements, thought of in their isolation" (Menger 1883/1985: 62). Moreover, Menger thought that the paradigm of (historical) development (*Entwicklung*) was overemphasized by the HS:

> Theoretical economics is the science of the general nature (the empirical forms) and the general connection (laws) of economy. In contrast to this comprehensive and significant task of our science the establishment of "laws of development" in economy . . . must appear as one that is by no means unjustified, but still quite secondary.
>
> (ibidem: 119)

Inama's disagreements with Menger's methodological approach are different from Schmoller's objections. For Inama, knowledge of general economic laws cannot primarily be the result of historical or empirical description. The "method of isolation" – that is the formulation of abstract hypotheses – is of equal importance. "The lowest and the highest knowledge of social life, beginning and end of social science, belong to speculation. In between lies the large area where exact historical-statistical research comes into play" (Inama-Sternegg 1903: 18). With respect to Schmoller's confusion of economic theory and history, Inama's critique of Schmoller concurs with Menger's characterization of Schmoller's method: "Theory embroidered with historical-statistical notes, interrupted with excursions – which claim to count as theory!" (Menger 1884: 50).

The fundamental disagreement between Inama and Menger was the latter's choice of the individual as "most original constitutive factor". In Inama's view, economics had to be "purged from the trivial discussion of individual actions and occurrences", with statistics as "science of mass phenomena" as an alternative (Inama-Sternegg 1908: 97). In the spirit of the GHS, Inama was primarily interested in the economy in its totality, viewed from the perspective of the state within which economic and social forces are combined to a higher unity. As a consequence, questions of economic policy, such as the case of state intervention in situations of economic crises, should not be treated as "problems of theoretical economics, but as problems of administration" (Inama-Sternegg 1903: 146).

Schumpeter's synthesis between the Austrian School and the GHS

If Gustav Schmoller remained confident about final victory of the GHS at least in Germany, with the emergence of the third generation of the GHS (Werner Sombart, Max Weber, Arthur Spiethoff) it became more and more obvious that the better arguments had been on the side of Menger and his followers, at least as far as epistemological foundations of economics and the principal importance of analytical theory are concerned. On the other hand, the neglect of empirical foundation was increasingly recognized as a weak spot of the Austrian School. It is Joseph Schumpeter who deserves credit for having produced the most convincing synthesis of the two.

The books and journal articles which Schumpeter published between 1905 and 1917 deal with issues of economic theory, of statistics and of economic policy, and he also wrote extensively on the history of economic doctrines. In the famous "Seventh Chapter" (*"Das Gesamtbild der Volkswirtschaft"*) of his *Theory of Economic Development*, which was omitted in the later editions of this book, he distinguished between two tasks.

On the one hand, economic development is a problem of economic history and economic geography. This approach is concerned with the concrete course of development in a particular time and at particular locations, with changes in industrial organization, in methods of production and quantities produced . . . On the other hand, one can look at an additional group of questions . . . First, how and by what process do concrete changes occur? Second, is it possible to recognize regularities in the way that everything new arises?

(Schumpeter 2003: 63)

In the period when he wrote his *Theory of Economic Development*, he contented himself with stating that the descriptive treatment and the theoretical treatment of economic development "stand beside each other and supplement each other" (Schumpeter 2003: 63), without embarking on the task of elaborating in historical detail the regularities which he analyzed theoretically.

It was always Schumpeter's ambition not only to be a champion of economic theory but also to display sovereign command of economic and social history in order to demonstrate the empirical validity of his theoretical propositions. The fields where he first analyzed problems of economics and sociology primarily in a historical setting were not directly related to his central theme of economic development. In his essay of 1918 on the crisis of the tax state, he approached the problem of the financial burden imposed by World War I from a historical perspective. He pursued the same approach when, in his essay of 1919 "On the Sociology of Imperialisms", he took up the question of what was underlying the imperialistic drives of governments and states, and in particular the relationship between capitalism and imperialism.

The question of precedence of history or theory was left open in the seventh chapter, and in his 1914 "*Epochen der Dogmengeschichte*" Schumpeter took great care in doing justice to both parties in the *Methodenstreit*. It was after he had accepted the call of the University of Bonn in 1925 that Schumpeter discussed in detail one of the major works of the HS in his review of the third volume of Werners Sombart's "*Der moderne Kapitalismus*". He also took up the question of the relationship between historical (empirical) work and theoretical analysis in his essay on "*Gustav v. Schmoller und die Probleme von heute*".

Even though Schumpeter at that time was widely accepted as one of the leading scholars in economic theory, for him perfection and refinement of abstract analytical thinking was not the ultimate purpose of economics as a social science. In the fourth (German) edition of his *Theory of Economic Development* he praised Sombart's approach towards an exposition of the evolution of the European economy as "the highest aim after which ambition can strive today" (Schumpeter 1934: 91).

In his 20-page review article Schumpeter acknowledged the final volume of Sombart's *opus magnum* as a major achievement in economic theory – in the sense of a general explanation and concrete investigation of historical processes (Schumpeter 1927: 199). But he also pointed to serious deficiencies of Sombart's theoretical apparatus. Schumpeter's critical remarks mainly pertain to one aspect of Sombart's work: his lack of theoretical rigor – here theory is understood as comprising the analytical tools for the explanation and understanding of economic phenomena. This is interpreted by him as a consequence of Sombart's tendency to neglect all the last 60 years' achievements in economic theory in the latter sense

> with the healthy scorn of the creative thinker who disregards everything that is uncongenial to his thought . . . Where Marx analyzes, Sombart draws sketches. Marx wrestles for solutions, Sombart scatters around aspects which he leaves to their destiny. Marx is interested in the answer, Sombart in the question.
>
> (Schumpeter 1927: 204–205)

When Schumpeter asks for a "combination of Sombart and Edgeworth" (ibidem: 214), this is probably his own ideal which he tried to fulfil in *Capitalism, Socialism and Democracy*, which has been greatly inspired by Sombart's writings.

One year earlier, Schumpeter had published his article on Schmoller where he discussed the relationship between theory and history from a principal perspective. Once again, Schumpeter emphasized that theory and history were complementary and not contradictory approaches to the understanding of economic phenomena. Progress in economics cannot be achieved through sharp separation between theory and history, nor does the establishment of sharp borders between the disciplines of the social sciences lead to a better understanding of the realm of the social. If the essence of the Schmoller program consists in "approaching the factual substrate with a minimum of (theoretical) Apriori in order to comprehend interrelationships, therewith augmenting this Apriori and elaborating new forms of understanding which are then applied to other material" and so forth, this program can be considered a success also in the sense that it has become generally accepted (Schumpeter 1926: 192–193). But Schumpeter also reiterates his criticism that Schmoller underestimated the significance of work on the improvement of the theoretical apparatus, and that he had not found an adequate modus of how to verify or reject theoretical propositions (ibidem: 179–180).[20]

I Schumpeter acknowledged the achievements of the GHS and recognized the necessity for himself that "in order to explain things, . . . the economist, for his part, cannot behave towards historical facts in any other way than the historian. To find relationships, to reflect on these, to formulate them and explain them – that is something that both of them do" (Schumpeter 1926: 173). As a model for a synthesis between theory and history in this concrete sense, Schumpeter intended to make his book *Business Cycles: A Theoretical, Historical and Statistical Analysis of the Capitalist Process* (published 1939) his *magnum opus*, where history was elevated to a position even superior to theory:

> General history (social, political cultural), economic history, and more particularly industrial history are not only indispensable but really the most important contributors to the understanding of our problem. All other

materials and methods, statistical and theoretical, are only subservient to them and worse than useless without them.

(Schumpeter 1939: 13)

In the light of this statement, E. Streissler's (1994: 37) judgment that Schumpeter's "Business Cycles may in fact be considered the last (and one of the most important) monographs of the Younger German Historical School" does not appear exaggerated.

But at a time when the new macroeconomic paradigm was taking shape, Schumpeter's *Business Cycles*, with its meticulous elaboration of patterns of interlocking cyclical movements, received little attention from the academic public. Sombart's *Moderner Kapitalismus* fell into oblivion after World War II. Schumpeter's efforts for a synthesis between the two approaches did not have a lasting impact on the development of economics. In the second half of the twentieth century, the ideal of a synthesis of theory and history vanished from the agenda of economics.

The end of the historical school in Austria

Development of economic thought in Austria is characterized by a parallel rise of the Austrian School and an HS after 1870. When an increasing number of disciples of Menger were appointed to economic chairs at Austrian universities after 1880,[21] the Austrian School continuously extended its position in Austria and became clearly dominant before World War I. The University of Vienna and the central statistical office remained strongholds of historicist economic thinking in Austria until World War I.

Of the other universities only Prague was of significant relevance, where Arthur Spiethoff (1873–1957) held an extraordinary chair at the German University of Prague[22] from 1908 to 1918. He had studied in Berlin and was habilitated by Schmoller in 1907. During his time in Prague, Spiethoff published several articles in *Schmollers Jahrbuch* in which he developed his theory of economic crises (*Konjunkturtheorie*), upon which he based his seminal contribution *Krisen* to the *Handwörterbuch der Staatswissenschaften* of 1925. In the spirit of the HS, he took detailed empirical observations as a starting point, from which he developed a scheme of successive developments in the real and in the monetary sector of the economy, which produced recurrent cycles of expansion and contraction of overall economic activity. Psychological factors also played an important part in Spiethoff's theory of business cycles. His final aim was to derive a generalized pattern of cyclical movements from historical investigation of economic fluctuations in a variety of individual cases. Spiethoff left Prague to accept a chair at the University of Bonn in 1918. He is also known for his concept of *Wirtschaftsstil* ("economic style"), which he proposed as an alternative to Sombart's concept of *Wirtschaftssystem.*

After the war, which had resulted in the dissolution of the Habsburg monarchy, the leading representatives of the historicist approach to economics left

Vienna: in 1924 Grünberg went to Frankfurt, and Pribram moved from the ministry of social affairs to Geneva. Schumpeter, who had not returned to academic teaching after his resignation as Austrian minister of finance, left for Bonn in 1925. The succession of Grünberg was one of the steps towards the "decline of economics at the University of Vienna" (Klausinger 2013). Schiff retired (involuntarily) from the statistical office in 1922. Some influence of historicism was still noticeable among Austro-Marxist authors, especially Otto Bauer (1923, 1925).

Concluding remarks

As the detailed account of the writings and other activities of economists with historicist orientation shows, the impact of the HS on economic thinking as well as on economic and social policy in Austria was significant.

With a wealth of studies on Austria's economic development, the members of the HS established economic history as a separate field among the social and human sciences. Yet Austria's historicist economists largely abstained from theoretical work and did not produce any generalizing syntheses, not of the type of Karl Bücher's stage theory, not to speak of economic textbooks comparable to those of Roscher and Schmoller. Obviously, the Austrian authors of the HS shied away from the "highest knowledge of social life", which, according to Inama, belonged to speculation.

In the debate about method, the Austrian historicist economists did not take sides with Schmoller. Obviously, they considered detailed historical and statistical investigation more important for achieving progress in economic knowledge than what Menger called "exact science", but in contrast to Schmoller they thought that analytical tools gained through abstraction from concrete reality were no less important.

There was an important implicit message from the studies on Austria's economic history: that the state played a positive role in the economic development of the monarchy. This was made explicit by Inama, who analyzed economic development from the perspective of the state. In accordance with Stein and the "Schmoller program",[23] he considered the science of public administration (*Verwaltungswissenschaft*) and the analysis of institutions as part of political economy.

If social legislation had a comparatively early start in Austria with the introduction of factory inspection in 1885, accident insurance for factory workers in 1887 and health insurance in 1888, this was essentially a spillover effect of Bismarck's social legislation in Germany, for which Schmoller and the *Verein für Socialpolitik* had prepared the ground. With its stronghold in the Austrian statistical office after Inama's appointment, the empirical work of members of the HS (Inama, Schiff) made important contributions to further steps in social policy, such as pension insurance for white collar employees (1906), protection of labour in retail trade and the establishment of a special office of labour statistics (1908).

The survey of writings of Austrian authors of the HS highlights an important difference between the HS in Austria and Germany: a difference in political perspective. According to Schumpeter (1926: 387), "for Schmoller the Hohenzollern state was not simply an object of study". A certain historical teleology often motivates the authors of studies in the economic history of their country, but there is a difference in political perspectives of this historical teleology between Austria and Germany. For German historicism (not only economic) this perspective is progress towards unity of empire in a Prussian-dominated Reich. The unification of Germany under Chancellor Bismarck was essentially the unification of a homogenous German people through subordinating a variety of independent territorial states to the Prussian dynasty. In contrast, the political unity of the Habsburg monarchy was constantly threatened by the ethnical diversity of its population. Successful economic development was essential for the survival of the monarchy as a major European power, to be promoted by transformation of the monarchy into a single market – for example through abolishment of obstacles resulting from premodern traditions. Hence, a promarket, pro-Smithian perspective (combined with Marxist "second thoughts") is implicit in many studies of authors of the HS in Austria, compared to an antimarket, anti-Manchester, "pro-organization" perspective of the German HS.

In the actual political context of the Habsburg monarchy, history and development had an ambivalent meaning. In contrast to Prussian Germany, historical developments put the unity of the Austrian empire increasingly at risk. The emergence of an ahistorical, apolitical type of economic theory, such as the new economics of the Austrian School, should be viewed against the background of this situation, and also its early triumph over the historicist approach to political economy in Austria.

Notes

This contribution has benefitted from comments on previous versions from the editors, José Luís Cardoso and Michalis Psalidopoulos, from Harald Hagemann and from three anonymous referees.

1 According to Streissler (1990, 1994).
2 On the relations between the economists of the historical school in Austria and the historical science in Austria, see Fellner (2002: 36ff.). Due to restrictions of space, the related issues cannot be pursued in further detail in the present contribution.
3 For more detailed biographical information, see Rauchberg (1909).
4 See, for example, Kulischer (1928, Vol. 1: 49ff.) and Sombart (1916, Vol. 1: 1).
5 See his report on the personal situation of the poor in Vienna (Inama-Sternegg 1899).
6 See Stein's introductory chapter in his textbook *Die Volkswirthschaftslehre* (1878: 1–12).
7 See his article "*Vom Nationalreichtum*" in Inama-Sternegg (1908: 139–157).
8 An excellent biography of Grünberg is Nenning (1966).
9 Nenning (1966: 94) calls him "Vater des Austromarxismus".
10 Among the contributors to the *Festschrift für Carl Grünberg* (1932) there are seven of his former Austrian students, five of them Marxists and/or Social Democrats.

11 Max Adler (1873–1937) studied law and state sciences and, as a philosopher, became one of the leading theoreticians of Austro-Marxism.

12 Helene Landau (1871–1942), economist, later married Otto Bauer, theoretician of Austro-Marxism and one of the leaders of the Austrian Social Democratic party.

13 Henryk Grosssmann (1881–1950) studied in Krakau (Galicia, Austrian province) and moved to Vienna to continue his studies under Grünberg and Eugen von Böhm-Bawerk. After World War I he served in the statistical office of Poland and moved to Frankfurt in 1925 to work as an economist for the *Institut für Sozialforschung.*

14 Walther Schiff (1866–1950) started his career in the statistical office under Inama. He was habilitated at the University of Vienna 1899 and later awarded the title "Ordinarius".

15 Karl Pribram (1877–1973) was appointed extraordinary professor at the University of Vienna in 1914. From his post with the statistical office he changed to the Austrian ministry of social affairs after World War I, and later to the International Labour organization (ILO) in Geneva. In 1928 he was appointed professor at the University of Frankfurt. He moved to the US after the Nazi takeover.

16 Johann/Ivan Slokar (1884–1970) was born in Slovenia. He studied at the University of Vienna and returned to Yugoslavia after World War I. He held leading positions at the finance ministry of Yugoslavia; thereafter he became director of a Slovenian credit cooperative.

17 This difference is also emphasized by Schumpeter (1934: 90–91).

18 Anton Menger (1841–1906), brother of Carl Menger, was professor of civil litigation at the University of Vienna.

19 Eugen von Philippovich (1858–1917) studied at the universities of Graz and Vienna. He became professor of economics at the University of Freiburg (Germany) in 1885, and was appointed to ordinary professor at the University of Vienna in 1893.

20 In his posthumous "History of Economic Analysis", Schumpeter criticized Schmoller for his tendency towards an "illimited extension" of the subject matter of his economic analysis. "Nothing in the social cosmos or chaos is really outside of Schmollerian economics. In principle, if not quite in practice, the Schmollerian economist was in fact a historically minded sociologist in the latter terms' widest meaning. On this level, specialization would indeed impose itself again if decent work is to be turned out" (Schumpeter 1954b: 812). This sounds like an echo of Inama's review of Schmoller's "*Grundrisse*", quoted earlier.

21 For names and appointments see Lehmann (1977: 200ff.).

22 The University of Prague, the oldest university in the Holy Roman Empire, was founded in 1348 by Emperor Charles IV. It was divided into a Czech and a German university in 1882.

23 On the "Schmoller program" see Backhaus (1993: 9ff.).

References

Adler, E. (1898). *Über die Lage des Handwerks in Österreich*, Vol. 1/1 of *Wiener Staatswissenschaftliche Studien,* Franz Deuticke, Wien und Leipzig.

Adler, M. (1903). *Die Anfänge der merkantilistischen Gewerbepolitik*, Vol. 4/3 of *Wiener Staatswissenschaftliche Studien,* Franz Deuticke, Wien und Leipzig.

Archiv für die Geschichte des Sozialismus und der Arbeiterbewegung (Grünbergs Archiv). (1910–30). Hirschfeld, Leipzig (15 vols.).

Backhaus, J. (ed.) (1993). *Gustav von Schmoller und die Probleme von heute*, Duncker & Humblot, Berlin.

Bauer, O. (1923). *Die österreichische Revolution*, Verlag der Wiener Volksbuchhandlung, Vienna.

Bauer, O. (1925). *Der Kampf um Wald und Weide*, Verlag der Wiener Volksbuchhandlung, Vienna.

Chaloupek, G. (2006). Approaches of the Austrian School to the Soziale Frage before World War I – Wieser and Böhm-Bawerk, in *Journal of Economic Studies* 33, 177–188.

Deutsch, H. (1909). Die Entwicklung der Seidenindustrie in Österreich 1660–1840, in *III. Heft der Studien zur Sozial-, Wirtschafts- und Verwaltungsgeschichte*, ed. Carl Grünberg, Carl Konegen, Vienna.

Deutsch, J. (1908). *Geschichte der österreichischen Gewerkschaftsbewegung*, Verlag Anton Hueber, Vienna.

Fellner, F. (2002). *Geschichtsschreibung und nationale Identität*, Böhlau Verlag, Vienna.

Festschrift für Carl Grünberg zum 70. Geburtstag (1932). C. L. Hirschfeld, Leipzig, reprint Verlag Detlev Auvermann KG, Glashütten im Taunus 1972.

Grossmann, H. (1916). Die Anfänge und Geschichte der amtlichen Statistik in Österreich, in *Statistische Monatsschrift* 21, 331–423.

Grünberg, C. (1894). *Die Bauernbefreiung und die Auflösung des gutsherrlich-bäuerlichen Verhältnisses in Böhmen, Mähren und Schlesien*, Duncker & Humblot, Leipzig.

Grünberg, C. (1899). Die Grundentlastung, in *Geschichte der österreichischen Land- und Forstwirtschaft und ihrer Industrien 1848–1898*, Vol. 1/1, Commissions-Verlag Moritz Perles, Vienna, 1–80.

Grünberg, C. (1910–11). Vorwort zum I. Band, in *Archiv für die Geschichte des Sozialismus und der Arbeiterbewegung* 1.

Grünberg, C. (1922). Agrarverfassung, in *Grundriss der Sozialökonomik*, 8. Abt., Mohr, Tübingen, 131–167.

Hatschek, H. J. (1886). Das Manufakturhaus auf dem Tabor in Wien, Vol. 6/1 of *Staats- und sozialwissenschaftliche Forschungen*, ed. Gustav Schmoller, Duncker & Humblot, Leipzig.

Inama-Sternegg, K. T. von (1872). *Untersuchungen über das Hofsystem im Mittelalter*, Wagner'sche Universitätsbuchhandlung, Innsbruck.

Inama-Sternegg, K. T. von (1876). *Adam Smith und die Bedeutung seines Wealth of Nations für die moderne Nationalökonomie*, Wagner'sche Universitätsbuchhandlung, Innsbruck.

Inama-Sternegg, K. T. von (1878). *Die Ausbildung der großen Grundherrschaften während der Karolingerzeit*, Duncker & Humblot, Leipzig.

Inama-Sternegg, K. T. von (1879–1901). *Deutsche Wirtschaftsgeschichte*, Vols. 1–3, Verlag Duncker & Humblot, Leipzig.

Inama-Sternegg, K. T. von (1899). *Die persönlichen Verhältnisse der Wiener Armen*, Selbstverlag des Vereins gegen Verarmung und Bettelei, Vienna.

Inama-Sternegg, K. T. von (1903). *Staatswissenschaftliche Abhandlungen*, Verlag Duncker & Humblot, Leipzig.

Inama-Sternegg, K. T. von (1908). *Neue Probleme des modernen Kulturlebens*, Verlag Duncker & Humblot, Leipzig.

Klausinger, H. (2013). Krise und Niedergang der Nationalökonomie an der Wiener Universität nach 1917, manuscript.

Klimburg, R. (1900). Die Entwicklung des gewerblichen Unterrichtswesens in Österreich, Vol. 2/1 of *Wiener staatswissenschaftliche Studien*, Franz Deuticke, Wien und Leipzig.

Kulischer, J. (1928). *Allgemeine Wirtschaftsgeschichte des Mittelalters und der Neuzeit*, 2 vols., Duncker & Humblot, Munich.

Landau, H. (1906). *Die Entwicklung des Warenhandels in Österreich*, Wilhelm Braumüller, Vienna.

Lehmann, H. (1977). *Grenznutzentheorie*, deb-Verlag, Berlin.

Menger, A. (1908). *Das bürgerliche Recht und die besitzlosen Volksklassen*, Mohr, Tübingen.

Menger, C. (1883/1985). *Investigation into the method of the social sciences with special reference to economics*, translation of the German original (1883) by F. J. Nock, New York University Press, New York.

Menger, C. (1884). *Die Irrtümer des Historismus in der deutschen Nationalökonomie*, Alfred Hölder, Vienna.

Mises, L. von (1902). Die Entwicklung des gutsherrlich-bäuerlichen Verhältnisses in Galizien bis zu seiner Auflösung 1772–1848, Vol. 4/2 of *Wiener staatwissenschaftliche Studien*, Franz Deuticke, Wien und Leipzig.

Mises, L. von (1905). Zur Geschichte der österreichischen Fabriksgesetzgebung, in *Zeitschrift für Volkswirtschaft, Sozialpolitik und Verwaltung* 14, 209–271.

Mises, L. von (1978). *Erinnerungen*, Gustav Fischer, Stuttgart.

Nenning, G. (1966). Biographie Carl Grünberg, in *Indexband zu Archiv für die Geschichte des Sozialismus und der Arbeiterbewegung*. Reprint, Akademische Druck- und Verlagsanstalt, Graz, 1–224.

Philippovich, E. von (1883–1907). *Grundriß der Politischen Ökonomie*, 3 vols., Mohr, Tübingen.

Philippovich, E. von (1910). *Die Entwicklung der wirtschaftspolitischen Ideen im 19. Jahrhundert*, Mohr, Tübingen.

Pribram, K. (1907). Geschichte *der österreichischen Gewerbepolitik 1740–1860. Erster Band: 1740–1798*, Duncker Humblot, Leipzig.

Pribram, K. (1912). *Die Entstehung der individualistischen Sozialphilosophie*, Hirschfeld, Leipzig.

Pribram, K. (1921). Die Sozialpolitik im neuen Österreich, in *Archiv für Sozialwissenschaft und Sozialpolitik* 48, 645–680.

Pribram, K. (1983). *A history of economic reasoning*, Johns Hopkins University Press, Baltimore.

Rauchberg, H. (1909). Karl Theodor von Inama-Sternegg, in *Zeitschrift für Volkswirtschaft, Sozialpolitik und Verwaltung* 17, 1–28.

Roscher, W. (1874). *Geschichte der National-Ökonomik in Deutschland*, Oldenbourg-Verlag, Munich.

Schiff, W. (1898). *Österreichs Agrarpolitik seit der Grundentlastung*, Laupp'sche Buchhandlung, Tübingen.

Schiff, W. (1913). Die Kinderarbeit in Österreich, in *Archiv für Sozialwissenschaft und Sozialpolitik* 37, 131–174, 483–520.

Schmoller, G. (1901–1904). *Grundriß der Allgemeinen Volkswirtschaftslehre*, 2 vols., Verlag Duncker & Humblot, Leipzig.

Schüller, R. (1899). *Die Wirthschaftspolitik der Historischen Schule*, Carl Heymanns Verlag, Berlin 1899.

Schumpeter, J.A. (1926) [1954a], Gustav v. Schmoller und die Probleme von heute. Schmollers Jahrbuch für Gesetzgebung, Verwaltung und Volkswirtschaft 50. Reprinted in Schumpeter 1954a, 148–199.

Schumpeter, J.A. (1927) [1954a] Sombarts Dritter Band. Schmollers Jahrbuch für Gesetzgebung, Verwaltung und Volkswirtschaft 51. Reprinted in Schumpeter 1954a, 220–240.

Schumpeter, J. A. (1934). *Theorie der wirtschaftlichen Entwicklung*, Duncker & Humblot, Berlin.

Schumpeter, J. A. (1939). *Business cycles: A theoretical, historical and statistical analysis of the capitalist process*, McGraw-Hill, New York.

Schumpeter, J. A. (1954a). *Dogmenhistorische und biographische Aufsätze*, Mohr, Tübingen.

Schumpeter, J. A. (1954b). *History of economic analysis*, Allen & Unwin, London.

Schumpeter, J. A. (2003). The theory of economic development: The seventh chapter, translated by Ursula Backhaus, in J. Backhaus (ed.), *Joseph Alois Schumpeter: Entrepreneurship, style, vision*, Kluwer Academic, Boston, 5–116.

Slokar, J. (1913). *Geschichte der österreichischen Industrie und ihrer Förderung unter Kaiser Franz I.*, Tempsky, Vienna.

Sombart, W. (1916). *Der moderne Kapitalismus, Band I: Einleitung – Die vorkapitalistische Wirtschaft – Die historischen Grundlagen des modernen Kapitalismus*, Duncker & Humblot, Munich.

Sommer, L. (1920/1925). *Die österreichischen Kameralisten in dogmengeschichtlicher Darstellung, Heft XI und XII der Studien zur Sozial-, Wirtschafts- und Verwaltungsgeschichte*, ed. Carl Grünberg, Carl Konegen, Vienna. Reprint, Scientiaverlag Aalen, 1967.

Sommer, L. (1932). Das geisteswissenschaftliche Phänomen des "Methodenstreits": Analogien und Präzedentien, in *Festschrift für Carl Grünberg zum 70, Geburtstag*, Leipzig, 486–537.

Spiethoff, A. (1909). Die äußere Ordnung des Kapital- und Geldmarktes (3 parts), in *Schmollers Jahrbuch 33*, 17–39, 33/3, 65–89, 33/4, 43–63.

Spiethoff, A. (1918). Die Krisenarten, in *Schmollers Jahrbuch 42*, 223–266.

Spiethoff, A. (1925). Krisen I., in *Handwörterbuch der Staatswissenschaften 4*, 8–91.

Spiethoff, A. (1933). Die allgemeine Volkswirtschaftslehre als geschichtliche Theorie: Die Wirtschaftsstile, in *Festgabe für Werner Sombart*, ed. A. Spiethoff, Duncker Humblot, Munich, 51–84.

Stein, L. von (1878). *Die Volkswirthschaftslehre*, Wilhelm Braumüller, Vienna.

Streissler, E. W. (1990). The influence of German economics on the work of Menger and Marshall, in *Carl Menger and his legacy in economics*, ed. B. J. Caldwell, Duke University Press, Durham, 37–68.

Streissler, E. W. (1994). The influence of German and Austrian economics on Joseph A. Schumpeter, in *Schumpeter in the history of ideas*, ed. Y. Shionoya & M. Perlman, University of Michigan Press, Ann Arbor, 13–38.

2 The reception of the German Historical Schools among French economists (1857–1900)

Jean-Pierre Potier

Among historians of economic thought, general consensus is that during the second half of the nineteenth century, the German Historical School of economics had virtually no influence in France, with French economists being either completely indifferent or very hostile towards it. According to Joseph Schumpeter,

> Although some leaders [. . .] did some or most of their work in the field of economic history, it would hardly occur to anyone to speak of an Italian historical school in the sense of a distinct scientific party. *The same holds true for France* [. . .]. Some economists did historical work. I shall mention only Levasseur.
>
> (1954: 820; italics added)

According to John Kells Ingram, in France unlike in Italy, "the historical school has not made so strong an impression – partly, no doubt, because the extreme doctrines of the Ricardian system never obtained much hold there" (1919: 212).

For his part, Charles Gide asserted,

> The influence of Germany on French economic literature did not begin to be felt until the last two decades of the 19th century. Until then it was almost non-existent – vastly different to its influence on philosophical teaching which was very great.
>
> (1908: 7)

Charles Rist, who was in charge of writing the chapter devoted to "L'Ecole historique et la querelle des méthodes" in *Histoire des doctrines économiques depuis les physiocrates jusqu'à nos jours* (Gide and Rist, 1909) – a book collaboratively prepared with Gide – gives us more precise information. He asserts that in France, unlike in England, "a true school of economist historians" did not emerge, but he adds,

> The effect of the new ideas, however, did not miss to penetrate by numerous channels in the scientific thought. Firstly in 1878 an official teaching in political economy was introduced in Law faculties, and just afterwards, with

a direct contact with the legal disciplines, this teaching took on a new character, all penetrated with a historical spirit. At the same time, professional historians were increasingly interested in the issues in economic history [. . .]. Many among the liberal economists, without pitting themselves against the old school, dedicated their works either to the detailed observation of contemporary facts or to historical research.

(1909: 448)

Rist mentions Emile Levasseur as being among these liberal economists (see p. 27). He carries on his analysis, remarking that a new group came to join the economists – the sociologists. In their study of the economic system, at various times, they have brought "mistrust of abstractions, worry about meticulous observations, a preference for induction as opposed to deduction which rightly characterizes the historical school" (1909: 448–449). To this end, it must be noted that during the 1870s only a few students attended the lectures of the members of the historical school in German universities, the majority of whom were sociologists rather than economists: Émile Durkheim is a good example (see p. 28).

In fact, the question of the French reception of the German Historical School of economics is rarely studied in both older and more recent literature (see especially Breton, 1988, Le Van-Lemesle, 1994a, and Grimmer-Solem and Romani, 1998). It would thus be useful to reconsider this question and to examine the diverse aspects of the reception of German economic thought (the "older" and the "younger" historical schools) within the various trends of French economic thought during the second half of the nineteenth century. We can identify hostile as well as positive reactions.

The first part of this chapter examines the reception of the "older" German Historical School in France under the Second Empire. It is during this period that the first debates appear, mainly focusing on method (1857–1868). The second part of this chapter deals with the reception of the "younger" German Historical School in France during the Third Republic until the end of the nineteenth century. In this period, the debates are not limited to methodology; questions of economic policy are also involved (1874–1900).

The reception of the "older" German Historical School among the French economists: First debates on method (1857–1868)

During the first half of the nineteenth century, the so-called French liberal school emerged in Paris. Schumpeter rightly stated that this group had a "too exclusive concentration upon economic policy" and "lacked interest in purely scientific questions" (1954: 497). Within this group, broadly speaking, it is possible to distinguish two families. The ultraliberal economists – namely Pellegrino Rossi (1787–1848), Charles Dunoyer (1796–1862), Frédéric Bastiat (1801–1850), Léon Faucher (1803–1854), Joseph Garnier (1813–1881) and Gustave de Molinari

(1819–1912) – were the biggest supporters of the natural laws of political economy and the most uncompromising about the arbitrariness of the state. On the other hand, the moderate liberal economists – namely Adolphe-Jérôme Blanqui (1798–1854), Louis Wolowski (1810–1876) and Michel Chevalier (1806–1879) – were more interested in the "labour question" and its solutions. For example, according to Blanqui, the cause of pauperism is mostly in the development of the manufacturing system, in "excessive competition", in the submission of workers to machines, but also in industrial and commercial isolation – that is to say in protectionism, which closes the markets and keeps wages very low. On the other hand, according to Wolowski the cause of pauperism is an insufficiency of production. Thus, industrialization, the increase of production thanks to mechanization and the rise of wages would solve the labour question in the long term. During the 1840s and 1850s, all these liberal economists denounced the utopian character of the socialists' ideas and programs. They criticized the ideas of the followers of Saint-Simon, Fourier and Cabet, but also of Pierre Leroux, Philippe Buchez and Louis Blanc.

These liberal economists had the Guillaumin publishing house (established in 1839) and a monthly review, the *Journal des économistes* (since December 1841) at their disposal. They were active in the "Political Economy and Statistics" section of the Academy of Moral and Political Sciences (restored by Guizot in 1832) and the *Société d'économie politique* in Paris (founded in 1842). They had a true monopoly over the few teaching posts in political economy, such as at the *Conservatoire des Arts et Métiers* or at the *Collège de France* (until 1877, this discipline was not introduced to universities – see p. 29[1]).

These economists were mostly followers of Jean-Baptiste Say, according to whom Adam Smith used the right method: ascending from facts the more constantly observed to the general laws which govern them (unfortunately, Ricardo was doing the reverse). Otherwise they thought that history and statistics as purely descriptive sciences could not explain the facts and could not go from effects to causes or, inversely, from causes to effects (Le Van Lemesle, 2004: 304). Midway through nineteenth century, during the Second Empire, these economists had some knowledge of German economic thought, and particularly of Friedrich List and Karl Rau (M. Block, 1853). Among liberal economists, Maurice Block (1816–1901) represented a special case: he was born in Berlin and studied at the universities of Bonn, Heidelberg and Tübingen, where he received a doctorate in philosophy. Granted French citizenship in 1848, he worked in the office of the *Statistique générale* in the Ministry of Agriculture, Trade and Civil Engineering (1844–1853), and then became "sous-chef" of the *Statistique générale de la France* until 1861.[2] In 1854, he published a translation into French with annotations of a book by Wilhelm Roscher, *Ueber Korntheuerungen: Ein Beitrag zur Wirtschaftspolizei* (1847).[3]

Friedrich List's major work, *Das nationale System der politischen Ökonomie* (1841), mostly written in Paris during 1839–1840, is known in France thanks to Henri Richelot's translation, which was published in 1851 (second ed., 1857). "Chef de bureau" in the Ministry of Trade and author of the book *L'Association douanière allemande* (1845), Henri Richelot (1811–1864) began his translation in 1847. The immediate context of this publication was the fight between the *Association pour la liberté des échanges*, run by Frédéric Bastiat and then by Michel Chevalier, and the *Association pour la défense du travail national*, which was driven by various groups of manufacturers and supported by the politician Adolphe Thiers. In June 1851, thanks to Thiers, a resolution in favour of free trade failed in the Legislative Assembly (Todd, 2008: 400–403). It was not until January 1860 that Michel Chevalier, Emperor Napoléon III's personal adviser, finalised the signature of a trade treaty between France and Great Britain (the so-called Cobden-Chevalier treaty), which put France in the way of free trade for around 20 years.

According to Richelot, apart from the *Wealth of Nations*, *Système national d'économie politique* was the most important book about the theory of international trade. So List's theories were not purely German. Protective duties were useful because the consumers' temporary loss of values of exchange was compensated for by a lasting increase of the producers' productive powers, and thus the nation's prosperity (Richelot, in: List, 1851: xii, 8). Therefore, it was not possible to support private interest against public interest. Concerning List, the translator added,

> By doing justice to the ambitious systems which claim to manage all places and times with a formula, by teaching that the majority of economic truths are relative and not absolute, by exploiting history, he proposed a historical method, which appears to have a bright future.
>
> (Richelot, in: List, 1851: xiv)[4]

While the works of Bruno Hildebrand (*Die Nationalökonomie der Gegenwart und Zukunft*, 1848) and of Karl Knies (*Die politische Ökonomie von Standpunkte der geschichtlichen Method*, first ed., 1853; second ed., 1883) have never been translated into French, Wilhelm Roscher's textbook, *System der Volkswirthschaft*, vol. 1, *Die Grundlagen der Nationalökonomie* was translated by Wolowski with the author's permission (1857).[5] Louis Wolowski (1810–1876), of Polish origin, and a political refugee from 1832, was a lawyer and an economist; he obtained a doctorate in law from the University of Heidelberg and a doctorate in economics from the University of Tübingen. In 1839, he became the professor of industrial legislation[6] at the *Conservatoire des Arts and Métiers* (see Markiewicz, 1994).[7] In 1841, having carried out a mission to study the different economic and social legislation in the German states on behalf of the Ministry of Agriculture, Industry and Trade, he came into contact with Wilhelm Roscher in Leipzig (Van-Lemesle, 1994b: 682). He added a number of annotations and a lengthy introduction to his translation of Roscher's book; the translation was almost finished in 1855, but he modified it in line with the second German edition.

In his introduction, Wolowski wished to rehabilitate the role of history in economics.[8] According to him, until the eighteenth century, political economy was mixed in with philosophy, ethics, law and history. After that it was entirely isolated from history and from the moral sciences. In fact, German economists such as W. Roscher sought to align political economy with the other fields of knowledge. Wolowski criticized Pellegrino Rossi's distinction between pure or rational economics and applied economics – that is to say between science and art. According to Rossi, pure economics, inquiring into the nature, causes and movement of wealth, is based on general and constant factors about human nature and the world, while applied economics takes external factors into account: nationality, time and space (1857: liii–liv). In fact, according to Wolowski, applied economics must be developed using historical induction and not the "dogmatic deduction" of pure science. He asserts,

> The abstract deductions in pure science do not leave us without worry, as they treat man as a material force much more than as a moral force; in contact with the rigorous processes of mathematical speculation, man becomes a *constant*, for all time and in all nations, while in reality he is a *variable*.
>
> (1857: lv–lvi; italics in original)[9]

This text sparked some debates among liberal economists (see Gislain, 2000). In articles from the *Journal des économistes* and some papers read at the *Société d'économie politique*, the reactions are contrasted. Roger de Fontenay (1809–1891), a disciple of Frédéric Bastiat, was clearly hostile to the historical method. According to him, the historical method in Germany was the "logical consequence and direct application of the great philosophical doctrine of evolution and progress"[10] (Fontenay, 1858: 62). Wolowski was wrong when he said that the "rationalist method" considers man as a "material force" and a "constant". In fact, this method is "much more historic than one would think", as it rests on notions such as goodness, justice and usefulness, which are "essentially progressive" (1858: 64). Later, in 1864, on the occasion of a discussion of the *Société d'économie politique* devoted to the usefulness of the division between pure and applied economics, Wolowski took the opportunity to reassert that "the best method is the historical method", taking into account the facts of the past and present in the nations. (Wolowski, in : Société d'économie politique. Réunion du 5 janvier 1864 : 455).

In 1866, the opening lecture of Henri Baudrillart (1821–1892) for his course in political economy at the *Collège de France* was devoted to method in economics. Baudrillart accepted Rossi's distinction between pure and applied economics. First, economics is a pure science raising universal principles. Unfortunately, economists such as Ricardo, using the "idealist method", were lead to some overstatements considering man only as an economic being (and not as a moral being); so economics has been brought closer to mathematics. Then, economics is also an applied science, or art; it shows the reasons which can modify the applications of the principles. But the only method in economics is the experimental method, considering concrete man with his needs, ideas and faculties (Baudrillart, 1866: 13–19). The historical method is a complement for the experimental method because history is a means to verify the teachings of economics. Thanks to history we can understand the succession and the mistakes of political economy's systems, like the mercantile, *agricole* (Physiocracy) and *industriel* (Adam Smith) systems. In order to successfully implement reforms, the historical method and knowledge about the past and tradition are needed (1866: 28–31).[11]

At the suggestion of Jean-Gustave Courcelle-Seneuil (1813–1892), who wished to reconsider the content of Wolowski's introduction to Roscher's book, the *Société d'économie politique de Paris* chose the following topic for discussion on January 5, 1868: "What is the historical method? How can it be applied to political economy?" Courcelle-Seneuil thought that the only method for economists was the one used in "natural and physico-chemical sciences", the observation of facts suggesting assumptions. History provides only facts but not a method of reasoning (Courcelle-Seneuil, in: Réunion de la Société d'économie politique, 1868: 145–146).[12] On the contrary, according to Wolowski,

> political economy, elucidated through the historical method, recognizes that, while the constant and manageable forces of their nature are governed by mathematical laws, fickle and free men are only governed by moral laws. In effect, in this field we do not see a gathering of passive forces, but the harmony of free forces, and we can clearly see that man is the primary source, as he is the unique goal of the production of goods.
>
> (Wolowski, in: Réunion de la Société
> d'économie politique, 1868: 146–147)

Henri Baudrillart rejected Courcelle-Seneuil's point of view. According to him, history is a complement, or a part of the experimental (observation), inductive method (Baudrillart, in: Réunion de la Société d'économie politique, 1868: 156). Léonce de Lavergne (1809–1880), historian of rural economics,[13] considered that the historical method (not to be confused with the observation and inductive method used in all sciences[14]) "does not make the theory", but "controls it and prevents it from being mislaid". The historical method took an interest in the "development of economic ideas during various eras and with various peoples; it shows how these ideas were born, how they grew, and how they can spread and be achieved". Clearly, its utility appears on the ground of the application. Indeed, according to him, "with pure theory, we are led to say: *let the colonies perish rather than a principle!* with theory completed by studying economic facts, we can reconcile the whole" (Lavergne, in: Réunion de la Société d'économie politique, 1868: 158; italics in original).

Among these liberal economists, a historical economist, Emile Levasseur (1828–1911), adopted a particular position. He was influenced by Roscher, whose lessons he attended at the University of Leipzig at the beginning of the 1850s (Breton, 1988: 410–411; 1991: 405). He was a secondary-school professor from 1852, and in 1857 he was admitted to the *Société d'économie politique* and befriended Louis Wolowski.[15] Member of the *Académie des sciences morales et politiques* in 1868, he was appointed as a professor at the *Collège de France* in the same year, for a complementary course entitled "Histoire des faits et doctrines économiques". According to him, economics is an observation science which can obtain laws only through studying facts.[16]

Soon after the German unification (1871), the "younger" historical school of economics, a group made up mainly around Gustav Schmoller, appeared. Claiming a historical and inductive approach in scientific research, it engaged politically in favour of social reforms and against economic liberalism and free trade. Which will be its echo in France, during the beginning of the Third Republic?

The reception of the "younger" German Historical School among French economists: New debates (1876–1900)

After the fall of the Second Empire, the Franco-Prussian War and the defeat of France in 1871, the situation changed dramatically. Some young French historians, such as Gabriel Monod, Ernest Lavisse and Charles Seignobos, completed their studies at German universities. These intellectuals believed that the explanation for Germany's victory came not only from its military institutions but also from its cultural institutions. According to them it was necessary to imitate the German universities' principles and methods in order to restore France. These intellectuals were influenced by the works of Leopold Von Ranke, Theodor Mommsen, Heinrich von Treitschke and so forth. According to Ranke, using documents, the historian records historical facts just like a mirror, with total objectivity ("reflect theory"). In 1876, with the creation of the *Revue historique* in Paris, the "methodical school" led by Gabriel Monod was born, which claimed to apply von Ranke's precepts (Bourdé and Martin, 1983: chap. 6).

Some philosophers and sociologists studied at German universities. Just after returning from Berlin, where he attended the lessons of Schmoller and especially of Wagner (1885–1886), the sociologist Émile Durkheim (1858–1917) deplored the lack of interest in the works of German economists in France. He stressed,

> We can see that at heart, liberal economists are Rousseau's reckless disciples, which they deny wrongly [. . .]. They only conceive of the nation as a great joint stock company whereby each receives just as much as he gives and where we only stay if we find our place. Moreover, it seems right that it should be as such [. . .]. In these conditions, economic activity can resort to nothing other than egoism and through this, political economy radically separates itself from morality, supposing that there are still some moral ideals in humanity once all social links are broken.
>
> (Durkheim, 1887: 37)[17]

For his part, Charles Andler (1866–1933), a socialist and lecturer in German literature at the *Ecole Normale Supérieure* and the *Sorbonne*, who lived in Berlin from 1889 to 1891, where he attended H. von Treitschke's lectures, prepared a doctorate thesis on German state socialism, which was published under the title *Les origines du socialisme d'Etat en Allemagne* (Paris: F. Alcan, 1897).

During the 1870–1890s, French economic science was in a very different situation from in 1850–1860. Indeed, several groups were then in competition and the liberal school was no longer prevalent. Under the Third Republic, economics received official standing in the Faculty of Law with the decree of March 26, 1877: economics was then included in the bachelor of laws coursework, and lessons were developed by lawyers (12 faculties at first in 1878). This was the only group of economists potentially suited to receive some influence from the German Historical School. According to the universities' statutes no one could fill a chair in a law faculty unless he got the *agrégation en droit* or eventually a doctorate in law. So in this period as before, it was impossible for Léon Walras (1834–1910) to obtain a teaching post in France, and in 1870 he got a chair in political economy at Lausanne's Faculty of Law in Switzerland. There, until 1892, he taught according to his own division of economic science: pure, social and applied economics. Paul-Emile Cauwès (1843–1917), graduate of the *Ecole des Chartes* and professor of economics at the Faculty of Law in Paris (from 1873 teaching as a substitute for A.-P. Batbie), was antiliberal and very attracted by the ideas of the "younger" German Historical School and by the historical method, but also by interventionism as regards economic and social policy.[18] He borrowed his ideas from Friedrich List and Henry C. Carey but also from Gustav Schmoller and Adolf Wagner.[19]

In 1887, Charles Gide (1847–1932), professor in the Faculty of Law at Montpellier (1880–1898), founded a new economic journal, *Revue d'économie politique*, which challenged the supremacy of the *Journal des économistes*. In fact, the economics professors led by Gide in this journal were mostly trained in legal studies. The *Revue* editors' board displayed an open-mindedness both towards the social sciences (the *Revue* published the works of not only economists but also lawyers and sociologists) and towards foreign contributions, most of which came from German-speaking countries. The content of the *Revue d'économie politique* remains very eclectic, and contributions were accepted from all trends of thought from England, Germany and Austria, without favouring any one school.[20] In this way, Léon Walras had the opportunity to publish eight articles in the *Revue* between 1887 and 1898. Henri Saint-Marc (1855–1896), professor at the Law Faculty of Bordeaux, secretary of the *Revue d'économie politique* and a supporter of the historical school, translated, for example, two articles written by Ludwig Josef Brentano (1889a, 1889b).

In this period, the publishing house Guillaumin in Paris was still active in the promotion of liberal ideas in economics. But we must mention V. Giard & E. Brière as being among the publishing houses specialized in social sciences from 1893. This publishing house launched several collections: in 1896, the "Bibliothèque sociologique internationale" and the "Bibliothèque socialiste internationale", and in 1899 the "Bibliothèque internationale d'économie politique". This last collection was directed by Alfred Bonnet (1866–1933),[21] whose background was in mathematics (he wished to study at the *École Polytechnique*) and Marxism. He gained comprehensive knowledge of economics around the world. Thanks to him, many books were translated, such as works by Luigi Cossa (1899),

W.J. Ashley (1900), Gustav Schmoller (1902, 1905–1908), Adolf Wagner (1904–1914, 1909–1913), Ferdinand Lassalle (1904) and Karl Rodbertus (1904), but also by Eugen Böhm-Bawerk (1902), Vilfredo Pareto (1902) and Alfred Marshall (1906–1909).

After this brief description of the French context, we have to present the debates about the "younger" German Historical School.

Jean-Gustave Courcelle-Seneuil (1877), Maurice Block (1876, 1878, 1890), André Liesse (1854–1944) (1891–1892), Paul Leroy-Beaulieu (1843–1916) (1880, 1896) and several colleagues at the *Société d'économie politique de Paris* violently criticized the ideas of the "younger" German Historical School, not only on the rejection of natural laws in economics but also on the necessity of social reforms and labour legislation.[22] In particular, Block wished to defend the "scientific (liberal) school" against the "new authoritarian school" – that is to say the "socialists of the chair", who in his opinion were Roscher, Hildebrand, Knies and Schmoller (Block, 1876).[23] The most balanced, although critical, presentation of the German Historical School that can be found in the *Journal des économistes* was written by a young Austrian student, Eugen Schwiedland (1863–1936). He distinguishes three groups: "economic historism", which is influenced by the absolute laws' doctrine (Roscher), "economic-ethical historism" (Hildebrand, Knies, Kautz) and "neo historism" (Schmoller). He mentions Carl Menger's book, *Untersuchungen über die Methode der Sozialwissenschaften und der Politischen Ökonomie insbesondere* (1883), and the *Methodenstreit*. According to him, "In France, historism has not taken root and has only influenced the views of a few economists in so far as it holds just principles" and he alludes to Wolowski and Levasseur (Schwiedland, 1885: 30).[24] From 1876 to 1907, the liberal economist Emile Levasseur succeeded Louis Wolowski as the chair of Political Economy and Industrial Legislation in the *Conservatoire des Arts et Métiers*. During his chair of the Collège de France, he taught from 1871 "Histoire des doctrines économiques" and from 1885 "Géographie, histoire et statistiques économiques". Levasseur considered economic history as essential for history and economics, and he paid respect to the German Historical School. In favour of the inductive method in economics, he took up an eclectic position by recognizing the utility of the abstract method (1898a: 292–294).[25] A critic of Knies's ideas, he could not bring himself to call the existence of universal laws into question. But Levasseur did not accept his colleagues' great hostility against the *Revue d'économie politique*, and between 1892 and 1911 he published 13 articles in this journal.

Levasseur's (1898a) methodological point of view was accepted by Auguste Béchaux (1854–1922) in his book *L'école économique française* (1902: 18–19, 21–22). Born in Switzerland, Béchaux studied political economy in Germany during the 1870s and taught political economy at the Catholic Faculty of Law in Lille (1882–1900). Frédéric Le Play's personal secretary, in 1888 he became one of the trustees of the *Société d'économie sociale*. He was a critic of the "German authoritarian school" and the "socialism of the chair". According to him, the "French economic school" (distinguished from the English and German schools) combines the abstract deductive and the observation methods about natural economic laws; this school accepts only *"demonstrated laws"* – that is to say laws confirmed by observation and comparison of economic phenomena.[26] So if the liberty of work is the normal system of modern society, the state must intervene when private initiative is powerless to work (1902: 8–9; italics in original).

Charles Gide was a representative of the "solidarist-interventionist" group and cooperative movement (Pénin, 1996). He believed that the inductive method used by the historical school of economics, whose aim was to find historical laws about men living in a determined society and epoch, was not as powerful as the deductive method used by the classics. The observation of economic facts can be only a collective work and requires the use of statistics. Furthermore, it is impossible to directly apply experimentation to social sciences in the manner of natural sciences. We can make only comparisons which give uncertain conclusions. Unfortunately, the historical school accumulated facts and did not shed light on permanent relations and general laws.[27] Rejecting the scholastic opposition between deductive and inductive methods, Gide asserts that only one method exists (used by the physical and natural sciences) with three steps: observation of the facts, formulation of a hypothesis and testing the hypothesis while observing (Gide, 1884: chap. 2; 1890: 127–128).

In a long study prepared for a six-month mission to Germany and Austria funded by the Ministry of Public Education, Henri Saint-Marc gave for the *Revue d'économie politique* precise information about the German Historical School and also about the Austrian School of economics (Saint-Marc, 1892). In this work, he translated the majority of Schmoller's maiden speech to the Eisenach Congress (October 6–7, 1872) into French, and he tried to answer Block, who accused the German Historical School of rejecting science and confusing science and art. According to Saint-Marc, the "historic-ethical school" did not refute science but considered that the materials and results obtained at that time were not sufficient to even outline a general universal science of political economy (1892: 227–231).

In the group of Durkheim's followers, we must mention François Simiand (1873–1935), "agrégé" in philosophy, who contributed from 1896 to *L'Année sociologique* on economic sociology matters.[28] If he was not convinced by the pure historists' works, his reviews (1901, 1905) of Schmoller's *Grundriss der allgemeinen Volkswirtschaftslehre* were overall positive. He praised Schmoller for the quality of his experimental method applied to the study of economic phenomena and his step towards the preparation of a "truly positive economic science". Moreover, he was not convinced by his classifications and his teleological approach.[29]

In the first volume of his *Précis du cours d'économie politique* (1878–1879), Paul-Emile Cauwès supported the historical school's approach, saying that the "historical critic" must be considered as one of the observation methods in economics; he praised also the monographic works about families done by Frédéric Le Play. Concerning economics, Cauwès did not dispute the existence of a very limited number of universal economic laws but not the ones of the "metaphysical political economy". However, in the third edition of his *Cours d'économie politique*, more reluctant about the "too exclusively realistic character" of many monographic works of the historical school, he ended up taking an openly eclectic position (1893, vol. 1: 23–24, 59–60; vol. 4, Appendix 1: 595). Cauwès's *Précis du cours d'économie politique* was strongly criticized by the liberal economists; J.-G. Courcelle-Seneuil laughed at the author for "speaking about political economy without knowing a single word of it" (1878: 318).

According to Léon Walras, in pure economics the rational, mathematical method is used for both research and exposition of the results, without expecting confirmation from experience.[30] In his writings in social and applied economics, he used a theory of stages or "economic regimes",[31] but he asserted, "We must study history after the economic principles because political economy throws light on history (and not the reverse)" ("Exposition et conciliation des doctrines sociales", 1872, in: Walras, 2000: 668, note 251). During the 1870s, Walras learned about the "younger" German Historical School through two means: several articles collected in Lausanne[32] and his correspondence with some Italian followers of the German "socialists of the chair". According to him, the German Historical School believes in contributing to economic science, but deals only with history and statistics. This school was satisfied with gathering a large number of facts, certainly with great scholarship, but refused abstraction and searching for laws, and therefore the construction of pure and applied science.[33] In particular, Walras corresponded with Vito Cusumano (1843–1908), a former student of Adolf Wagner and Ernst Engel in Berlin.[34] After reading the first part of the *Eléments d'économie politique pure* (1988 [1874–77]), Cusumano sent a letter to Walras (October 15, 1874) indicating their divergences:

> If you believe, as it is true, that the current economic order is not *natural* and *divine*, as the Phisiocrates [sic] called it, it must also be believed that the economic laws are not *natural*, it must also be believed that the *current economic order* is not *the only possible one*, State intervention must also be admitted *a priori* [. . .]. These are the questions which separate us from the Manchester School.
>
> (Quoted in Jaffé, 1965: 441; italics in original)

Soon Walras answered him:

> The social and economic order, otherwise known as the organization system of industry and property, is certainly artificial in the sense that it depends on us to modify it, to transform it. In applied economics and in social economics, we are free to direct the natural tendencies suited to social wealth as in applied mechanics, we are free to direct the natural properties inherent to the matter. However, as to construct good machines one must know the natural properties of the matter, to well organize the economic society one

must know the natural tendencies of social wealth. We cannot command the exchange value, like gravity, except by obeying them.

(Quoted in Jaffé, 1965: 443–444)

According to Walras, the German school was not able to contribute to pure economics; for example, on the *entrepreneur*, or the theories of rent and wages.

Finding Walras badly informed about the recent developments in German economics, Cusumano asserts on January 3, 1875,

> German economists do not want to create a new system of Political economy, nor develop new theories about *profit* or *rent*; they do not deny the progress that political economy has made in the hands of the English and French [. . .]. The issue that divides one and all is that of State intervention [. . .]. German economists want the *laissez-faire* as a *rule* [. . .] arguing social questions, they are rejecting the *absolute principle of self-help* and are deciding the intervention of the State and of society in social matters [. . .]. If they make use too much of *numbers* and *history*, no one will ever be able to deny that *numbers* and *history* are necessary in the field of application as no one will be able to deny the progress obtained from this century's statistics. The best Germans support the *deductive method* in Theoretical Political Economy: they appreciate the value of the theory but want to study social *facts* at the same time.
>
> (Quoted in Jaffé, 1965: 462–463)

This wish to keep the unity of induction and deduction is very typical of the approach of Adolf Wagner, Cusumano's master. In his letter written on February 15, 1875, Walras reacted as follows:

> At present, it is quite certain that we are in perfect accord on certain points which are the most essential, for example: the fact that to really speak there are *natural* laws only in *pure economics*, and also on nature and the role of the State and on the necessity of its intervention for social progress". However, these divergences remain on the "respective limits of rational method and historical method in political and social economy.
>
> (Quoted in Jaffé, 1965: 468–469)[35]

Concerning the social reforms carried out in Germany by Bismarck with the support of the historical school of economics, the hostility of the French liberal school was very strong. In his letter to Walras (January 3, 1875), quoted before, Cusumano indicated that the Italian disciples of the German School wished for the state to adopt laws on factories and mines, create post-office savings banks and support the creation of funds for workplace accidents, health care and old-age pensions (Jaffé, 1965: 462–463). If Walras seems to agree with him about the necessity of state intervention concerning factories, mines and so on, on the last point about social laws, he was not really convinced. Later, he confronted the social laws promoted by Bismarck, setting up a compulsory workers insurance system with laws relating to health insurance (1883), workplace accidents (1884) and a disability and pension scheme (1889) in German industry. About this question, his position was the same as that of French liberal economists. In France, compulsory insurance was introduced with the laws of April 9, 1898, on working accidents and of April 5, 1910, on the *retraites ouvrières et paysannes*. In particular, Walras criticized the projects aimed at setting up an insurance system managed by the state. According to him, insurance must involve individual initiative. Of course, it is not the position defended by Cauwès.

In the third edition of his *Cours d'économie politique*, Cauwès thought that inside the "socialism of the chair",[36] it was possible to differentiate three main groups. The first group, represented by Wagner and von Scheel, is close to socialism and wanted various reforms, such as progressive tax, state insurance, land collective property in the cities and so forth. The second group, represented by Brentano (see Brentano, 1885), relied on the spontaneous creation of free organizations, such as workers' associations. Between these two groups, the third one, represented by Schmoller, advocated for the implementation of social legislation: in fact, the government of Chancellor Bismarck partly carried out this program (Cauwès, 1893, vol. 4, Appendix 1: 601–602). According to Cauwès, "Labour is not an ordinary commodity [. . .]. The State has a right of guardianship in general interests for humanity and a right to police in order to assure people's security" (1893, vol. 3: 98). Mutual societies and cooperatives born from private initiatives as recommendations of the liberals were insufficient. The state needed to take charge of social protection. Cauwès approved the creation of an *Office du travail* with the July 20, 1891, law. He became the president of the commission to organize the *Congrès international de la protection légale des travailleurs* (*Musée Social*, Paris, July 25–28, 1900). This international congress in Paris was important because it led to the creation of the International Association for Legal Protection of the Workers, whose constituent assembly was held in Bale in 1901. This association, organized in national sections,[37] played a decisive part in the adoption of international labour standards, a movement which in 1919 led to the birth of the International Labour Organization.

According to Cauwès, the transition from "agricultural state" to "industrial complex state" requires a "rational protection". He asserts, "The protection of national industries [. . .] is not the most perpetual; it is a transition regime devoted to favour industrial education; it is a guardianship which must naturally stop at the age of full economic development" (1893, 2: 482). He was harshly criticized by the liberal economists on this question. Henri Baudrillart reacted to the *Cours* of Cauwès as follows:

> The way in which Mr. Cauwès treats free trade will surely not satisfy economists. We admit that the historical method and experience can prevent us to see in free trade one of these absolute truths which imposes itself in all places at all times. A certain degree of guardianship in fledgling industries,

the necessity of transitions, the opportunity for certain exceptions can be indicated with as much force as one would want. Moreover, it is necessary that free trade would be sufficiently shown so as not to be suffocated under reserves to the point that it seems to die before the contrary system.

(1885: 184)

Baudrillart could not have put it better. Indeed, Cauwès became the leader of the "national political economy" group[38] and during the 1890s supported the strong protectionism of the minister of Commerce, Jules Méline.[39]

Concluding remarks

We can confirm the overall absence of a French Historical School of economics and of a strong intellectual influence of the German Historical School during the nineteenth century. The only economists who were primarily influenced by the German economists were Henri Wolowski in the first half and Paul Cauwès in the second half of the nineteenth century. Most of the French economists influenced by the German Historical School were liberal and attached to the existence of universal economic laws. However, from the 1870s, the works of French liberal economists took an increasing role in statistical and historical research. This was the case, for example, for Paul Leroy-Beaulieu and his students.

While the influence of the German Historical School concerning methodology is weak, until the First World War, its influence was more significant in regards to economic policy, labour legislation and protectionism.

Notes

1 There is only one exception: the teaching of economics at the Faculty of Law in Paris, introduced in 1864, entrusted to Anselme-P. Batbie, professor of public law.
2 Block also published the *Dictionnaire de l'administration française* (Paris: Berger-Levrault, 1856, second ed., 1877) and the *Annuaire de l'économie politique et de la statistique* (1856–1879).
3 *Du commerce des grains et des mesures à prendre en cas de cherté* (Paris: Guillaumin, 1854).
4 The translator then referred to W. Roscher's works.
5 His first book, *Grundriss zu Vorlesungen über die Staatswirthschaft, nach geschichtlicher Methode* (1843), was not translated into French.
6 In 1834, Wolowski founded the *Revue de législation et de jurisprudence*.
7 In 1864, the title of this course became "Political Economy and Industrial Legislation".
8 Wolowski (1857: i) was preparing a book on political economy in Germany, but it would never be published.
9 Instead, Wolowski would publish the *Traité de la première invention des monnaies* of Nicolas Oresme and the *Traité de la monnaie* of Copernic (Paris: Guillaumin, 1864).
10 He refers to Hegel.
11 Baudrillart published *Jean Bodin et son temps. Tableau des théories politiques et des idées économiques au XVIe siècle* (Paris : Guillaumin, 1853), *Des rapports de la*

morale et de l'économie politique. Cours professé au Collège de France (Paris : Guillaumin, 1860) and *Histoire du luxe privé et public depuis l'Antiquité jusqu'à nos jours* (Paris: Hachette, 1878–1880, 4 vols.).

12 Courcelle-Seneuil would support later this point of view in the *Journal des économistes* (1877: 320–321).

13 Léonce de Lavergne published *Essai sur l'économie rurale de l'Angleterre, de l'Ecosse et de l'Irlande* (Paris: Guillaumin, 1854), *Economie rurale de la France depuis 1789* (Paris: Guillaumin, 1860) and *Les Assemblées provinciales sous Louis XVI* (Paris: M. Lévy, 1864).

14 He refers to Bacon.

15 Levasseur married Wolowski's niece.

16 Levasseur used this methodological approach in his book *La question de l'or* (Paris: Guillaumin, 1858). He also published *Recherches sur le système de Law* (Paris: Guillaumin, 1854) and *Histoire des classes ouvrières en France de 1789 à nos jours* (Paris: Rousseau, 1867).

17 On Durkheim and the German economists, see Steiner (1994) and Nau and Steiner (2002).

18 Ironically, Schumpeter said that Cauwès "was a man of sense and force even if not much of a scientific economist" (1954: 843).

19 For the history of the last impact of the historical school among the French economists, a follower of Cauwès must be mentioned: Lucien Brocard (1870–1936), professor at the University of Nancy from 1906, author of *Principes d'économie nationale et internationale* (Paris: Sirey, 1929–1931) and later *Les conditions générales de l'activité économique* (Paris: Sirey, 1934).

20 Articles by L.J. Brentano (10 between 1889 and 1902), K. Bücher (three between 1892 and 1894), G.F. Knapp (one in 1891) and G. Schmoller (three between 1889 and 1894) were translated into French for the *Revue d'économie politique*. Knowledge about German state socialism was also present in the *Revue d'économie politique*.

21 On Bonnet, see Rist (1933).

22 Otherwise, they criticized Karl Marx's *Capital.*

23 Baudrillart wrote a review (1874) on the French translation of Roscher's book *Recherches sur divers sujets d'économie politique* (1874).

24 In 1890, Eugen Schwiedland was appointed by Gide as a member of the *Revue d'économie politique*'s board of editors; he published 13 articles in the *Revue* between 1888 and 1902.

25 In 1898b (pp. 34–35) (whose English translation is *The American Workman*, Baltimore: Johns Hopkins University Press, 1900), he paid attention to Alfred Marshall's point of view ("Each study supplements the other, there is no rivalry or opposition between them"). He also published *La population française* (Paris: Rousseau, 1889–1892, 3 vols.).

26 In order to illustrate Béchaux's point of view, we can mention Paul Leroy-Beaulieu, who in his *Essai sur la répartition des richesses* (Paris: Guillaumin, 1881) tried to put to the test by means of history and statistics the classical theory of distribution, particularly the Ricardian theory of wages.

27 Gide quoted the famous scientist Claude Bernard, who widely used the experimental method: "the observer who does not know what he is searching for will never understand what he finds" (1890: 128).

28 In 1904, Simiand defended his doctoral thesis prepared under the supervision of Paul Cauwès, which would be expanded under the title *Le salaire des ouvriers des mines de charbon en France: Contribution à la théorie économique du salaire* (Paris: Cornély, 1907).

29 Previously in 1899, F. Simiand published a review of the second edition (1897) of Karl Bücher's *Die Entstehung der Volkswirtschaft.*

30 When Walras presented "Principe d'une théorie mathématique de l'échange" in the *Académie des sciences morales et politiques* (August 16 and 23, 1873), Levasseur opposed him on the impossibility of an exact measurement of the "intensity of the need" for the purchasers: the fluctuations of the needs cannot be precisely calculated and, in short, human freedom cannot be put in an "algebraical expression". Wolowski criticized Walras for making political economy an "exact science", whereas it can be only a "moral science, which has man as starting point and purpose" (Walras, 1987: 530–532).

31 See Potier (2014).

32 For example, Walras obtained French translations of three of Gustav Schmoller's works: "Arbeitseinstellungen und Gewerkvereine" (Report to the Eisenach Assembly, October 6–7, 1872), *Jahrbücher für Nationalökonomie und Statistik*, vol. 19, no. 6, 1872; "Die Entwicklung und die Krisis der deutschen Weberei im 19. Jahrhundert", *Deutsche Zeit – und Streit-Fragen*, vol. 2, no. 25 (1873); and *Die Natur des Arbeitsvertrage und der Kontrakt-bruch, Schriften des Vereins für Socialpolitik* Bd. 7, 1874 (translations preserved in the Bibliothèque Cantonale et Universitaire of Lausanne). The author of these French translations is unknown.

33 In a "note d'humeur" (undated), Walras remarked, "Gathering facts . . . is not the job of the scientist, but of the rag-and-bone man. Science starts the moment that we shine the light of reason on facts" (2000: 552). On the historical school, see also his review of Alberto Errera's book, *L'Italia industriale*, 1874 (Walras, 2000: 486–488) and his *Cours d'économie politique appliquée* (Walras, 1996: 448–449).

34 See Potier (1998: 127–131, Appendix 1: 138–140) (previously unpublished letter of Cusumano to Walras, October 24, 1874).

35 For more details about the correspondence between Walras and Cusumano, see Potier (1998).

36 Curiously, Cauwès asserted that Gide had some sympathy for "socialism of the chair" (1893, vol. 4, Appendix 1: 592, 603, note 3).

37 Cauwès became the first president of the French section.

38 In December 1897, he founded the *Société d'économie politique nationale* and was its president from the following year. See Cauwès (1898) and Ravix (2000).

39 Here we must remember the return of protectionism in France with 1881's and 1892's customs laws (the last one was called "Méline law").

40 The translator is unknown. At the opening we find an author's dedication: "A mon ami Louis Wolowski Membre de l'Institut, etc."

References

Baudrillart, H. (1866). "De la méthode en économie politique" [Leçon d'ouverture au Collège de France]. *Journal des économistes*, series 3, vol. 1, 15 January: 11–31.

Baudrillart, H. (1874). "Recherches sur divers sujets d'économie politique, par M. Guillaume Roscher [. . .]". *Journal des savants*, March: 173–186, July: 461–468, August: 501–514.

Baudrillart, H. (1885). " Le nouvel enseignement de l'économie politique dans les facultés de droit". *Revue des Deux-Mondes*, 1 May: 158–185.

Béchaux, A. (1902). *L'école économique française*. Paris: Arthur Rousseau/Guillaumin.

Block, M. (1853). "Des limites de l'économie politique en Allemagne". *Journal des économistes*, vol. 36, year 12, no. 148, 15 August: 245–254.

Block, M. (1876). "Les deux écoles économiques. I – La nouvelle école autoritaire ou les socialistes de la chaire". *Journal des économistes*, series 3, year 11, vol. 43, no. 128, 15 August: 153–174.

Block, M. (1878). "La quintessence du socialisme de la chaire. MM. Held, Wagner, Samter, De Scheele, Roesler, De Laveleye, etc.". *Journal des économistes*, series 4, year 1, vol. 4, no. 11, November: 173–213.

Block, M. (1890). *Les progrès de la science économique depuis Adam Smith*. Paris: Guillaumin, 2nd ed., 1897, 2 vols.

Bourdé, G. and Martin, H. (1983). *Les écoles historiques*. Paris: Le Seuil.

Brentano, L. (1885). *La question ouvrière*, trans. by L. Caubert (*Die gewerbliche Arbeiterfrage in Handbuch der politische Ökonomie*, ed. by G. Schönberg, 1882). Paris: Librairie des bibliophiles.

Brentano, L. (1889a). "Une leçon sur l'économie politique classique". *Revue d'économie politique*, vol. 3, 1–23.

Brentano, L. (1889b). "Des dernières causes de notre misère sociale: Un essai de morphologie économique". *Revue d'économie politique*, vol. 3: 341–365.

Breton, Y. (1988). "Les économistes français et les écoles historiques allemandes: rencontre entre l'économie politique et l'histoire? 1800–1914". *Histoire, économie et société*, no. 3, 3rd quarter: 399–417.

Breton, Y. (1991). "Les économistes français et les questions de méthode", in Y. Breton and M. Lutfalla (eds.), *L'économie politique en France au XIXe siècle*. Paris: Economica, 389–419.

Cauwès, P. (1878–1879). *Précis du cours d'économie politique professé à la Faculté de Droit de Paris*. Paris: L. Larose & Forcel, 2 vols. (2nd ed., 1881–1882).

Cauwès, P. (1893). *Cours d'économie politique*, 3rd ed. Paris: L. Larose & Forcel, 4 vols.

Cauwès, P. (1898). "L'économie politique nationale". *Revue d'économie politique*, vol. 12: 97–107.

Courcelle-Seneuil, J-G. (1877). "Situation et perspectives de l'économie politique". *Journal des économistes*, series 3, vol. 37, 15 September: 313–329.

Courcelle-Seneuil, J-G. (1878). Review of *Précis du cours d'économie politique* by P. Cauwès. *Journal des économistes*, series 4, vol. 2, May: 315–319.

Durkheim, É. (1887). "La science positive et la morale en Allemagne". *Revue philosophique*, vol. 24: 33–58, 133–142, 275–284.

Fontenay, R. de (1858). "De la méthode historique appliquée aux études économiques: Principes d'économie politique, par M. G. Roscher, traduits par M. Wolowski". *Journal des économistes*, series 2, year 5, vol. 17, no. 1, 15 January: 57–73.

Gide, C. (1884). *Principes d'économie politique*. Paris: L. Larose & Forcel.

Gide, C. (1890). "L'école nouvelle", in *Quatre écoles d'économie sociale: Conférences données à l'aula de l'Université de Genève*. Geneva: Librairie Stapelmohr, 99–154.

Gide, C. (1908). "L'Ecole économique française dans ses rapports avec l'Ecole anglaise et l'Ecole allemande", in *Die Entwicklung der deutschen Volkswirthschaftslehre in 19e Jahrhundert: Festschrift Gustav Schmoller*. Leipzig: Duncker & Humblot, vol. 1, chap. 16, 1–27.

Gide, C. and Rist, C. (1909). *Histoire des doctrines économiques depuis les physiocrates jusqu'à nos jours*. Paris: L. Larose & L. Tenin.

Gislain, J.J. (2000). "Le premier débat sur la 'méthode historique' (1857–1868): Louis Wolowski et Léonce de Lavergne", in P. Dockès, L. Frobert, G. Klotz, J-P. Potier and A. Tiran (eds.), *Les traditions économiques françaises, 1848–1939*. Paris: Ed. du CNRS, 101–113.

Grimmer-Solem, E. and Romani, R. (1998). "The Historical School 1870–1900: A cross-national reassessment". *Journal of European Ideas*, vol. 24, no. 4–5: 267–299.

Ingram, J.K. (1919). *A History of Political Economy*. New and enlarged ed. London: Black.

Jaffé, W. (ed.) (1965). *Correspondence of Léon Walras and Related Papers*. Amsterdam: North Holland, 3 vols.

Leroy-Beaulieu, P. (1880). "Le développement du socialisme d'Etat". *Journal des économistes*, vol. 9, series 4: 109–115.

Leroy-Beaulieu, P. (1896). *Traité théorique et pratique d'économie politique*. Paris: Guillaumin, 4 vols.

Le Van-Lemesle, L. (1994a). "Economie politique et histoire au 19e siècle en France: Quand l'économie retrouve l'histoire", in H. Moniot and M. Serwanski (eds.), *L'histoire en partage*. Paris: Nathan, 125–140.

Le Van-Lemesle, L. (1994b). "Levasseur Emile", in C. Fontanon and A. Grelon (eds.), *Les professeurs du Conservatoire national des Arts et Métiers: Dictionnaire biographique, 1794–1955*. Paris: INRP, vol. 2, 105–115.

Le Van-Lemesle, L. (2004). *Le Juste ou le Riche: L'enseignement de l'économie politique, 1815–1950*. Paris: Comité pour l'histoire économique de la France.

Levasseur, E. (1898a). "De la méthode dans les sciences économiques" [Lecture at Collège de France]. *Revue politique et littéraire: Revue Bleue*, series 4, vol. 9 (5 & 12 March): 291–296, 338–343.

Levasseur, E. (1898b). *L'ouvrier américain: L'ouvrier au travail, l'ouvrier chez lui – les questions ouvrières*. Paris: Larose.

Liesse, A. (1891–1892). "Méthode", in L. Say and J. Chailley-Bert (eds.), *Nouveau dictionnaire d'économie politique*. Paris: Guillaumin, vol. 2, 256–272.

List, F. (1851). *Système national d'économie politique*, annotated by H. Richelot (*Das nationale System der politischen Ökonomie*, 1841). Paris: Capelle (2nd ed., reviewed and corrected, 1857).

Markiewicz, P. (1994). "Wolowski Louis", in C. Fontanon and A. Grelon (eds.), *Les professeurs du Conservatoire national des Arts et Métiers: Dictionnaire biographique, 1794–1955*. Paris: INRP, vol. 2, 677–687.

Nau, H-H. and Steiner, P. (2002). "Schmoller, Durkheim, and Old European Institutionalist Economics". *Journal of Economic Issues*, vol. 36, no. 4, December, 1005–1024.

Pénin, M. (1996). "La *Revue d'économie politique* ou l'essor d'une grande devancière (1887–1936)", in L. Marco (ed.), *Les revues d'économie en France (1751–1994)*. Paris: L'Harmattan, 157–196.

Potier, J-P. (1998). "Léon Walras et l'"école lombarde-vénitienne" à travers sa correspondance (1874–1886)", in F. Michon (ed.), *L'Economie, une science pour l'homme et la société – Mélanges en l'honneur d'Henri Bartoli*. Paris: Sorbonne, 117–145.

Potier, J-P. (2014). "Espoirs et dangers du 'régime industriel et commercial' de l'humanité selon Léon Walras". *Innovations: Revue d'Economie et de Management de l'Innovation*, no. 45, 2014/3, 159–170.

Ravix, J-T. (2000). "Paul Cauwès et le concept d'économie nationale", in P. Dockès, L. Frobert, G. Klotz, J-P. Potier and A. Tiran (eds.), *Les traditions économiques françaises, 1848–1939*. Paris: Ed. du CNRS, 155–167.

Réunion de la Société d'économie politique. (1868). "De la méthode historique en économie politique, et de la méthode en général dans les sciences morales et politiques" (contributions by J.-G. Courcelle-Seneuil, L. Wolowski, A.-P. Batbie, H. Baudrillart), *Journal des économistes*, series 3, vol. 9, no. 25, 15 January: 145–162.

Rist, C. (1933). "Nécrologie: Alfred Bonnet". *Revue d'économie politique*, vol. 47, 1591–1592.

Roscher, G. [Wilhelm] (1854). *Du commerce des grains et des mesures à prendre en cas de cherté*, trans. by M. Block (*Ueber Korntheuerungen: Ein Beitrag zur Wirtschafts-polizei*, 1847). Paris: Guillaumin.

Roscher, G. [Wilhelm] (1857). *Principes d'économie politique*, 2nd ed., transl. and annotated by M.L. Wolowski (*System der Volkswirthschaft*, vol. 1, *Die Grundlagen der Nationalökonomie*, 1854). Paris: Guillaumin, 2 vols.

Roscher, G. [Wilhelm] (1874). *Recherches sur divers sujets d'économie politique*. Paris: Guillaumin.[40]

Saint-Marc, H. (1892). "Etude sur l'enseignement de l'économie politique dans les universités des pays de langue allemande". *Revue d'économie politique*, vol. 6, 217–249, 423–470.

Schumpeter, J-A. (1954). *History of Economic Analysis*. New York: Oxford University Press.

Schwiedland, E. (1885). "L'historisme économique allemand". *Journal des économistes*, series 4, year 8, vol. 31, no. 7, July, 17–36.

Schmoller, G. (1902). *Politique sociale et économie politique (Questions fondamentales)* (*Über einige Grundlagen der Sozialpolitik und der Volkswirtschaftslehre*, 1898). Paris: V. Giard & E. Brière.

Schmoller, G. (1905–1908). *Principes d'économie politique*, trans. by G. Platon and L. Pollack (*Grundriss der allgemeinen Volkswirtschaftslehre*, 1900–1904, 2 vols.). Paris: V. Giard & E. Brière, 5 vols.

Simiand, F. (1899). "La formation de l'économie nationale, conférences et essais" (review of K. Bücher's *Die Entstehung der Volkswirtschaft*, 2nd ed. 1897). *L'Année sociologique*, vol. 2, 440–448.

Simiand, F. (1901). "L'école historique allemande" (review of Schmoller's *Grundriss der allgemeinen Volkswirtschaftslehre*, 1900). *L'Année sociologique*, vol. 4, 486–496.

Simiand, F. (1905). "L'école historique allemande" (review of Schmoller's *Grundriss der allgemeinen Volkswirtschaftslehre*, 1904). *L'Année sociologique*, vol. 8, 515–520.

Société d'économie politique. (1891). Réunion du 5 janvier 1864. *Annales de la Société d'économie politique*, vol. 5, July 1862–December 1864. Paris: Guillaumin, 437–480.

Steiner, P. (1994). "Durkheim, les économistes et la critique de l'économie politique". *Economies et Sociétés. Cahiers de l'ISMEA*, vol. 28, no. 4, April, series PE no. 19: 135–159.

Todd, D. (2008). *L'identité économique de la France: Libre échange et protectionnisme: 1814–1851*. Paris: Grasset.

Wagner, A. (1904–1914). *Fondements de l'économie politique*, trans. by L. Pollack (*Grundlegung der politischen Ökonomie*, 1892–94, 3rd ed., 2 vols.). Paris: V. Giard & E. Brière, 5 vols.

Wagner, A. (1909–1913). *Traité de la science des finances*, trans. by H. Vouters, J. Ronjat, P. Hallier, E. Bouché-Leclercq and L. Cusinet (*Finanzwissenschaft*). Paris: V. Giard & E. Brière, 5 vols.

Walras, L. (1987). *Mélanges d'économie politique et sociale*, vol. 7 of *Œuvres économiques complètes*, ed. by C. Hébert and J.-P. Potier. Paris: Economica.

Walras L. (1988) [1874–77]. *Eléments d'économie politique pure*, vol. 8 of *Œuvres économiques complètes*, ed. by C. Mouchot. Paris: Economica.

Walras, L. (1996). *Cours (Cours d'économie sociale, Cours d'économie politique appliquée, Matériaux sur le Cours d'économie politique pure)*, vol. 12 of *Œuvres économiques complètes*, ed. by P. Dockès and J.-P. Potier with coll. of P. Bridel. Paris, Economica.

Walras, L. (2000). *Œuvres diverses*, vol. 13 of *Œuvres économiques complètes*, ed. by P. Dockès, C. Mouchot and J.-P. Potier. Paris: Economica.

Wolowski, L. (1857). "De l'application de la méthode historique à l'étude de l'économie politique". *Journal des économistes*, series 2, no. 15, July: 172–212. Published as "Préface: De l'application de la méthode historique à l'étude de l'économie politique", in G. Roscher, *Principes d'économie politique*. Paris: Guillaumin, vol. 1, ix–lxxiii.

3 Economics, statistics and history

The legacy of the German Historical School in Belgium

Guido Erreygers and Maarten Van Dijck

> Political economy can establish nothing without the aid of statistics and history; for it is only by consulting these two sciences that it can learn what it seeks to determine; that is to say, what are the laws which are useful or fatal to nations.
>
> (De Laveleye, 1884: 12)

Introduction

Belgium's intellectual climate in the second half of the nineteenth century was characterized by deep ideological cleavages, and heavily oriented towards France. It is, therefore, remarkable that many Belgian economists and historians, from a wide variety of ideological backgrounds, favourably received the writings of the German Historical School. In this chapter we explore the influence exerted by the German Historical School on economists and economic historians between 1870 and 1914. We argue that the German Historical School was an important factor in the development of economics and sociology in Belgium, and played a crucial role in the emergence of the discipline of economic history. Personal contacts and study periods of Belgian scholars in the German academic world were important ways to spread the ideas of the German Historical School. And even though a formal historical school never existed in Belgium, the themes and methods of the German Historical School were continuing sources of inspiration, at least until the beginning of the war in 1914.

Several reasons explain why the ideas of the German Historical School became a source of attraction. There was a strong interest in the inductive method and in the use of all kinds of empirical research (statistical studies, surveys, archival research) in the social sciences. Some economists were charmed by the multi-disciplinary character and the ethical dimensions of the work by members of the school. Moreover, at the end of the nineteenth and the beginning of the twentieth centuries broad support developed for economic and social policies aimed at improving the living conditions of the majority of the population. We illustrate the influence of the German Historical School by looking successively at the economists Émile De Laveleye and Victor Brants, the historian Henri Pirenne and the *Institut de Sociologie*.

An early follower: Émile De Laveleye

In his long outdated overview of economic thought in Belgium in the period 1830–1886, Paul Michotte (1904) devoted one chapter to the "Historical School – Socialism of the Chair". He saw two economists as representative of this current of thought: François Huet (1814–1869) and Émile De Laveleye (1822–1892). Although the inclusion of the Frenchman Huet seems highly debatable – its main motivation being the fact that Huet exerted a strong influence on De Laveleye during his student years at the University of Ghent – Michotte was certainly right to consider De Laveleye as an important representative of the historical school in Belgium. This independent and eclectic spirit was probably Belgium's most respected economist in the second half of the nineteenth century (Chlepner, 1972: 156–158; Lambert, 1970), even more so than the outspoken libertarian Gustave De Molinari (1819–1912). De Laveleye contributed much to the spread of the ideas of the historical school, both in Belgium and elsewhere, at the end of the nineteenth century.

De Laveleye revealed himself as a fellow traveller of the *Kathedersozialisten* in July 1875, when he published an article on "the new tendencies of political economy and of socialism" in *La Revue des Deux Mondes*, the French journal to which he was a frequent contributor. As he explained later, it was at John Stuart Mill's instigation that he decided to give wider publicity to their views. De Laveleye and Mill had started corresponding in 1868 (Bots, 1992: 151), and they met eye to eye in Mill's English residence in 1873. During their meeting, they mainly discussed the book De Laveleye was preparing at the time, *De la propriété et de ses formes primitives*, which he published in 1874 and dedicated "À la mémoire de John Stuart Mill et de François Huet". When De Laveleye talked about the German socialists, Mill informed him that he was familiar with their names but had never studied their work, and he encouraged De Laveleye to make their views known (De Laveleye, 1885: 25).

De Laveleye (1875c) started his article by observing that a wide variety of writers were challenging the prevailing orthodoxy in economics, by which he referred to the canon defended by those working in the tradition of Adam Smith and Jean-Baptiste Say. In different countries alternative views were expounded: in Germany by the socialists of the chair; in Britain by economists who paid a lot of attention to history and law, such as Thomas Edward Cliffe Leslie (1826–1882) and William Thomas Thornton (1813–1880); in Italy by those involved in the *Giornale degli Economisti*, such as Luigi Luzzatti (1841–1927), Fedele Lampertico (1833–1906) and Vito Cusumano (1844–1908)[1]; and in Denmark by those around the *Nationaløkonomisk Tidsskrift*, such as Niels Christian Frederiksen (1840–1905), Vigand Andreas Falbe Hansen (1841–1932) and Hans William Scharling (1837–1911). In De Laveleye's mind, it could not be doubted that "a scientific revolution [is] going on of a very serious character" (De Laveleye, 1879b: 1). He then described in some detail what he considered to be the essence of the criticism of orthodox economists, and especially of the free traders of the Manchester school, by the socialists of the chair. Political economy tended to present man "as a being who everywhere and always pursues his private interest" (ibid.: 2), expressed a very strong belief in the doctrine of *laissez-faire, laissez-passer*, and concentrated on questions relating to the production of wealth. By contrast, the socialists of the chair admitted that human beings are driven not only by self-interest but also by social motives, that the state is "the supreme organ of law and the instrument of justice" (ibid.: 5) and that questions of distribution should not be neglected. The largest part of the article consists of an assessment of what De Laveleye considered to be valuable in the arguments of the socialists of the chair. He endorsed their view of economics as a moral science, and sided with them in criticizing the tendency to conceive economics as an exact or natural science. He could not find any evidence for the natural laws which economists claimed they had discovered.[2] The reservations which De Laveleye expressed about the conceptions of the *Kathedersozialisten* remained very minor:

> The new doctrine is still somewhat vague both as to premises and conclusions, and when it endeavors to define the relations of political economy to morality and to law, it is less original and less new than some of its more enthusiastic followers are willing to admit.
>
> (Ibid.: 23)

On the whole, he praised their realistic approach to economic problems (he called them "realistic economists"), and thought that they offered more practical solutions to social issues than either utopian or scientific socialists.

There was an almost immediate reaction to what some saw as a frontal attack on the existing economic science. In August 1875 the French economist Henri Baudrillart (1821–1892) protested forcefully in the *Journal des Économistes* against "a critique which is too absolute and decidedly unfair" (Baudrillart, 1875a: 190). In his reply, dated 20 October 1875, De Laveleye (1875b) slightly softened his words and affirmed that he still considered himself to be an economist; his aim had been to show that in some respects economics had chosen the wrong road. However, Baudrillart (1875b) and even more prominently Joseph Garnier (1813–1881) thought that De Laveleye went much too far; Garnier (1875: 219) was convinced that De Laveleye's enthusiasm for the *Kathedersozialisten* and the "new economists" distorted his view of what economics had to offer. Interestingly, De Laveleye began his reply by saying that he had just returned from a trip abroad; what he did not tell was that he had attended the third general assembly of the *Verein für Socialpolitik* in Eisenach, from 10 to 12 October 1875. About this participation he wrote a detailed report, which he addressed to the editor of the recently founded Italian journal *Giornale degli Economisti*, Eugenio Forti, who published it in November 1875 (De Laveleye, 1875a).

De Laveleye's position in favour of the German Historical School was also noticed in the English-speaking world. When the Political Economy Club celebrated the centenary of the publication of Adam Smith's *Wealth of Nations* on 31 May 1876, De Laveleye was one of the invited speakers. In his speech, which was published in *The Times*, he argued that economists should pay more attention to the distribution of wealth than they had done so far. This is what he found attractive in the positions taken by the German Historical School:

> But it is chiefly upon this point that there has lately arisen a division in the ranks of the economists. On the one hand, the elder school, which, for want of a better term, I shall denominate the orthodox school, holds that every thing is governed by natural laws. The other school, which its adversaries have styled the Socialists of the Chair – *Katheder-Socialisten* – but which should more properly be called the historical school, or, as the Germans say, the school of the *realists*, maintains that distribution is regulated, in part, no doubt, by free contract, but still more by civil and political institutions, by religious beliefs, by moral sentiments, by customs, and by historical traditions.
>
> (De Laveleye, 1879b: 26)

On the other side of the Atlantic Ocean, the banker and financial writer George Walker (1814–1885) drew attention to De Laveleye's 1875 article by publishing a translation in the New York–based *The Banker's Magazine and Statistical Register*, which together with the 1876 speech was also published as a separate leaflet (De Laveleye, 1879a, 1879b).

In 1881 De Laveleye again published an article on "the new tendencies in political economy" in *La Revue des Deux Mondes* (1881b), this time focusing on England and more specifically on the work of Cliffe Leslie. He placed Cliffe Leslie in the line of "historical economists", such as Roscher and Knies, but did not see him as a representative of the *Kathedersozialisten*. The two "new tendencies" articles became the core of De Laveleye's book *Le socialisme contemporain* (1881a), of which the first edition was published in 1881. Over the years it was substantially revised and expanded, and also translated into English, German, Russian, Spanish, Swedish, Polish and Czech. The book clearly articulated De Laveleye's views on socialism and on the German Historical School. These views were much less explicitly present in his very successful textbook *Éléments d'économie politique*, first published in 1882, of which also numerous editions and translations were issued (see Erreygers and Van Dijck, 2012). Although in that book he argued for an interdisciplinary approach of economic issues, it is remarkable that he referred frequently to Adam Smith and John Stuart Mill, but only once to Roscher and never to Schmoller.

As a prolific writer De Laveleye exerted a considerable influence on many Belgian and non-Belgian economists, and undoubtedly he was instrumental in orienting some of them to the German Historical School. A prominent example is Ernest Mahaim (1865–1938), who was one of De Laveleye's students at the University of Liège. At the end of the 1880s Mahaim went to Berlin to study with Adolf Wagner and Gustav von Schmoller (Rey, 1983: 502); subsequently, he contributed to the *Schriften des Vereins für Socialpolitik*. In 1892 Mahaim took over De Laveleye's course on political economy, but this was only one of his many fields of expertise. In fact, throughout his academic career he taught courses on economics, international law and statistics. His research work was also of an interdisciplinary character (more on this in the final section). Moreover, Mahaim played a major role in national and international associations aimed at the improvement of the conditions of the labouring population, such as the *Association internationale pour la protection légale des travailleurs*, a precursor of the International Labour Organization.

Victor Brants and empirical research in a Catholic blend

At the Catholic University of Leuven the influence of the German Historical School can be seen in the work of Victor Brants (1856–1917), who started to teach the course of political economy at the Law Faculty in 1881. He succeeded Charles Périn (1815–1905), for whom economics had to be subordinated to Catholicism, and was intellectually related to this strain of Catholic economics (Erreygers and Van Dijck, 2012: 221). Yet Brants was, like De Laveleye, also a pioneer of economic history. His goal was to corroborate Périn's abstract moral and economic principles with historical studies, of which he wrote that "Cette méthode est fort en honneur aujourd'hui" (Brants, 1887: 66). From 1882 onwards Brants also taught courses in history at the Faculty of Arts and Humanities.

While Brants was primarily a Catholic economist, he was close to the German Historical School. Brants came into contact with the school through De Laveleye and the French group of researchers around Frédéric Le Play (Meerts, 1982: 207). Some correspondence between Brants and Schmoller has been conserved in Brants's papers (Van Molle, 1989: 78). In 1885 Brants started a seminar parallel to his lectures in political economy. The law students who enlisted for the seminar *Conférence d'économie sociale* studied contemporary socioeconomic topics and learned to work independently by analysing articles and books, by going on study trips and by doing individual research. Brants himself wrote that the German example inspired him to start the seminar (Brants, 1900: 120–121). Each year the best student of the *Conférence* received a grant to study abroad. In 1891 E. Dubois was sent to Berlin to attend the courses of Schmoller, Treitschke and Lamprecht (Meerts, 1982: 222–225).

Brants's publications in the years 1878 and 1882 were primarily concerned with economic history. As an antirevolutionary, Brants opposed the society of the Christian Middle Ages to the industrial society of the nineteenth century. While, according to Brants, history in the Ancien Régime had been a road towards intellectual and moral improvement, the French Revolution had blocked progress. The ideal societal order, as prescribed by Providence, had in its time been replaced by a life oriented towards profits and luxury (Meerts, 1983: 101–104). Brants researched the historical genesis of property rights in particular and distinguished two separate phases. In the first phase, the *communauté négative*, man used God's creation, while no man had any property. In the second phase, the *communauté positive*, man lived in community and had personal possessions. Possessions stimulated the spirit of enterprise and made production cheaper because of the specialization of labour. Possessions also created a responsibility towards the poor. In his historical exhibition of the genesis of property, Brants referred to the publications of Roscher and De Laveleye to show that appropriation was based on labour (Brants, 1880).

In his 1883 publication *Lois et méthode de l'économie politique*, Brants stated that he wanted to reconcile the inductive and deductive method (Brants, 1887: 75). At the beginning of his career Brants's ideas came from Périn. Brants wrote that Catholic economists had a fixed and indisputable point of departure for their deductive economics in Catholic principles. The moral guidelines for economic life were deduced from these first principles. He was a normative economist who saw religion, family and property as the foundations for society and economics. By an analysis of facts, be it of a historical, statistical or observational character, he hoped to verify these first principles of social life and to establish the corresponding economic and social laws.

In his research on the history of economic thought Brants identified the German Historical School as one of the acknowledged schools in European economic thought. Brants divided the field of economics into four groups: the "Manchester school of Adam Smith", socialists, mathematical economists and a group of economists that opposed the utilitarian principle as the basis for economics (Brants, 1887: 88–107). Brants subdivided the last group into the Mainz school of Wilhelm von Ketteler, the Périn school, the observational school of Le Play and the German Historical School (Almodovar and Teixeira, 2010: 129–131). Brants, while using the historical method as an economist himself, nevertheless warned against the tendency of the German Historical School to identify only laws specific to certain phases of history. All too often historical studies became a succession of facts. Brants, by contrast, acknowledged the existence of immovable rational principles from which economists could work deductively (Brants, 1887: 74).

According to Brants, the German Historical School also gave too large a responsibility to the state in governing economics, individual activity and social progress of society (Brants, 1887: 101–104). Initially he had hoped, like Périn expected, that Christian charity could solve the social problems that accompanied the industrial revolution. Certainly after the large wave of social protest in the industrial centres of Belgium in the year 1886, Brants's thoughts on the social question evolved. His observations in the 1880s led him to believe that the state should play a more active role in social and economic issues. His thoughts also evolved in the direction of corporatism.

In the 1880s the young professor became influenced by the observational method of Frédéric Le Play. Brants's approach became more sociological, and he wrote detailed monographs about subjects such as the working conditions of the labourers, agricultural problems, production cooperatives, corporatism and so on. In his textbook on political economy, written during the 1880s but reworked and published as *Les grandes lignes d'économie politique* in 1901, he made ample room for the description of economic legislation, associations and institutions. But, as a testimony to the lasting interest in history, his textbook included lengthy digressions on for instance the history of the corporations of the Ancien Régime (Erreygers and Van Dijck, 2012: 222).

Brants's blend of Catholicism, historical research and sociological studies inspired a number of followers at the Special School for Political and Economic Sciences that was founded at the University of Louvain in 1892. For example, Emiel Vliebergh (1872–1925) was influenced by the German Historical School through Brants, but also directly by studying in Berlin (Van Molle, 1989: 79). A similar blend can be found later in the work of Georges Legrand, who taught at the State Institute of Agronomy in Gembloux (Erreygers and Van Dijck, 2012: 227).

Henri Pirenne and the genesis of economic history in Belgium

The activities of Belgian historians and archivists before 1880 were oriented towards political and institutional history and the publication of sources for the national history. Economic history became an important topic after that date, in particular in the work of Henri Pirenne and his followers. The German Historical School was an important factor in the orientation of a number of historians towards economic history. The easy military victory of Germany over France in 1870 made German intellectual life attractive to a number of young historians (Pirenne, 1927a: 52). The first influence was the scientific spirit in critical source analysis used by German historians. In 1874 the historian Godefroid Kurth (1847–1916) introduced the formula of the German historical seminars, with exercises on source criticism and historical writing, at the University of Liège (Kupper, 2011: 412), and soon thereafter the practice was also adopted at other universities. The rigorous and critical approach of historical sources and practical research were crucial factors in lifting the scientific level of Belgian historians to international heights, with Pirenne as a prime example.

Pirenne, who had been a student of De Laveleye and Kurth at the University of Liège, was introduced to the subject of social and economic history during his studies in 1883–1884 at the *École Pratique des Hautes Études* in Paris. He took Arthur Giry's course on the history of the wool industry in the Middle Ages. But Pirenne was fascinated the next academic year by Schmoller. Pirenne started his stay in Germany in Leipzig at the end of 1884 and went to Berlin at the beginning of 1885, where he attended Schmoller's lectures on economic history and followed his seminar (Crombois, 1994: 101). Pirenne had enjoyed the course by Giry in Paris, but thought it lacked a foundation in method and theory. By contrast, Schmoller introduced the young Pirenne to the different schools of economic thought and their respective methods. The stay in Berlin became the basis for Pirenne's approach to the economic history of the Middle Ages as a professor at the University of Ghent (Lyon, 1974: 60–64). Of course, Pirenne was influenced not only by Schmoller. He was also greatly impressed by the work of Karl Lamprecht (1856–1915), whose PhD had been supervised by Roscher. Pirenne wrote approvingly about Lamprecht's *Deutsches*

Wirtschaftsleben im Mittelalter (1885–1886) as an example of history from the viewpoint of the social sciences. Pirenne was inspired by the "theorie-fähigkeit" of the Germans in historical discussions and was fond of their explanatory models and typologies (Warland, 2011: 245–247).

Throughout his career Pirenne kept close contact with the German historical world. Pirenne published in the *Vierteljahrschrift für Sozial- und Wirtschaftsgeschichte* and participated in the *Deutsche Historikertage*. In 1901 Pirenne wrote a preface for Alfred Hansay's (1871–1951) translation into French of Karl Bücher's (1847–1930) *Die Entstehung der Volkswirtschaft*. Pirenne showed himself well aware of the position of the German Historical School in the development of economic thought and the works of the principal economists, while he overestimated the influence of the historical method in economics, and did not seem to be aware of the *Methodenstreit* in economics.[3]

Pirenne became a famous economic historian with his theory on the renaissance of the cities in Western Europe in the tenth and eleventh centuries. He examined how the cities of the Middle Ages became politically and economically distinct from the countryside. Pirenne tried to show that the characteristics of cities came into being when merchants settled permanently in locations well situated with regard to transportation. He discarded the thesis that the cities of the Middle Ages originated on the sites of former Roman cities or the sites of abbeys or castles. These merchants in the *faubourgs* introduced long-distance commercial activities which would become the essential character of the cities. As soon as these centres became important, the necessary judicial and administrative institutions were created. Pirenne saw the distinct customs of the merchants, and the fact that they lived by their commerce and industry, as the nucleus of the cities to be (Ganshof, 1959). While his ideas were based on research of Belgian cities, he later strived to generalize them to Western and Central Europe (Pirenne, 1927b). On 3 December 1909 Schmoller wrote to Pirenne that he was renowned for his work and was an essential go-between between French and German science (cited in Warland, 2011: 242–243).

In the style of Werner Sombart and Max Weber, Pirenne also wrote an article on the stages of development of capitalism. His purpose was to do a social study of the capitalist, including a characterization of the capitalist during each of the various stages of economic history, and to search for his origins. Pirenne thought that in every stage of history a new group of courageous and enterprising capitalists would stand up. The capitalists of the previous epoch would, however, become the aristocracy of the new, and play a conservative role in the economy. Like many German historians Pirenne was also attentive to the influence of institutions, such as guilds and crafts and municipal authorities, and their regulations. Contrary to others, Pirenne saw capitalist merchants arising in the eleventh century, while keeping in mind that these individuals themselves did not create a complete capitalist economy (Pirenne, 1914).

Pirenne also introduced statistics, this cherished method of the German Historical School, into Belgian historical studies. In 1903 he wrote an article on the possibilities of statistical sources for the history of demography, based on the example of the population censuses of the city of Ypres in the fifteenth century, which was published in the *Vierteljahrschrift fur Sozial- und Wirtschaftsgeschichte* (Pirenne, 1903). With this kind of research Pirenne taught a whole generation of historians how to count, and pointed to the social and economic structures that grounded history (Ebels-Hoving, 1981: 37).

Like the German Historical School, Pirenne searched for the typical and the general in history based on meticulous historical research, without losing sight of the complexity and variation of the different epochs (Pirenne, 1901: vii–viii). Yet, Pirenne always considered himself to be a historian, not an economist. The aim of the economic historian was to improve the knowledge of history, and not to improve economics. Thus he clearly erected a disciplinary boundary between economics and history (Wils, 2011: 371).

Pirenne inspired many of his students to do research on economic and social history. Perhaps the most striking example is that of Guillaume Des Marez (1870–1931), who became archivist of the Municipal Archives of Brussels and professor of legal history and economic history at the University of Brussels (Sirjacobs, 1997: 27). Des Marez wrote his PhD under the supervision of Pirenne on property rights in medieval cities. Pirenne sent him to Berlin in 1897 and to Paris in 1898, where he attended the courses of many renowned historians (Billen and Boone, 2011: 461–462). In Berlin he was impressed by the seminars of Schmoller (Lyon, 1999: 1055). As will be explained ahead, Des Marez was also involved in the *Institut de Sociologie Solvay*. His interest in social issues is apparent in his 1913 study of *Les origines historiques du mouvement syndical en Belgique*. Other historians specialized in economic and social history formed by Pirenne include Herman vander Linden (1868–1956), who did research on Louvain and on merchant guilds, Victor Fris (1877–1925) and Hans Van Werveke (1898–1974), on Ghent, and Fernand Vercauteren (1903–1979), on the cities of the third to the eleventh centuries (Ganshof, 1936: 182). We should also mention Hubert Van Houtte (1872–1948), professor of institutional history at the University of Ghent, who studied with Schmoller and Lamprecht in Berlin and wrote extensively on economic history of the early modern period (Van Houtte, 1902, 1920; Verlinden, 1960).

The *Institut de Sociologie*

The influence of the German Historical School was particularly important at the *Institut de Sociologie*, founded in 1902 by the wealthy industrial Ernest Solvay, and more generally at the Free University of Brussels, to which the institute was closely linked and of which it eventually became a part. The institute succeeded the *Institut des Sciences Sociales*, which Solvay had founded in 1894 (Crombois, 1994: 25–33). The research there was narrowly related to Solvay's own preoccupations, such as inheritance taxation and monetary reform (Erreygers, 1998: 228–247). Solvay's main research associates at that time were Hector Denis (1842–1913), Guillaume De Greef (1842–1924) and Émile Vandervelde (1866–1938). The economist Denis and the sociologist De Greef had some affinity with the approach advocated by the historical school. Denis expressed his sympathy for the work of Roscher, Knies, Hildebrand and Schmoller in the introduction of his *Histoire des systèmes économiques et socialistes* (Denis, 1904, 1: 18–20, 33–35), while De Greef discussed the work of these authors in his *La sociologie économique* (De Greef, 1904: 13–15). Even though De Greef (1921) promoted the use of "the historic method" in his treatise on social economics, he certainly cannot be considered as a disciple of the German Historical School. On the whole, the influence of the German Historical School on the activities of the *Institut des Sciences Sociales* remained very limited.

Things changed with the creation of the *Institut de Sociologie Solvay*. Its first director, the engineer and sociologist Émile Waxweiler (1867–1916), ensured that Solvay's preferred lines of research were further developed. For instance, in his major sociological treatise, *Esquisse d'une sociologie*, published in 1906, Waxweiler repeatedly pointed out similarities with Solvay's energetic views. But much more was going on at the institute. In the first years of its existence the organizational structure consisted of four divisions: on technology and geography, on statistics, on history and on anthropology (Crombois, 1994: 35–40). Des Marez directed the history division, but he left the institute in 1910, apparently no longer able to cope with the dogmatism of Solvay and Waxweiler (Billen and Boone, 2011: 464, n. 18). Another early collaborator of the institute, the lawyer Louis Wodon (1868–1946), took position in the debates on the nature of primitive societies. He reacted very critically to the views of Karl Bücher, whom he accused of constructing a fiction of primitive man, a creature of dreams even further removed from reality than *homo œconomicus* (Wodon, 1906: 37). A similar critique was raised by the Hungarian sociologist Félix (Bódog) Somló (1873–1920), who visited the institute in the period 1906–1908 (Crombois, 1994: 102). His book on circulation in primitive societies (Somló, 1909) was published as Volume 8 of the institute's *Notes et Mémoires* series.

As far as economics is concerned, the three most active members of the institute in its early years were Georges De Leener (1879–1965), Jules Ingenbleek (1876–1953) and Maurice Ansiaux (1869–1943). De Leener was the most productive in terms of output. Together with Waxweiler and Wodon he co-authored a volume on the coal industry in the northern part of Belgium (De Leener, Waxweiler and Wodon, 1904). His research focused on industrial organization, more specifically on how employers organized themselves (De Leener, 1904; 1909). He reported extensively on surveys he conducted in Belgian industrial circles; he was keen to stress that he adopted a "realistic point of view" (De Leener, 1909, 1: 6–9). He did not want to be seen as a dogmatic defender of free competition; in studies on Belgium's foreign trade policy (De Leener, 1906) and on its transport policy (De Leener, 1913) he advocated specific forms of cooperation between the public and private sector. In this respect, his work resembles the views of some of the *Kathedersozialisten* on the role of the state in encouraging national prosperity (Crombois, 1994: 106–107). Of a similar strand is Ingenbleek's comparative research on income taxation. Judging that a direct tax on incomes would be infeasible in Belgium, he argued in favour of indirect taxes based on the expenses enabled by incomes (Ingenbleek, 1908: 377). He called for mildly progressive rates on the employment of domestic servants, the possession of horses and the like, and in support of this mentioned the theories of Wagner, Schäffle and Neumann (ibid.: 396).

The work of Ansiaux, who directed the technology and geography division of the institute, consisted of research on the future of domestic industries in Belgium (Ansiaux, 1904), and on exchange rate policies (Ansiaux, 1910). For his study of the first topic he made ample use of the data collected around the turn of the century by the Belgian Labour Office and published in the series *Les industries à domicile en Belgique*, a project in which he himself was involved. But he also referred extensively to similar data collected by the *Verein für Socialpolitik*, and he mentioned the work of Karl Bücher and Alfred Weber. With regard to exchange rates, he criticized the *laissez-faire* policy advocated by Ricardo and other classical liberals, and recommended a regulatory framework based on changing the discount rate supplemented by other policies. He was very well versed in the economic literature, and often referred to German economists, such as Georg Friedrich Knapp, Heinrich Dietzel and Roscher. In the economics textbook which he published in the 1920s, Ansiaux (1920–1926, 1: 6) expressed his approval for the inductive approach favoured by the German Historical School, but criticized its reluctance to make generalizations.

Although there undoubtedly was an influence of the German Historical School on the methods employed at the institute (with emphasis on empirical evidence and the institutional context), and some of its members shared the policy orientations of the *Kathedersozialisten*, the institute also supported research which criticized aspects of their approach. A good example of the critical attitude towards the German Historical School can be found in the work of the Polish economist and sociologist Jan Stanislas Lewinski (1885–1930), who was at the institute in the period 1907–1909. During his stay he did research on the industrial evolution in Belgium in the nineteenth century, which resulted in a volume (including an extensive bibliography) published in 1911 in the *Études Sociales* series of the institute. In his introduction, Lewinski stressed the need to combine deduction with induction (Lewinski, 1911: 5). He lamented that some schools of thought in economics, and especially "Schmoller's school", had given too much emphasis to the inductive method, generating studies in which one tended to get lost in the "chaos of the facts" (ibid.: 4). He clearly distinguished Schmoller's radical approach from that of the younger followers of the German Historical School, such as Werner Sombart and Max Weber, and from that of his younger brother Alfred Weber. He also objected to the tendency of the *Kathedersozialisten* to mix economic and social research with judgments of a political, religious or ethical nature (ibid.: 10).

In 1910 the institute was reorganized. Several "working groups" were formed to encourage multidisciplinary research within the institute and to increase the participation of external collaborators (for an overview of the members and the activities of these groups, see Warnotte 1946, 2: 560–566). The institute also created a bibliographic documentation service, for which it could build upon the foundations laid by Paul Otlet (1868–1944) and Henri La Fontaine (1854–1943), and started publishing the *Bulletin de l'Institut de Sociologie*. Moreover, it widened its international network by means of *L'Intermédiaire sociologique*, a service aimed at increasing international cooperation in the social sciences. This aroused considerable interest at the Academy of Sciences in Berlin; Daniel Warnotte, the institute's librarian, was even sent on a visit to Berlin in 1913, but the hoped-for collaboration with the German and Austrian societies for sociology did not come about (Mahaim, 1937: 182; Warnotte, 1946, 2: 555–560).

In 1910 the institute also published an incredibly detailed study by Ernest Mahaim, who was at that time not a full member of the institute, in which he not only presented data and maps on the system of railway passes for workers in Belgium, but also examined the social effects of their widespread use. Mahaim's ability to handle and analyse vast amounts of statistical data probably explains why the *Verein für Socialpolitik* asked him to make a survey of prices of industrial goods in Belgium, in the framework of a huge survey of price formation (*Untersuchungen über Preisbildung*) launched by the *Verein*. For this work Mahaim assembled a team of collaborators consisting of Edouard Mathus, Georges De Leener, Max Léo Gérard, Léon Lobet and Paul Stévart. Although the study was published under a German title in 1914, it is entirely written in French (Mahaim, 1914). It is the only one of the foreign surveys of industrial prices commissioned by the *Verein* which went to press.

Mahaim played a much more prominent role in the *Institut de Sociologie* in the interwar period. In 1916 Waxweiler died in a car accident in London. After a transitory period in which Ansiaux, Georges Barnich (1876–1948) and Georges Hostelet (1875–1960) managed the institute, Mahaim was appointed director in 1923. He oriented the research of the institute towards contemporary social and economic issues. This led to publications on the living conditions of labourers, by the historian Guillaume Jacquemyns (1897–1969), on the banking sector, by the economist Boris-Serge Chlepner (1890–1964), and on the reconstruction in Belgium, by a team of economists and sociologists under the supervision of Mahaim. He remained at the head of the institute until 1935, when the institute organized the twelfth International Congress of Sociology in Brussels.

Concluding remarks

The intellectual influence of the German Historical School suffered a serious blow when Germany breached the neutrality of Belgium in August 1914. The change is tellingly illustrated by what happened to Pirenne. Alerted by a number of his contacts and students about the nationalism and militarism that had taken hold of Germany, he initially kept faith in the good intentions of his German academic colleagues. During the war, however, he lost his confidence in German intellectuals. The first step came in October 1914 when 93 German scientists and artists, among whom were prominent academics, such as Schmoller, Lamprecht, Max Planck and Wilhelm Röntgen, signed the document *An die Kulturwelt! Ein Aufruf.* While the actions of the German army in Belgian villages and cities, such as Louvain, in August and September 1914 were widely perceived as atrocities and condemned as the Rape of Belgium, the German elite considered these to be legitimate military operations. The loss of one of his sons who had enlisted in the Belgian army was a second traumatic event. Pirenne's imprisonment and deportation to a German prison camp because of his resistance to the German language policy at the University of Ghent were the last steps in his disenchantment with Germany.

There is little doubt that the war severely damaged the position of German science and of the German Historical School in Belgium. But this did not mean the end of the developments which had been set in motion. Pirenne and his disciples continued to do research on economic history. Economists also remained interested in historical and empirical research. The Royal decree of 17 September 1934 that organized the curriculum of commercial sciences institutionalized the course of economic history (Buyst and Vandenborrre, 1998: 524). After 1928 historical and empirical research of the Belgian economy and of the business cycle formed an important part of the studies published by the new *Institut des sciences économiques* at the University of Leuven. What changed, however, was that the new generation of economists turned their backs to Germany and went to the US. Paul Van Zeeland (1893–1971) and Léon-H. Dupriez (1901–1986) studied in the US thanks to the Belgian American Educational Foundation (Buyst et al., 2005: 64–65). When Fernand Baudhuin (1894–1977) wrote his study *Histoire économique de la Belgique* (1928), the German Historical School was already history.

To sum up, the influence of the German Historical School in Belgium was particularly important in the period 1871–1914. This is at least partly due to the remarkable international mobility of the elites in that period. Many Belgian academics stayed at German universities during their studies, and quite a few historians and economists attended the courses of Schmoller in Berlin. Traces of the legacy of the school can be found in the emergence of the discipline of economic history, in the increased interest in various kinds of empirical research, and in the search for innovative forms of economic theory and social policy.

Notes

1 De Laveleye also mentioned Eugenio Forti and A. Morelli, both of whom are less well-known.
2 With one exception: "that man, in order to live, must make a living" (De Laveleye, 1879b: 17).
3 Pirenne was, of course, well aware of the *Methodenstreit der Geschichtswissenschaft* that had been going on between Karl Lamprecht, who, inspired by the German Historical School, saw collective forces active in history and historians that connected history to important individuals.

References

Almodovar, A. and Teixeira, P. (2010). Is there a Catholic economic thought? Some answers from the past, in D. F. Parisi and S. Solari (eds), *Humanism and Religion in the History of Economic Thought. Selected Papers from the 10th Aispe Conference.* Milan: FrancoAngeli, 125–147.

Ansiaux, M. (1904). *Que Faut-il Faire de nos Industries à Domicile?* Brussels: Misch & Thron.

Ansiaux, M. (1910). *Principes de la Politique Régulatrice des Changes.* Brussels: Misch & Thron.

Ansiaux, M. (1920–1926). *Traité d'Économie Politique.* Paris: Marcel Giard, 3 vols.

Baudhuin, F. (1928). Histoire économique de la Belgique, in *Histoire de la Belgique Contemporaine 1830–1914.* Brussels: Dewit, 233–348.

Baudrillart, H. (1875a). D'une soi-disant nouvelle économie politique. À propos d'un recent article de la Revue des deux mondes. *Journal des Économistes,* Year 34, 3rd series, Year 10, Vol. 39, no. 116, August: 185–190.

Baudrillart, H. (1875b). Les nouveaux économistes. II. Observations de M. H. Baudrillart. *Journal des Économistes,* Year 34, 3rd series, Year 10, Vol. 40, no. 119, November: 214–215.

Billen, C. and Boone, M. (2011). Pirenne in Brussels before 1930: Guillaume Des Marez and the relationship between a master and his student. *Revue Belge d'Histoire Contemporaine,* 41(3–4): 459–485.

Bots, M. (Ed) (1992). *Lettres Adressées à Emile de Laveleye.* Ghent: Liberaal Archief.

Brants, V. (1880). *Essai Historique sur la Condition des Classes Rurales en Belgique jusqu'à la Fin du XVIIIe siècle.* Leuven: Peeters.

Brants, V. (1887). *Lois et Méthode de l'Économie Politique.* Louvain: Peeters-Champion, 2nd ed.

Brants, V. (1900). *L'Université de Louvain. Coup d'Œil sur son Histoire et ses Institutions, 1425–1900.* Brussels: Charles Bulens.

Bücher, K. (1901). *Études d'Histoire et d'Économie Politique* (Trans. A. Hansay). Brussels: Lamertin-Alcan.

Buyst, E. and Vandenborre, H. (1998). 100 jaar Toegepaste Economische Wetenschappen aan de K.U. Leuven. *Tijdschrift voor Economie en Management,* 43(4): 513–548.

Buyst, E., Maes, I., Plasmeijer, H. W. and Schoorl, E. (2005). Comparing the Development of Economics during the Twentieth Century in Belgium and the Netherlands. *History of Political Economy,* 37(1): 61–78.

Chlepner, B.-S. (1972). *Cent Ans d'Histoire Sociale en Belgique.* Brussels: Éditions de l'Université de Bruxelles, 4th ed.

Crombois, J.-F. (1994). *L'Univers de la Sociologie en Belgique de 1900 à 1940.* Brussels: Éditions de l'Université de Bruxelles.

De Greef, G. (1904). *La Sociologie Économique.* Paris: Félix Alcan.

De Greef, G. (1921). *L'Économie Sociale, d'après la Méthode Historique et au Point de Vue Sociologique.* Brussels: Office de Publicité.

De Laveleye, É. (1874). *De la Propriété et de ses Formes Primitives.* Paris: Librairie Germer Baillière.

De Laveleye, É. (1875a). Il congresso dei socialisti della cattedra ad Eisenach. *Giornale degli Economisti,* 2(8), November: 81–89.

De Laveleye, É. (1875b). Les nouveaux économistes. I. Lettre de M. de Laveleye à M. Baudrillart. *Journal des Économistes,* Year 34, 3rd series, Year 10, Vol. 40, no. 119, November: 210–213.

De Laveleye, É. (1875c). Les tendances nouvelles de l'économie politique et du social-isme. *La Revue des Deux Mondes*, Year 45, 3rd period, Vol. 10: 445–468.

De Laveleye, É. (1879a). The new tendencies of political economy. *The Banker's Magazine and Statistical Register*, Series 3, Vol. 13, No. 8: 601–609, No. 9: 698–706, No. 10: 761–767.

De Laveleye, É. (1879b). *The New Tendencies of Political Economy* [With an appendix containing the remarks of M. de Laveleye at the Adam Smith centenary in London]. New York: The Office of The Banker's Magazine and Statistical Register.

De Laveleye, É. (1881a). *Le Socialisme Contemporain*. Brussels: Librairie Européenne C. Muquardt.

De Laveleye, É. (1881b). Les tendances nouvelles de l'économie politique en Angleterre – Cliffe Leslie. *La Revue des Deux Mondes*, Year 51, 3rd period, Vol. 44: 623–646.

De Laveleye, É. (1882). *Éléments d'Économie Politique*. Paris: Hachette; Brussels: Merzbach et Falk.

De Laveleye, É. (1884). *The Elements of Political Economy*. London: Chapman & Hall.

De Laveleye, É. (1885). Lettres inédites de Stuart Mill. *Revue de Belgique*, Year 17, Vol. 49: 5–25.

De Leener, G. (1904). *Les Syndicats Industriels en Belgique*. Brussels: Misch & Thron.

De Leener, G. (1906). *Ce qui Manque au Commerce Belge d'Exportation*. Brussels: Misch & Thron.

De Leener, G. (1909). *L'Organisation Syndicale des Chefs d'Industrie*. Brussels: Misch & Thron, 2 vols.

De Leener, G. (1913). *La Politique des Transports en Belgique*. Brussels: Misch & Thron.

De Leener, G., Waxweiler, É. and Wodon, L. (1904). *Le Charbon dans le Nord de la Belgique*. Brussels: Misch & Thron.

Denis, H. (1904). *Histoire des Systèmes Économiques et Socialistes. Vol. 1: Les Fondateurs*. Paris: V. Giard & E. Brière.

Ebels-Hoving, B. (1981). Henri Pirenne (1862–1935), in A. H. Huussen Jr., E. H. Kossmann and H. Renner (eds), *Historici van de Twintigste Eeuw*. Utrecht-Antwerpen: Het Spectrum, 26–40.

Erreygers, G. (1998). The economic theories and social reform proposals of Ernest Solvay (1838–1922), in W. J. Samuels (Ed), *European Economists of the Early 20th Century. Volume 1: Studies of Neglected Thinkers of Belgium, France, The Netherlands and Scandinavia*. Cheltenham: Edward Elgar, 220–262.

Erreygers, G. and Van Dijck, M. (2012). "A powerful instrument of progress": Economic textbooks in Belgium 1830–1925, in M. M. Augello and M.E.L. Guidi (eds), *The Economic Reader: Textbooks, Manuals and the Dissemination of the Economic Sciences during the Nineteenth and Early Twentieth Centuries*. London: Routledge, 214–247.

Ganshof, F.-L. (1936). Henri Pirenne and economic history. *Economic History Review*, 6(2): 179–185.

Ganshof, F.-L. (1959). Pirenne, Henri, in *Biographie Nationale*, vol. 30. Brussels: Bruylant, 671–722.

Garnier, M. J. (1875). Les nouveaux économistes. III. Observations de M. Joseph Garnier. *Journal des Économistes*, Year 34, 3rd series, Year 10, Vol. 40, No. 119, November: 216–219.

Ingenbleek, J. (1908). *Impôts Directs et Indirects sur le Revenu: La Contribution Personnelle en Belgique, l'Einkommensteuer en Prusse, l'Income Tax en Angleterre*. Brussels: Misch & Thron.

Kupper, J.-L. (2011). Godefroid Kurth and Henri Pirenne: An improbable friendship. *Revue Belge d'Histoire Contemporaine*, 41(3–4): 411–426.

Lambert, P. (1970). Emile de Laveleye (1822–1892). *History of Political Economy*, 2(2): 263–283.

Lamprecht, K. (1885–1886). *Deutsches Wirtschaftsleben im Mittelalter*. Leipzig: Alphons Dürr, 3 vols.

Lewinski, J. S. (1911). *L'Évolution Industrielle de la Belgique*. Brussels: Misch & Thron.

Lyon, B. (1974). *Henri Pirenne: A Biographical and Intellectual Study*. Ghent: Story-Scientia.

Lyon, B. (1999). Guillaume Des Marez and Henri Pirenne: A remarkable rapport. *Revue Belge de Philologie et d'Histoire*, 77(4): 1051–1078.

Mahaim, E. (1910). *Les Abonnements d'Ouvriers sur les Lignes de Chemins de Fer Belges et leurs Effets Sociaux*. Brussels: Misch & Thron.

Mahaim, E. (Ed) (1914). *Preisbildung Gewerblicher Erzeugnisse in Belgien*. Munich: Duncker & Humblot.

Mahaim, E. (1937). Notice sur Émile Waxweiler. *Annuaire de l'Académie Royale de Belgique*, 104: 173–271.

Meerts, K. (1982). De Leuvense hoogleraar Victor Brants: een brugfiguur in het sociaal-katholicisme (1856–1891). *Bijdragen tot de Geschiedenis*, 55: 197–233.

Meerts, K. (1983). De Leuvense hoogleraar Victor Brants: sociale ideeën tussen katholieke romantiek en realisme (1856–1891). *Bijdragen tot de Geschiedenis*, 56: 101–130.

Michotte, P. L. (1904). *Étude sur les Théories Économiques qui Dominèrent en Belgique de 1830 à 1886*. Louvain: Peeters.

Pirenne, H. (1901). Préface, in K. Bücher *Études d'Histoire et d'Économie Politique*. Brussels: Lamertin; Paris: Félix Alcan, v–xii.

Pirenne, H. (1903). Les dénombrements de la population d'Ypres au XVe siècle (1412–1506). *Vierteljahrschrift für Sozial- und Wirtschaftsgeschichte*, 1(1): 1–32.

Pirenne, H. (1914). Les étapes de l'histoire sociale du capitalisme. *Bulletin de l'Académie Royale de Belgique, Classe des Lettres*, 5: 258–299 (translated as "The stages in the social history of capitalism", *American Historical Review*, 19(3): 494–515).

Pirenne, H. (1927a). Belgique, in *Histoire et Historiens depuis Cinquante Ans. Méthodes, Organisation et Résultats du Travail Historique de 1876 et 1926*. Paris: Félix Alcan, 51–71.

Pirenne, H. (1927b). *Les Villes du Moyen Âge: Essai d'Histoire Économique et Sociale*. Brussels: Lamertin.

Rey, J. (1983). Mahaim (Ernest Aimé Joseph), in *Biographie Nationale de Belgique*, 43, cols. 501–509. Brussels: Académie Royale de Belgique.

Sirjacobs, I. (1997). *L'Économiste dans le Temps. 100 Ans de Sciences Économiques à l'ULB*. Brussels: Archives de l'ULB.

Somló, F. (1909). *Der Güterverkehr in der Urgesellschaft*. Brussels: Misch & Thron.

Van Houtte, H. (1902). *Documents pour Servir à l'Histoire des Prix de 1381 à 1794*. Brussels: Kiessling & Cie.

Van Houtte, H. (1920). *Histoire Économique de la Belgique à la Fin de l'Ancien Régime*. Ghent: Van Rysselberghe & Rombaut.

Van Molle, L. (1989). *Katholieken en Landbouw: Landbouwpolitiek in België, 1884–1914*. Louvain: Leuven University Press.

Verlinden, C. (1960). Hubert Van Houtte (1872–1948), in *Rijksuniversiteit Gent, Liber Memorialis 1913–1960, Vol. 1: Faculteit Letteren en Wijsbegeerte*. Ghent: Rijksuniversiteit Gent, 139–142.

Warland, G. (2011). Rezeption und Wahrnehmung der deutschen Geschichtswissenschaft bei belgischen "Epigonen": Paul Fredericq (1850–1920), Godefroid Kurth (1847–1916) und Henri Pirenne (1862–1935), in H. Roland, M. Beyen and G. Draye (eds), *Deutschlandbilder in Belgien 1830–1940*. Münster: Waxman, 219–261.

Warnotte, D. (1946). *Ernest Solvay et l'Institut de Sociologie: Contribution à l'Histoire de l'Énergétique Sociale*. Brussels: Émile Bruylant, 2 vols.

Waxweiler, É. (1906). *Esquisse d'une Sociologie*. Brussels: Misch & Thron.

Wils, K. (2011). Everyman his own sociologist: Henri Pirenne and disciplinary boundaries around 1900. *Revue Belge d'Histoire Contemporaine*, 41(3–4): 355–380.

Wodon, L. (1906). *Sur quelques Erreurs de Méthode dans l'Étude de l'Homme Primitif: Notes Critiques*. Brussels: Misch & Thron.

4 On the surface things seemed quiet

The reception of the German Historical School in the Netherlands

Bert Tieben and Evert Schoorl

Introduction

According to Schumpeter (1954: 861), 'On the whole things were quiet' with regard to the influence of the historical school in the Netherlands. Judging by the mainstream teaching in the state universities of Leyden, Groningen and Utrecht, one can only agree with this statement. Also, in a number of influential articles the leading Dutch economist Nicolaas G. Pierson attacked the ideas of Roscher and other German economists in a polite but nonetheless very critical way. Yet in the two Amsterdam universities – one municipal, the other reformed Protestant – the historical school received a warmer reception. And in political discussions in parliament and in the press, the historical approach was defended with great zeal. The conclusion of this chapter is that we have identified an important historical undercurrent in Dutch economics which continued well into the twentieth century.

We examine more closely the ideas of the 'historical' Quack, the 'neoclassical' Pierson and the 'compromising' Greven. When Pierson became prime minister in 1897, the Protestant opposition leader Kuyper explicitly attacked him with the ideas of the German Historical School. In the first decades of the twentieth century, historical and chair-socialist economics remained an influence in Dutch economics.

Our conclusion is that the influence of the historical school in the Netherlands was greater and longer-lasting than Schumpeter estimated, not just in economists' discussions but also in political debates. Moreover it affected university appointments, given that the appointment of professors was the responsibility of government bodies like the Dutch state. This did not impede the transmission of the ideas of the historical school in the Netherland, which largely ran through the channels of both economic and general journals. The debate on the historical school inspired clashes between the younger and the older generation of Dutch economists, the liberal and more socialist-inspired, the Christian and the secular politicians and economists. In short, the historical school left its traces not only in Dutch economics as an academic discipline but also in society at large.

The Dutch anticlassicals

In the united kingdom of the Netherlands and Belgium, soon after 1815 a broad academic institutionalization of economics took place. King William the First encouraged the teaching of the subject in the faculties of law. So from the 1820s onwards, economics was taught in Leyden, Groningen, Utrecht and Amsterdam. Scholars from the Northern Netherlands taught the subject in Belgium, like Ackersdijck in Liège and Thorbecke in Ghent; after the revolt of 1830 they moved to Utrecht and Leyden respectively.

Judging by the Belgian lecture notes of Ackersdijck's course, his teaching was fairly Saysian. For most of his colleagues as well, Smith and Say were the stock-in-trade. Ricardianism got its first disciple only by the middle of the century, in the person of The Netherlands Bank president W. C. Mees. However, an early protester against the harsh gospels of the classicals was the Leyden professor Tydeman (1778–1863). Already during the Napoleonic reign, he had been appointed as a professor of civil law in 1812, primarily for teaching the Code Civil.

Tydeman was the translator of Jane Marcet's *Conversations on Political Economy* in 1825. Although he legitimized the relevance of this work by pointing to the ideas of Malthus and McCulloch, he was equally influenced by Sismondi's concerns with the poor. Between 1817 and 1822 he published a periodical about poor relief in the Netherlands.

In the stagnating Dutch economy, the debate on poor relief became more intense around the middle of the century, as described in Boschloo (1989). W. C. Mees in 1844 published a pamphlet on the economic aspects of workhouses for the poor, in which he used a Malthusian reasoning. Subsidized production would lead to higher costs, to the crowding-out of free market production, to moral degradation and ultimately to more instead of fewer poor people. In his opinion the only useful instruments were educational, moral and religious elevation of the poor.

Less concerned with the Malthusian limits to growth, and the possibility of gluts, was the moderately classical economist Jeronimo de Bosch Kemper (1808–1876), who in 1851 published his historical study of poverty in the Netherlands. On the one hand, Kemper's interpretation of classical economics was limited to a material concept of production and welfare, but on the other he found it necessary to embrace a broader view of social science, leading to a greater knowledge of 'the nature, development, and destination of human society' (de Bosch Kemper 1860–1871: 2). To that purpose he was equally active as a member of parliament, as the author of 'practical' studies on poverty, and as the establisher of the foundation 'The Friend of the Poor and the Rich' (1851), which published a brief weekly periodical with practical advice on daily life till Kemper's death in 1876.

Tydeman was a nonclassical interventionist; de Bosch Kemper distinguished himself from his purely analytical, classical contemporary Mees by his historical description and analysis of poverty in the Netherlands. Towards the end of the century, this Christian tradition of concern for the poor found another representative in the economics professor and Netherlands Bank director H.P.G. Quack (1834–1914). As a student of Kemper in the 1850s, Quack had heard him teach that 'for the emancipation of factory workers, it is more important to study the history of the workers in British mills than to read theoretical discourses about them' (Quack 1915: 43). And after having defended a dissertation on the Middle Ages, as a contributor to Kemper's popular weekly he wrote economic reviews. As a professor of economics in Utrecht since 1868, he taught a kind of Christian evolutionary economics in which not the individual agent but the social structure was the most important element. He rejected the abolition of the guilds, and deplored the isolation of the individual worker, brought about by the industrial revolution. In his autobiography he wrote that 'what I taught my students on the subject of economics – mostly following the historical school – was nothing but an orderly consequence of the once, in my student years, proposed principles of de Bosch Kemper' (Quack 1915: 168). As Quack was a student in the 1850s this is an interesting statement, labelling Kemper as a forerunner of the historical school in the Netherlands.

In his autobiography, Quack reports on his 'wanderings in society' as a necessary complement of, and sometimes a superior approach to 'reading dry and dusty discourses on political economy in the vein of J.B. Say' (Quack 1915: 97). In 1862 he considered his wanderings still incomplete, so when de Bosch Kemper proposed him as his successor at the Amsterdam Athenaeum – not yet fully a university – he negotiated about combining this appointment with his job at the Amsterdam Chamber of Commerce.[1] The chairman of this chamber opposed the combination, so Quack declined the proposal of the academic chair.

When in 1868 a vacancy fell open in the Utrecht law faculty, de Bosch Kemper pushed both his former pupil Quack and his friend in the supervisory board to have Quack appointed. From the beginning the latter's teaching was controversial. In the editorial board of the literary and social journal *De Gids* (The Guide) Quack confronted the older, classical economist and textbook author Vissering with the statement that he could not share Bastiat's ideas on the dynamics of society, in a spontaneous and freely operating harmony of interests. Vissering could not distance himself from 'the rules of the doctrinary, absolute, closed science of political economy – with its constant and permanent laws-science, imagined as the doctrine of wealth in a so-called free exchange traffic' (Quack 1915: 140–141).

In the end, not scientific controversies but the combination of financial considerations with his research programme of writing a history of socialist ideas determined the end of Quack's Utrecht professorship. At the international statistical conference of 1876 in Buda-Pesth, a German colleague had labelled him as a socialist of the chair. This only strengthened him in his plan to expand his lectures on socialism into a book, and to implant social ideas in the 'rigid and individualist economics' (Quack 1915: 237). His professorial salary was insufficient for purchasing an adequate library, and he wished to become again a participant in society instead of just an academic observer, so he applied successfully for the job of secretary of The Netherlands Bank: 'I threw myself again into real life, with the secret agenda of becoming a historian of socialism' (Quack 1915: 239).

Without ever calling himself a socialist, the Christian-inspired Quack wrote and published his six-volume historical overview *De Socialisten* (1875–1897). When the first of these had just been published in 1876, Quack, still teaching in Utrecht, was seated at a dinner next to the chairman of the university's supervisory board, central bank president Mees. The latter attacked Quack's criticism of exclusively regarding human labour as a good, subject to supply and demand, and of considering in economics only material riches (Quack 1915: 275–276):

> Mr. Mees was not amused: he did not easily admit objections against the absolute, closed rules of doctrinary science. I had the impression that he did not rate me highly as a scholar of economics. Or rather that he wished me to understand that an economist, in dissecting and unveiling facts and relationships in society, had nothing to do with the moral appreciation of these relationships. Accordingly, he later had appointed prof. d'Aulnis [de Bourouill] as my successor in the economics chair in Utrecht, who in his inaugural lecture combated the socialism of the chair.

Almost 30 years later Quack and D'Aulnis crossed swords again in a meeting of the Royal Academy of Sciences (KNAW), where the latter argued that Proudhon had been a Hegelian socialist. According to Quack he was an idealist anarchist (van Berkel 2008: 511).

In the first two thirds of the nineteenth century, classical economics was the dominant school in economics in the Netherlands. However, an important undercurrent of moral concerns was continually present. Tydeman, de Bosch Kemper and Quack were its most prominent scholars. Towards the end of the century, classical economics as well as classical liberal politics were increasingly subject to criticism from younger liberals, from followers of the historical and Austrian schools, and from Christian-inspired politicians. The great liberal politician Thorbecke, father of the constitution of 1848, was challenged by the young Sam van Houten. His first writings were still published in the Thorbeckean literary and political monthly *De Gids*, but soon he was one of the founders of its competitor *Vragen des Tijds* (Questions of Today). Altogether it is remarkable that so many distinguished economists were among the editors of the *literary* journal *De Gids*: Vissering, Quack and Buys. Aerts (1997: 360) even concludes that apparently in economics this periodical had a professional stature, comparable to the journal *De Economist*.

Pierson continued to be the foremost contributor of economic reviews in *De Gids*. In most of these he criticized the new German school, first known as the historical school, and later as socialism of the chair. His great authority was largely responsible for the fact that this movement never got a strong foothold in the Dutch state universities.

In a broader context, *De Gids* was a focussing point for the shift from an 'abstinent state' liberalism to a more socially concerned movement which did not blame the poor themselves for their condition, and did not shut its eyes to the social question. According to Aerts (1997: 368), Pierson and van Houten arrived at their criticism of self-indulging liberalism by philosophical and methodological studies; Quack had observed great social changes abroad and wished to warn against these developments.

The debate gets going

In the period under consideration, the Dutch professional association *Vereeniging voor Staathuishoudkunde* had been firmly established. The same could be said of the professional journal *De Economist*, which was founded in 1852. But economics had also become a subject on which the educated general reader wished to be informed.

In the mid-nineteenth century Dutch economics was first and foremost a practical affair. It lacked theoretical acumen (van Maarseveen 1981: 53–54). This partly explains why, as a professional journal, *De Economist* had a slow start. In the early years it hardly published serious contributions to economic theory. It professed to further 'public welfare' and paid attention to a wide array of subjects: recipes for good health, gymnastics, fertilizer for improvement of the soil and so forth (De Vries 1952). Most of these publications accepted economic theory as a given, if they mentioned theory at all. Smith, Ricardo and the other classical authors functioned merely as an introduction to the description of highly practical issues. There existed among Dutch economists no critical discourse about the assumptions and implications of economic theory, and original contributions to theory were scarce.

It is this practical bend of mind which Pierson in the early period of his career aimed to change. His article in 1866 entitled 'Value and Production Costs' was in fact one of the first serious articles on economic theory published in *De Economist*, foreshadowing the advent of marginal utility theory (Pierson 1866).

Paradoxically the focus on economic theory per se brought the work of the German Historical School to the attention of Dutch economists. The Leyden professor Vissering, a clear proponent of a stronger theoretical focus in economics, was among the first to comment on the historical school in what is typically called his *Practical Handbook of Political Economy* (Vissering 1860–1865). This 'Dutch Bastiat' criticized the historical school for its strong rejection of natural laws in economics. Vissering and Pierson stood in close contact, and it is not surprising that Vissering's rejection of the historical school had an impact on Pierson at this early stage of his economic education. But it is testimony of Pierson's originality that he developed his own interpretation of historicism, seeking a midway point between Vissering's rejection and his own positive appreciation of this school.

This attempt at reconciliation typifies Pierson's stance on the historical school from the start. In 1861 he wrote an essay on the logic of political economy for the *Association of Political Economy* (Staatshuishoudkundige Vereeniging), of which Vissering was also a member (Pierson 1861). This essay critically compares the deductive and the inductive method in economics and concludes that '[logical] speculation and history need to interact; speculation needs to explain history, history needs to support speculation. Both need each other' (Pierson 1861: 11).

This essay provided the foundation of his 1862 review of Roscher's *Ansichten*, which contains a discussion of the 'mathematical' versus the historical method (Pierson 1862). Pierson's review of the sixth edition of Roscher's *Grundlagen*, published in 1866, is characteristic of his critical attitude towards the historical school:

> Roscher is not just the head, he is the most perfect type of the historical school; and whoever cannot agree to the spirit reigning in this school, to the method it follows and to the direction in which it operates, he will not appreciate those writings in which this method, this spirit, and this direction are exposed on every page. Every criticism of Roscher, whether it is an effort to make him better appreciated, or one to diminish his fame, must therefore necessarily start with a criticism of his approach. Therein lies his power and his weakness; the sympathy of one observer, and the indifference of another, can thus be explained. Are you a kindred soul to Roscher? Then you must be particularly attracted to his works. And if not, then the peculiar *charm* he possesses for many will always remain a secret for you.
>
> (Pierson 1868: 403–404)

According to Pierson, defining the historical school is hardly possible. On the one hand, for Hildebrand its central tenet is never to search for natural laws. On the other, Roscher not only repeatedly uses this concept but also tells us about his disagreement with Hildebrand. The only member of the school explicitly discussing methodology is again Roscher. He distinguishes between two approaches in social science: one asking the question, 'What exists, what has been, how has this come about?' and the other asking, 'What ought to be?'. Pierson's verdict is that he does not deny the value of historical empiricism, but accuses Roscher of doing only 'systematically half a job' (Pierson 1868: 412).

Pierson praises the historical school for having done a lot to promote the study of the history of economic thought. If only this approach would be more common in the education of every economist, then the level of economics as a science would markedly rise, and it would get the ranking it deserves.

In his concluding methodological remarks, Pierson looks to John Stuart Mill's *Logic* for guidance: 'Generally spoken there is only one method of reasoning applicable for economics, to wit, the one of *deduction*' (Pierson 1868: 425). Inductively searching for causality by comparing special cases is nearly always impossible in economics. This makes the historical method relevant only for studying large and long-term phenomena.

Pierson's essay in *De Gids* from 1864 on the concept of national wealth provided the next key to the unlocking of the teachings of the historical school to the Dutch public. This essay strongly criticizes Adam Smith for his attempt to explain the mechanism of economic growth in terms of universal laws valid for all times and all places. In this sense Pierson (1864) is strongly anti-Vissering in spirit and content. According to Pierson, Smith viewed society as the sum total of individual activities, which could be examined in isolation and aggregated in order to provide a clear picture of the social mechanism. For Pierson, this reductionist approach was impossible. Approvingly he quoted Roscher, who described production and consumption as phenomena of society seen as an economic organism (Pierson 1864: 29). The problem is that producers and consumers need each other. The one cannot subsist without the other. This makes the degree of interdependency between the members of society much stronger than, for instance, the members of a family. In Pierson's view only the term organism captures this characteristic of the economy seen as a whole. He subsequently treated the organic nature of the economy as a self-evident axiom for the theory of national wealth (Pierson 1864: 63–67).

On this conceptual level the attack of the historical school on Adam Smith's universalism was clearly successful. But their historical alternative went to the other extreme and could likewise not find approval in the eyes of Pierson. The historical school substituted the study of concrete historical cases for the study of the natural laws of the economy. This approach implied that it was impossible to draw any kind of general lesson from the study of history. Pierson could not accept this inference. He stated that Roscher and his colleagues could not see the wood for the trees, but that Smith failed to see the trees in the wood. The 'new approach' needed to consider both the trees and the wood. By way of conclusion Pierson complimented the historical school for its 'great achievement' but stated that it went too far in the application of its fundamental principles (Pierson 1864: 96).

Pierson's reviews and essays show that for Dutch scholars the German Historical School marked a new development in economics, which was followed with great interest. An example of this attitude is the doctoral thesis of H. J. Hamaker, *De historische school in de Staathuishoudkunde* (The Historical School in Political Economy), which appeared in 1870. Hamaker defended his thesis at Leyden University as a legal scholar, and it is exactly the legal aspects of the historical school which had an impact on his scientific career. He became a law professor in Utrecht and is known in the Netherlands as a pioneer of the sociology of law. Legal principles had to reflect the opinion of the general public on what constituted right and wrong in the legal arena, rather than compliance with written and unwritten fundamental principles of law. This was Hamaker's historical-positivist interpretation of the law.

Hamaker was not extremely well-read in economics, but his summary of what he views as the contribution of the historical school is nonetheless interesting as a contemporary statement of curiosity regarding what the school had to offer. This included, first, an acknowledgement of the relativism of 'truths in any system, institutions and policies' (Hamaker 1870: 24) and, second, the call to study the historical development of economic society and to draw lessons from this historical study. Needless to say, the scope of these lessons was limited given the particularities of time and place. Third, the historical school promoted the development of economics into a normative science, generating statements about the proper goal of economic life. The historical school aimed to remove the distinction between science and art. This point would prove a bone of contention for a later generation of Dutch economists crossing their swords with the proponents of the 'socialism of the chair'.

For the time being the historical school managed to gain adherents in the Netherlands, which changed the course of economic science in our country. The victim of this change was the classical liberalism of Vissering and others that had dominated Dutch economics since the revolutionary year 1848. A key event in the spread of the ideas of the historical school was the establishment of the journal *Vragen des Tijds* in 1874/1875 as a direct competitor of *De Gids*, of which Vissering was an editor. Ironically, most of the lead men of the new journal were former students of Vissering and other laisser-faire economists (Boschloo 1989: 241). This new generation did not dismiss liberalism per se, but believed that economics could not turn a blind eye to the negative impact of economic development. In particular this concerned the social question. This was also a key issue for the historical school, as it 'proved' that the laws of economics lacked universal application. The social question so brought the teaching of the historical school under the purview of the Dutch economists.

The spring meeting of the Dutch Statistical Association in 1875 put the 'dangers' of this modern form of socialism on its agenda. One of these dangers was the wrong course for a political economy journal trying to promote the cause of socialist economics, which explicitly referred to the new journal *Vragen des Tijds*. The minutes of this meeting neatly summarize the spirit of this time and the growing gap between the generations. The older, orthodox generation re-emphasized its belief in the natural law character of economic science. The younger liberals, like Levy, retorted that cause and effect relationships were determined by the circumstances of time and place. This position directly referred to the historical school, which promoted historical research in order to establish the connection between social-economic conditions and economic performance. According to Boschloo (1989: 237–244), here we witness a clash of generations. This clash signalled the end of the dominance of classical liberalism in the Netherlands and marked the advent of new economic doctrines, such as the historical school.

The debate intensifies, and the rift widens

The change of liberalism to socialism was certainly not a prime example of a paradigm shift in the sense of Kuhn (1970). There was no quick change of positions, as demanded by Kuhn's notion of a scientific revolution. The 1875 meeting of the Statistical Association was just the starting point of an extended debate. More importantly, this debate lacked a clear winner. For a while the political cause of the socialists of the chair reinforced the scientific interest in the economics of the historical school. But ultimately the marriage between politics and science also proved its Achilles heel, which allowed the liberal school to regain its position in Dutch academia.

D'Aulnis de Bourouill was one of the first exponents of the marginalist school in the Netherlands, applying Jevons's felicific calculus in his dissertation of 1873. In spite of the rapid theoretical developments in this field, D'Aulnis chose 'katheder socialisme' – socialism of the chair – as the prime target for his professional lecture in 1878 (D'Aulnis de Bourouill 1878). He argued that the members of the German *Verein für Sozialpolitik*, like Schmoller, failed to understand the distinction between political prescriptions like laissez-faire and the economic analysis supporting this type of policy. According to D'Aulnis there was nothing analytical in the classical doctrines of Adam Smith and David Ricardo which necessitated following a liberal economic policy agenda. Hence the advocacy of the *Verein* for a socialist policy agenda confused the analytical quality of economics and the political consequences that one could reach by applying the insights of this analytical toolkit to specific social and economic conditions.

This started a lively debate between Dutch economists. The Dutch politician Goeman Borgesius retorted in a 'letter to the public', published in *Vragen des Tijds*, that the historical school was the first approach in economics to recognize the limits of economic laws, which in his view were valid only under specific, historically determined conditions (Goeman Borgesius 1878). J. A. Levy published a long book on English socialism of the chair, partly in reaction to Pierson (1878). In no less than 450 pages Levy defended the socialism of the chair, for which he considered the label of 'ethical-historical' school to be a more correct name (Levy 1879). Levy's objections against classical economics are threefold. First, man is driven by greed, and his behaviour is subject to natural laws. Second, the classicals make a sharp distinction between economic theory and economic policy. In the third place, they practice the deductive method where they should be using the 'inductive-historical' one.

Pierson (1878) published an answer to Goeman Borgesius's defence of the socialism of the chair. Regarding its form, Pierson's comment is a model example of his erudite, polite and careful reasoning. He starts by describing the socialism of the chair as 'a plant of German soil' and 'a reaction against the influence of the French school' (Pierson 1878: 211–212). In a few pages, the reception of Adam Smith in Germany and the attitudes of the most important German economists are summarized. The socialism of the chair is the most recent form of the opposition to Smith in Germany, and its ideas are those of the historical school in a stronger wording. It is 'a direct descendant of Roscher, Knies, and Hildebrand. To its merit we can add that until now it has not recommended List's protective system' (Pierson 1878: 215). By recommending state intervention with regard to improving production and distribution the school deserves praise, but it has not proposed any new ideas. This is even more the case among its Dutch representatives.

Goeman Borgesius had warned against the interpretation of economics as a system teaching only the promotion of self-interest. Pierson drily replies that every merchant prefers a higher price to a lower one, and every worker a higher wage. This is not egoism, but a realistic observation of the kind recommended by the socialists of the chair. On the one hand, some traditional economists have made their discipline an instrument for defending the interests of the bourgeoisie; on the other, socialists of the chair use it to justify prejudices and practices of the labouring class. Pierson elaborates three arguments against the reasonings of the latter.

First he deplores their lack of respect for the achievements of Smith, Ricardo and other classical economists, and their enthusiasm for the superficial and even wrong analyses of Lassalle. Second he attacks the role taken by socialists of the chair as advocates of trade unions, and approvingly quotes D'Aulnis, who has identified the attitude of this school with regard to the labour movement as its weakest point. The third and methodological criticism concerns the new school's denial of the existence of economic laws. There may be a difference between physical and economic laws, as the functioning of the latter is dependent on psychological mechanisms. This implies a conditionality of economic laws, which must always be observed by the economist, regardless of whether he explicitly mentions the conditions under which the laws prevail.

Pierson's concluding remarks evaluate the recent German contribution to economics, and praises its achievements in economic history. The work of Schmoller, Stahl and Brentano in this field in recent years is 'more than an everyday's job':

> The Dutch chair-socialists had better follow the example of their German kindred spirits in this respect. Thereby science would gain more than by spreading a number of false ideas which, on the other side of the Rhine, are in my opinion already past their best period.
>
> (Pierson 1878: 247)

Subsequently both Pierson (1879) and D'Aulnis de Bourouill (1880) commented on Levy's book. D'Aulnis found this book a muddle, lacking any kind of economic logic. If this was support for the historical method, then this approach lacked 'method' altogether. D'Aulnis also repeated his earlier point that he believed the opposition between 'old' economics and 'new' historical economics to be a straw man. There was nothing new in the work of exemplary German socialist economists like Held and Wagner. If one studied their work in more detail, it was old-fashioned classical economics from start to finish (D'Aulnis de Bourouill 1880: 150–151).

To underline the old wine in new bottles argument D'Aulnis remarked that John Stuart Mill was a socialist of the chair long before the German economists ever thought of this movement. It was all in Mill, and the Germans just copied his idealism concerning the issue of improving social conditions.

Pierson's rejoinder is threefold (1879). He disagrees with Levy's definition of economic questions, attacks his melting together of economics and economic policy and criticizes his methodological inductivism. He protests against the narrow interpretation of economics as the study of material maximizing: value judgments always leave room for decisions correcting market outcomes. With sardonic pleasure he points to Levy's inconsistencies:

> By insisting upon a strict distinction between economics and economic policy, we state first of all that material interests, however important, do not naturally deserve precedence; we maintain – for an instant I speak Mr. Levy's language – *the ethical element.* Secondly we state: the life of a nation is unity; whatever affects welfare, more or less affects the entire social framework. By this second statement we maintain – again I speak Mr. Levy's language – *the organic character* of society.
>
> (Pierson 1879: 270)

In the concluding methodological section, Pierson corrects Levy's misinterpretation of John Stuart Mill's and his own viewpoints on induction and experimentation. And finally he ridicules Levy's interpretation of Adam Smith as an inductivist scholar. Yet he generously concludes by praising Levy for his contribution to a serious debate on economics, far above the level of many superficial and popularizing booklets.

In 1868 Pierson had been mildly critical about the tenets of the historical school. A decade later his judgment was much stricter about the relevance of the socialism of the chair. This widening rift with Dutch mainstream economics also became apparent in the professorial appointments in the state universities.

The reconciliation that failed

The inaugural lecture of H. B. Greven, in 1880 at Leyden University, already in its title made clear that in the Netherlands a struggle between old and new economics was going on: *Old and New Economics: An effort at reconciliation.*

Greven's appointment was remarkable because the first select list of three candidates exclusively counted three followers of the historical school: Goeman Borgesius, van Houten and Kerdijk. These 'younger liberals' were to make their mark in politics, the first as a cabinet minister in Pierson's ministry (1897–1901), also known as the Cabinet of Social Justice, and the second as the father of the first bill regulating child labour. The proposal carrying their names was put aside, and a new selection started. This was possible in a system where professorial appointments – Amsterdam excepted – were an affair of the state, and where classical and marginalist economics prevailed.

Remarkably the scientific opponents Pierson and van Houten were good friends. Van Maarseveen (1981: 45) argues that their friendship was based on their joint opposition to orthodox economics and appeal for social reform. The former had even proposed the latter as a candidate for the vacant Utrecht chair that would be occupied by Quack in 1868. And when van Houten's bill against employing children under age 12 was passed in 1874, Pierson wrote to him approvingly but also voiced his concern about the enforcement of the new rules. He recommended the appointment of independent inspectors, and referred to the discussions at the German Eisenach conference (1872) of socialists of the chair, where the discussions had demonstrated that local labour inspectors were ineffective because in practice they were dependent on the employers to be inspected.

The passing of van Houten's bill can be regarded as the first victory in practice of socially concerned economics – whether labelled historical or chair-socialist. In theory Pierson and other mainstream Dutch economists continued to preach value-free economics, and to condemn the value-laden historical school as well as the socialism of the chair.

A confidential and sharp letter to Pierson from the Leyden law professor Buys, written in September 1879 (van Maarseveen 1990: 667–670), reveals the problems around the appointment of a new economics professor after the retirement of Vissering. Buys had been an economics teacher and a professor in Amsterdam, as the successor of de Bosch Kemper. For many years he was one of the editors of *De Gids*. Pierson had recommended Greven and another candidate for the vacant Leyden chair. Buys replied that Greven was an able man, but a failure as a secondary school teacher in Leyden. To the great regret of Vissering, the law department had proposed three 'men of *Vragen des Tijds*' (to be read as 'socialists of the chair') to the supervisory board of the university (van Maarseveen 1990: 668). This body chose to present Kerdijk as the candidate to the responsible cabinet minister, although two of its members deplored that 'the department wished to throw the academy in the arms of socialism' (van Maarseveen 1990: 669). But then a lobby – of which Buys suspected Vissering – convinced the minister to decline the proposal. Bitterly Buys commented,

> What a liberality! Germany does not object to entrusting its most prominent chairs to pronounced socialists of the chair. Held in Bonn, Brentano in Breslau, Schmoller in Strasbourg, and earlier Schäffle in Vienna, and we liberal Dutchmen believe the slightest tinge of heterodoxy to be enough for disqualifying a professor. As if a movement, thus systematically excluded, would not exert an endlessly larger influence upon young men.
>
> (Van Maarseveen 1990: 667–670)

Buys concluded by asking permission to approach the minister with Pierson's letter and suggestions. The latter's reply is unknown, but the outcome was that Greven – indeed one of Pierson's two names – was appointed.

In his inaugural Greven set off with a comparison between the natural and the social sciences. Perhaps he wished to demonstrate that he was no lesser methodologist than Samuel van Houten, who had tackled this subject in an article in 1871 (van Houten 1871):

Whoever devotes himself to Economics, while being not totally uninformed about the method and progress of the exact sciences, will often be seduced to jealousy with regard to the practitioners of these sciences. Every man's task is precisely defined; there is agreement about research methods; every labour, once diligently accomplished, is a permanent asset for science.

(Greven 1880: 5)

But in the social sciences, everything is contested:

The question is contested, whether a science of society is possible at all, whether a division of labour in this field is desirable, where the domain and the boundaries of every subfield are located, what is the right method, what is the link between theory and practice – just to name a few of the cardinal points.

(Greven 1880: 6)

Greven continues on the efforts of 'the economists of the historical school in Germany, who have accepted the label of Socialists of the Chair' (Greven 1880: 7). From Germany this movement has reached the Netherlands and England, and everywhere the struggle between old and new economics is taking place: 'While one discussant accuses the other of tampering with the *bourgeoisie*, the latter throws back the accusation of flirting with *socialism*' (Greven 1880: 8).

According to Greven, in Germany the two schools are aiming at reconciliation. Unfortunately in the Netherlands this is not the case. It is Greven's purpose to hold a plea for reconciliation in the Netherlands as well. Economics is a science and an art: theoretical economics is the science, practical economics the art. But the question of whether material welfare is always a legitimate goal is a matter of morals or politics. To a certain extent there are natural laws in economics, but it is wrong to justify every resulting distribution of incomes on grounds of these laws, and wrong to deny any possibility of interfering in this distribution.

Regarding method, Greven does not choose between deductivism and inductivism:

Induction is infinitely more difficult than deduction; while the latter is deducing the consequences from known causes, and develops the results from given theorems, for induction inversely the question is, what have been the causes of known consequences, and which theorems have led to the known results.

(Greven 1880: 18)

The old theoretical economics should not be discarded. On the other hand, historical and statistical researches are indispensable. And when it comes to the art of practical economics, Greven does not accept the reproach to the old economics of (selfish) individualism, contrasting the organic nature of society. In his opinion, a healthy individualism can go hand in hand with the recognition that society is an organism. He concludes his inaugural by praising the positive dimensions of the 'old' and the 'new' school in economics:

> With the old one, a healthy individualism is maintained against the elevation of the State as final objective; with the new one, the big influence of regulation is recognized, particularly in matters of distribution of wealth, and the State is asked, as far as is possible within its powers, to improve conditions in society.
>
> (Greven 1880: 37)

Greven's effort at reconciliation between the two schools was commendable but hardly effective. The representatives of the old and the new continued combating each other.

Bordewijk (1931) claims the historical school really took hold in the Netherlands with the inaugural lecture of M.W.F. Treub. On 23 November 1896 Treub accepted his professorship at the University of Amsterdam with a lecture entitled 'The Development of Political Economy (*'Staathuishoudkunde'*) towards a Social Science'. Treub attacked the very popular textbook of Pierson (1884–1890) and used the economics of the historical school to support his arguments. In particular he adopted historical arguments to counter the individualistic foundation of Pierson's economics and supported the case of 'social economics', which for Treub implied an approach addressing the inequality of wealth and income in society as a key economic problem. For Treub the historical school with its focus on the social conditions for economic progress stood in the same tradition as Marx.

The appointment of Treub was a small victory for the historical school in Dutch economics, because Treub 'beat' C. A. Verrijn Stuart, who also applied for the job. Verrijn Stuart later became the great advocate of Dutch 'Austrian' economics, not in the least through his successful economic textbook, *Grondslagen der Volkshuishouding* (Foundations of the General Economy, 1920), which ran through six editions until 1947.

Treub was a typical example of the Dutch economist of the late nineteenth century, trained in law with a strong interest in history and politics. Just before his appointment Treub was alderman of the city council in Amsterdam. In this function he succeeded in founding an impressive array of municipally owned utilities, such as the provision of water, telecommunications, the tramway and the local gas company. Previously these companies had all been exploited by private firms. In spite of his zeal to get public services under government control, politically he is best characterized as a progressive socialist in the modern meaning of that word (Nouwen 1970). He entered parliament, and in 1913 became minister of agriculture and in 1914 became minister of finance in the wartime cabinet of Cort van der Linden. Pragmatic as he was, after the war he became a representative of the Dutch corporate interests in the Dutch East Indies, with the intention to moderate the consequences of impending social law and policies for Dutch firms. Treub's career characterizes the strong connections between academia, the corporate sector and politics. In this period a scientific career for economists was never entirely devoted to pure science. On the contrary, Treub's lecture demonstrates that in this period there was just a thin line running between the historical school and the socialist political agenda of Dutch economists claiming to adopt the historical school as a framework for their thinking. Consequently, the debate about the meaning of the historical school became quickly drawn into the trenches of political disagreement. The institutional setting of Dutch economics, with its interdependent interests, promoted this type of political debate about issues that first emerged as scientific issues proper.

Political controversy: *Ethical* against *Mammonist*

In 1897 the new liberal cabinet under Pierson presented itself in parliament with a programme of social reform. Remarkably the new minister of justice was Goeman Borgesius, whose application for the Leyden economics chair had been thrown into the dustbin because of his chair-socialist leanings. The leader of the Antirevolutionary (orthodox reformed Protestant) party, Abraham Kuyper, did not fail to point this out, and attacked the government by stating that the liberals were misrepresenting the economists' consensus on what social reform meant. Abraham Kuyper (1837–1920), nicknamed Abraham the Colossal, was a towering figure in Dutch politics and society in the later nineteenth and early twentieth centuries. He founded a political party, a journal and a university (the Free University in Amsterdam).[2] In the parliamentary session of 1 December 1897 he presented himself as a follower of the historical school:

> Regarding social reform there is *not one road for all*. Many people may think so, and in most organs of the liberal school a picture is sketched as if there is only *one school* in economics. But when one looks across borders, and follows academic studies abroad, one knows better. No, there is not one school, but two competing almost like fire and water, to wit the old-orthodox school of Smith, Say, and Ricardo, and the younger one of Carey, List, and Roscher.
>
> (Kuyper 1897: 274)

Kuyper then asked the question of whether the cabinet, in its social reform, would follow the ideas of the old or of the new school. He put forward the hypothesis that the prime minister would embrace the former, and the justice minister the latter school. Kuyper stated that not only Protestant but also Roman Catholic politicians have united against old-school economics. They denounced deductivist methods and individualist policies, which are contrary to the national and ethical interest:

> When gradually in the economic discipline, by men like Carey in America, like Friedrich List and others, quite different social-historical ideas in economics

were pronounced, in almost all countries men of Christian conviction immediately voiced their sympathy.

(. . .)

On the foundation of their social principle, Christian parties had to take a stand against the individualist economic school, and could only applaud the stepping forward of the ethical, social-historical school. It must have their sympathy that people like List, Schäffle, Roscher, Knies, Schmoller and others, were bringing forward again the *national* element against the *cosmopolitan*, the *social* and *organic* against the *individualist*, and no less the *ethical* against the *Mammonist*.

(. . .)

Isn't it natural that Christian parties, not putting *material* values first, but *spiritual* ones, and not being of recent origin but *historically* having a genealogy of centuries behind them, – Isn't it natural, I'm asking, that Christian parties, eminently representing the social and organic element, in full appreciation of the many good and excellent things with which the orthodox-economical school has enriched us materially, must be thankful that finally the hour came which liberated us from its dominance, and in which a youthful and fresh economic school stepped forward that by appreciating the *social* and *ethical* element of man, can now be said to be *the* economic school of the future in Germany?

(Kuyper 1897: 274–275)

In the following debate on the education budget, Kuyper's hidden agenda became clear. He was not primarily interested in propagating the historical school, but much more in getting recognition and financing for his Protestant Free University, founded in Amsterdam in 1875.[3] This private institution did not have the academic *ius examinandi* and *ius promovendi*. So in practice it was an institute preparing students for examinations at the Amsterdam municipal university. The official argument against its recognition was that the programme of the sciences – speaking with one voice – was already taught in Amsterdam. Kuyper's first counterexample was, of course, his belief in creationism versus the theory of evolution, and now he was glad to present another example of scientific disagreement within another discipline. That had most probably been his true motive behind his praise for the historical school, when he came back to it in the education discussions.

It is remarkable that in the Netherlands not only an academic strand of opposition against the tenets of classical political economy was running through the entire nineteenth century, but also this criticism echoed in political debates in parliament.

What, in the meantime, was the fate of true socialism in Dutch academia? In 1899, after a lively public debate, Franc van der Goes was admitted as 'privaat-docent' (unpaid private lecturer) in socialist economics at the Amsterdam municipal university, against the vote of the largest possible majority of professors in the law faculty – only Treub was in favour (Van Heerikhuizen 1974). Van der

Goes was the Dutch translator of *Das Kapital*. In the background of the public debate, the question was looming of whether economics or sociology would rise to the status of most prestigious social science. S. R. Steinmetz, admitted as a private lecturer of ethnology in Utrecht, and of sociology in Leyden, was van der Goes's fiercest opponent. J. A. Levy, the liberal lawyer who had written the pamphlet defending the socialism of the chair in 1879, came to the defence of van der Goes. He labelled Steinmetz's first public lecture in Leyden as 'a mixture of rubbish, crazy wisdom, arrogance, and affectation' (Van Heerikhuizen 1974: 355). Nevertheless van der Goes was admitted, and commenced his course called Scientific Foundations of Marxism in March 1900. His admission was prolonged until 1912, but already in 1906 his audience had dwindled to four students (Van Heerikhuizen 1974: 357).

Kalshoven (1993) typifies this period as the weak foundation for Dutch Marxist economics ('a house of straw'), which enjoyed its best theoretical period from 1900 to 1916 ('a house of stone'). During these years, Dutch Marxists had a common platform which allowed them to exchange ideas and to join forces, the journal *De Nieuwe Tijd* (The New Era), which was politically and financially independent. The demise of this platform started a quick change of Dutch Marxism, which became a variant of neoclassical socialism. The typical features of Marxism – the labour theory of value and the prominent role for class struggle – were replaced by considerations of central planning in a general equilibrium setting, using the tools of marginalistic calculation.

By and large the Dutch discussion about the relevance of socialism of the chair followed the course of the international debate, which more or less ended with Brentano's final clarion call in 1918.

The final stage: Symbiosis

The turn of the century marked the breakthrough of Austrian economics in Dutch economics. Pierson had been greatly interested in the work of the Austrians, but professed to be more of a Marshallian. For the next generation, this was certainly not the case. C. A. Verrijn Stuart was beaten to the chair in Amsterdam by Treub, but got his chance in the new Technical High School in Delft in 1906. His professional lecture frontally attacked the type of approach followed by proponents of the historical school and socialists of the chair, which mixed up science and art. For Verrijn Stuart, this led to an approach which was devoid of any type of economic logic, which was not worthy of the name economics. In line with this defence of the pure approach to economic science, Verrijn Stuart (1920) wrote the first textbook in Dutch economics written primarily for academic curricula (Pierson's textbook had its origin as a secondary school manual; Pierson 1884–1890). This marked the process of institutionalizing economics as a scientific discipline with the foundation of separate economic faculties. In 1913 the new Higher School of Economics in Rotterdam was founded, soon to be followed by faculties in Tilburg and Amsterdam. So this was the first textbook for economic students, and it was thoroughly Austrian in outlook and content. In their history of the Dutch economic textbooks, Schoorl and Plasmeijer (2012) describe this period as the heyday of Dutch Austrianism.

H.W.C. Bordewijk's (1931) *Theoretical-Historical Introduction to Economics* reviews the achievements of the historical school in the Netherlands in similar terms, but concludes on an optimistic note. The relevance of Bordewijk's book is that it summarizes the state of thinking of Dutch economists on the position of the historical school in the early decades of the twentieth century. He provides an in-depth analysis of the development of the school, starting with Friedrich List, Wilhelm Roscher and Karl Knies, up to Gustav Schmoller, Adolph Wagner, Lujo Brentano, Gustav Cohn and Werner Sombart as representatives of the younger historical school.

Bordewijk greatly praises the school for what he considers its greatest contribution – namely its relative historicism, which posits that economic thinking can never be judged independently of the historical conditions pertaining to a specific place and time. *Vice versa* economic science it must take notice of the influence of historically determined conditions and institutions when developing theories and policies. This is the lesson that Dutch economists could learn from studying the historical school, according to Bordewijk. For him this was certainly not a school belonging to the atheoretical domain, as suggested by the Method-enstreit. In many fields, the historical school advanced economic theory, such as price theory, monetary theory and the theory of capital and growth. In this regard, the Methodenstreit should be considered 'a storm in a glass of water' (Bordewijk 1931: 577), which Bordewijk with a nice sense of humour typifies as a clear case of 'roundabout production' within the economic domain. The greatest error of the historical school is not hidden by Bordewijk and consisted in its political bias, which affected much of its work. This was a point in favour of the Austrian School, which on the whole was better able to separate economic theorizing from the political implications following from it.

All in all Bordewijk's extensive reading of the historical school nicely under-lines the core thesis of this chapter: there was no smooth transition from classical economics to Austrian economics. The historical school left its skid marks in virtually every domain of economics, and with the appointment of Treub in Amsterdam had its moment of victory over the emerging Austrian paradigm.

Conclusion

In the Netherlands, on the whole things were not altogether as quiet as Schum-peter stated. In academic economics a fairly smooth transition took place from classical economics to marginalist, Marshallian and Austrian economics. This was largely the merit of Nicolaas Gerard Pierson, the figurehead of Dutch eco-nomics at the time. But in public and parliamentary discussions, the historical school received a warmer appraisal. This can at least partly be explained by the specifically Dutch political climate of the period, in which confessional parties of Protestant and Roman Catholic denomination came to the fore and challenged the traditional dominance of the liberal politicians. In a similar manner the rise of socialism provided ammunition to a critical debate about the meaning and relevance of the historical school.

This chapter showed how this debate developed as a clash of generations. The older generation was trained in the tradition of the classical school of economics and upheld its orthodox-liberal position towards economic policy. The younger generation was sympathetic towards the ideas of the socialists of the chair and its foundation in the teachings of the historical school. This clash affected university appointments, which initially prevented adherents of the historical school from becoming part of the academic establishment. This happened only with the likewise politically inspired appointment of Willem Treub in 1896 in Amsterdam.

The proponents and opponents of the historical school crossed swords in the economic and general journals of the time. The role of the general journals in this regard is noteworthy. They proved a more important transmission channel for economic ideas – new or old – than the more specialized economic journals. In part this can be explained by pointing out that the economics profession in the Netherlands at this time was still going through its initial phases of development. Specialized economic journals initially strongly focused on matters of practical relevance. New economic ideas, with their stronger political profile, seemed more suitable for general journals, which attracted a wider audience, like *De Gids*. Hence it was here that the combatants exchanged their articles and letters on the historical school, sometimes fired on by academic publications, like the inaugural lecture of D'Aulnis, which was devoted to the socialism of the chair. Later on ideas for and against the historical school and related calls for social policies were further developed in books, such as Levy's long book on historicism in Britain and Pierson's dismissal of the school in his influential textbook (Pierson 1884–1890).

It is telling that it was a textbook with the title *Theoretical-Historical Introduction to Economics* (Bordewijk 1931) that summed up the debate with a lengthy analysis of the contributions of the historical school, both the older and the younger. By and large the Dutch economists always kept an open eye for the theoretical advancements of the members of the historical school, who were greatly valued on their own merit.

These examples indicate that first and foremost the historical school impacted the political discourse in the Netherlands. But for Dutch economists the historical school certainly did not pass unnoticed in the Low Countries. On the whole things were not quiet with regard to the historical school, and Dutch economists continued to teach and apply the basic tenets of German historicism until well into the twentieth century.

Notes

1 In the old Republic, every Dutch province was allowed to have one university. For Holland, this was Leyden University. In practice the municipal Amsterdam Athenaeum Illustre taught courses at university level since 1632, without the 'ius promovendi'. In 1877 it received the status of a fully fledged university under the municipal aegis, in

contrast with the state universities of Leyden, Groningen and Utrecht. The other pro-
vincial universities did not survive.

2 In 1901 Kuyper succeeded Pierson as prime minister of the Netherlands. In 1903, after
a large railway strike, he designed a strict antistrike legislation, known as Kuyper's
Strangling Laws.

3 With a PhD in theology, he served as a Protestant reverend. As a strict Neo-Calvinist
he promoted the split between the Dutch Protestant Church and the Dutch Reformed
Church. The founder of the Antirevolutionary Party, he is considered one of the orga-
nizers of the modern political party system in the Netherlands, with the accompanying
'pillarization' of society into groups with their own social organizations (including – but
not always – churches), journals, and schools and universities.

References

Aerts, R. (1997). *De Letterheren – Liberale cultuur in de negentiende eeuw: Het tijdschrift.
De Gids*, Groningen: Meulenhoff.

Berkel, K. van (2008). *De stem van de wetenschap; Geschiedenis van de KNAW I:
1808–1914*. Amsterdam: Bert Bakker.

Bordewijk, H.W.C. (1931). *Theoretisch-Historische Inleiding tot de Economie*. Groningen:
Wolters.

Boschloo, T. J. (1989). *De Productiemaatschappij: Liberalisme, economische wetenschap
en het vraagstuk der armoede in Nederland 1800–1875*. Hilversum: Verloren.

D'Aulnis de Bourouill, J. (1878). *Het katheder-socialisme: Redevoering bij de aanvaard-
ing van het hoogleraarsambt aan de Rijks-Universiteit te Utrecht op den 23sten maart
1878 uitgesproken*. Utrecht: Beijers.

D'Aulnis de Bourouill, J. (1880). Nederlandsch Kathedersocialisme. *De Economist*, vol.
29(1), 133–160, 305–324.

De Bosch Kemper, J. (1860–1871). *Handleiding tot de kennis van de wetenschap der zamen-
leving en van het Nederlandsche staatsregt*, 3 vols. Amsterdam: Johannes Müller.

De Vries, F. (1952). Honderd jaar theoretische economie. *De Economist*, vol. 100(1),
829–879.

Goeman Borgesius, H. (1878). Open brief aan Mr. J. Baron d'Aulnis de Bourouill. *Vragen
des Tijds*, vol. 4(2), 219–278.

Greven, H. B. (1880). *Oude en Nieuwe Economie: Eene poging tot verzoening*. Utrecht:
J. Greven.

Hamaker, H. J. (1870). *De Historische School in de Staathuishoudkunde*. Leiden: Gebroe-
ders van der Hoek.

Heerikhuizen, B. van (1974). Fanatische docenten ongewenscht! De toelating van Franc
van der Goes als privaatdocent aan de Universiteit van Amsterdam. *De Gids*, vol.
137(5), 352–358.

Houten, S. van (1871). De methode der natuurwetenschap in verband met die der geestelijk-
en wetenschappen, *De Gids*, reprinted in S. van Houten (1883), *Bijdragen tot den
strijd over God, Eigendom en Familie*, 2nd edition. Haarlem: Tjeenk Willink, 17–31.

Kalshoven, F. (1993). *Over marxistische economie in Nederland, 1883–1939*. Amsterdam:
Thesis.

Kuhn, T. S. (1970). *The Structure of Scientific Revolutions*, 2nd edition. Chicago: University of Chicago Press.

Kuyper, A. (1897). Handelingen Tweede Kamer 1897–1898 (parliamentary records), 1
December, 269–275.

Levy, J. H. (1879). *Engelsch Katheder-Socialisme.* 's-Gravenhage: Belinfante.

Nouwen, L.J.M. (1970). *Willem Treub, een remarkabel man.* Deventer: Kluwer.

Pierson, N. G. (1861). De logica der Staatshuishoudkunde, in C. A. Verrijn Stuart (ed.), *Verspreide economische geschriften van mr. N.G. Pierson: Volume 1, 1910.* Haarlem: Erven F. Bohm, 1–13.

Pierson, N. G. (1862). Wilhelm Roscher: Ansichten der Volkswirthschaft aus dem geschichtlichen Standpunckte. *De Gids,* vol. 26(1), 588–595.

Pierson, N. G. (1864). Het begrip van volksrijkdom, in C. A. Verrijn Stuart (ed.), *Verspreide economische geschriften van mr. N.G. Pierson: Volume 1, 1910.* Haarlem: Erven F. Bohm, 14–103.

Pierson, N. G. (1866). Waarde en productie-kosten, in C. A. Verrijn Stuart (ed.), *Verspreide economische geschriften van mr. N.G. Pierson: Volume 1, 1910.* Haarlem: Erven F. Bohm, 104–125.

Pierson, N. G. (1868). Wilhelm Roscher, Die Grundlagen der National-oekonomie, in C. A. Verrijn Stuart (ed.), *Verspreide economische geschriften van mr. N.G. Pierson: Volume 2, 1910.* Haarlem: Erven F. Bohm, 402–433.

Pierson, N. G. (1878). Het katheder-socialisme, in C. A. Verrijn Stuart (ed.), *Verspreide economische geschriften van mr. N.G. Pierson: Volume 1, 1910.* Haarlem: Erven F. Bohm, 248–247.

Pierson, N. G. (1879). Werkkring en methode der staatshuishoudkunde, in C. A. Verrijn Stuart (ed.), *Verspreide economische geschriften van mr. N.G. Pierson: Volume 1, 1910.* Haarlem: Bohm, 248–286.

Pierson, N. G. (1884–1890). *Leerboek der Staathuishoudkunde I & II.* Haarlem: Bohn.

Quack, H.P.G. (1915). *Herinneringen uit de levensjaren van mr. H.P.G. Quack,* 2nd edition. Amsterdam: Kampen & Zoon.

Schoorl, E. and Plasmeijer, H. (2012). From ruminators to pioneers: Dutch economics textbooks and their authors in the nineteenth and early twentieth century, in: M. M. Augello and M.E.L. Guidi (eds), *The Economic Reader: Textbooks, manuals and the dissemination of the economic sciences during the nineteenth and early twentieth centuries.* Oxford: Routledge, 248–284.

Schumpeter, J. A. (1954). *History of Economic Analysis.* New York: Oxford University Press.

van Maarseveen, J.G.S.J. (1981). *Nicolaas Gerard Pierson: Handelsman, Econoom en Bankier. Eerste periode 1839–1877.* PhD dissertation, Rotterdam.

van Maarseveen, J.G.S.J. (1990). *Briefwisseling van Nicolaas Gerard Pierson 1839–1909: Part 1, 1851–1884, NIBE-bankhistorische reeks VIII.* Amsterdam: De Nederlandsche Bank.

Verrijn Stuart, C. A. (1920). *De Grondslagen der Volkshuishouding.* Haarlem: Erven F. Bohm.

Vissering, S. (1860–1865). *Handboek van Praktische Staathuishoudkunde I & II.* Amsterdam: Van Kampen.

5 The German Historical School of economics in the Italian debate (1870–1890)

Vitantonio Gioia

Introduction

In 1874 Ferrara published "*Il germanismo economico in Italia*" (Economic Germanism in Italy), followed in 1876 by two other articles: "Gli equivoci del vincolismo: Il Congresso di Milano" (Misunderstandings of protectionism) and "L'italianità della scienza economica: Lettera all'On. Sen. Fedelo Lampertico" (The Italian Features of Economics: Letter to Senator Fedele Lampertico). These three articles marked the birth of the idea of an Italian historical school of economics and the birth of a distorted debate about the German Historical School (GHS).

Harsh debates and ferocious criticisms occurred. Messedaglia, Lampertico, Cossa, Rabbeno and others were considered representatives of this new school of economics; Ferrara, Pantaleoni and Pareto became standard-bearers of a norest struggle against the historicist degeneration of economics. Nobody wondered whether such a school really existed in Italy, or what its features and its purposes were. The existence of the Italian historical school of economics was accepted, and it was accepted that it was characterized by an antitheoretical attitude in the scientific field and by an antiliberal perspective in the political vision. So scientific tradition persisted in the idea of a harsh contrast in Italy between two economic schools: between a theoretical school (Ferrara, Pantaleoni, Pareto) and an antitheoretical school (Messedaglia, Lampertico, Cossa), and between a liberal school and an antiliberal school.

Nevertheless, if we try to overcome the impression created by Ferrara's work and by the radical criticisms of Pantaleoni, Pareto and others, if we do not accept immediately the interpretation they suggest about the evolution of Italian economic thought and if we make a systematic analysis of the works of the Italian economists considered representatives of the historical school or, even, *Kathedersozialisten*, we can observe a different reality. In particular, we do not find any scientific production proving explicit support for the scientific program of the GHS. Strictly speaking, it is therefore very difficult to talk about the existence of a historical school of economics in Italy.

As we will show, the Italian historical school of economics was a Ferrarian invention caused by political reasons (linked to the organization of the Italian State following political unification), but the uncritical acceptance of Ferrara's view produced serious interpretative distortions. As a result, there are still no

acceptable explanations in the scientific reconstruction of the evolution of economics in Italy after 1870. In particular, we need more thorough inquiries into
these aspects:

- The reasons for the strong influence in Italy of the GHS of economics;
- The reasons for the harsh controversies that occurred, linked to such influences;
- A rigorous analysis of the limits of Ferrara's work trying to show the exis-
tence of an Italian historical school of economics.

As we will see, the analysis of the ideological barriers built up during the harsh
debates of this period explains the difficult reception of the GHS authors not only
at the end of nineteenth century but also in the following century. Scientific interest in some representatives of the GHS (above all, Max Weber and Sombart)
increased in Italy after World War II (Pisanelli 2015: 166ff.), and in the last decade
of the twentieth century, Schmoller and the general experience of the GHS underwent a thorough reconsideration (Gioia 1990; Schiera & Tenbruck 1989).

Ferrara's and Pareto's Criticism

Let's start from the reasons which determined the influence and spread throughout
Italy of ideas and scientific approaches which can be traced back to the GHS of
economics. Such reasons – as we will see – are broader and more variegated
than we usually think. In the second half of the nineteenth century for Italian
philosophers and social scientists Germany assumed a more and more significant
role for various reasons:

- It was an important reference point in the immediate postrisorgimental phase
for "the more advanced part of the post-risorgimental Italian intelligentsia"
(Garin 1974: 9).
- As well as the many similarities in their political history, there was great
interest in Germany's rapid economic growth (Germany was a particularly
attractive model for a latecomer like Italy).
- That model of economic and social growth seemed able to successfully deal
with the problem linked to the *soziale Frage* and to the socialist challenge
(Cognetti de Martiis 1895: 688; Rabbeno 1891: 440).
- Finally, some innovative approaches of the GHS were perceived by Italian
economists as serious contributions to the discovery of new fields of inquiry,
and to the overcoming of that "theoretical stagnation" (to use the Schum-
peterian expression) which had followed the crisis of the classical paradigm
(Rabbeno 1894: 456–458).

Given such reasons the strong interest of Cossa and other Italian economists
in the German economic model seems fully understandable. The legitimacy of
this attention towards the German economic model and its scientific achievements
was also confirmed by Ferrara's scientific judgment. The great critic of "economic

Germanism" had showed explicit appreciation for the methodological approach and the analytical results of the representatives of the GHS (Ferrara 1934, 1: 18).

From this point of view, Pareto's attitude and his refusal to be interested in what was happening in Germany in that period both on the economic and theoretical front seem extremely surprising. They seem even more surprising if we consider the way Pareto worked as a social scientist with his proclaimed positivistic attitude in the evaluation of the role of empirical facts in social analysis. This meticulous and indefatigable gatherer of little empirical facts from which he constructed – inter alia – his *Trattato di sociologia generale* (Bobbio 1973) felt no scientific interest in Germany, its economy and the theoretical results of its economists. He therefore jeered at the young people who "allèrent . . . dans les universités allemandes" to study the German model or to learn the "principes de l'économie politique historique ou socialisme de la chaire". In his opinion, they only were antiliberal economists and followers of socialism: one of the causes of the ruin of Italian liberalism (Pareto 1965: 233).

Of course, Pareto did not find it relevant that the "German model" was not the sole model of reference of the Italian economists he criticized, and he simply ignored their explicit statement about the preference for the "English model" (Romani 1985), concerning political and economic matters (Cammarano 1992; Cossa 1883: 80ff.; Luzzatti 1880: 495; Scaldaferri 1992).

Pareto did not consider that for the Italian economists he criticized, the conceptions of Roscher, Hildebrand, Knies, Schmoller and Wagner were seen as a "liberal response" to the challenges of a historical phase, which run the risk of assuming the threatening features of socialist revolt. After all – as Schumpeter stated – the great loser of that historical period was none other than "old liberalism" which had constituted the philosophical frame of the paradigm of the classical political economy (Schumpeter 1990, 3: 932).

The second reason that can explain the fast spreading of ideas of the GHS among Italian economists is certainly to be found in the radical changes in the general cultural climate due to the spread in Italy of the idealist philosophy. Italy was, at that stage, traversed not only by strong political tensions connected to the making of a modern state, but also by an intense effort to achieve cultural renewal, aiming to overcome the old forms of spiritualism which had in prevalence characterized the philosophical tradition of the country before its political unification. Idealism, positivism and Marxism helped – beyond the significant differences within them – to spread an acute historical sensibility and to press for an intense effort to face reality (through historical analysis, empirical inquiries, statistical research, sociological surveys, etc.) in order to explain and modify it (Garin 1997, 1: 4–5).

Idealism – which developed in the southern Italian environment, through Francesco De Sanctis, Silvio and Bertrando Spaventa and Benedetto Croce – had a great significance for the making of a liberal experience in Italy (Tessitore 1988). It would be impossible to understand Italian liberalism without referring to this philosophical and cultural experience. From this point of view, I again find the Paretian judgment on the role of Italian idealism interesting, because he seemed absolutely incapable of understanding the effort to modernize the Italian state within a liberal perspective produced by this component of the national culture. Pareto regarded Italian idealism simply as a sort of Trojan horse which contributed to the ruin of the "liberal party" and to the penetration of socialist ideas in Italy (Pareto 1965: 234).

While the diffusion of idealistic historicism was an important precondition for the further spreading of views – like those of the GHS – which attributed great significance to history in explaining economic phenomena, we must not forget that positivism and Marxism also made a significant contribution in this direction (Jannaccone 1899: 106ff.).

Positivism spread the concept of evolution, the emphasis on the analysis of "facts" and empirical realities, the idea of a necessary relationship between scientific theories and historical reality and, as a result, that of scientific relativism, even though it did not avoid the degeneration of positivism itself into a new kind of metaphysics (Garin 1997, 1: 10).

Marxism also contributed to spreading the historicist vision with its reference to the idea that "understanding history" – as Antonio Labriola pointed out – was the only way both to explain economic and social phenomena (Labriola 1968a: 23; 1968b: 97ff.) and to modify it, overcoming the utopias which had ravaged the evolution of socialism (Labriola 1968a: 28ff.; on this see Cognetti de Martiis 1895; Messedaglia 1921; see also Gioia 2000).

Italian Economists and the Crisis of Classical Economics

Obviously neither the reference to the "German model" nor the modifications in the cultural climate can completely explain the changes in economic science and the heated debates they produced. As a matter of fact, these elements exercised a decisive influence on economics, because of the sense of dissatisfaction which characterized the economists' world in that period. As is well known, such dissatisfaction was connected with the crisis of the classical paradigm and had an international dimension. Already considered an illusion was the idea – explicitly expressed by J. Stuart Mill and Torrens – that concerning fundamental principles in economics there was nothing more to discover. It was also considered an illusion that economics was founded on principles which would soon acquire a general consensus among economists, putting an end to all controversy. These unfortunate prophecies – Cairnes pointed out – have not been fulfilled, and the controversies among economists have increased enormously, on those very same fundamental principles which J. Stuart Mill and Torrens believed almost accepted (Cairnes 1965: 20).

Moreover, such a level of dissatisfaction grew not only because of the awareness of the theoretical limits of the classical paradigm and because of the disputes internal to the field of political economy, but also because of the external criticisms which questioned the role of economics as a social science. From Comte to Marx to Knies, Hildebrand, Schmoller and so on, harsh attacks against the cognitive capability of economics found crowds of followers among social scientists and economists. Economics – the most developed social science – in such circumstances demonstrated great fragility, showing a significant level of permeability to the influence of sociology and other social sciences. From J. Stuart

Mill to Marx, to Cairnes, to Ingram and, coming to Italian economists, to Minghetti, Messedaglia, Lampertico, Cognetti de Martiis, Pareto and so forth, the relation between political economy and other social sciences had a central role in the disputes of that period (Cognetti de Martiis 1886; Messedaglia 1921; Minghetti 1859; Pareto 1980: 130–139).

In Italy too, we find general dissatisfaction concerning the condition of economics, but we also find an unexpected peculiarity concerning the relationship between Italian economists and classical political economy. Lampertico, Cossa, Cognetti de Martiis and so forth, who generally demonstrated a certain sensibility towards the theoretical approach of the GHS, retained a constant connection to the scientific paradigm of the classical school. The heritage of the classical school – Lampertico stated in 1875 – and its "doctrines are still universally accepted" (Lampertico 1875, 2: 277). The English classical school – Rabbeno insisted – has given "economic science a coordinated body of doctrines" which still represents the great reference point for economists, even though in this phase the system of the classical school "is shaken by every part" and "its conclusions and its principles are universally debated" (Rabbeno 1894: 852).

But in their opinion, the inadequacy of some theoretical devices created by classical economy did not mean the end of the classical heritage. England – Cossa wrote – had had "for a long time the old supremacy" in economics (Cossa 1892: 342). Such a supremacy is now contested "especially by Germany which in the last twenty years has become a great reformer of science"; nevertheless the "supremacy" of the English classical heritage is now confirmed thanks to the publication of "very important works which highlight, on the one hand, the link between the force of the abstraction and the great practical sense and, on the other, the deep knowledge of the results of the foreign investigations, which it once lacked". So, the "crisis of classical political economy", which for some should have led to its "failure", and for others, "to the substitution of it with a new science", produced instead "important corrections and new additions to the old science" (Cossa 1892: 362).

Italian economists regarded the crisis of the classical paradigm as an inevitable effect of scientific evolution, but in their view it still represented for them an essential point of departure, even though requirements to update some of its aspects were generally expressed (Cognetti de Martiis 1895: 686; Cossa 1878; 1892: 362ff.; Lampertico 1875: 277; Rabbeno 1891; 1894: 852). They did not see the contribution of the GHS and marginalism as a presupposition for the birth of a new scientific paradigm (Barucci 1980).

Moreover, given their strong interest in historical interpretation of economic phenomena, the marginalist view left a sense of disappointment in many Italian economists. As a matter of fact – in a phase of profound and rapid change in economic reality – it seemed to evade the problem of explaining original aspects of contemporary capitalism and – through the isolation of the phenomena of the market, the idea of perfect competition, through the exclusive emphasis on individuals and the disregard for the institutions – it seemed interested above all in creating a theoretical construct pervaded by a pronounced indifference and diffidence towards history and towards the problems of historical changes (Rabbeno 1894: 860ff.; Ricca

Salerno 1892: 9). As Cognetti de Martiis said with reference to Menger, his *Erscheinungsformen* recall "in a worrying way" the medieval debates on "the universalia ante rem, in re o post rem", which involved realists and nominalists, determining a de-historicized view of economic phenomena (Cognetti-de-Martiis 1886: 188).

In Search of a Synthesis

All this certainly created a favorable climate for the spreading of ideas and analytical approaches typical of the GHS. Italian economists appreciated not only the effort of German economists in building theoretical devices which were able to analyze new phenomena of the capitalist economy, but also their attempt at providing a general theoretical basis, for a deeper and more constant reflection on the changes in economic reality. They emphasized the following:

- The elements of scientific originality of authors like Roscher, Wagner and Schmoller, in the partial redefinition of the subject of political economy, which after their reflection, is not confined to the analysis of private economies, but includes a profound inquiry into the economic role of the state (Rabbeno 1894: 856ff.).
- The fact that such a view was supported by a strong reconsideration of those methodological aspects of the economic inquiry long neglected after David Ricardo. From this point of view, they generally did not consider the historical approach as an anticlassical approach, but if anything an attempt to restore a more balanced way of dealing with theory within a historical perspective. It was a way to reconcile induction and deduction in economic inquiry. In their opinion, the attempt of GHS authors was not very different from that made by authors like Cairnes in *The Character and Logical Method of Political Economy* and in *Essays in Political Economy* or Marshall in *The Present Position of Economics* (Cognetti de Martiis 1886: 188; Cossa 1878: 137ff.; Luzzatti 1894: 10ff.).
- The fact that the representatives of the GHS opened original fields of inquiry for economics: economic analysis thanks to Hildebrand, Schmoller and so forth can avail itself of the contribution of statistics, historical and empirical surveys, and sociological inquiries in order to pursue a better understanding of the economic reality (Jannaccone 1899: 108).

Of course, these evaluations confirm the close attention of Italian economists towards the GHS and the reasons its views spread, but do not show whether such a spread led to the creation of a true historical school in economics in Italy.

Normally, by an 'economic school' we mean a group of scholars strongly coordinated in order to work systematically to achieve a new paradigm, characterized by an original vision of economic relations and a radical break with the dominant paradigm, in order to build new scientific tools for economic analysis. Of course, in Italy, we do not have a historical school in this sense. As a matter of fact, the setting of a common scientific program did not exist among the economists whom Ferrara considered representatives of an Italian historical school of economics. The Congresso di Milano (1875), which was considered a foundation act of the Italian historical school, was not characterized by a scientific program and was mainly based on the idea of the introduction in Italy of political reforms in order to launch social legislation which could allow better control of the labor market, supporting the industrialization process.

In a similar fashion, we might compare this experience with the *Verein für Sozialpolitik* (founded in 1872), but it is useful to remember that the *Verein* was the result of theoretical reasoning and was conceived – wrongly or rightly – as a way to create a link between scientific explanation of the world and the attempt to change it through state intervention and appropriate economic policies (Schmoller 1898: 67ff.). Besides, it had a duration that made the *Verein* a complex experiment which, in many respects, has remained unique (Bruch 2004: 39–51; Nau 1998: 13–41; Priddat 2004: 53–73). In Italy, that did not occur.

At the "Congresso di Milano", conceived and managed by Luigi Luzzatti, the professional economists had a marginal role, and the same thing happened at the second meeting: the "Congresso di Palermo". In the *Giornale degli Economisti*, E. Forti pointed out that the Palermo conference was devoted to the suggestion of new social policies, and not to the making of a new scientific paradigm: "about our science, there is nothing really relevant to say concerning that Conference" (Forti 1876: 67).

Moreover, Luzzatti, in his answer to Francesco Ferrara, insisted on the fact that an Italian economic "school" did not exist (Luzzatti 1874) and, on the other hand, Ferrara too stated that the historical school in Italy was "acephalous" (Ferrara 1874). And that this should correspond to reality is shown by the failure to give continuity to political initiatives (like the Congresso di Milano and Palermo) and by the failure of scientific initiatives linked to the foundation of the *Giornale degli Economisti*, which, as is well known, lasted only a few years as the journal of the economists of historicist orientation and then – by a twist of fate – became the flag of Italian marginalism (Cardini 1995).

Of course, we might understand by 'economic school', in a broader sense, a group of economists who, without any coordination and also using different scientific tools, worked towards similar scientific purposes with an attitude we might link back to a common scientific program. But, even by using this broader meaning of economic school, I find it difficult to consider those economists indicated by Ferrara as components of an Italian historical school. This difficulty derives not only from the significant scientific differences among them, but also from the fact that while we generally find in their work explicit support for the idea of economic analysis carried out within a historical perspective, we rarely find explicit support for the scientific program of the GHS. And when we do find partial support, it is full not only of many specifications and distinctions but also of serious theoretical criticisms, concerning both methodological aspects and analytical results of the proposal of the GHS. So, for example, Cossa, in reviewing Fedele Lampertico's *L'economia dei popoli e degli stati*, points out that not all the doctrines of the GHS were "acceptable" and that Italian economists have to produce a significant effort in order to choose those contributions which "an adequate and impartial criticism will have demonstrated to represent a true progress in the scientific inquiry of economic phenomena" (Cossa 1878: 133).

In some cases the criticism of the GHS is too harsh, especially when directed against a certain approach, common in young German scholars, of collecting empirical facts and neglecting the exigencies to build theoretical generalizations. Cossa reproaches Schmoller for falling "into the serious mistake of thinking of the impossibility of applying the deductive method to the inquiries of economic science in a meaningful way, which, in Schmoller's opinion, could not exist without complete historical and statistical materials concerning the economic conditions of all the times and all the places" (Cossa 1892: 432–437).[1] Rabbeno, too, maintains that "while, thanks to the German historical school new life had penetrated into economic science, opening onto new horizons to the science, what was scarce – so to speak – was the theoretical fecundity of the new studies" (Rabbeno 1894: 860–862). Rabbeno, Cossa and others are therefore convinced that in many respects the German economists had played a significant and innovative role, but also that we cannot be satisfied with their "overly vague and indefinite generalizations" (Cossa 1892: 417). On the other hand, Cossa insists, we can say that German economics is not able to compete with the English supremacy. It is not possible "to admit the idea of a German supremacy in the entire field of economic sciences, similar to that which Germany has still in the philosophical, historical and juridical sciences" (Cossa 1892: 417).

So while Lampertico, Cossa and Rabbeno appreciate the fact that German economists like Roscher, Schmoller and Wagner paid close attention to the role of the state in modern capitalist economies, at the same time they criticize the excesses shown in their faith in the "omnipotence of the state" and the fact that the tasks it was given in the control of the economy were too onerous (Cognetti de Martiis 1886: 189; Cossa 1878: 134). "We have to consider", Cossa points out, ". . . as a good effect of the juridical culture of the German professors, a more correct idea concerning state functions", but at the same time we cannot ignore the fact that they often fall "into the theoretical mistake of confusing the sound economic liberty sustained by classical economists, with the absolute dogma of laissez faire, advocated by the optimists" (Cossa 1892: 418).

In this respect, the opinion of Giuseppe Ricca Salerno, Cossa's pupil and one of the founders of the Italian science of public finance, is very interesting. On the one hand, he did not accept the attempt, made by radical liberals like Ferrara, to consider the public economy simply as a private economy (Ricca Salerno 1878: 188); on the other, he made an effort to define the boundary markers concerning state intervention. In this attempt he, who studied in Berlin with Wagner, explicitly distances himself from Wagner and from those representatives of the GHS who advocated an expansion of state power over the economy. The state – he points out – cannot and must not change "the natural distribution of wealth" and the "relative economic position of the contributors" (Ricca Salerno 1878: 175). Instead, considering "the legitimate aims" and the "needs of the different social classes", the state must guarantee that they retain "their economic position". Otherwise, we would be assigning to the state – as Wagner and other German economists tend to do – a task which does not belong to it: that of "correcting the defects of society's economic order". We do not accept – Ricca Salerno insists – a kind of public policy which, through an excessive extension of state intervention, aims to surreptitiously create "an expedient used for ulterior plans in politics and social economy" (Ricca Salerno 1878: 177–178).[2]

The same thing is found in reference to the theory of free trade. Moreover, in this case Italian economists do not highlight the limits of the classical theory, but underline the "sharp contrast" existing between it and the present situation of international trade. The problem – Rabbeno writes – does not lie in a mistake in classical theory but rather in the fact that on the one hand we have a "perfectly accomplished theory" and on the other we have "an historical interpretation of the facts" which "is still all to build" (Rabbeno 1898: 8). Rabbeno focuses on the relevant theoretical innovations brought about by List and the historical school in this field, above all, in their ability to correctly analyze "the historical forms of the social evolution", but at the same time he radically criticizes the "exaggerations and scientific unilateralities of List" (Rabbeno 1898: 433). He particularly indicates four theoretical "defects" in the Listian analysis:

1   Exaggerations in the List's criticisms of the classical school;
2   The overestimation of the historical facts examined;
3   The overestimation of "the concept of nationality";
4   The fact that List "gives an excessive and exorbitant importance to the role of international trade" with reference to the issue of the economic growth of a single country (Rabbeno 1898: 436).

These scientific defects pull List towards a warped vision of the economic science; in fact "while he reproaches the orthodox economists for considering only the abstract economic life of mankind, List commits the opposite mistake, giving too much space to economic policy and not much to the general economy" (Rabbeno 1898: 436–437). In this way – Rabbeno continues – we are certainly able to consider the historical conditions of economic activity in reference to a country, but do not build a "general theory", forgetting the fact that economic science "has to reach more general conclusions" (Rabbeno 1898: 437ff.).

We can trace the first conclusions. Among the authors who were inspired by the GHS only Lampertico and Cusumano (Cusumano 1875) completely supported its scientific program. Cusumano, however, did not have the scientific personality needed to transplant to Italy an experience like that of the GHS. So the only scientific attempt to translate to Italy the scientific program of the GHS remains that made by Lampertico in the work *L'economia dei popoli e degli stati*. The other authors accepted only a few general scientific indications and did so with such specifications and distinctions that it is difficult to describe them as clear followers of the GHS (Romani 1992: 180).

If we cannot speak of an economic school on a scientific level, we can perhaps use the idea of a "school" in reference to the fact that these economists shared the same view concerning the role of the state and the economic policies to use in order to promote the country's growth. After all, the idea of an "Italian historical school" was a rhetorical invention by Ferrara in order to dramatize the confrontation concerning the effects of different economic policies on the growth of the Italian economy.

However, if we accept this meaning of "school" (convergence of such a group of Italian economists in the field of economic policies), we cannot accept the Ferrarian definition of them as economists who shared an antiliberal, authoritarian and pro-socialist view. The "liberal ideas" – Rabbeno points out in response to Ferrara's attacks – are accepted in great part by Italian economists" and "all or nearly all Italian economists favor free trade". Certainly, it cannot "be denied that the ideas of protectionists have made headway in Italy", they have "gained ground among farmers and business men" and in the "chambers of commerce", which have "repeatedly taken up the cause" and have pressed for protectionist policies, but upon Italian economists and "upon students of economic sciences in Italy, the doctrines of the protectionists have as yet made no impression". Therefore, it is not "possible in Italy to speak of a protectionist school in contrast to the liberal school" (Rabbeno 1891: 446–448).

On the other hand, it is a mistake to attribute solely to Germany this idea of state intervention in order to solve the *soziale Frage*: "English people already do what Germans are thinking" (Luzzatti 1874: 48). Besides, other European countries (Scandinavia, Hungary, Belgium, Holland, France, etc.) adopt the same kind of social legislation, so we can conclude – Luzzatti insists – that differences in "political regimes" do not seem able to modify tendencies which are deeply rooted in the evolution of the economic systems (Hay 1984; Hennock 1984; Luzzatti 1894: 18ff.; Mommsen 1984).

So – Ciccone points out – it is not possible to consider these authors as socialists or socialists of the chair:

> I dared not name any of the Italian economists among the socialists of the chair . . . because none of them, except perhaps Cusumano, has really propounded the doctrine. They call for broader action by the government in economic matters, but they remain loyal to orthodox economic principles.
> (Ciccone 1876: 72)

The writings of these economists – Rabbeno adds – show full support for liberalism, and the idea "if necessary" of "the intervention of the state" is accepted " very cautiously and in such a way as not to paralyze individual and associated action but rather to foster its development" (Rabbeno 1891: 438). What they contest are those aspects of Ferrarian ultraliberalism whose "line of thought" was closer to the views of Bastiat and to "the French optimistic school" rather than to "Smith's theories" (Rabbeno 1891: 466). So we find two common elements in their conception of liberalism: a kind of temperate liberalism, rooted in the theoretical approach of the classical school, and a resolute "anti-Ferrarian" attitude (Faucci 1995: 252; Gioia 2003a: 281ff.; Parisi 1997: 11–15). The former and the latter were not an exclusive heritage of the Italian economists, but were shared – again – by much of the national culture and constituted the backbone of the attempt to carry out a liberal experiment in postunification Italy (Are 1974; Gherardi 1989; Gozzi 1984).

From this point of view, it is sufficient to recall the bitter evaluation of the philosopher Silvio Spaventa, who, critically reflecting on the limits of the "old" liberalism, dwelled on the "abstract" and de-historicized concept of liberty which it implied. That liberalism is pervaded by a "scrupulous, elusive (almost bashful) desire to defend the freedom of the individual at all costs, which ends up proving to be indifferent to that very freedom", and leads to an unacceptable doctrinarianism which produces a

> strange confusion of ideas and words, as if we should consider liberal the Russian government, which leaves its railway in private hands, and authoritarian the Belgian government, which on behalf of the State rules the majority of the railways of that country.
>
> (Spaventa 1910: 43)

Concluding Remarks

But, things being thus, why did this mild historicist orientation and that (largely accepted) sort of tempered liberalism arouse such fierce reactions and such a "long and stubborn controversy"? Why were those controversies over the approach of the historical school so intense and enduring?

The keystone of such a persistent opposition is to be sought in the fact that – as Pareto said – we cannot admit any exception concerning the role of the state in the economy. The idea – shared by the representatives of the GHS of economics and its Italian followers – to accept even limited "interference by the state" or "the extension of its power" entails going back to the first "principles" on which economics is constructed and forces us to define the set of relations that economics can legitimately study (Pareto 1980: 75). In other words – as Pantaleoni stated – it involves excessively expanding "the extent of the field that is recognized as belonging to economics" (Pantaleoni 1963: 174–176).

Considered unacceptable were both the German definitions of economics as Staatsökonomie or Nationalökonomie (Hagemann 1996: 77) and Lampertico's proposal to consider the state "neither as an institution outside [the economic order], nor above it" (Lampertico 1874: 302), but "as an integral part of the economic order". As a matter of fact, while it is true that Lampertico – like Ferrara, Pantaleoni and Pareto – insisted on the existence of "a natural order we cannot violate unscathed", it is also true that he considered the "natural laws" to be "borderline laws" (Lampertico 1875: 468–469). These laws have a coercive character (and are therefore comparable to natural laws), but also a social dimension, since by varying the conditions set for their realization, it is possible to change the social reproduction of the economic order.

Ferrara, Pareto and Pantaleoni had a different vision of the "natural order of the economy". Natural order is, as in Lampertico, Luzzatti and Cossa, a result of economic activity of individuals, but individuals are conceived as a priori for the society. So, the "natural laws" are seen not as logical constructs derived from the effort to explain factual relations beyond the changing features of historical phenomena, but as a constant ontological relationship between facts, arising from an unchanging natural behavior. Ferrara expresses this view in this way:

> Every new analysis of economic phenomena on a purely theoretical order has discovered new links between the metaphysical truths and the obstinate attachment to freedom; just as every observation of events in the sphere of politics has confirmed the advantages of applying it and the harm of violating it.
>
> (Ferrara 1976a: 177–178; see also Pareto 1974: 144)

The only economic activity of the state compatible with the individual's behaviors, thus conceived, is that which guarantees safety and social order (Ferrara 1934: 551–552). Every other economic activity of the state might determine forms of "slavery" and "oppression" of the citizens, a mortal danger for their liberty. The state is always a terrible Leviathan which, with its intervention, modifies the "natural laws" arising out of individual activity, thus representing an unacceptable disturbance in the natural economic order. Reflecting on this Ferrararian view, Luigi Luzzatti emphasizes the survival in economics of a metaphysical approach typical of the philosophy of the seventeenth century, indicating Bastiat as its source. Bastiat is for economic science what Leibniz was for philosophy in the seventeenth century. Leibniz "saw the pre-established harmony of the universe in the monads"; Bastiat "observed in a more detailed way the pre-established harmony in the economic world" (Luzzatti 1952: 38).

The conclusion of this controversy and the predominance of pure economics became a formidable obstacle for the subsequent spread of the theories and methodological approaches of the GHS in the Italian social sciences, involving authors like Max Weber, A. Spiethoff and W. Sombart. Besides, the economists' hostility was reinforced by a significant change in those components of Italian culture which at the end of nineteenth century had favored the penetration of the GHS. In fact, while in that phase Italian Marxists and idealist philosophers had had a decisive role in spreading the methodological approach of the German economists, with whom they shared the same view on the historicity of economic and social phenomena, in the first quarter of the twentieth century, this syntony was replaced by the emphasis on the differences between the methods of inquiry (Pisanelli 2015: 156ff.).

Marxist authors were disappointed by the criticisms of historical materialism put forward by many representatives of the GHS, especially by M. Weber and Sombart. They appreciated only the Sombartian commentary on the third volume of *Das Kapital*, on the basis of Engels's partial approval (Engels 1970: 35–36). Croce, on the other hand, expressed radical criticism of theories that he considered superficial in many respects, because of their neo-Kantian basis (Croce 1902, 1938; on this see Rossi 1957: 322ff.), and the use of overgeneric categories in the explanation of modern capitalism (Croce 1918: 298; 1927: 29ff.). As a result, Croce's influence and his philosophy of history became a strong and enduring obstacle for a serious "confrontation between Italian and German sociology" (Scaglia 1991: 166).

Another aspect needs to be added. As Michels pointed out, the studies on the relationship between religion and capitalism developed by M. Weber (Weber 1904–05) and Werner Sombart (Sombart 1911) gave rise to persistent disapproval in Italy, helping to create further distrust in theories and inquiries made by the representatives of GHS (Michels 1934: 31). It was only after World War II that a new interest arose in the theoretical experience of the GHS, especially through the rediscovery of some aspects of the work of Sombart and M. Weber by economic historians and sociologists (Barbieri 1964: 151–167; Cavalli 1978: 7–49; Ferrarotti 1988: 15ff.; Scaglia 1991: 159–191).

Notes

1 Cossa's interpretation actually seems incorrect to me. Concerning this aspect it is sufficient to see what Schmoller writes in Schmoller (1894, 1898). On this see Abelshauser (2004), Backhaus (2003–04), Bruch (2004), Campagnolo (2004: 98ff.), Gioia (1990, 1991), Nau (1998), Priddat (2004), Schefold (1993) and Shionoya (2005).
2 As is well known, Ricca Salerno developed this approach further and, accentuating his distance from Wagner and from the GHS (also in methodology), after 1887 (date in which Sax published his *Die Grundlegung der theoretischen Staatswissenschaft*) supported a scientific view closer to the Austrian School (Griziotti 1960: 201; see also Gioia 2003a: 341ff.).

References

Abelshauser, W. (2004). L'école historique et les problèmes d'aujourd'hui, in Bruhns 2004: 19–38.
Are, G. (1974). Luigi Luzzatti e il socialismo della cattedra in Italia, in *Alle origini dell'Italia industriale*. Naples: Guida Editore, 257–285.
Backhaus, J. (2003–04). Gustav Schmoller and the Problems of Today. *History of Economic Ideas*, 1–2: 3–25.
Barbieri, G. (1964). Werner Sombart ed il valore dello 'spirito economico' nella ricostruzione storiografica, in A. Fanfani (ed.), *L'opera di Werner Sombart nel centenario della nascita*. Milan: Giuffré, 151–167.
Barucci, P. (1980). La diffusione del marginalismo: 1870–1890, in M. Finoia (ed.), *Il pensiero economico italiano: 1850–1950*. Bologna: Cappelli Editore, 67–92.
Barucci, P. (2003). *Le frontiere dell'economia politica: Gli economisti stranieri in Italia: dai mercantilisti a Keynes*. Florence: Edizioni Polistampa.
Bobbio, N. (1973). *Pareto e il sistema sociale*. Bologna: Sansoni.
Bruch, R. (2004). Gustav Schmoller entre science sociale et reforme sociale, in Bruhns 2004, 39–52.
Bruhns, H. (2004). *Histoire et économie politique en Allemagne de Gustav Schmoller à Max Weber: Nouvelles perspectives de l'école historique de l'économie*. Paris: Éditions de la Maison de sciences de l'homme.
Cairnes, J.E. (1965 [1875]). *The Character and Logical Method of Political Economy*. New York: Kelley.

Cammarano, F. (1992). Il modello politico britannico nella cultura del moderatismo italiano di fine secolo, in Camurri 1992: 309–338.

Campagnolo, G. (2004). *Critique de l'économie politique classique*. Paris: Presse Universitaires de France.

Camurri, R. (1992). Introduction to *La scienza moderata: Fedele Lampertico e l'Italia liberale*. Milan: Franco Angeli, 1–52.

Cardini, A. (1995). La serie padovana del "Giornale degli economisti" e il dibattito tra le scuole (1875–1878), in M. M. Augello (ed.), *Le riviste di economia in Italia (1700–1900): Dai giornali scientifico-letterari ai periodici specialistici*. Milan: F. Angeli, 403–424.

Cavalli, A. (1978). Introduction to W. Sombart, *Il Capitalismo Moderno*. Turin: UTET, 7–49.

Ciccone, A. (1876). *La nuova scuola economica tedesca detta socialismo della cattedra*. Naples: Tip. e Stereotipia della R. Università.

Cognetti de Martiis, S. (1886). L'economia come scienza autonoma. *Giornale degli Economisti*, 1: 166–203.

Cognetti de Martiis, S. (1895). Lo spirito scientifico negli studi sociali. *La Riforma Sociale*, 2: 673–691.

Cossa, L. (1878). L'economia dei popoli e degli stati di Fedele Lampertico, in *Saggi di Economia Politica*. Milan: Hoepli, 132–151.

Cossa, L. (1883). Una pagina di storia dell'economia politica. *La Nuova Antologia*, 38: 80–92.

Cossa, L. (1892). *Introduzione allo studio dell'Economia Politica*. Milan: Hoepli.

Croce, B. (1902). Estetica come scienza dell'espressione e linguistica generale. *La critica*, 29: 301–303.

Croce, B. (1918). *Materialismo storico ed economia marxista*. Bari: Laterza.

Croce, B. (1927). *Di un equivoco concetto storico: La "borghesia"*. Naples: Sangiovanni.

Croce, B. (1938). *La storia come pensiero e azoine*. Bari: Laterza.

Cusumano, V. (1875). *Le scuole economiche della Germania in rapporto alla questione sociale*. Naples: G. Marghieri.

Engels, F. (1970). Preface to K. Marx, *Il Capitale*, vol. 3, 1. Rome: Editori Riuniti, 31–52.

Faucci, R. (1995). *L'economista scomodo: Vita e opere di Francesco Ferrara*. Palermo: Sellerio Editore.

Ferrara, F. (1874). Il germanismo economico in Italia. *La Nuova Antologia*, 26: 983–1017.

Ferrara, F. (1934). *Lezioni di economia politica*, edited by G. De Mauro Tesoro. Bologna: Zanichelli.

Ferrara, F. (1976a). Gli equivoci del vincolismo: Il Congresso di Milano, in R. Faucci (ed.), *Opere Complete*, vol. 8. Rome: Istituto Grafico Tiberino, 165–180.

Ferrara, F. (1976b). L'italianità della scienza economica: Lettera all'on. Sen. Fedele Lampertico, in R. Faucci (ed.), *Opere Complete*, vol. 8. Rome: Istituto Grafico Tiberino, 295–319.

Ferrarotti, F. (1988). Introduction to M. Weber, *Sociologia delle Religioni*, vol. 2. Turin: UTET, 13–43.

Forti, E. (1876). Rassegna dei fatti economici. *Giornale degli Economisti, Serie Padovana*, A. 2: 59–77.

Garin, E. (1974). Appunti sulla formazione e su alcuni caratteri del pensiero crociano, in *Intellettuali italiani del XX secolo*. Rome: Editori Riuniti, 3–32.

Garin, E. (1997). *Cronache di filosofia italiana (1900–1960)*. Bari: Laterza.

Gherardi, R. (1989). L'Italia dei compromessi: Politica e scienza nell'età della Sinistra, in P. Schiera and F. Tenbruck (eds.), *Gustav Schmoller e il suo tempo: La nascita delle scienze sociali in Germania e in Italia.* Bologna: Il Mulino, 217–251.

Gioia, V. (1990). *Gustav Schmoller: La scienza economica e la storia.* Galatina (Lecce): Congedo Editore.

Gioia, V. (1991). Teorie economiche e storia nel Methodenstreit: Alcune riflessioni. *Economia Politica*, 7, no. 2: 279–299.

Gioia, V. (2000). German and Italian Economists between 1961–1930: Some Points to Consider, in V. Gioia and H. Kurz, *Science, Institutions and Economic Development: The Contribution of "German" Economists and Their Reception in Italy.* Milan: Giuffré Editore, 1–39.

Gioia, V. (2003a). Gli economisti italiani e la scuola austriaca: Dalla teoria del valore alla scienza delle finanze, in Barucci 2003: 325–351.

Gioia, V. (2003b). Gli economisti italiani e la scuola storica tedesca dell'economia: Storia di un equivoco, in Barucci 2003: 273–306.

Gozzi, G. (1984). Legislazione sociale e crisi dello Stato di diritto tra Otto e Novecento. Due modelli: Italia e Germania. *Annali dell'Istituto storico italo-germanico in Trento*, 10: 195–230.

Griziotti, B. (1960). Primi lineamenti delle dottrine finanziarie in Italia nell'ultimo cinquantennio, in E. Morselli (ed.), *Storia e storiografia del pensiero finanziario.* Padua: CEDAM, 187–215.

Hagemann, H. (1996). German Economic Journals and Economic Debates in the Nineteenth Century. *History of Economic Ideas*, 4: 77–102.

Hay, J.R. (1984). The British Business Community, Social Insurance and the German Example, in Mommsen 1984: 107–132.

Hennock, E.P. (1984). The Origins of the British National Insurance and the German Precedent 188–1914, in Mommsen 1984: 84–106.

Jannaccone, P. (1899). Il momento presente negli studi economici. *La Riforma Sociale*, 9: 101–128.

Labriola, A. (1968a). In memoria del Manifesto dei Comunisti, in *Saggi sul materialismo storico.* Rome: Editori Riuniti, 11–71.

Labriola, A. (1968b). Del materialismo storico: Dilucidazione preliminare, in *Saggi sul materialismo storico.* Rome: Editori Riuniti, 73–168.

Lampertico, F. (1874). *Economia dei popoli e degli stati.* Milan: Fratelli Treves.

Lampertico, F. (1875). Della italianità nella scienza económica. *Giornale degli economisti*, 1, no. 1: 459–479.

Luzzatti, L. (1874). L'economia politica e le scuole germaniche. *La Nuova Antologia*, 27: 174–192.

Luzzatti, L. (1880). La embriologia e la evoluzione delle costituzioni politiche: A proposito di alcuni recenti studi sulla costituzione inglese. *La Nuova Antologia*, 49: 115–131.

Luzzatti, L. (1894). *Le odierne controversie economiche nelle loro attinenze colla protezione e col socialismo.* Rome: Ermanno Loescher, 5–38.

Luzzatti, L. (1952). Le perturbazioni economiche (1879), in *Opere: L'ordine Sociale.* Bologna: Zanichelli, 32–41.

Messedaglia, A. (1921). L'economia politica in relazione colla sociologia e quale scienza in sé, in *Opere scelte di economia e altri scritti*, vol. 2. Verona: Accademia di Agricoltura, di Scienze e Lettere, 553–576.

Michels, R. (1934). Preface to *Politica ed Economia*, vol. 12. Turin: UTET, ix–li.

Minghetti, M. (1859). *Dell'economia pubblica e delle sue attinenze colla morale e col diritto*. Florence: Le Monnier.

Mommsen, W.J. (1984). Preface to *The Emergence of the Welfare State in Britain and Germany. 1850–1950*. London: Croom Helm, 1–5.

Nau, H.H. (1998). *Gustav Schmoller: Historish-etische Nationaloekonomie als Kulturwissenschaft*. Marburg: Metropolis Verlag.

Pantaleoni, M. (1963). Del carattere delle divergenze d'opinione esistenti tra economisti, in *Erotemi di Economia*. Padua: CEDAM, 147–176.

Pareto, V. (1965). *Libre-échangisme, protectionisme et socialisme*. Geneva: Librairie Droz.

Pareto, V. (1974). *Scritti politici: Lo sviluppo del capitalismo (1872–1895)*. Turin: UTET.

Pareto, V. (1980). *Scritti sociologici minori*. Turin: UTET.

Parisi, D. (1997). L'economia come scienza "utile" e "interessata": Sapere tecnico e cultura economica a Milano tra otto e novecento. *Quaderni dell'Istituto di Teoria Economica e Metodi Quantitativi*, 7: 1–45.

Pisanelli, S. (2015). Werner Sombart and His Reception in Italy. *Dada – Rivista di antropologia post-globale*, 1: 155–182.

Priddat, B.P. (2004). Gustav Schmoller: L'économie comme moralité institutionnalisée, in Bruhns 2004: 53–73.

Rabbeno, U. (1891). *The Present Condition of the Political Economy in Italy*. New York: Ginn. Reprinted from *Political Science Quarterly*, 1891, 6, no. 3: 439–473.

Rabbeno, U. (1894). L'odierna crisi nella scienza economica. *La Riforma Sociale* 1, no. 2: 850–879.

Rabbeno, U. (1898). *Protezionismo americano: Saggi storici di politica commercial*. Milan: Fratelli Dumolard Editori.

Ricca Salerno, G. (1878). Dell'imposta progressiva secondo alcune recenti dottrine tedesche. *Il Giornale degli Economisti*, 1: 175–203.

Ricca Salerno, G. (1892). *Sullo stato presente dell'economia politica*. Palermo: Stabilimento Tipografico "Virzi".

Romani, R. (1985). L'anglofilia degli economisti lombardo-veneti. *Venetica*, 4: 5–27.

Romani, R. (1992). Romagnosi, Messedaglia, la "scuola lombardo-veneta": La costruzione di un sapere sociale, in Camurri 1992: 177–210.

Rossi, Pietro (1957). Benedetto Croce e lo storicismo assoluto. *Il Mulino*, 67, no. 6: 322–354.

Scaglia, A. (1991). La sociologia tedesca. *Italia, in Studi di Sociologia*, 29, January–March: 159–191.

Scaldaferri, R. (1992). I modelli stranieri nel socialismo della cattedra italiano, in Camurri 1992: 235–244.

Schefold, B. (1993). Schmoller come teorico, in V. Gioia (ed.), *Gustav Schmnoller: Metodi e analisi nella scienza económica*. Galatina (Le): Congedo Editore, 39–63.

Schiera, P. and Tenbruck, F. (1989). *Gustav Schmoller e il suo tempo: La nascita delle scienze sociali in Germania e Italia*. Bologna: Il Mulino.

Schmoller, G. (1894). L'economia politica, la sua teoria e il suo método. *La Riforma Sociale*, 1: 28–46, 218–238, 337–352, 445–458.

Schmoller, G. (1898). Teorie vaganti e verità stabili nel campo delle scienze sociali. *La Riforma Sociale*, 8: 29–44.

Schumpeter, J.A. (1990). *Storia dell'analisi economica*, vol. 1. Turin: Bollati Boringhieri.

Shionoya, Y. (2005). *The Soul of the German Historical School: Methodological Essays on Schmoller, Weber and Schumpeter*. New York: Springer.

Sombart, W. (1918 [1911]). *Die Juden und das Wirtschaftsleben*. Munich: Duncker und Humblot.

Spaventa, S. (1910). *La politica della Destra*. Bari: Laterza.

Tessitore, F. (1988). *Da Cuoco a De Sanctis: Studi sulla filosofia napoletana nel primo Ottocento*. Naples: ESI.

Weber, M. (1904–05). Die protestantische Ethik und der 'Geist' des Kapitalismus. *Archiv für Sozialwissenschaft und Sozialpolitik*, vol. 20, 1904: 1–54; vol. 21, 1905: 1–110.

6 The German Historical School in Spain

From the fringes to mainstream (1870–1936)

Jesús Astigarraga and Juan Zabalza

Introduction

In spite of the long-standing influence of French, Italian and British economic traditions in Spain, there are strong indications that Spanish economists did not overlook the advances made by political economy in the German-speaking territories from the second half of the nineteenth century, precisely when political economy was emerging as a relatively autonomous discipline. The political elite in Spain turned its attention to the agrarian and economic reforms promoted by Frederick II the Great and Austrian empress Maria Theresa, the remarkable institutionalisation of economic knowledge in Vienna, Uppsala or Milan, and particularly the treatises of the cameralists. Authors such as Sonnenfels, Justi and Bielefeld were well-known by advocates of the Spanish Enlightenment, and some of their works were translated into Spanish. Their approaches were highly influential in the territories that had belonged to the Aragonese Crown, where the distinctive economic organisation was more prone to receiving the industrialist and regulatory ideology inherent in cameralism (Lluch 1999).[1] Furthermore, as late as the early nineteenth century cameralism was kept alive in the writings of some Spanish authors, such as Jaumeandreu, Valle-Santoro and Espinosa, who combined it with other German intellectual sources, such as the agronomists Thaër and Liebig, the economists K.H. Rau and the experts on public finance Storch or Jakob (Lluch-Argemí 2000). Jakob's eclecticism that brought together the Smithian and the cameralism traditions proved to be particularly successful in Spain in the mid-nineteenth century. His *Die Staatsfinanzwissenschaft* (1821), in particular, was belatedly translated into Spanish twice in 1850 and 1855, and together with Rau's *Lehrbuch der Politischen Oekonomie* (1826) was profusely consulted by Spanish economists in their French and Italian translations.

This article examines the influence of the so-called German Historical School in Spain up until the outbreak of the Spanish Civil War in 1936. The turn of the century represents a sharp delimitation between two periods in this respect. The late nineteenth century was characterised by the indifference towards the new advances experienced by economic science, such as marginalism and, in a different way, historicism. Conversely, German neo-historicism played a crucial role in the catching-up process experienced by political economy during the early twentieth century.

German historicism in Spain during the late nineteenth century

There are no indications of the German Old Historical School having any great impact in Spain during the last third of the nineteenth century. This fact does not mean that German historicism was absent, but it seems apparent that its influence was "peripheral". The term "peripheral" refers to the fact that the main Spanish economists, despite being well aware of its existence, did not pay particular attention to German historicism for reasons which will be explained ahead. But it is also due to the fact that German historicism during this period mainly influenced the economists and entrepreneurs of Catalonia, and was generally supported not by scholars but by publicists and businessmen who were connected to such industrial interests.

A forerunner of German historicism: Friedrich List and the debate on commercial policy in the second half of the nineteenth century in Spain

Some historians categorise List as a forerunner of the German Historical School. Obviously, we do not seek to contribute to this debate, as our objective is to discuss the impact that the German economists had in Spain. Such influence is interesting enough by itself. From our point of view, however, it is also significant as the economists who were inspired by List were those who eventually were influenced more strongly by the German Historical School.

According to the most reliable accounts, List's reception became known in Spain basically within the context of the debate on commercial policy, which in practice monopolised the economic discourse of the mid- and late nineteenth century (Spaletti 2002). Classical political economy had slowly spread – without entirely removing the intellectual heritage of mercantilism – through the work of Condorcet and Garnier and mainly through Say's treatise more than through Smith or Ricardo's work. Say's optimistic disciples, such as Rossi, Garnier and Blanqui, reinforced the traditional influence of French economics in Spain, contributing to providing a plausible alternative strategy to protectionism during the 1840s. Likewise, the first institutions, periodicals and newspapers that promoted free trade were founded, which, together with Cobden's tour of Spain in 1846 and the far-reaching influence of Bastiat, greatly helped to unite the defenders of free trade. From then on, during the 1850s and 1860s, the so-called economist school, which grouped together the main defenders of free trade in Spain – mostly scholars based in Madrid – had quite a hegemony over any other economic school and promoted the foundation of the *Asociación para la Reforma de los Aranceles de Aduanas* (Association for the Reform of Custom Duties) (1857), which lobbied for transforming custom duties into a mere fiscal tool. The school reached its peak of success and influence when some of its members became part of the government of the so-called Democratic Six-Year Period (1868–1874), contributing to the reform of the custom duties system.

This intellectual – an institutional – dominance in academic circles caused a reaction from the industrial lobbies, in particular in Catalonia. Classical political economy in Catalonia was basically disseminated by E. Jaumeandreu, professor of political economy at the Junta de Comercio de Barcelona (Board of Commerce of Barcelona). Jaumeandreu made a protectionist interpretation of Say's Law by swinging it back and, thus, assuming that the demand would boost supply. This peculiar change in Say's doctrine sought to justify the protectionism of the Catalonian production against foreign competition (Lluch 1973). Henceforth, the evolution of Catalonian economic thought until the end of the century took Jaumeandreu's work as a point of reference. However, protectionism was not restricted solely to Catalonian economists, although they were its main support- ers. The influence of Friedrich List, together with H. G. Carey, emerged within this intellectual context, and it was used for counterbalancing Say's and Bastiat's ideas and their consequences for commercial policy.

List was also well-known by the advocates of free trade, who strongly criticised him as a supporter of protectionism. A paradigmatic example is the free-trader economist G. Rodríguez's criticism of the Spanish supporters of protectionism in 1861.[2] According to Rodríguez, the intellectual source of them was List, from whom they took the distinction between political economy and cosmopolitan economy on the one hand, and the differences between value of exchange and productive forces on the other. Rodríguez claimed that List's approach had no scientific foundation contrasting with Say's Law and Smith's division of labour – he did not use com- parative costs theory – and consequently, the resulting economic policy was com- pletely wrong (Spaletti 2002). Rodríguez's criticism of List's doctrines was published in *Gaceta Economista*, which was the main periodical of the free trade group; interestingly enough, he tried to respond to the almost unknown group of protec- tionists from Madrid, which demonstrates that List was also known outside Catalonia. As a matter of fact, the only Spanish translation of List's *National System of Political Economy*, symbolically entitled *Comercio internacional con relación a la Industria y a la Agricultura* (International Commerce Concerning Industry and Agriculture) (1849), was not drafted in Catalan circles. Nevertheless, this Spanish version was incomplete and barely included the introductory and historical chapters. Therefore, List's work was mostly quoted from its French translations.[3]

The protectionists, on the contrary, and in particular the most outstanding of them – namely the Catalan protectionists, such as Güell i Ferrer, Bosch i Labrús and Illas i Vidal – were not scholars but publicists, intellectuals and businessmen who were members of the Catalan industrial bourgeoisie. As such, most of the authors who supported protectionism did not, paradoxically, adopt a very differ- ent theoretical framework to the free traders, as they basically focused on practical issues. Therefore, List was interpreted in terms of the debate on commercial policy. However, there were some exceptions, such as the book review of the *National System of Political Economy* by the Catalan J. L. Feu, who compared protectionism to what he called the Manchester or English school on different standards. According to Feu, the subjectivism of the latter is replaced by a moral approach to political economy; the individualism that reduces the role of the state to a minimum is substituted by the "national principle", which leads to the intervention of the state; the goal of low prices is replaced by the development of national productive forces; and finally, the principle of the international division of labour is substituted by the rejection of specialisation and the simultaneous development in all national industries to which the individual economic rights are subordinated (Feu 1862: 378–379).

In addition to his contributions on commercial policy, List was also used in a second sphere: the emergence of the national dimension in economic issues. Particularly significant in this respect was the rise of the national consciousness in Catalonia – in those days, it took the form of regionalism – during the last third of the nineteenth century. Nevertheless, there are indications in nonscholarly spheres that List's influence survived until late into the twentieth century, as demonstrated by the works of G. Graell, who considered that List's system was the seed of the idea of economic nationalism not only in Germany but throughout the world. Obviously, he was referring to Catalonia (Artal 2000).

In general, it should be said that the simplification of List's theory was quite obvious. On the whole, Spanish free traders as well as Spanish protectionists focused on the practical consequences of commercial policy, without paying much attention to the theory of productive forces, referring to the set of conditions to produce wealth – the ability of creating wealth more than the wealth in itself – which is considered the core of List's theoretical contributions.

The fate of the German Historical School in the last quarter of the nineteenth century: Awareness but not influence

German historicists were well-known in Spain by some of the critics of classical political economy, who in some cases were also economists who had been influenced by List. However, it is generally admitted that his influence was scant and his ideas did not take root among Spanish scholars. This is explained by the reaction to or criticism of classical political economy in Spain. Such criticism first emerged within the circle of the so-called *krausist* economists.[4]

The Spanish krausists were followers of the German philosopher Karl Christian Friedrich Krause and his disciple H. Ahrens. The main doctrinal tenet of krausism might be summarised as follows: man is made out of nature and spirit, and thus he should strive for achieving maximum harmony within himself and the rest of humanity. Krausism spread throughout Spain in the 1840s thanks to the endorsement of J. L. Sanz de Río – who was Krause's direct disciple – and other influential followers, such as the active F. Giner de los Ríos, who founded the educational institution *Institución Libre de Enseñanza* (Free Institution of Education), which greatly contributed to furthering the influence of Krause's idealism. From the beginning krausism had some influence on Spanish economists, both those who supported free trade and those who did not. In fact, there were no discrepancies between the members of the "economist school" – Bastiat's followers – that ruled political economy during the 1850s and 1860s and the krausist's doctrine. Moreover, some members of the school adopted the general principles of krausism.

The breakup of the Spanish economists took place in 1874 when J. M. Piernas and G. Azcárate, who had close connections to Giner de los Ríos, shifted away from Bastiat's approach.[5] In short, krausist economists criticised classical political economy based on two principles: the lack of ethical foundations and the restricted role attributed to state interventionism. Nevertheless, they called for competition operating within a legal framework organised by the state, which they believed should also assume social policy. The doctrinal divide with Bastiat's followers widened when the krausist economist A. Buylla, based on Cusumano's *Le scuole economiche della Germania in rapporto alla questione sociale* (1875), made a famous speech on *Sozial-Kathederen* in 1877 at the opening of the academic year at the University of Oviedo in the context of the emergence of the so-called social question or proletarian question.[6] Nevertheless, in spite of moving away from classical political economy, Buylla did not accept the principles of *Sozial-Kathederen*, such as the prevalence of the inductive method, the rejection of the existence of economic natural laws, the overinterventionism of the state and the predominance of protectionism. Conversely, he held an ambivalent, midway stance between individualism and heterodox *Sozial-Kathederen*, which was, indeed, the krausist harmonic ideology that included methodological pluralism. This explains why he preferred the ethical current of German historicists led by Schäffle.

The timing of the criticism of classical political economy is crucial for understanding the reception of German historicism in Spain. It is now accepted that Spanish krausists did not embrace the methodological tenets of historicism as they found the economic doctrine of krausism was an effective and sufficient response to classical political economy. This response, indeed, preceded in time the criticism of German historicism of the classical economists. Krausists seem to have considered this response as appropriate for overcoming the weaknesses of classical political economy. This does not mean that Spanish economists overlooked historicist contributions. On the contrary, Wagner, for example, after Leroy-Beaulieu, was the most quoted expert on public finance, and Engel's statistical method or Schäffle organicism was relatively well-known by Spanish economists. It should be mentioned in this respect that Álvarez-Buylla promoted some translations into Spanish of significant historicist works, such as the famous *Handbuch der politischen Oekonomie* by Schönberg, which incorporated the contributions of distinguished German economists, such as Kleinwächter, Nasse, Wagner, Neumann, Mithof and Lexis,[7] or Schäffle's *La quintaesencia del socialism* (The Quintessential Expression of Socialism). Nevertheless, on other subjects, such as methodology, social policy and theoretical issues, a consensus of indolence prevailed. For example, despite the attention received by the founding conference of the *Verein für Sozialpolitik* at Eisenach, Spanish economists did not distinguish between the more radical proposals of Wagner and the more tempered contributions of Schmoller or Brentano. This attitude is exemplified by G. Azcárate, the main representative of the Spanish krausist economists, when he wrote Roscher's obituary. According to Azcárate, Roscher had opened four lines of research: the ethical and social line; evolutionist research; the relativist line; and historical and statistical research. He accepted only the first, as, in his opinion, the others might pull political economy out of the scientific path (Malo 1998).

The influence of German old historicism, however, was wider in some spheres outside the academic community, such as the then-emerging Catalan regionalism, in which List's *National System of Political Economy* had been relatively influential in some aspects. Feu, who, as mentioned, had drafted the only book review on List's *System* available in Spanish, considered that Roscher had continued List's work. According to Feu, Roscher had applied the historicist method of the leading German jurists of the early nineteenth century – F. Eichorn and F. K. Savigny; likewise, he believed that it was Roscher who had established the limits to Smith's division of labour and who had pointed out how in some cases the economic interests of individuals led to falling production and other symptoms of economic crisis – the removal of financial and physical capitals and unemployment (Feu 1862: 384). Something similar might be said of P. Estasén, who seems to have been influenced by German historicism and more specifically by Roscher in issues such as the significance given to economic history, the inductive method and the profuse use of statistics, the criticism of classical political economy, and the emergence of the national framework as an analytical object (Artal 2000). Finally, the members of the so-called *regeneracionismo* movement – social thinkers who, after the loss of the last Spanish colonies in 1898, focused their thoughts on the causes and remedies of Spanish decadence and economic backwardness – were also influenced by German historicism. In particular, the promotion of a culture of radical protectionism as strategy of economic development that characterised *regeneracionismo* seemingly emerged from the German historicists.

German neo-historicism and the catching-up process of political economy during the early twentieth century

The early twentieth century coincided with the period of modernisation of Spanish economics thanks to the leading role played by three economists – J. M. Zumalacárregui, A. Flores de Lemus and F. Bernis. Zumalacárregui has been traditionally considered as the economist who introduced marginalism into Spain – it is believed that he had stayed at Lausanne, where he allegedly met Vilfredo Pareto. Although he acknowledged that Schmoller had rectified the failures of the old historicism, he explicitly rejected the historicist methodology, arguing that it was not able to link deductive and inductive research. Flores de Lemus, who brought together a group of disciples, and Bernis, on the other hand, were – although not exclusively – highly influenced by German historicism as they had been brought up in Germany. German economic historicism is also visible in many publications on public finance and in many translations of original German texts into Spanish.

Flores de Lemus as the prime driving force of modern economics in early twentieth-century Spain

Flores de Lemus's German instruction on economics

As most Spanish economists of the early twentieth century, A. Flores de Lemus (1876–1941) had studied law. Although he first attended courses at the University of Grenade, Flores de Lemus voluntarily moved to the University of Oviedo, where he was intellectually seduced by the founder of the *Institución Libre de Enseñanza* and reputed krausist, F. Giner de los Ríos. By then, Giner de los Ríos had spent a quarter of a century promoting the modernisation of the Spanish educational and scientific systems in order to catch up with the intellectual development of the main European countries. In this intellectual environment, Giner seems to have encouraged Flores de Lemus to move to Germany in order to shape his academic background as an economist.

There are indications that Flores de Lemus first went to the Faculty of State Sciences at the University of Tübingen, where he attended courses taught by F. J. Neumann and Schöenberg. Then he moved to the Department of State Sciences at Humboldt University in Berlin, where he attended lectures taught by prestigious professors, such as L. von Bortkiewicz. These early contacts with German economic scholarly spheres do not reveal a particular historicist background. Conversely, Flores de Lemus also learned about neoclassical economics and in particular *Marshallian* economics during this first period in Germany. Nevertheless, there are strong signs that Flores de Lemus attended courses by L. Brentano, A. Wagner, which profoundly influenced his views on public finance (which we will explain ahead), G. Schmoller, from whom he inherited an admiration for the Prussian bureaucracy, and W. Sombart (Velarde 1976). Despite such a wide range of influences, and in particular the weight of the Marshallian tradition, most historians remarked that the influence of German historicism on Flores de Lemus prevailed over other economic schools of thought. In fact, Flores de Lemus's contributions always retained a neo-historicist hallmark, which he also passed on to some of his disciples. As late as 1929, for example, the content and bibliography of the syllabus that he drafted were still biased towards neo-historicism (Flores de Lemus 2011).

Flores de Lemus's disciples at the University of Barcelona

After returning to Spain in 1903, Flores de Lemus was appointed as professor of public finance and political economy at the Faculty of Law at the University of Barcelona, where he gathered together his first group of disciples.[8] The earliest influence of German neo-historicism in Spain was exercised within this group of disciples. This is the case of J. M. Tallada, who was highly committed to the construction of the Catalan national identity. Tallada regretted that German historicism had had little impact in Spain and suggested that the old economic ideas of the nineteenth century that had been instrumental for supporting protectionist policies in Spain – which had been strongly upheld by Catalan industry – had become anachronistic in the early twentieth century and, therefore, needed to be replaced by a new approach – namely the methodology of German historicism – that would provide scientific support to protectionism (Artal 1979).

On the other hand, Flores de Lemus encouraged some of his Catalan disciples to undertake academic placements in Germany. M. Vidal i Guardiola, for example, spent four years studying economics and public administration and working in Germany. His admiration for the German economic system and public administration was apparent, and his first contribution attempted to apply the Prussian model of urban and territorial management to Catalonia (Vidal 1907). Vidal, indeed, is considered to be the main propagator of German neo-historicism in Catalonia as he was highly influential among the economists who worked around the political organisation of Catalan regionalism – *Lliga Regionalista* – which constituted the seed of modern Catalan nationalism. Something similar might be said about M. Reventós. Although historians agree about his personal relationship with Flores de Lemus, there are some disagreements about the effective influence on Reventós's economic thought. Whatever the influence that Flores de Lemus had on him, however, it is undisputed that Reventós kept close ties with German neo-historicism as the Spanish government awarded him a grant to study postgraduate courses at Humboldt University in Berlin, where he had contact with some of the leading German neo-historicists. There are also indications that he had read Wagner's principal works and kept intellectual and personal ties with W. Sombart, whose *Der Bourgeois* (1903) he regarded as the "spiritual history of the modern homo oeconomicus" (Gómez-Rojo 2006).[9] Besides all the German neo-historicists, however, Reventós seems to have been influenced most by G. Schmoller.[10] In 1928, he outlined the evolution of pure economics, attributing a central role in the development of economics to Schmoller's *Grundriss der Allgemeinen Volkswirtschaftslehre* (1900–1904), to whose methodological approach he enthusiastically adhered. In particular, he opposed the excessive theoretical abstractions of pure economics and the deductive approach that prevailed in England, which he strongly criticised, that contrasted with the empirical and inductive basis that dominated American economic thought thanks, according to him, to the influence of German historicism. On the other hand, Schmoller's influence on Reventós went beyond methodology as the history of the theory of wages, the criticism of Henry George's theory and the analysis of the phenomena of the middle class were also taken from Schmoller (Gómez-Rojo 2007).

Flores de Lemus and the spread of German
neo-historicism in Madrid

Flores de Lemus spent some months at the University of Barcelona, but in 1905 he moved definitively to Madrid to organise the *Laboratorio de estadística* (Statistics Workshop) – which adopted the German *Seminarien* educational model, consisting in practical classes that used statistical data for complementing lessons – at the prestigious Athenaeum of Madrid, a private institution that greatly influenced Spanish intellectual and political circles. The annual reports of the Athenaeum show how Lemus acknowledged Schmoller's influence and how he insisted on the empirical approach to economic research which used the intellectual source, according to his own account, of the German statistician Ernst Engel. Although Flores de Lemus continued for a while in his position at Madrid's Athenaeum, thanks to his growing prestige as an expert on public finance, he moved to the Spanish Department of Public Finances, where he undertook his most significant practical achievement: the gradual transformation of the Spanish tax system from product taxation into personal taxation. Nevertheless, he never abandoned his commitment to training young Spanish economists until the Spanish Civil War broke out in 1936. As a matter of fact, he trained three groups of disciples in Madrid: the group of Marshallians who concentrated on the neoclassical components of Flores de Lemus's thought, the young group of economists in *Junta de Ampliación de Estudios e Investigaciones Científicas* (The Council for the Extension of Studies and Scientific Research), which evolved after the Spanish War towards the new approaches that emerged after the Keynesian revolution, and finally, the group at the Department of Public Finances in Madrid, formed by R. Carande, A. Viñuales, G. Franco and J. Álvarez-Cienfuegos, which was clearly inclined towards neo-historicism (Velarde 2001). All of them, advised by Flores de Lemus himself, moved to Germany in order to undertake academic placements with grants awarded by the *Junta de Ampliación de Estudios* and regularly attended Flores de Lemus's workshop at the Department of Public Finances, which was based on the *Seminarien* model and used some historicist handbooks on political economy by the Italian C. Supino or the Germans Klein-wächter and Conrad.

Flores de Lemus and the so-called Spanish realistic approach to political economy

The numerous texts that Flores de Lemus produced during the two long decades at the beginning of the twentieth century are characterised, in spite of contemplating the new advances of economic theory, by the profuse use of statistical information, which was processed by the most advanced empirical methods, and historical analyses that consider the significance of the national environment in economic issues. This methodological approach became known as "Spanish economic realism". As V. Gay, one of Flores de Lemus's principal neo-historicist disciples, pointed out, the term sought to define the historical and empirical methodology of the school:

> . . . which lays the rational, abstract and idealist approach of the classical school – that tried to formulate general laws of economics for the economic administration of the nations – aside. Conversely, the *realistic school*, however, focused on the sources, on the plain facts, on the specifics. It works historically, positively, and experimentally through the institutions of the

different countries and outlines their respective economies in relation to their material and physical conditions, customs, people, history and so on.

(Gay 1906: xi–xii)

This methodology is apparent throughout the work of Flores de Lemus. This is the case in the analysis of the structural trends of Spanish agriculture, his famous report about the possible accession of Spain to the gold-exchange standard, the influential memorandums in the Department of Public Finances and his influential analysis of the Spanish economy as a whole –which some historians have called "structural analysis" – from which proposals on the commercial, industrial and agricultural policies emerged. All of them exemplify how Flores de Lemus combines economic theory, empirical methodology and historical analysis in which qualitative and ideological elements are apparent, giving the analysis an undisputable neo-historicist feel. Some written notes taken during his period in Germany seem to confirm that this combination of theory and limitations imposed by material, physical and historical conditions comes from his German period (Flores de Lemus 1903). Flores's writings were widely read by many Spanish economists at the time, even by those who were not his direct disciples, such as R. Perpiñá and M. de Torres. They were a point of reference for many applied works on the Spanish economy during the 1920s and particularly the 1930s.

Finanzwissenschaft as the prevailing school in public finance in Spain in the early twentieth century

The German influence was particularly significant in the field of public finance. The main Spanish economists at the time highlighted the need to reform the Spanish tax system as a requisite for the economic development and social stability of Spain. The Italian school of public finance, but also the German tradition in public finance, was self-evident in the works of the leading experts in the field at the time: A. Flores de Lemus and his disciples, F. Bernis and, on a second level, L. V. Paret and P. Ballesteros. There is no doubt that they were greatly influenced by Wagner, who continued the process of transferring German public finance doctrines that dated back to the influence of Storch and particularly Jakob during the early and mid-nineteenth century.

Flores de Lemus, his disciples and Finanzwissenschaft

Flores's main practical achievement was probably his contribution to the transformation of Spanish public finances from his strategic technical position at the Spanish Department of Public Finances, which he held for three decades. Therein, he drew up numerous reports, reform plans and memorandums for advising the successive heads of the Department, which were highly influenced by Wagner himself and the German experiences of tax reform. Wagner's influence on Flores de Lemus was concentrated in three main areas. First, taxes are not conceived individually as a means to finance the activities of the state but as a part of a wider social, political and economic framework. Second, Flores de Lemus's interpretation of the principle of "ability to pay" in taxation is also taken from Wagner. And third, the reform of the Spanish local tax system was based on the German municipal reforms model (Fuentes Quintana 1976).

These influences were interpreted in a way so that they could be adapted to the Spanish financial and economic context. According to Flores de Lemus's disciple V. Gay, the so-called Spanish realistic approach to political economy applied to the field of public finance was shaped around four main principles: empirical research would determine the content of the role of the state and its size, and therefore it cannot be determined a priori; public finance must be organised according to the goals attributed to the state; the tax system must be analysed globally; and finally public credit is a permanent and not a temporary resource of public finances (Gay 1906). This approach was disseminated by Flores de Lemus's group of neo-historicist disciples (V. Gay, A. Viñuales, E. Rodríguez Mata, J. Álvarez-Cienfuegos, G. Franco, R. Carande), who predominantly taught public finance in some of the most significant Spanish faculties of law and undertook academic placements in Germany, encouraged by Flores de Lemus himself; some drafted handbooks on public finance which were used at their respective faculties and contributed to spreading the historicist approach to public finance and which clearly displayed Flores de Lemus's intellectual footprint.

Indeed, V. Gay's treatise, which was the first original Spanish textbook on public finance of the twentieth century, drew mainly upon German sources (Moll's, Wagner's and Eheberg's treatises are continuously used and quoted in the handbook), and it was structured along the lines of Wagner's treatise. Gay's starting point was Wagner's organicism and evolutionary approach. In particular, he based the text on the idea of the unitary nature of the state, which has to satisfy its own needs. Thus, public expenses must be connected to the different public sources of revenues. Nevertheless, the textbook was by no means a passive reception of the German *Finanzwissenschaft* approach as Gay adapted it to the context of Spanish public finance (Zabalza 2004).

German Finanzwissenschaft in Spain beyond the scope of Flores de Lemus

Besides Flores de Lemus's disciples, the German tradition in public finance penetrated Spain through other means: directly, through F. Bernis and P. Ballesteros, who visited Germany with grants awarded by the Spanish government, and indirectly, through the considerable influence of the American institutionalist Edwin R. A. Seligman on a group of Spanish experts in public finance.

As many other Spanish economists of the last nineteenth century and early twentieth century, F. Bernis was also influenced intellectually by the philosopher F. Giner de los Ríos, and, like many of them, he also moved to Germany (1903–1905) to attend courses by Schmoller and other German economists and immersed himself in German economic culture. Wagner's seminar on statistics and state science, in particular, made a great impression on Bernis. Nevertheless, German historicism was not the exclusive intellectual source of Bernis's economic thought as he was also influenced by the English and American traditions, after having studied in both countries. In fact, he became familiar with F. Edgeworth and came into contact with some outstanding American economists, among whom he particularly admired E.R.A. Seligman and his work on public finance. Bernis's contributions mirrored the methodological ancestry of the German Historical School. His main contribution in the field of public finance, however, *La hacienda española – Los impuestos – Como son en España – Como son en otras haciendas – Como deben ser en la nuestra* (Spanish Public Finance – Tax System – The Spanish Case – The Tax Systems in Other Countries – How It Should Be in Spain) (1917) was reviewed by Edgeworth, who assessed it in a positive light once he had understood that Spanish economists did not seek to doctrinally contribute to public finance. Nevertheless, Edgeworth complained about the German influence on Bernis and his support of higher custom duties to protect Spanish markets (Zabalza 2007). Edgeworth was not ill-informed as Wagner's decisive influence is clearly noticeable throughout *La hacienda española*'s pages: the historical analysis of taxation that considers wants, public incomes and expenditure as continuously changing; the "communal" approach to the financial activity of the state that imposed a certain amount of restriction on individual economic freedom and considered that economic agents were mobilised for something other than self-interest, which was also noteworthy (Zabalza 2007); and the adoption of the so-called realistic or empirical approach to taxation, which formed the basis of the analysis of the different national tax systems. In fact, behind this outlook lies the organic vision of the economic process that attributes goals to the state and wants of its own, which, at the same time, are not comparable to the goals and wants of other different states.

Within this doctrinal framework and following a historicist approach, Bernis identified the main problem of contemporary public finance: the gradual separation and contradiction between the new context of economic inequality that characterised modern societies at the beginning of the twentieth century and the obsolescence of tax systems. This historicist tone is even more apparent when he tackled the problem of the distribution of income:

> The distribution of national income is not, as classical economists held, the economic phenomena that render the contribution to the final product by the different factors of production into returns. Conversely, crucial legal phenomena in which the competence of the state prevails, inasmuch as only such institution shapes the law, constituted the "nerve" of the distribution of income.
>
> (Bernis 1917: 114)

This theoretical framework together with the premises supported his proposal for reforming the Spanish tax system that used Wagner's interpretation of the principles of taxation (principles of sufficiency and elasticity) and justice (principles of generality and equality) within the context of the limitations imposed by the Spanish institutional framework (Zabalza 2007).

During the 1930s, the predominance of German *Finanzwissenschaft* was gradually replaced by the Italian tradition in public finance. Such a shift in intellectual sources might be partially explained by the fact that Spanish experts in public finance perceived the Italian tradition as a continuation and modernisation of German *Finanzwisenschaft*. It was P. Ballesteros who most faithfully adopted this stance by pointing out, for example, the Wagner–Viti di Marco link regarding the concept of the state or the influence of political, moral and psychological phenomena on the financial activity of the state. Nevertheless, Ballesteros, as well as the most outstanding Spanish experts in public finance, was not an exception, and he also adopted the so-called realistic approach to public finance and highlighted the need to transform the institutional environment in order to guarantee the success of tax reform, which required a profound knowledge of economic, administrative and fiscal frameworks (Zabalza 2004).

In his classical article, Dorfman stressed the significance that German historicism had had in American political economy during the late nineteenth century (Dorfman 1955). Besides the educational method of seminars and the statistical approach, Americans were attracted by the systematic and unitary approach to public finance that characterised German *Finanzwissenschaft*. Although parts of the German doctrinal heritage, such as social organicism and centralised interventionism, were not adopted by the Americans, there is a clear connection between *Finanzwissenschaft* and some of the outstanding American economists. E.R.A. Seligman, who became one of the leading authorities on taxation in economics, had converted to the German neo-historicism that followed an institutional and historical approach to public finance.

Seligman became well-known in Spain in the 1910s, 1920s and 1930s as some of his publications – which we will mention in the next paragraph – were translated into Spanish. Particularly significant was the Spanish translation of Seligman's *Progressive Taxation in Theory and Practice* (1913) by L. V. Paret as it tackled the main concern of the Spanish experts in public finance at the time: the problem of distributing the tax burden. Seligman, as it is well-known, was a campaigner for the progressive income tax system and one of the primary researchers of the incidence of taxation. Both aspects, indeed, were used by L. V. Paret, who also, following Seligman, argued that a progressive tax structure fit perfectly with the requisites imposed by this principle of justice. Furthermore, Seligman's treatise seems to have inspired Paret to modify theoretical premises by introducing the limitations imposed by political and institutional contexts and the practice of taxation in Spain. Seligman had known Wagner while he was studying in Germany, and *Progressive Taxation* displays a clear intellectual influence from German *Finanzwissenschaft*. Paret recognised this connection and pointed out how, despite their obvious differences, Seligman had furthered Wagner's contributions by adding the positive analysis of progressive taxation. In fact, Paret never abandoned Wagner's conceptualisation as a remote intellectual source: taxation was not the mere contribution of individuals to public expenditure but also the way through which the state intervened in economic and social issues (Zabalza 2004).

German historicist literature in Spain

The obvious difficulties encountered by Spanish people in understanding the German language were, on an educational level, a serious obstacle for the diffusion of German historicism. This difficulty, however, was attenuated by the translations of German works into the French and Italian languages, which were profusely consulted by Spanish economists. Nevertheless, there was a perfect match between the influence of German economic thought and the number of works translated in Spanish. As a result, German old historicists' works were not, in general, translated into Spanish during the 1870s and 1880s. During the 1890s, however, there was a noticeable increase in the interest in German neo-historicism, and thus the translations into Spanish began. Therefore, the krausist A. Álvarez-Buylla – without making any clear reference to historicism – drafted the prologue to *Economía* (Economics) by Neumann, Kleinwächter, Nasse, Wagner, Mithof and Lexis, which was published twice during the period (Zabalza 2004).

For the most part, however, German translations were carried out in the early twentieth century, coinciding with the growing interest for neo-historicism. It is worth mentioning Schmoller's *Política social y economía política* (Social Policy and Political Economy) (1905), which corresponds to a volume published in German in 1897 that contained two booklets previously published by the same author: his open letter to Heinrich von Treitschke originally published in *Jahrbücher für Nationalökonomie und Statistik* (1875) that summarised his social ideology, and his work on the methodology of political economy originally published in *Handwörterbuch der Staatswissenschaften*, which, later on, and duly extended, became *Der Grundriss der Allgemeinen Volkswirtschaftslehre* (1900–1904). Schmoller himself highlighted the instructional nature of the materials included in the volume, which served as a guide to neo-historicism for students. In this respect, the role played by Flores de Lemus as the promoter of some translations of neo-historicist handbooks which he recommended to his closest disciples should be noted. This is the case of the successful Kleinwächter's *Economía Política* (Political Economy), which was published successively in 1925, 1929, 1934, 1940 and 1946, Conrad's *Historia de la Economía* (History of Economics), published in 1914, 1928, 1933 and 1941, and Weber's *Introducción al estudio de la Economía Política* (Introduction to Political Economy).[11] German historicism, however, also had public repercussions, thanks to M. Sánchez-Sarto, who had been awarded grants by the Board of Extension of Studies to study in Germany. Sánchez-Sarto, who became editor of Labor Publishers, promoted – and in some cases translated into Spanish and prefaced – a collection of educational books, including texts by W. Lexis, E. Wagemann and A. Weber.

The aforementioned weight of German *Finanzwissenschaft* in Spain was embodied in translations of German publications (Vocke, Scheel-Mombert) from the very beginning of the twentieth century. Later on, during the 1920s the translation of German works was resumed. *Hacienda Pública* (Public Finance) by Van der Borght was published three times, in 1925, 1929 and 1934, as part of the aforementioned collection of educational texts of Labor Publishing. Van der Borght was inspired by Conrad's approach to public finance, which in fact was a vulgarisation of von Stein's and Wagner's treatises. Von Eheberg's handbook, however, is a much more substantial and complete treatise, although its intellectual sources and doctrinal background are not very different from Borght's work, with the exception of the focus on non-German literature. Nevertheless, it was not an innovative text and did not incorporate the then recent advances in public finance. In fact, Neumark classified von Eheberg's treatise alongside those written by Cotz, which symbolised the period of decadence of the German tradition of public finance (Neumark 1994).

Wagner's strong influence on Spanish experts in public finance was not accompanied by the translation of any of his major works, and he was mainly read in his original German or in some cases in his French and Italian versions. This gap was filled, as mentioned, by *El impuesto progresivo en la teoría y en la práctica* (Progressive Taxation in Theory and Practice) (1913) by E.R.A. Seligman. Consequently, Seligman's handbook filled a serious gap in the Spanish literature on public finance, and despite the uniqueness of his contribution, it must be classified, from the point of view of the circulation of economic ideas, as part of the German tradition of public finance. Seligman was quite influential in Spain, and two further publications were translated into Spanish in Flores de Lemus's spheres (Zabalza 2004).

Summary

An evaluation of the fate of the German Historical School in Spain for half a century sheds light on the particularities of the evolution of Spanish political economy around the turn of the century. The criticism of the so-called economist school – the Spanish representatives of classical political economy during the mid-nineteenth century – by krausist economists as early as 1874 seems to be crucial for understanding why the German old historicist school was not so influential. Most Spanish classical critics deemed that the major tenets of krausism – that supported a tutelary role for the state in economic issues without challenging the methodological principles of classical political economy – provided an appropriate framework for addressing the problems caused by the growing level of industrialisation. Furthermore, some proposals of *Sozial-Kathederen* were seen as being too radical by Spanish economists who in fact supported the English model of social reform, which was finally implemented in Spain. Nevertheless, there was a sphere of influence of German historicism and its forerunners in the late nineteenth century outside scholarly circles. This reception, however, had nothing to do with methodological or theoretical questions but with economic policy: German historicists were quite influential in the business and political circles of the region of

Catalonia as they provided a rationale for supporting commercial protectionism and later on a kind of political regionalism that evolved over time towards
nationalism.

German neo-historicism is a crucial element for understanding the nature of
the modernisation of Spanish political economy in the early twentieth century
as it inspired most of the advances experienced by political economy in Spain
during the period, and thus contributed to establishing an approach to economics
that constituted a genuine national style or tradition for approaching economic
problems. German historicism in particular proved to be influential in the diffusion of an empirical methodology, the prevalence of historical-institutional analyses and the prominence given to social policy, which was embedded within the
reform of the Spanish tax system that was addressed from the socio-economic
perspective that characterised *Finanzwissenschaft*. The growing prestige of German academic and educational institutions among Spanish intellectuals and
scholarly circles and the continuous outflow of Spanish economists to German
universities greatly contributed to the influence of German historicism in Spain
during this period, which was mainly concentrated in scholarly spheres.

Notes

1 For a complete overview of the spread of cameralism in Spain, see Lluch (1997).
2 Echegaray, who won the Nobel Prize for Literature in 1905, seems to be the other
   intellectual economist who paid more attention to List's ideas, in a similar way
   to Rodríguez. Obviously, he was also referred to by many other Spanish classical
   economists in their different treatises, but mainly in brief and peripheral works.
3 List's work would not be completely translated into Spanish – not in Spain, but in
   Mexico – until 1942.
4 At the end of the century and particularly after the *Rerum Novarum* encyclical of
   Pope Leo XIII was published, social Catholics began criticising classical political
   economy. In some cases, some social Catholic authors who were quite influential in
   Spain, such as the Italian Christian Democrat G. Toniolo, used some kind of historical
   methodology (Grimmer-Solem and Romani 1999).
5 The breakup was reified in the appendix by J. M. Piernas to the then most-used
   handbook on political economy in Spanish universities by the classical economist M.
   Carreras.
6 Cusumano's work is considered to be the only positive acceptance of German historicism in Italy (Gioia 2006).
7 This work was translated into Spanish twice in 1894 and 1901.
8 Vidal i Guardiola, B. Amengual, J. Pi i Sunyer, M. Reventós, J. M. Tallada, C. Massó
   and A. Bauxili.
9 Reventós drafted a report for the *Junta de Ampliación de Estudios*, the research
   institute that awarded him a grant for his stay in Berlin. This report focused on real
   state taxation, was profoundly influenced by Wagner's approach to public finance and
   reveals that Reventós had been knowledgeable about the works of other renowned
   German experts on public finance, such as Schanz, Vocke, Neumann and Schäffle
   (Zabalza 2004). See a complete and erudite interpretation of Reventós's work in
   Gómez-Rojo (2007).
10 Reventós proved to have a profound knowledge of Schmoller's works as he echoed a
   wide number of them. Apart from *Grundriss* he demonstrated his familiarity with "Über
   einige Grundfragen des Rechts und der Volkswirtschaft: Ein offenes Sendschreiben an

Herrn Heinrich von Treitschke" (in *Jahrbuch für Nationalökonomie und Statistik,* 1875: 2) and "Geschichte der Lohntheorien" (in *Jahrbuch für Gesetzgebung, Verwaltung und Volkswirtschaft im Deutschen Reich,* 38 [1914]: 1113–1140) (see Gómez-Rojo 2006).
11 On the problems of categorising authors such as Kleinwächeter as neo-historicists, see Senn (1997).

References

Artal, F. (1979). Tallada i Paulí, Josep Maria, in *Ictineu: Diccionari de les ciències de la societat als països catalanes.* Barcelona, Edicions 62, 465–467.

Artal, F. (2000). El desarrollo del pensamiento proteccionista catalán en la segunda mitad del siglo XIX, in E. Fuentes-Quintana (ed.), *Economía y economistas españoles. Vol. 4: La economía clásica.* Barcelona, Galaxia-Gutenberg, 543–555.

Bernis, F. C. (1917). *La Hacienda Española – Los impuestos – Como son en España – Como son en otras haciendas – Como deben ser en la nuestra.* Barcelona, Minerva.

Dorfman, J. (1955). The Role of the German Historical School in American Economic Thought. *American Economic Review,* vol. 45, no. 2, May: 17–28.

Feu, J. L. (1862). Sistema Nacional en Economía Política. *Revista de Cataluña,* vol. 1: 317–375.

Flores de Lemus, A. (1903). Notas bibliográficas sobre Oldenburg-Berufzühlingen: La relación entre la agricultura y la industria en el Imperio alemán. *Flores de Lemus' Personal Archive,* Signature 1–1010.

Flores de Lemus, A. (2011) [1929]. Programa de un curso de Economía Política, in A. Flores de Lemus, *Obras. Vol. 2: Estudios teóricos y de economía española en general.* Madrid, Real Academia de Ciencias Morales y Políticas, 341–418.

Fuentes Quintana, E. (1976). La ideología de la reforma tributaria silenciosa: Un análisis del pensamiento financiero de Flores de Lemus. *Hacienda Pública Española,* no. 42–43: 105–144.

Gay, V. (1906). Prólogo, in F. Flora, *Ciencia de la Hacienda.* Madrid, Librería General de Victoriano Suárez, 4–12.

Gioia, V. (2006). Los economistas italianos y la escuela histórica alemana. *Mediterráneo Económico,* no. 9: 199–210.

Gómez-Rojo, M. E. (2006). *Historiografía Jurídica y Económica y Pensamiento Jurídico-Público, Social y Económico de Manuel Reventós i Bordoy (1888–1942).* PhD dissertation, Málaga, Universidad de Málaga.

Grimmer-Solem, E. and Romani, R. (1999). The Historical School 1870–1900: A Cross National Reassessment. *History of European Ideas,* vol. 24, n. 4–5: 267–299.

Lluch, E. (1973). El pensament ecònomic a Catalunya *(1760–1840): Els origens ideològics del proteccionisme i la presa de consciència de la burgesia catalana.* Barcelona, Edicions 62.

Lluch, E. (1997). Cameralism beyond the Germanic World: A Note on Tribe. *History of Economic Ideas,* vol. 2: 85–99.

Lluch, E. (1999). *Las Españas vencidas del siglo XVIII: Claroscuros de la Ilustración.* Barcelona, Crítica.

Lluch, E. and Argemí, Ll. (2000). La influencia alemana en España (1800–1860): Desde el cameralismo tardío a Jacob, Krause y List, in E. Fuentes-Quintana (ed.), *Economía y economistas españoles. Vol. 4: La economía clásica.* Barcelona, Galaxia-Gutenberg, 451–458.

Malo, J. L. (1998). *Pensamiento económico y filosofía social en la España del siglo XIX: Liberalismo, Krausismo y reformas sociales.* Unpublished PhD dissertation, Zaragoza, Universidad de Zaragoza.

Neumark, F. (1994). Principios de la imposición, in J. F. Corona (ed.), *Lecturas de economía española.* Madrid, Minerva Ediciones, 285–304.

Seligman, E.R.A. (1913). *El impuesto progresivo en la teoría y la práctca.* Madrid, Librería General de Victoriano Suárez.

Senn, P. R. (1997). Problems of Determining the Influence of Gustav Schmoller and Adolph Wagner on American Fiscal Policy and Taxation Systems. In J. G. Backhaus (ed.), *Essays on Social Security and Taxation.* Marburg, Metropolis-Verlag, 35–141.

Spaletti, S. (2002). Friedrich List en las historias nacionales del pensamiento económico italiana y española. *Revista de Historia Industrial*, no. 22: 79–107.

Velarde, J. (1976). Antonio Flores de Lemus: Las lejanas raíces. *Hacienda Pública Española*, no. 43–46: 43–68.

Velarde, J. (2001). Las cuatro escuelas de Flores de Lemus, in E. Fuentes-Quintana (ed.), *Economía y economistas españoles. Vol. 6: La modernización de los estudios de economia.* Barcelona, Galaxia-Gutenberg, 269–272.

Vidal i Guardiola, M. (1907). *La reforma de los impuestos directos en Prusia (1891–1893) ante el estado actual de la tributación española.* Barcelona.

Zabalza, J. (2004). Más allá de Flores de Lemus: La literatura hacendística en España en el primer tercio de siglo XX (1901–1936). *Colección de Documentos de Trabajo AEHE*, DT-0401.

Zabalza, J. (2007). Los fundamentos doctrinales de "La Hacienda Española" de Francisco Bernis, in *Miscellània Ernest Lluch i Martín. Vol. 2.* Vilassar de Mar, Fundació Ernest Lluch, 151–160.

7 The influence of the German Historical School in Portugal

António Almodovar and José Luís Cardoso

Introduction

The process of diffusion and influence of the German Historical School (GHS) in Portugal was similar to what occurred with every other school or current of thought that was acknowledged, assimilated and appropriated by Portuguese economists and publicists in different historical moments: due to a pervasive eclectic attitude regarding the so-called moral and political sciences, the commitment to any new doctrine was as a rule limited, biased and institutionally inconsequent. It was limited because the references made to representative figures of every economic doctrine were fragmentary, without a systematic reading of the imported sources, with no translation of the main books and textbooks of the authors occasionally quoted. Biased means the lacking of a vision on the ensemble of the features of the school behind such doctrine, whose ideas and principles were selected or evoked insofar as they served certain and precise commitments concerning intellectual argumentation in the public sphere or doctrinal support in the political arena. Finally, the influence of the doctrine was inconsequent because it did not give rise to the creation or institutionalization of a school, of a set of uncompromising disciples coherently gathered under the patronage of a mentor or a follower.

This caveat notwithstanding, it is nevertheless evident that, like it happened with other economic doctrines, there has been a significant number of Portuguese economists of the second half of the nineteenth century who have acknowledged and shown a selective receptiveness of the ideas spelt by the GHS, especially when they served to challenge the unconvincing universal laws of political economy. The spreading was facilitated by the strong influence of the German tradition in the fields of law, history, philosophy and, above all, the sciences of administration. This chapter will therefore pay a deliberate attention to the antecedents that help to explain the willingness to follow and appropriate the German tradition(s) on economic and policy issues, in opposition to cosmopolitan political economy, as discussed in the next section.

Antecedents and preconditions

The type of state administration doctrines currently associated with German cameralism surfaced in the political thought and in the economic agenda of the Portuguese state in the second half of the eighteenth century. This was a period when the king's direct involvement in the creation of laws and regulations was deepened – that is the ruler acted first and foremost as a legislator. The same situation was to be found in other contexts shaped by the political rule of enlightened absolutism, which provided the ideal political conditions and background for the emergence and development of the police state that lay at the core of cameralist doctrines.

In Portugal, police matters were the king's main concern as a legislator during the second half of the eighteenth century – namely during the consulate of the Marquis of Pombal (1750–1777). Before assuming his functions as head of government, Pombal served as Portuguese ambassador in London (1739–1743) and in Vienna (1745–1749), these diplomatic experiences being quite relevant for his own intellectual formation.[1]

The attention given by Pombal to the rationalization of state administration can be clearly seen in the multiplication of decrees, permits and laws throughout the period of his government, dealing with such themes as the organization of economic activities (with special attention being paid to manufactures and trade circuits), the centralization of the public finance system, the creation of fresh knowledge about natural resources, and the incentives designed to help increase the size of the population (i.e. through legislation directed at native Brazilians), as well as the educational reform and its receptiveness to enlightened ideas. Finally, issues relating to the overseas economic and political administration were also the subject matter of a significant part of the crown's legislative activity over this period.

The theme of the rational centralization and administrative organization of state finance was one of the most prominent issues in eighteenth-century cameralist literature. In Portugal, the quasi-cameralist doctrines and practices were neither grounded nor expressed in philosophical terms and were not developed in the same distinctive way as von Justi's "political metaphysics" (see Schmidt am Busch, 2009).[2] Nevertheless, there were clear signs of a different kind of practical attention being paid to the process of the rational centralization of public policies, as illustrated by the establishment of the Royal Exchequer (*Erário Régio*) in 1761.

The rationale of Pombal's rule was a combination of the mercantilist canon (more specifically a certain kind of Colbertism) with an attention to police matters (which in Portugal meant the combining of quasi-cameralist doctrines with the understanding of "police" that was prevalent at that time in the French political literature of enlightened despotism). Thus, "police" was seen as referring to a set of procedures designed to secure public authority and to strengthen the state's power.

The formation of a new economic and political discourse in Portugal throughout this period was also influenced by the philosophy of jusnaturalism. The developments that had taken place in natural law since the seventeenth century clearly contributed to the gradual definition of economic aims and policy and offered further conceptual instruments and methodologies for the development of political economy. In this context, the connection between self-interest and social welfare, conceived as a relationship of harmony and equilibrium, stood out as being particularly relevant, because it also fitted in with the cameralist tradition of economic thought. In fact, the very notion of "police" (associated here with the internal order established through the action of the state, based on the production of the common good and public happiness) took on an important role as the point of convergence of the different discourses that led to the emergence of political economy as the science of the legislator, hence providing the necessary means for promoting political reform and economic change. This rationale was followed in the reform of the University of Coimbra by the Marquis of Pombal in 1772, thus paving the way for a renewal of the education of the administrative staff for an enlightened state.

The dissemination of German reading was minimal at that time in Portugal, which is certainly one of the reasons why the influence of the cameralist tradition was primarily channelled through the reading of Bielfeld's *Institutions Politiques*, hence allowing the use of the term quasi-cameralism (Bielfeld 1774). Much of the text is devoted to the administration of the public finance system and to the praise of the centralization of financial functions by the state. The discussion of themes relating to colonial policy, associated with political decision making in the European sphere, is obviously one of the main reasons behind the interest in Bielfeld's work within the Spanish-Portuguese context. This influence of the cameralist formulations in Bielfeld's *Institutions Politiques*, mixing together the topics of the centralization of the public finances, colonial policy and general considerations about the science of government, was to continue until the first decades of the nineteenth century, with important effects on the formation of the Brazilian state.

The quasi-cameralist way of thinking proved its usefulness when applied to the discussion of matters relating to police and administration. And it also proved possible to join the state administration science and the new science of political economy together, thus paving the way for the inclusion of political economy in the syllabus of law studies.

The reception of Smithian political economy in Portugal was to a large extent mitigated by this inherited zeitgeist. As the work by Acúrsio das Neves illustrates (1814–1817), the economic policies followed by the Marquis de Pombal were to blame mainly on account of a number of mercantilist misconceptions regarding the proper way to promote national wealth – thus the need for adjusting the administrative action by adopting a modern economic policy rationale, which Acúrsio das Neves believed to be available in the writings of Adam Smith. Modern political economy was therefore to be incorporated in the Portuguese quasi-cameralist administrative tradition.

The liberal revolution that took place in Portugal in the early 1820s did not change this orientation. The decay experienced by the Portuguese economy in the aftermath of the Napoleonic wars favoured the rise of a backwardness conscience and the search for viable defensive strategies for the nation. Unsurprisingly, this fostered a tendency towards *eclecticism*, an unwillingness to accept the existence of general, abstract and universal rules of economic policy (a distrust of cosmopolitism), a limited acceptance of laissez-faire and a very limited acceptance of laissez-passer all along the first half of the nineteenth century.

A major source of information regarding the alternative economic doctrines came from the expatriates. One of them – Francisco Solano Constâncio – conveyed a notion of political economy as a practical science, as a "science of proportions", stressing the need for incorporating the social and national elements in political economy (Constâncio 1821). Another one – José Ferreira Borges – after a lengthy disquisition on the doctrines of Jean-Baptiste Say on the benefits of free trade, cared to make clear that in several instances it was absolutely necessary to accept exceptions to the theory conveyed by the systems of political economy:

> The freedom of trade is a thesis that accepts no exception regarding importations, absolute freedom necessarily bringing forth a benefit to the society that adopts it; but it doesn't follow that each nation, due to the present international scene – all being in a more or less open state of hostility regarding this principle – should alone proceed to adopt such freedom when the other keep with restrictions; the game would be uneven, and the loss certain.
>
> (Borges 1834, 19)

The same kinds of precautions were also present in the doctrines expended by Portuguese political economists who were currently living in Portugal. Some of them, like António Oliveira Marreca, stated even more clearly the type of measure that ought to be taken in order to bring forth national economic development, stressing the necessary role to be performed by the state regarding industrial organization, transport infrastructures, industrial education and credit. According to this author, since factories were instrumental for Portuguese economic recovery, the state should supply them with "what enlightened governments usually offer to their national industry" – such as "the building of good roads and sailing channels", "the loan of capitals without interest by the State to honest and active entrepreneurs, like it happens in England", "the lessening of taxes on industrial products" and "the spread of professional schools" (Marreca 1838, 2: 44).

Concurring with Ferreira Borges regarding the need to impose limits to the general principle of free trade, Oliveira Marreca developed the argument in a more openly nationalistic tone:

> If the principle of freedom, in spite of being so true and fruitful, is limited by acquired rights, shouldn't it also be limited by the national interests? The national interests are not limited to the interests of one year, one month, or

those of the present day, they include future interests and are not limited to the interests of the present generation for they include the future ones; because a nation is a progressive series of generations that perpetuate themselves in a territory. The transient calculations of individual egoisms are not applicable. The prospect of its economy is larger than the petty rule that commands to buy in the cheapest market. It should get hold of the instruments of wealth that are the foundation of the prosperity and glory of the modern peoples. In a word, it should have its own factories, even if at the cost of temporary sacrifices.

(Marreca 1838, 2: 25)

The possible influence of List – and the actual importance of List's doctrines for a backward economy, as was the case of Portugal (cf. Bastien 1997) – is suggested by the following considerations:

The branch of the social sciences that embraces the national economy has few absolute principles. The laissez faire and the laissez passer, a dogma of the economists, which gives to commercial freedom an unrestricted latitude, is the enemy of all infant industry, the opponent of the progresses that industry is performing among the peoples whose products cannot compete with those of other nations that manufacture them at lower price. In order to establish factories, keep them, and improve them, less developed countries must keep the foreign artifacts that they cannot match either in quality and price away from their markets. Protective or restrictive taxes are the indispensable defense of peoples that aspire to enter into a factory career.

(Marreca 1838, 2: 41)

The ensuing reception of the doctrines of Jean-Baptiste Say and other classical political economists was therefore performed with a view to the training of the administrative staff that the Portuguese state needed in order to resume growth.

German influences in the Portuguese culture

Before accompanying the evolution of Portuguese economic thought, a mention must be made regarding the evolution of the nineteenth-century intellectual milieu. The development of modern Portuguese historiography owes much to the German historical canon and deserves particular attention.

The *Monumenta Historica* German model by Georg Heinrich Pertz was followed by Alexandre Herculano, the most important nineteenth-century Portuguese historian. In 1852, Herculano submitted a proposal to the Academia das Ciências de Lisboa regarding the publication of a set of national historical sources. Between 1836 and 1854, the German historian Heinrich Schaefer published a four-volume history of Portugal (*Geschichte von Portugal*), which was widely acclaimed by contemporary Portuguese historians – namely by Alexandre Herculano, Oliveira Martins, Pinheiro Chagas and Teófilo Braga.

Schaefer's history helped to call into question the religious explanations of the origins of Portuguese nationality – namely by stressing the importance of economic and geographic factors behind lagging the fifteenth-century north Atlantic expansion. This history was eventually translated in the last decade of the nineteenth century (Schaefer 1893–99).

The characteristic vision of German romanticism was present in several Portuguese authors, who did their best to downplay the historical role played by individuals and random influences, stressing instead the importance of collective social and institutional phenomena. This approach, which was also present in other historiographical traditions (i.e. in the French approach by Guizot), had its roots in the enlightened historicism of Vico and Herder. It implied thorough and accurate archival research, the sources being subsequently interpreted in order to establish a sequence of epochs of national development and decay according to a number of different elements – the psychological character of the historical agents, their economic and social interactions, the political drive and the cultural context.

According to Herculano, the proper historiographical approach was epitomized by Leopold von Ranke, Justus Moeser, Friedrich Karl von Savigny and Karl Friedrich Eichhorn, all of whom did stress the need for a history of civilization based on social rather than individual agents. Such conceptualization of history was based on the study of traditions and laws, institutions and other ways of organizing the collective livelihood, also taking into consideration the artistic, literary and scientific manifestations that displayed the specificities of national histories – thus the view, expressed by Herculano among other, that the adoption of any foreign institutional was to be carefully performed, taking in due account the national specificities. In his opinion, it would be absurd to adopt any doctrine that did not take into account the "moral, political and material situation" of the nation; and, even when such doctrines were "excellent and liable of being established among us", it was certain that their "beneficial results would only take place when properly adjusted to the national mores" (Herculano 1841, 141).

Like Alexandre Herculano, Joaquim Pedro de Oliveira Martins also stood for an historical approach that could explain the national evolution as a process of qualitative progress, one that was not only material but also spiritual. The writing of history thus becomes a civic and political imperative, implying the will to bring about a social change – whose effectiveness was unequivocally related to an awareness of the actual characteristics of the nation.[3]

This approach paved the way for the reception of the GHS in Portugal. Believing that the essence of the nineteenth-century evolution and revolutions was necessarily economic, Oliveira Martins (1873, 47) searched for guidelines that could help to design a development strategy for Portugal. Given the need for freedom and competition – but also for equity and solidarity between nations in the same civilizational stand – the merging of the national political economy tradition and the German historicism seemed to offer a promising doctrine.

In a tribute to Emile de Laveleye, Oliveira Martins lists the authors who helped to build the aforementioned approach:

> A school that had its origins in the writings of Rodbertus, Lueder and Soden, whose founding fathers were von Thünen, Müller, Bernhardi, List, Stein, Roscher, Knies, Hildebrand, Hermann, and that enrols among its countless current followers Nasse, Schmoller, Brentano, Schaenberg, Raesler, Dühring, Wagner, Schäffle, Cohn, von Scheel, Samter, Engel.
>
> (Martins 1885, 94)

The diffusion of the doctrines of the GHS in Portugal – be it through an enhanced attention to the social question, to the socialist movement, or to the appropriate national strategies for economic growth – is also present in the writings of Portuguese liberal political economists.

For Oliveira Martins, these were basic tenets of this school, which he quoted whenever in need of an argument of authority against free-trade doctrines. But even for some supporters of free trade, like José Luciano de Castro, it was impossible to ignore the importance of Roscher – "an author whose opinion is worthy of being considered" (Castro 1856, 55). Consequently, instead of ignoring or dismissing the opposing views, he cared to refute Roscher's arguments in favour of (exceptional) export prohibitions: "[Roscher] believes that export prohibitions should take place in some exceptional situations. We do not share such view" (ibid.). In order to show that Roscher's arguments were illusory[4] Luciano de Castro pointed out that the initial fall of agricultural prices following the prohibition would eventually cause a rise of demand, thus leading to an inevitable rise of those prices to the previous high levels.

Another example of the influence of the GHS over liberal political economists is to be found in J.J. Rodrigues de Freitas.[5] Even if he defined himself as an "economist, and consequently as anti-socialist", the arguments set forth by the supporters of the GHS led him to accept that political economy was not incompatible with a more significant state intervention:

> Which other functions would Adam Smith give to the State if he was to write today? Whatever his thought might be in the present circumstances of the economic world, under the spell of the philosophical ideas of the nineteenth century, he would not have to revise his doctrines to avoid the criticisms against excessive individualism. His doctrine belongs without a doubt to those that organise private enterprises, those that socialise or assign to the State some activities beside those related to peace and freedom. Without any fundamental modifications, and without any logical breach, one could advance from it to the very Katheder socialism. The legislation to protect the workers and meant for their wellbeing is not incompatible with the ideas professed by Adam Smith.
>
> (Freitas 1883, 2: 212)

The emergence of the German Historical School as a scholarly reference

The major hub for the diffusion of ideas among the cultured circles – economic ones included – was the University of Coimbra, the sole Portuguese university until the establishment of the University of Lisbon in 1911.

When the teaching of political economy was eventually established in the syllabus of law studies at the University of Coimbra (in 1836) its role as the science of the legislator at the service of public institutions and political administration was firmly secured. To the cameralist background inherited from Pombal (Jakob Friedrich von Bielfeld, Christian von Wolff), liberalism brought not only a new discipline but also the philosophical influence of Immanuel Kant (1724–1804) and the less celebrated Karl Christian Friedrich Krause (1781–1832). German philosophical and law traditions played a decisive role in the structuring of the teaching of political economy and jurisprudence.[6] As foreseen by one of the temporary lecturers of political economy at the University of Coimbra, the development of economic science in Europe was largely dependent on the achievements of German authors, considering that "it is in Germany that, above all countries, this science presents further developments" (Carneiro 1850, 60).

The appointed professor, Adrião Forjaz de Sampaio, performed his duties with professional engagement, publishing regularly updated versions of his lessons between 1837 and 1874. This long career allows us to appreciate the gradual development of an eclectic approach that started with a translation of Jean-Baptiste Say's *Catechisme d'économie politique* and ultimately evolved to a handbook displaying an elaborate array of influences.

The French political economists are pervasive in the references – François-Xavier-Joseph Droz, Alban de Villeneuve-Bargemont, Frederic Bastiat, Charles Dunoyer, Michel Chevalier and so forth. However, they are stapled on a basic framework that was provided by the French translation of the German economist Karl Heinrich Rau, which Forjaz de Sampaio picked as the epitome of a proper organization of the principles of a science (Rau 1839).[7] And, as Forjaz de Sampaio explicitly acknowledges, one of the advantages of such organization was that it allowed the teacher to skip several of the

> minute and little useful issues that engross some economists and move as soon as possible to the analysis – more important than anything else – of the theory of the relations of the State with the industrial sphere (. . .) I have abridged as far as possible the theory of the economy of nations in order to expand the theory of economic policy.
>
> (Sampaio 1858, xxiii–xxiv)

Along the text, we may find once again evidence of the administrative "practical" approach to political economy: one the one hand, it is acknowledged that

> the strict observance of the principle of industrial freedom once applied to commerce reduces the action of governments to the mere defense of order

and justice (. . .) and to the levy of taxes that are absolutely indispensable for traders to contribute to State expenses.

(Sampaio 1874, 2: 49–50)

But then it is stressed that

since both the work and capital have not followed the free movement that the philosophy of industry demands; and some industrial efforts, appropriate for the soil, climate and national genius, may be jeopardized by the absolutely free competition of similar foreign initiatives, characterized by considerable superiority, it is convenient, in such cases, for some time, to support those national efforts, prudently, by means of protective duties – but always moderate ones.

(Ibid., 51)

Another influence that emerges in the lessons by Forjaz de Sampaio is at the origin of the duty of the state to perform a "special direct interference on the transactions regarding the labour of children; for if performed in complete freedom, they may imply an abuse of power, and severe moral and political future damages" (Sampaio 1874, 2: 49). Here echoes the ethical approach developed by Droz and Villeneuve-Bargemont, which was to be subsequently developed by the Christian (both French and German) political economists.

The replacement of Adrião Forjaz de Sampaio in 1870 allowed for some changes in the course on political economy at the University of Coimbra. Alberto dos Reis and Marnoco e Sousa (1907) vividly describe those changes as a process of catching up with the historical trends that marked the evolution of the economic thought in the second half of the nineteenth century: after Forjaz de Sampaio, who had never recanted the doctrines of the liberal school, "the socialist ideas soon gained visibility (. . .) the classical orientation being abandoned in view of the fact that it no longer matched the aspirations of the times" (Reis and Sousa 1907, 10) – thus the emergence of a new approach to political economy, one that now informed the students of both the "individualist and socialist" views. Then, the "sociological form of socialism" was also incorporated, to be followed by the "the doctrine that wishes to assign a national character to political economy" (ibid., 12). Ultimately (i.e. 1910), due to the permanent concern to ensure that the course on political economy was kept in tune with "the foreign scientific movement", the course began to encompass an analysis of "the most recent economic theories". As the authors mentioned, this recent effort led to the inclusion of references not only to "the individualists of the Austrian school" and to "the socialist doctrines of Bernstein and Kautsky, which represent two different contemporary interpretations of Marxism", but also to "Anton Menger's doctrines of juridic collectivism", to the "anarchist doctrines of Kropotkine, Tucker, Tolstoi, Reclus, Grave, Malato, etc.", to the ideas of "the Le Play school, modernly reconstructed by Tourville and Demolins", and last but not least to the ideas of "the Lorian solidarism" (ibid., 13).

This pedagogical concern with supplying the students with a complete, unbiased and updated set of references did not prevent the teachers from ultimately expressing their own preferences.

Still, according to Alberto dos Reis and Marnoco e Sousa, it was not difficult to see that José Frederico Laranjo

> was already under the spell" of the "doctrines of List, which subordinated entirely the economic life to the political national goals, also of the historical school, which believed that political economy could not progress if it didn't study the institutions of each particular people.
>
> (Reis and Sousa 1907, 12)

J. F. Laranjo's lessons do in fact display an adherence to a few tenets of the GHS – namely the need to bring "together the idealist (deductive spiritualist) method and that of historical observation" (Laranjo 1891, 9), the view of the object of political economy as encompassing not only men "as a sensitive, moral, progressive being" but also "the results of institutions over human happiness, the ideal of public and individual conscience, [and] the historical evolution" (ibid., 10). Roscher is extensively quoted,[8] either regarding the proper method for political economy, the description and classification of the sectors of economic activity, or the theory of value. So, even if Laranjo did not assume an explicit doctrinal affiliation for his lessons, there is no doubt that the influence of the GHS school was present in the overall approach to the organization of economic activity, the guarded approach to the adoption of abstract principles and the sympathy regarding the Katheder socialists' reformist agenda.

A few years later,[9] the course on political economy was assigned to José Ferreira Marnoco e Sousa. This young professor performed his duties with an exceptional proficiency,[10] lecturing for an impressive number of different courses – that is finance, political law, ecclesiastic law, commercial law, penal law, colonial administration and history of law. In the successive editions of his lessons on political economy (i.e. in the 1900s and 1910s) and in those on finance (1908, 1911, 1913) both the main thesis and the representative authors of the GHS were now explained to the students in a detailed, neutral textbook approach.

In the historical introduction to the course on finance, Marnoco e Sousa acknowledges the founding role played by the cameralists, who "offered an abstract theory, a systematisation of the administrative rules regarding the fulfilment of the financial needs of the prince and the state" (Sousa 1908, 18). This school, starting with Seckendorff in the seventeenth century and ending with Sonnenfels in the eighteenth century, "had Justi as its best representative" (Sousa 1908, 19).

The second milestone in the history of financial science was also German:

> It was the German authors such as Eiselen, Malchus and principally Rau that, influenced by the cameralism, studied finance independently from economics.

And the value of Rau is such that we can consider him as the true founder of the science of finance.

(Sousa 1913, 23)

Regarding the current stage in the development of the science of finance, four schools are reported: the historical, Katheder socialism, the Austrian school and the socialist school.

Concerning this phase in the evolution of the science of finance, Marnoco e Sousa reminds his students that they have already been taught in the course of political economy that

> the doctrine of [the historical] school was in favour of the gathering of data and the description of the needs, the economic characteristics and the institutions of a nation, without the concern of formulating the laws that govern those phenomena. This last task should be allotted to future generations, better equipped than us to perform it, since presently we do not command a sufficient number of facts so to safely attempt to formulate laws. These doctrines were followed by the partisans of the historical school in economics, and were passed to the study of finance. Their main representative author was Roscher. This orientation is fundamentally empirical, but it gave a major contribution to the development of the science of finance due to the huge amount of information that it gathered on financial phenomena.
>
> (Sousa 1913, 23)

The Austrian school allegedly emerged as a reaction to these doctrines. According to Marnoco e Sousa, this school believed that "financial phenomena should be studied solely from an economic perspective (. . .), the dominant principle in the science of finance [being] the hedonistic principle" (Sousa 1913, 24). This doctrine, which was at the origin of a so-called pure finance, was unacceptable to Marnoco e Sousa due to the fact that it "leads to utter abstractions within the science of finance" – namely by unduly ignoring the "political and juridical elements [that] are immanent to the principles of justice and equity of the political organisation of the State" (ibid., 10).

Marnoco e Sousa also dismisses the socialist school, not only because they almost "despise the study of financial and economic subjects" but also because "none of them has produced any remarkable treatise on the science of finance" (Sousa 1913, 25).

Thus the importance of the Katheder socialists:

> In Germany, which never surrender to the Austrian school doctrines, the school of Katheder socialism ruled in economics, also influencing the study of finance. Its main author is Wagner. According to this school, the State should provide all the necessary means for the betterment of the working classes. Taxes should be established so that they had a social goal besides their fiscal one, i.e. they should provide tax revenue for the State and also

better the situation of the working classes. They should, therefore, have a political and social goal. *Actually, this is the current tendency of modern fiscal systems.*

(Sousa 1913, 24, italics added)

A similar approach is to be found in the various editions of the course on political economy. As a rule, they comprise a lengthy historical review of the schools of economic thought, not only describing in detail the major tenets of each school and specifying its most representative authors but also including a critical assessment.

The development of economic doctrines is divided into three periods: a *fragmentary* epoch, during which economic doctrines surface as part of moral and political discourses; a *formative* period, during which political economy was founded; and finally a period of *development*, which comprises a process of simultaneous improvement and growing intricacy of the economic doctrines (Sousa 1910, 32).

According to Marnoco e Sousa, this last period corresponds to the establishment of the individualist school by Adam Smith, and to its ensuing development – first in England (Malthus, Ricardo), then in France (J. B. Say) and also in Germany (Rau, von Thünen). With this development, a number of more *radical* varieties also emerged – like the Manchester school of Cobden and Bright, its French counterpart played by Bastiat and Chevalier, and the German equivalent by Prince Smith and Schulze-Delitzsch.

In absolute opposition to this school, and particularly to its extreme developments, a socialist one emerged. Either collectivist or communist, Marnoco e Sousa considers that the socialist school gradually evolved into a chaotic array of doctrines, eventually leading to a number of socialist experiences totally deprived of a doctrinal basis.

In the face of these two major increasingly radicalized orientations, it was only natural that a number of intermediate schools would emerge – first the school of national political economy of List and of Carey; then the historical school, which had Sismondi as a forerunner and Hildebrand, Knies and Roscher as founding fathers, being also supported by Cliffe Leslie, Thorold Rogers and Ingram; finally came the Katheder socialists, comprising Lorenz von Stein, Schmoller, Schönberg, Adolph Wagner, Rösler, Held, Brentano, Scheel and Laveleye.[11]

In a more detailed analysis of the history of this latter school, Marnoco e Sousa explains that the Katheder socialists were in fact an offspring of the historical school,

some economists staying faithful to the principle of natural laws and the absence of state intervention, while others, by being impressed by the contrast between the extraordinary growth of wealth and the simultaneous growth of the proletariat, ultimately stood in favour of a distribution of wealth in accordance with the principles of morals and law, free competition being not enough for establishing a rational and equitable social order.

(Sousa 1910, 77)

According to Marnoco e Sousa, the basic tenets of the Katheder socialists' school were (a) the rejection of natural economic laws, (b) the condemnation of individualism and (c) the need for an enlargement of state action in support of national development. And, as a final characteristic of this school, Marnoco e Sousa mentions their allegiance to the historical or realist method in political economy, meaning that they were of the opinion that

> in view of the changes, according to the several phases of civilisation, of the ways of producing, distributing and consuming wealth, the economic problems do not admit an *a priori* solution, and must be addressed in each nation by means of statistics and history.
>
> (Sousa 1910, 78)

Although sharing the aforementioned tenets, there were nevertheless some practical divergences among the members of this school. Some, like Wagner and Scheel, were closer to socialism; others, like Brentano, "favoured the spontaneous establishment of free organisations, supportive of the interests of the weak (. . .) corporative institutions acting as a means for the transition to a socialist collective organisation"; finally, there was the intermediate approach followed by Schmoller, "rejecting the assail to property rights of the former, and asking for more intervention than the latter" (ibid., 79).

Even if Marnoco does not express his doctrinal preferences, it is nevertheless meaningful that he cares to highlight the fact that all modern states do follow this intermediate orientation. And it is plausible to believe this type of remark would induce the students if not to adhere to the doctrines of the historical school at least to acknowledge their practical importance.

The subsequent development of Portuguese economic thought within law studies was also marked by the attraction towards intermediate schools, an attraction that caused a series of regular attempts to detach the element of truth that was present in the extreme – that is purely individualist or purely socialist – approaches in order to build up a reasonable (i.e. nonpartisan) doctrine.

As J. Frederico Laranjo remarked, this attitude was unlikely to bring forth a meaningful development of any school of thought in Portugal:

> They say that English girls cut pictures that please them and past them in their albums. The characteristic of the Portuguese science is a scissor: with it, on its working days, it cuts paragraphs and chapters of those who thought in other countries in order to build its own books. A fat lady, our science does not have stomach, she merely stores but doesn't digest; reflection troubles us, we declare ourselves to be children, and we don't even act as parasites of other people's ideas because we don't even care to extract their juice, we only grasp them in a fragmentary way.
>
> (Laranjo 1871, v)

Concluding remarks

The fragmentary assimilation of foreign ideas – as expressed in the earlier sug-
gestive quotation – is a common feature of the processes of transmission, adaptation and appropriation of economic knowledge. Portuguese economists picked
up from the GHS the useful bits and pieces that could be accommodated into a
global vision of both the functioning and the improvement of economic life.
Although not always aware of the analytical and doctrinal framework where the
fragments could gain a meaningful sense, Portuguese economists intuitively
acknowledged the merits of a school of thought that responded positively to
their cherished concerns. The GHS could serve, and has served, as an additional
element of a conceptual matrix appropriate to the study of economic phenomena,
where historical and political elements should play a relevant role. The mélange
of ideas inherited from both the GHS and the representative messengers of
Katheder socialism is perhaps the most meaningful sign of a high propensity to
single out the virtues of relativism and eclecticism as a methodological framework
to the study of societies.

The history of Portuguese economic thought throughout the first decades of the
twentieth century is largely the outcome of a knowledge structure that resisted the
incorporation of the triumphant neoclassical orthodoxy, and thus accepted some
of the views offered by the GHS. The rescue of nationalist, organicist, historicist
and ethical references and values was responsible for the emergence of innovative
lines of research that aimed at incorporating a corporatist blueprint, a kind of a
third-way approach to the ideal organization of societies. By arguing against the
shortcomings of both socialism and capitalism, by stressing the need to enhance
the qualities of an economic organization that could harmonize individual motivations with state economic intervention, the ideologues of corporatism were also
paying tribute to the authors and schools of thought that had provided the best
arguments on that direction, of which the GHS was worth remembering.

Notes

1 In London, he moved in the circle of the Royal Society and built up a personal library
   that included the most relevant books representative of the mercantilist literature, such
   as those of Joshua Child, Charles Davenant, Charles King, Thomas Mun and William
   Petty. In Vienna, Pombal was well placed in the aristocratic milieu of the Austrian
   empire and his connections were crucial for the development of new ideas on issues
   related to education reform and pedagogical innovation, which later become one of
   the most acclaimed outcomes of his political career. It is also likely to admit that his
   stay in Vienna gave him a new perception of general problems concerning political
   administration and the sciences of the state.
2 When referring to the Portuguese historical experience we shall use the term quasi-
   cameralism to emphasize that the influence and spread of a genuine German cameralist
   tradition has been mostly indirect. On this topic see Cardoso and Cunha (2012).
3 On the Portuguese historiography of this period see Catroga (1996) and Matos (1998).
4 Roscher's argument being explained as stating that "exports should be exceptionally
   prohibited in less wealthy nations, lacking both capital and a strong commercial fleet,
   whenever the crops are scant both at home and abroad" (Castro 1856, 55).

5 Rodrigues de Freitas was one of the few authors who could read German authors in the original. His readings encompass original works by Fröbel, List, Albert Schäffle, Wilhelm Lexis and Wilhelm Georg Friedrich Roscher.

6 Roughly speaking, all disciplines of the syllabus were supposed to abide by the philosophical orientation endorsed by the established philosophy of law. When the course of political economy was established at Coimbra, the transition from a preliberal to a liberal philosophy of law was still underway. Vicente Ferrer, who is unanimously considered as the major Portuguese reference of the second half of the nineteenth-century philosophy of law, performed this transition. His books convey a peculiar attempt to merge the individualist views of Kant with Krause's organic societal archetype (cf. Ferrer 1850). Being an eclectic approach, this *sui generis* philosophical merger was prone to evolve towards the ascendancy of one of its component parts. J. Martens Ferrão was one of the first to replace the liberal views of Kant by those of Hegel, while keeping with the philosophy of Krause. In his academic dissertation (Ferrão 1854), this new philosophic approach allowed Martens Ferrão to support the idea that a proper juridical organization of the relations between labour and capital should be based on labour-free associations within a corporative organic state (cf. Moncada 1938, 65).

7 The other German economists mentioned by Sampaio are Ludwig Heinrich von Jakob, Theodor Schmalz and Wilhelm Georg Friedrich Roscher. The latter was read in the French translation by Wolowski (Roscher 1857), and is often quoted on the discussion of the general concepts of value, prices and distribution, although without a global presentation of Roscher's system of thought.

8 Albert Schäffle is also regularly quoted by Laranjo.

9 In the meantime, the course was assigned to Abel de Andrade, who was allegedly a follower of the historical school (Andrade 1898).

10 See Fátima Brandão (1996, x): "between 1898 and 1910, Marnoco e Sousa published eighteen textbooks".

11 Marnoco e Sousa also mentions two recent new intermediate schools – the solidarism school of Charles Gide (to which also belonged Durkheim and Worms) and the Lorian school, established by Achille Loria at the University of Turin, whose disciples were Camillo Supino and Mellusi.

References

Andrade, A. (1898). *Ciência Económica: Apontamentos das prelecções*. Coimbra: Minerva Central.

Bastien, C. (1997). Friedrich List and Oliveira Marreca: Some odd coincidences. Working papers GHES, ISEG-UTL.

Bielfeld, B. (1774). *Institutions Politiques (Tome III)*. Leipzig: Chez J.F. Bassompierre.

Borges, J. F. (1834). *Instituições de Economia Política*. Lisbon: Imprensa Nacional. (New edition: Lisbon: Banco de Portugal, 1995, Series of Portuguese Economic Classics, edited by A. Sousa Franco.)

Brandão, M. F. (1996). Introduction to J. F. Marnoco e Sousa (1910).

Cardoso, J.L. and Cunha, A. (2012). Enlightened reforms and economic discourse in the Portuguese-Brazilian Empire (1750–1808). *History of Political Economy*, 44: 4, 619–641.

Carneiro, B. (1850). *Lições de Economia Política*. Coimbra: Imprensa da Universidade.

Castro, J. L. (1856). *A questão das subsistências*. Lisbon: Tipografia Universal.

Catroga, F. (1996). Alexandre Herculano e o historicismo romântico. In F. Catroga, L. F. Torgal and J. A. Mendes (eds.), *História da História em Portugal*. Lisbon: Círculo de Leitores, 39–85.

Constâncio, F. S. (1821). Lettres à M. Malthus, etc. ou Cartas a M. Malthus sobre diversos assuntos de economia política, e particularmente, sobre as causas da estagnação do comércio. Por J.-B. Say etc., Paris, 1820. *Anais das Ciências, das Artes e das Letras*, Vol. 12, Part 1, 28–51. (Reprinted in F. S. Constâncio, *Leituras e Ensaios de Economia Política*. Lisbon: Banco de Portugal, 1995, Series of Portuguese Economic Classics, edited by J. L. Cardoso.)

Ferrão, J. B. Martens (1854). *Sobre o Melhoramento das Classes Trabalhadoras*. Coimbra: Imprensa da Universidade.

Ferrer, V. (1850). *Princípios Gerais de Filosofia do Direito*. Coimbra: Imprensa da Universidade.

Freitas, J. J. Rodrigues (1883). *Princípios de Economia Política*. Porto: Livraria Universal. (New edition: Lisbon: Banco de Portugal, 1996, Series of Portuguese Economic Classics, edited by A. Almodovar.)

Herculano, A. (1841). Instrução pública. In *Opúsculos* (vol. 5). Lisbon: Livraria Bertrand, 105–163.

Laranjo, J. F. (1871). *O Conteúdo e o critério do Direito*. Coimbra: Imprensa da Universidade.

Laranjo, J. F. (1891). *Princípios de Economia e Política Social*. Coimbra: Imprensa da Universidade. (New edition: Lisbon: Banco de Portugal, 1997, Series of Portuguese Economic Classics, edited by C. Bastien.)

Marreca, A. O. (1838). *Noções Elementares de Economia Política*. Lisbon: Tipografia do Contador-Mor. (New edition: A. O. Marreca, *Obra Económica* (2 vols.). Lisbon: Instituto Português de Ensino à Distância, 1983, edited by C. Barreira.)

Martins, J. P. Oliveira (1873). *Portugal e o Socialismo*. Lisbon: Guimarães Editores.

Martins, J. P. Oliveira (1885). Review of *Le Socialisme Contemporain* de Emile de Laveleye, (2nd ed. 1883). In *Política e Economia Nacional*. Lisbon: Guimarães Editores, 89–101.

Matos, S. C. (1998). *Historiografia e Memória Nacional no Portugal do século XIX*. Lisbon: Colibri.

Moncada, L. Cabral (1938). *Subsídios para uma história da filosofia do direito em Portugal (1772–1911)*. Coimbra: Coimbra Editora.

Neves, J. A. (1814–1817). *Variedades sobre objectos relativos às artes, comércio e manufacturas consideradas segundo os princípios da economia política* (2 vols). Lisbon: Impressão Régia. (New edition: *Obras Completas* [vol. 3]. Porto: Edições Afrontamento, 1985, edited by A. Almodovar and A. Castro).

Rau, K. H. (1839). *Traité d'economie nationale, traduit de l'allemand*. Brussels: Hauman & Cie.

Reis, A. and Sousa, J. F. Marnoco (1907). *A Faculdade de Direito e o seu ensino*. Coimbra: França Amado.

Roscher, W. (1857). *Principes d'économie politique* (transl. L. Wolowski). Paris: Libraire de Guillaumin et Cie.

Sampaio, A. F. (1858). *Novos Elementos de Economia Política e Estadística*. Coimbra: Imprensa da Universidade.

Sampaio, A. F. (1874). *Elementos de Economia Política e Estadística*. Coimbra: Imprensa da Universidade. (New edition: A. Forjaz Sampaio, *Estudos e Elementos de Economia Política, 1839–1874* [vols. 1–2]. Lisbon: Banco de Portugal, 1995, Series of Portuguese Economic Classics, edited by A. Pedrosa.)

Schaefer, H. (1893–99). *História de Portugal: Desde a fundação da monarquia até à revolução de 1820* (5 vols.). Porto: Empresa Editorial.

Schmidt am Busch, H.-C. (2009). Cameralism as "political metaphysics": Human nature, the state and natural law in the thought of Johann Heinrich Gottlob von Justi. *European Journal of the History of Economic Thought*, 16: 3, 409–430.

Sousa, J.F. Marnoco (1908). *O Capitalismo Moderno.* Coimbra: França Amado Editor.

Sousa, J.F. Marnoco (1910). *Ciência Económica.* Coimbra: França Amado Editor. (New edition: Lisbon: Banco de Portugal, 1996, Series of Portuguese Economic Classics, edited by F. Brandão.)

Sousa, J.F. Marnoco (1913). *Tratado da Ciência das Finanças.* Coimbra: França Amado Editor.

8 The legacy of the German Historical School in Greek economic thought and policy

*Michalis Psalidopoulos and
Yorgos Stassinopoulos*[1]

1893 and after: From liberalism to historical economics

The Greek nation, since its very inception, has been receptive to political and cultural influences from abroad. Before the Greek War of Independence and immediately thereafter, the Greek merchant class "endowed schools and libraries, and subsidised the publication, principally outside the boundaries of the [Ottoman] Empire, of a growing, and increasingly secular, body of literature" (Clogg, 1992: 27). This created fertile ground for the reception and cultivation of liberal economic ideas, on both a theoretical and a policy level, which remained dominant throughout the nineteenth century.

In the context of the political elite's aspirations to transform a breakaway province of the Ottoman Empire into a modern European state encompassing all Greeks living in southeastern Europe, liberal economic thought was seen as a complement to political democracy. According to a study about parliamentary debates in nineteenth-century Greece, "all economists in the Greek Parliament were basically of a liberal persuasion in that they believed in the free enterprise economy" (Psalidopoulos & Syrmaloglou, 2005: 246). Additionally, economists such as Professor Ioannes Soutsos (Psalidopoulos & Stassinopoulos, 2009) and Aristides Economos (Psalidopoulos, 1996) advocated liberal reforms that would free the Greek economy from government control and crowding-out effects. The liberalism of these two economists was not a crude transfer of foreign ideas. Soutsos acknowledged that economic policy should take account of national peculiarities. He believed that institutions were crucial in shaping economic activity and stressed that the adoption and "immediate implementation of absolute principles" (meaning British classical ideas) in economic policy were out of the question for him (Soutsos, 1851: 4). Moreover, Soutsos opposed what he perceived as paternalistic and short-sighted economic action by Greek governments and conceded that "the issue of the wider economic action by governments has proved to be a relative one that defies an absolute solution" (Soutsos, 1882–85: 12). Aristides Economos, on the other hand, as editor of the monthly journal *Oikonomiki Epitheorisis* [Economic Review] from 1877 to 1890 and as a member of Parliament, constantly criticized Greek economic policy as being incompatible with the postulates of liberal public finance (Psalidopoulos, 1996).

The Greek politician who dominated economic policy in 1882–1885 and 1887–1893 was Charilaos Trikoupis (1832–1896). He was an archetypal liberal-pragmatist who "admired England realistically as a naval and industrial power instead of sentimentally as a legendary figure of Liberalism and Democracy" (Mavrogordato, 1931: 69). In principle his economic policies were liberal. Amid rising nationalism in southeastern Europe after the Congress of Berlin in 1878, his growth strategies involved heavy public borrowing and large budget deficits, thereby jeopardizing the convertibility of the currency (Stassinopoulos, 2002) and the state's ability to service its foreign obligations. Due to an agricultural export crisis, Greece defaulted in 1893 and after losing a war with the Ottoman Empire in 1897 was subject to International Financial Control (IFC). Thus ended an era of (mostly) liberal hopes that the country could achieve rapid growth through liberal monetary and trade policies.

After 1893, new economic models were sought. Protectionism and support of industry came of age. As was pointed out, the "failure of the attempt to develop along liberal lines in mid-century inevitably strengthened the protectionist movement but until the 1890s manufacturing industry was too weak to bring any effective pressure to bear on the government" (Milward & Saul, 1977: 251). Socialist ideas also emerged during that period in Greece, with unionists and intellectuals criticizing the status quo and demanding socialism.

The most popular of these novel approaches in Greek economic thought was the German economic tradition. In particular, the younger GHS put forth the idea "of fostering development in accordance with a national perspective and a national spirit" (Schefold, 2010: 3) and called for a pragmatic, less abstract and more historically oriented approach to economic research (Grimmer-Solem & Romani, 1999). These principles increasingly appealed to intellectuals in Greece.

The German tradition in economics was not totally new in Greece. Even before default, prominent economists who opposed Trikoupis's policies, such as Ioannes Zographos (1844–1927) and Nikolaos Gounarakis (1853–1932), had argued in favour of the GHS and against economic liberalism, criticizing economic liberalism on theoretical and policy terms.

Zografos studied in Heidelberg, receiving a PhD in 1868, supervised by Karl Heinrich Rau. After a short tenure as professor of public finance at the University of Athens (1885–1886), he got into politics with the National Party, becoming its main economic spokesperson. In his writings he adhered to the tripartite division of Rau's *Lehrbuch*, which was "the most successful textbook in economics" in the German-speaking area (Hagemann & Rösch, 2012: 98), and emphasized economic policy and public finance issues, which had come strongly to the fore after the 1893 default. In one of his earliest writings, *An Essay on Money* (1876, prefaced by Lorenz von Stein), he questioned the monetary policy of the National Bank of Greece and criticized the political authorities for being eager to receive large loans from the bank, instead of letting the bank channel credit to the productive agents of the economy. Zografos was also critical of the tariff system, which left domestic industrial and agricultural production unsheltered, leading to huge current account deficits (Zografos, 1878).

Nikolaos Gounarakis studied in Greece, and in his *habilitation* thesis, on monetary theory and policy, he defended bimetallism as the proper monetary standard for Greece, as opposed to the classical gold standard. After the death of Ioannes Soutsos, Gounarakis succeeded him as professor of economics at the University of Athens (1890–1920), with long pauses in between, because of his participation in the political arena. In his inaugural lecture, he declared the state as the instrument for equitable income distribution and maximum domestic production and asserted that there is no sound theoretical reason for the limitation of the role and scope of state action (Gounarakis, 1892: 13). On these grounds he praised the protective policy expounded by List and followed by Bismarck and proposed an economic policy for Greece with a focus on encouraging domestic industry. Later, Gounarakis stressed the need for policies customised to the specific requirements of the country and supported the historical investigation of economic phenomena as essential to any well-founded economic theory (Gounarakis, 1913).

Thus, after 1893 mainstream economic thought in Greece shifted gradually from a more or less liberal to an interventionist mode. The aim of this chapter is to trace the influence of the GHS in Greece and its evolution from the sidelines of theory in the 1890s to becoming an influential, majority position in the first decades of the twentieth century and up to the late 1930s. Despite its loss of appeal in Germany after 1918, the GHS sustained its dominant status in Greece due to several reasons, to be explained ahead. The rest of the chapter is structured as follows: the first section provides an overview of economic and institutional developments that contributed to the increased influence of the GHS in Greece. Subsequent sections focus on individual economists, mostly academics and in one case a prominent politician, who followed the teachings of the GHS, and examine aspects of their contribution to economic thought in Greece. Reference is also made to economists who, although not GHS supporters, espoused a historical approach in their research, thereby contributing to a domination of the GHS in Greece in the interwar period and up to WWII. We close with concluding remarks.

The gradual rise of the GHS to prominence in Greece

The first decades of the twentieth century saw a flourishing of economics in Greece. The economic environment of the period was marked by austerity under the IFC from 1897 to 1910, heavy government regulation and mass migration; still, the currency was stabilised and fiscal balance was restored. Numerous economic studies were published on domestic and on international economic issues. Intellectuals started forming societies and clubs, such as the *Sociological Society* (1908–1935), the *Society of Political Economy and Statistics* (1914–1916) and the *Society of Social and Political Sciences* (1916–1935). The *General Statistical Service of Greece* was inaugurated in 1916. It conducted various censuses and released statistical data going back to the nineteenth century. In the 1930s the *Association of Greek Banks* published yearly a volume with studies about the state of the Greek economy. Areas such as business cycles, the labour market and industrial economics became the subject of scientific scrutiny. Long-established theories and approaches of a liberal kind were criticized. These tendencies were intensified by the tectonic political and economic changes that took place in Greece before and after World War I (WWI). Greece's victorious participation in the Balkan Wars and along the Entente forces in WWI provided the historical chance for territorial expansion and the long-sought national and political integration of the Greek nation. The dominant political figure of the period and the architect of the Great Idea was Eleftherios Venizelos, a statesman who envisioned a pro-western modernization of the country. He brought sweeping political and economic changes in 1910s and later between 1928 and 1933 (Kitromilides, 2006). After the liberals lost the elections in 1920 the pro-royal Popular Party took over and Greece was defeated in its Asia Minor campaign in 1922. The Great Idea collapsed, and the country, at the time having a population of 4 million, had to deal with an influx of 1.2 million refugees and enormous financial challenges.

Against this background, economists were in great demand, and this was reflected in the academic landscape that emerged after 1920. The increasing institutionalisation of economic studies was manifested also by the creation of new universities and commercial schools and the multiplication of academic chairs for economists, while degrees in economics started being awarded from the mid-1920s. This was the period when economic science in Greece forged stronger ties with German economic thought. Many young economists went abroad for graduate studies, showing a growing preference for German-speaking universities. In the late nineteenth and early twentieth centuries, Germany was the cultural and scientific beacon of Continental Europe and attracted many foreign students to its universities (Ben-David, 1971).

As shown in Figure 8.1, the number of postgraduate Greek students in German universities was growing since the early twentieth century, but soared during the interwar period, with 55 doctorates awarded to Greeks between 1918 and 1939. Of course, not every student who pursued postgraduate studies in state sciences (economics) at German universities should be regarded as a follower of the GHS, which was then in constant decline, squeezed between liberal and socialist ideas. The records of many German universities reveal a strong preference by Greek students for *specific* historical school economists as supervisors. The universities that particularly attracted young Greek economists and other social scientists were Berlin and Munich (Figure 8.2). Highly distinguished scientists, such as Karl Bücher and Werner Sombart, supervised the doctoral theses of some Greek students. Other notable professors of economics preferred by Greeks were, in Berlin, Heinrich Herkner, who supervised four doctorates, and Hermann Schumacher, who was responsible for three doctorates, while in Leipzig Alexander von Hoffmann supervised three doctorates. These statistics show a strong scientific link between the two countries and evidence the extensive influence exerted by the members of historically minded economic research in interwar Greek economic thought.

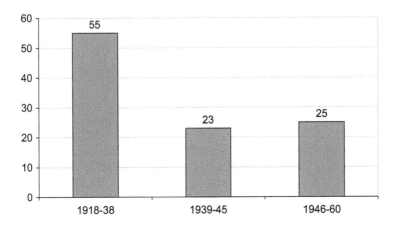

Figure 8.1 Completed doctorates by Greek students at German-speaking universities in state sciences, by period of study.

Source: Psalidopoulos (2013).

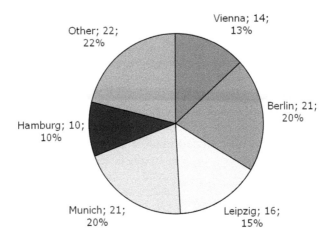

Figure 8.2 Geographical breakdown of doctorates by Greek students at German-speaking universities (1918–1960).

Source: Psalidopoulos (2013).

The influence of the younger GHS on Greek economists is manifested by a growing interest in historical economic studies concerning the development problems of the Greek economy and specific historical surveys of its major sectoral aspects, such as tobacco, currants, banking, land reform, industry and handicraft, shipping and so forth. However, what most characterised the followers of the GHS in Greece was the fact that they not only sought to suggest ways for overcoming economic backwardness but also stood for social engineering and gearing economic policy towards a radical transformation of the Greek economy through extensive state intervention and social protection. A case in point is the Society of Social and Political Sciences, founded in 1916 in the model of the *Verein für Sozialpolitik*. Its purpose was to encourage and promote scientific studies focused on pressing socio-economic problems that demanded cautious state action, ultimately aimed at steering economic and social politics towards social reforms. These studies were published in the periodical *Archive of Economic and Social Sciences*. Other important periodicals were *Ergasia* (Labour) and *Peitharchia* (Discipline).

The key economic challenges after 1922 referred to stabilising the currency, rehabilitating the refugees and setting up a development plan to expand the internal market. Greek economists debated many policy issues. Followers of neoclassicism advocated the gold standard, the purchasing power parity theory of the exchange rate, a balanced budget and a minimal role for the government. Historical economists argued in favour of the gold-exchange standard, the balance of payments theory of the exchange rate and deficit spending and wanted the government to assume whatever task was necessary to better economic conditions (Psalidopoulos, 1989). After the crash of 1929 and the European banking crisis of 1931, Greece defaulted once again. It adopted protectionism and a highly regulated economic system, which practically all economists endorsed, seeing it as a necessary path taken by all European economies.

Andreas Andréadès

The most important academic economist in Greece in the first three decades of the twentieth century was Andreas Andréadès (1876–1935). Andréadès won international acclaim with his dissertation at the University of Paris, titled *History of the Bank of England* (1899, English translation 1909), universally acknowledged as a milestone in financial history. Returning to Greece, he became a professor of public finance and statistics at the University of Athens (1902–1935). He was a prolific author and mentor to many young economists, and his *magnum opus* was *History of Greek Public Finance*, from antiquity to his days (translated into German in 1931 and into English in 1933; Bigg, 1987).

Andréadès was a staunch liberal economist, yet he strongly believed in the national character of economic science and, following the lead of the historical school, tried to infuse historical inquiry into economic reasoning. For him, the coupling of pure economic theory and economic history should be at the heart of every modern systematic approach to theoretical analysis and public policy, especially in economically backward countries (Andréadès, 1927). Historical explanation provides backing and does not substitute for theory, as this has been articulated by the classical economists, and pure economic analysis is indispensable for the scientific explanation of the economic process. Delving into ancient and modern Greek economic, in particular fiscal, history, Andréadès drew theoretical lessons for the financial and economic organisation of the contemporary Greek state and showed that imprudent fiscal management was the main reason behind the 1893 default. He was also a strong critic of government intervention in the economy, although he recognized that the refugees after the Asia Minor debacle had to be resettled and taken care of.

Despite his historical perspective, he never questioned the classical approach to economic theory and to public finance in particular. He regarded classicist principles as the solid foundation of economic science and therefore remained highly sceptical about the project of the GHS and state interventionism in general, especially in the domain of public finance. On the other hand, he showed remarkable scientific integrity. When in the early 1920s academic economic education was expanded and new appointments were due, he helped many interventionist economists to be appointed to academic positions, thus promoting plurality as *the* guiding principle in the Greek economics profession.

Andréadès was Greece's delegate in all major economic summits after WWI, such as the Danube Conference in Paris during 1920–1921, the Assembly of the League of Nations in 1923, 1924 and 1929, and the World Economic Conference in London in 1933, and he edited a volume on the economic and social effects of the WWI on the Greek economy, sponsored by the Carnegie Endowment of International Peace (Andréadès, 1928). However, due to his constant criticizing of Greek economic policy, his influence as a policy maker was marginal, in spite of his prestige and wide-acclaimed authority. His orthodox policy prescriptions were against the political priorities of all interwar Greek governments.

Alexandros Papanastasiou

Alexandros Papanastasiou (1876–1936) was an intellectual who tried in the early stage of his career to combine scientific research with political activity. However, his preoccupation with politics finally prevailed. He wholeheartedly participated in the political arena and became a major political figure, serving twice as prime minister (in 1924 and 1932). An ardent republican and social reformer, he was in charge when the monarchy was abolished, in 1923. He represented and personified the ideals of social democracy in Greece. He is considered the father of social insurance in Greece and the politician *par excellence* who created a safety net for the lower income strata. He also founded the Sociological Society in 1908, an intellectual forum in the footsteps of the Fabian Society that exerted considerable influence on labour reform and legislation throughout the 1920s, comprising many progressive scientists who later joined academia or became high-ranking civil servants.

After completing his PhD in Greece, Papanastasiou studied *Staatswissenschaften* in Berlin (1908–1910) under Adolph Wagner and Gustav Schmoller (Psalidopoulos, 2010). His speeches and political practice reveal a considerable influence from Wagner, in terms of methodology and of the importance of social legislation for the stability of the political system. Schmoller, on the other hand, was credited by Papanastasiou for his thorough historical investigations that lay solid foundations for future economic theorising.

In his seminal paper on economic methodology (Papanastasiou, 1988a), Papanastasiou supported the national character of economic discourse and rejected the notion of rational and narrowly self-interested actors, which, for him, blurred the human element in economic and social practice. Following Wagner, he accepted, however, that for expediency reasons resorting to economic rationality may be fruitful in the short term. This epistemological distinction became for Papanastasiou the pivotal point of his critique of Greek political and economic institutions of the time. For any critique to be scientifically and politically valid, according to Papanastasiou, one had to take into account the historical terms that ultimately have shaped the economic and political conditions underlying each nation's state of affairs. In order to understand patterns of change and to devise appropriate policies to accommodate that change (Grimmer-Solem & Romani, 1999: 334), policy had to respect national peculiarities. Political economy should therefore be policy-oriented, while a politico-economic reform programme had to address the specific social and economic relations that hindered the growth of the economy according to its capabilities.

Thus Papanastasiou advocated the *national* character of economic policy and reassessed the role of the state, especially on social issues, such as the regulation of wages and of working hours (1988b). What was politically right and socially good should count more than the pursuit of economic efficiency. Ethical issues in economic theorising, argued Papanastasiou, were not of secondary importance and should be accounted for in the formulation of economic policy, an idea clearly based on Schmoller (Betz, 1997: 96–101; Shionoya, 1997: 71ff.). This normative dichotomy implied a wider scope of action for the state, seen as the instrument for achieving social welfare. On the other hand, Papanastasiou admitted that the government could be easily manipulated by social groups with the power to promote their economic interests. Moreover, a gradual reform programme, the political inclusion of the working class and more equitable income redistribution were the only ways of keeping social unrest at bay and averting a violent overturn of modern democracies. These principles guided Papanastasiou's political career and action in support of workers' and peasants' rights.

Demetrios Kalitsounakis

A major exponent of the GHS approach at an academic level was Demetrios Kalitsounakis (1886–1982). He received his PhD in Greece, but soon afterwards he moved to Berlin, where he lived between 1910 and 1918. He defended a habilitation thesis on the work of Gustav Schmoller at the University of Athens, where he lectured before becoming a professor of economics at the Athens School of Economics and Business (1920–1960). During his 40-year tenure he introduced novel courses, such as Applied Economic Policy, Introduction to Social Policy, The Condition of the Working Classes and, for the first time at a Greek university, History of Political Economy. In his lectures, Kalitsounakis emphasized the transient and historically conditioned character of economic theories. He also edited the journal *Archive of Economic and Social Sciences* (1920–1971), translated Heinrich Herkner's *Die Arbeiterfrage* into Greek (1919–1920) and wrote extensively on almost all fields of economics (e.g. economic methodology, business cycle theory, Greek tobacco, cooperative unions). However, his main research interests were labour and social legislation, unemployment and alleviation of the lower social strata from interwar economic distress.

Kalitsounakis stood critically against established (liberal) economic theories and challenged their ability to adequately construe the complex socio-economic relationships that emerged during the interwar period. He disregarded abstract economic theory and focused on economic history and the history of economic thought. This methodological stance not only accentuated the national character of economic discourse but also aimed at gaining "deeper scientific knowledge. It is a historical critique" (1925: v), he stressed. Kalitsounakis tried to expand the field of economic research in Greece to encompass all social sciences, an enterprise analogous to that of Max Weber and other members of the younger GHS, which would strengthen the foundations of economic theorising and responsiveness to the unstable social and financial environment that emerged after the Great War. Kalitsounakis followed the scientific programme of his mentor, Gustav Schmoller, when he entitled his major book *Political Science*. It was Schmoller, Kalitsounakis reminded us, who successfully incorporated political and social aspects in his economic analysis in order to explain economic evolution and examined the broader socio-economic issues "from the point of view of the responsible administrators, who should adjust their stance according to the established constitutional rules and [the wishes of] the majority" (1925: 25). Although for Kalitsounakis the GHS did not supply a new coherent economic theory, it ought to be praised for "shedding light on fallacies intruding into the research of real [socio-economic] relationships by Classical Political Economy, because of the latter's abstract methodology" (1925: 28; see also 1929: 266ff.). Moreover, the confrontation of the GHS with classical economics on policy issues articulated alternatives and gave the chance to the European governments of the interwar period to comprehend and advance policies that improved the conditions of the lower strata (Kalitsounakis, 1929: 274). Kalitsounakis criticized certain aspects of the historical method, reminding us that historicism could mislead away from a right understanding of economic evolution and process, since "pure economy devoid of economic categories is incomprehensible" (1930b: 187). Thus, economic inquiry should include the essential characteristics of any economy, "not of course in abstracto, but in their historically specified form" (ibid.: 189).

Kalitsounakis was deeply convinced that the economic turbulence of the 1920s bore the seeds of the overthrow of modern capitalism. Orthodox economic policies and the anxiety to restore prewar exchange rates, along with the efforts to restore the gold standard, undermined the stabilisation of the world economy and threatened not only world trade and credit institutions but the very political foundations of modern western states (1925: 231–235). He was of the opinion that the pressing problem of the relative high unemployment experienced in the western world should be remedied through expansionary fiscal policy, a freeze on prices, the containment of inflation and the establishment of all-embracing social insurance and institutions that guarantee the inclusion of the working class in the process of policy formation. Nevertheless, he criticized Schmoller's conviction that business cycles could be efficiently resolved by just injecting credit into the economy, or by an anticyclical economic policy; the duration and vehemence of business cycles indicated for Kalitsounakis a need for a more radical approach, encompassing deeper aspects of economic and political organisation of modern states (1930a: 358ff.). It was only through the close collaboration of employers, employees and the state and the fostering of a cooperative spirit in the economy that economic and social crises could be overcome. It was for that reason that he praised Lujo Brentano for his moderate and pragmatic approach to political-economic issues and his emphasis on social aspects of economic organisation. This approach guaranteed that the Marxian theory of class struggle could "evolve as soon as possible into an advantageous context for the collective" (Kalitsounakis, 1931: 541).[2]

It was not a coincidence that Kalitsounakis favoured the politics of Eleftherios Venizelos, who introduced social policy, a social insurance scheme and labour legislation in Greece.[3] This helped Greek society to avoid "violent social riots, (by) improving the condition of the working masses to the point that is required by our modern civilisation" (Kalitsounakis, 1929: 170). Moreover, he acknowledged that Venizelos's political project was a major step towards economic and political modernization, a much-needed process for the reformation of the Greek economy (Kalitsounakis, 1936).

Kalitsounakis believed that a new era had arrived in economic policy which called for close cooperation between society and the state, a collective action that would "tend to substitute the private with the social economy, whenever this collaboration is not contradicted by economic, technical and other reasons" (1943: 107). This new era was characterised also by a growing trend towards nationalisations, which represented state efforts to coordinate and regulate the economy as a whole. In the period of late capitalism, the involvement of the government in economic activity guaranteed for Kalitsounakis that national and social interests were harmoniously accommodated and social conflicts were avoided (1921: 53, 59, 69).

Kyriakos Varvaressos

The case for enlarging the scope of state action found a powerful and eloquent champion in Kyriakos Varvaressos (1884–1957), who distinguished himself as an expert on economic policy and was second only to Andréadès in prestige and academic status. After completing his PhD in Athens, Varvaressos pursued advanced studies in Berlin (1908–1911), working in parallel as an intern in the Prussian Statistical Office. Upon returning to Greece, he engaged in several official activities, most notably the organisation of Greece's General Statistical Service. He was professor of economics at the University of Athens (1918–1946) and minister of finance after the Greek default in 1932, deputy governor (1933) and governor of the Bank of Greece (1939) and finally deputy prime minister in 1945. According to Varvaressos, political economy should abandon its doctrinal character and become an empirical social science that respects the peculiarities of national economies (1937). Moreover, phenomena such as the business cycle, income disparities among nations and the aggravation of the social question, especially after the Russian Revolution and the Great War, necessitated a reevaluation of the role of the state in economic activity. Varvaressos questioned also the capacity of the classical liberal world system "to be adequate according to modern social views and claims" (1937: 406). For him, the new orthodoxy rejected comparisons with the prewar era and pronounced that the state should intervene to solve not only market failures but also collective action problems. In his words,

> General harmony, as much declared as a necessary effect of the free play of economic forces, is only a mental artifact that does not correspond to real facts. It cannot seriously be doubted that the dominant characteristic of economic competition is opposition rather than commonality of goals and interests
>
> (Ibid.)

The emphasis on the struggle for resources and on socio-economic power rather than on competition and cooperation among economic agents, on political aspects of the economic process and on the historical – that is transient – character of fundamental economic institutions, such as property, all suggested for Varvaressos a reassessment of the role of the state. The government apparatus was the instrument *par excellence* "for the domination of social ends over the private ones [. . .], no matter what political organisation prevails each time" (ibid.: 410). Varvaressos insisted that the economic system he favoured went beyond capitalism and socialism; it was a command economy along the lines of étatisme, an authoritarian state analogous to that envisioned by Sombart (Tamura, 2001: 115–117). He regarded the state as a powerful institution that could control and influence fundamental macroeconomic variables, such as production, prices and wages, in favour of general interests. Private interests should be subordinate to national interests and to the state's priorities in order to build a "powerful national economy [. . . and] serve higher national or political purposes" (ibid.: 409). This antiliberal rhetoric was one of the reasons for his political failure in 1945.

Demosthenes Stefanidis

One of the most hostile opponents of economic liberalism was Demosthenes Stefanidis (1895–1975), professor at the University of Thessaloniki (1928–1945) and the University of Athens (1950–1965). He was a strong critic of classical political economy and free trade theories and a proponent of protectionism, in the tradition of List. Stefanidis studied in Frankfurt with Franz Oppenheimer and inherited from him the organic concept of the state (Oppenheimer, 1926). However, he moved away from Oppenheimer's liberal-land reformer views and adopted an authoritarian outlook blended with influences from economic romanticism. He regarded liberalism as a doctrine propagated internationally by developed countries, not suited to the circumstances of the Greek postwar economy. Stefanidis praised the scientific work done by the younger GHS and exalted the ideal of *Gemeinwirtschaft* (1948–49: 418–419), yet his emphasis was not on the strengthening of social bonds and the protection of the lower social strata but on the reinforcement of the Greek economy. The GHS's inductive and historical approach had decisively shaken the classical hypotheses and diluted the free trade arguments, he believed, rejecting thus the very notion of the value-free science of economics, since "absolute objectivity of the arguments expressed on social and economic issues is non-existent" (ibid.: 82). Hence economic policy was rather a matter of values than principles. The prominence he gave to social and national *power* and his emphasis on the aggressive and competitive character of the global economy were juxtaposed with the premises of the pure theory of foreign trade expressed by classical political economy (ibid.: 379). The decisive element that permeates Stefanidis's *œuvre* is the *national interest*, as the key guiding principle of socio-economic organisation; all the means and goals of economic policy should be subordinated to the imperative of national economic growth. It is not a surprise that Stefanidis was sympathetic to the fascist regimes of Germany and Italy (1937) and openly supported the 1936–1940 Metaxas dictatorship in Greece, since he believed that an autocratic form of governance is better suited to the attainment and protection of national interests.

Xenophon Zolotas

The challenges against liberal ideas were too big to be left unanswered. Just as Andréadès did almost 40 years earlier, the task of vindication of orthodox economics was taken on by a young economist with extensive knowledge of the German economic literature of the time, who was going to be the most important Greek economist in the postwar period, Xenophon Zolotas (1904–2004). Zolotas started his undergraduate studies in Greece and continued at the Handels-Hochschule Leipzig, where he earned his first degree in 1924. He continued at the University of Leipzig, where he got his doctorate in 1925. His supervisor was Ludwig Pohle, a follower of Gustav Cassel, who also exerted a strong influence on Zolotas (Psalidopoulos, 2008). After his return to Greece, Zolotas was appointed professor of economics at the University of Thessaloniki (1928) and later at the University of Athens (1930–1967). He served as governor of the Bank of Greece (1955–1967 and 1974–1981) and as prime minister in 1990–1991. Zolotas was an advocate of the stages of development theory of the GHS. He believed that in the interwar years Greece had entered the industrialization phase. In his later works he always weaved historical insights into his studies (e.g. origins of Greek industrialization, agricultural policy, trade policy), but criticized the GHS for having caused theoretical confusion among professional economists. As a Cassel follower and with arguments close to those used by Lionel Robbins against the institutionalists (Robbins, 1930: 20ff.), he rejected the separation of inductive and deductive methods and defended the classical and neoclassical theories and their theoretical assumptions which integrated, in his view, economics in a solid theoretical framework, enabling the emergence of "a positive economic theory" that "could lead to the development of exact or quasi-exact theories that typically possess economic laws' status" (1934: 17, 21). Zolotas pointed out that economic science in Greece lagged behind the theoretical developments "in economically advanced states, where a strong effort of development and cultivation of economic science is taking place" (1929: 55–56). He chastised the extensive use of the GHS methodology by Greek economists, which undermined the faith in sound liberal principles and fostered contemporary Greek interventionism. He discredited the claims that Greece's industrial backwardness resulted from a supposed adherence to liberal economic policies. Zolotas criticized protectionist policies and the crowding out of the private sector (Zolotas, 1926). Also, he pointed out that the tax system in Greece was burdening the private sector excessively and called for more business-friendly economic policies. He favoured the promotion of infrastructure, investment in human capital and in technological innovation and the liberalisation of the national market. His argumentation gradually gained authority among economic policy makers at the expense of interventionist economists. Zolotas's rise to superior fame after 1955 sealed in a way the withering away of the influence of the GHS in Greece. The traces of the GHS methodology became sparse, and the Anglo-Saxon economic paradigm gradually became the dominant one in post–WWII Greece.

Concluding remarks

In this chapter we offered evidence explaining how and through which institutional and public policy channels ideas related to the GHS were disseminated to Greece. These ideas suited Greek economic policy at that time and found widespread approval. The GHS was foremost the propagator of the German model of economic growth to the rest of Europe, rather than a radical critic of the classical economic model (cf., among others, Kurz, Nishizawa & Tribe, 2011; Psalidopoulos & Mata, 2002). The German economy, along with the American one, stood out in the late nineteenth century as the most dynamic economy of the world and as an archetype of economic modernization for the underdeveloped peripheral European nations. The GHS paradigm stood up to economic liberalism, questioning the ability of liberal economic policy to cope with the pressing economic and financial issues of the late nineteenth century, as was the case with Greece, especially after the default of 1893. Germany was also the model behind another form of the GHS influence: the strength and dynamics of the German economy were identified with German unification, which gave impetus to Greek nationalism. The aspirations for the unification of all Greeks in the Balkans under a Greek state (Great Idea) went hand in hand with the industrialization and modernization of the economy, and the archetype of this ambition was Germany of the Wilhelminian era.

Economics as practiced and taught at Greek universities strongly favoured *induction*; abstract thinking and analytical works were uncommon, and economic research was invariably tied to policy making and the tackling of practical policy challenges, in particular monetary stability, industrialization and public finance.

A striking similarity with the German economic tradition and especially with the GHS was the preoccupation of most Greek economists, academic or not, with practical economic problems and historical analysis, rather than with analytical arguments and theoretical contributions.

The high affinity between the GHS and Greek economists during the interwar period could also be identified on the basis of common scientific practices, most notably the emphasis on historical economic analysis as a "problem-oriented strategy" (Grimmer-Solem & Romani, 1999: 345), focusing on the deeper economic rigidities as well as the political obstacles that impeded the take-off of the Greek economy, especially after the Asia Minor disaster and the 1929 economic crash. In other words, WWI and the Balkan Wars acted as catalysts for the accentuation of the social and national issues which occasionally took the form of antiliberal and pro-interventionist positions. The most striking fact about the German influence on Greek economic thought and policy was that despite the fading of the GHS in Germany, the theoretical attachment of Greek economists to the younger GHS dominated the domestic scene in Greece until the early post–WWII period. In Germany, after 1914, "the aging founders of the *Verein* passed from the scene, [and] they left no coherent system to replace them" (Lindenfeld, 1997: 321). In Greece they dominated in academia and in public discourse for far longer.

Overall, the dominance of historical analysis in the interwar period and the economic policy-oriented approach of the majority of Greek economists of that period mark the transition of Greek economic thought from liberalism to interventionism. This process was a major episode not only in the intellectual but also in the economic and political history of the country. It was an attempt to reform the economic, social and political structures and boost economic growth along the lines of state action, shifting the emphasis from markets to government.

Notes

1 The authors have benefited from comments by Harald Hagemann. The usual disclaimer applies.
2 For the *Arbeiterversicherung* system proposed by Brentano, and his overall views on social policy, see Kaku (2001: 78ff.).
3 A recent appraisal and exposition of Venizelos's economic policy are presented by Psalidopoulos (2014).

References

Andréadès, A. (1924). *History of the Bank of England, 1640 to 1903*. London: King.
Andréadès, A. (1927). Griechenland, in H. Mayer et al. (eds.), *Die Wirtschaftstheorie der Gegenwart*. Vienna: Springer, vol. 1, 236–246.

Andréadès, A. (ed.) (1928). *Les Effets économiques et sociaux de la guerre en Grèce.* Paris: Presses Universitaires de France.

Andréadès, A. (1939). *Works*, ed. by K. Varvaresos, G. Petropoulos & I. Pintos. Athens: University of Athens, vol. 2 (in Greek).

Ben-David, J. (1971). *The Scientist's Role in Society: A Comparative Analysis.* Englewood Cliffs: Prentice Hall.

Betz, H.K. (1997). The Role of Ethics as Part of the Historical Methods of Schmoller and the Older Historical School, in Koslowski (1997): 81–103.

Bigg, R.J. (1987). Andreades, Andreas (1876–1935), in J. Eatwell, M. Milgate & P. Newman (eds.), *The New Palgrave: A Dictionary of Economics.* London: Macmillan, vol. 1, 94.

Blaug, M. (1992). *The Methodology of Economics, or How Economists Explain.* Cambridge: Cambridge University Press.

Clogg, R. (1992). *A Concise History of Greece.* Cambridge: Cambridge University Press.

Gounarakis, N. (1883). *Inaugural Lecture on Political Economy.* Athens: Paligenesia (in Greek).

Gounarakis, N. (1892) [1890]. Inaugural Lecture on Political Economy (October 30, 1890), in *Elements of Political Economy.* Athens: Paligenesia (in Greek), 1–25.

Gounarakis, N. (1913) [1895]. *Elements of Political Economy.* Athens: Petrakos (in Greek).

Grimmer-Solem, E. (2003). *The Rise of Historical Economics and Social Reform in Germany, 1864–1894.* Oxford: Oxford University Press.

Grimmer-Solem, E. & Romani, R. (1999). In Search of Full Empirical Reality: Historical Political Economy, 1870–1900. *European Journal of the History of Economic Thought*, 6 (3): 333–364.

Hagemann, H. & Rösch, M. (2012). Economic Textbooks in the German Language Area, in M.M. Augello & M.E.L. Guidi (eds.), *The Economic Reader: Textbooks, Manuals and the Dissemination of the Economic Sciences during the Nineteenth and Early Twentieth Centuries.* London: Routledge, 96–123.

Kaku, S. (2001). Lujo Brentano on the Compulsory Insurance System for Workers in Germany, in Shionoya (2001): 72–86.

Kalitsounakis, D. (1921). The Present Trends towards Nationalisation. *Archive of Economic and Social Sciences*, 1: 49–72 (in Greek).

Kalitsounakis, D. (1925). *Political Science: Characterisations, Economic, and Social Studies.* Athens: Eleftheroudakis & Barth (in Greek).

Kalitsounakis, D. (1929). *History of Political Economy: Economic History and History of Economic Doctrines.* Athens: Eleftheroudakis (in Greek).

Kalitsounakis, D. (1930a). Economic Forecast – The Pace in Economy: Contribution to the Morphology of Capitalist Society. *Archive of Economic and Social Sciences*, 10: 266–362 (in Greek).

Kalitsounakis, D. (1930b). Werner Sombart and the Systemization of Political Economy. *Archive of Economic and Social Sciences*, 10: 165–212 (in Greek).

Kalitsounakis, D. (1931). Lujo Brentano (18-XII-1844) (9-XI-1931). *Archive of Economic and Social Sciences*, 11: 536–542 (in Greek).

Kalitsounakis, D. (1936). Eleftherios K. Venizelos (1864–1936). *Archive of Economic and Social Sciences*, 16: 99–101 (in Greek).

Kalitsounakis, D. (1943). *Economic Forecast: Contribution to the Morphology of the Capitalist Society*, 2nd ed. Athens: Papazisis.

Kitromilides, P. M. (ed.) (2006). *Eleftherios Venizelos: The Trials of Statesmanship.* Edinburgh: Edinburgh University Press.

Koslowski, P. (ed.) (1997). *The Theory of Ethical Economy in the Historical School: Wilhelm Roscher, Lorenz von Stein, Gustav Schmoller, Wilhelm Dilthey and Contemporary Theory*, 2nd ed. Berlin: Springer.

Kurz, H. D., Nishizawa, T. & Tribe, K. (eds.) (2011). *The Dissemination of Economic Ideas*. Cheltenham: Edward Elgar.

Lindenfeld, D. F. (1997). *The Practical Imagination: The German Sciences of State in the Nineteenth Century*. Chicago: University of Chicago Press.

Mavrogordato, J. (1931). *Modern Greece: A Chronicle and a Survey, 1800–1931*. London: Macmillan.

Oppenheimer, F. (1926) [1908]. *The State: Its History and Development Viewed Sociologically*, trans. J. M. Gitterman. New York: Vanguard Press.

Papanastasiou, A. (1988a) [1908]. Methodological Problems of Economics, in X. Leukoparides (ed.), *Alexandros Papanastasiou: Studies, Speeches, Articles*. Athens: Agricultural Bank of Greece, vol. 1: 4–21.

Papanastasiou, A. (1988b) [1916]. Nationalism, in X. Leukoparides (ed.), *Alexandros Papanastasiou: Studies, Speeches, Articles*. Athens: Agricultural Bank of Greece, vol. 1: 221–258.

Psalidopoulos, M. (1989). *The Crisis of 1929 and the Greek Economists: A Contribution to the History of Economic Thought in Interwar Greece*. Athens: Foundation of the Commercial Bank of Greece for Research and Education (in Greek).

Psalidopoulos, M. (1996). Aristides Economos and the 'Oikonomiki Epitheorissis': The Rise and Fall of an Economic Journal in 19th-Century Greece. *History of Economic Ideas*, 4 (3): 149–167.

Psalidopoulos, M. (2008). *Xenophon Zolotas and the Greek Economy: A Historical Reconstruction*. Athens: Metamesonychties Ekdoseis (in Greek).

Psalidopoulos, M. (2013). Greek Holders of Doctorates in Economics in Interwar Germany, in M. Psalidopoulos (ed.), *Scientific Exchanges among Greece and Germany, 1870–1933*. Athens: Metamesonykties Ekdoseis, 93–113 (in Greek).

Psalidopoulos, M. (2014). New Liberalism and the Economic Policy of Eleftherios Venizelos, in N. Papadakis (ed.), *Eleftherios Venizelos: The Formation of His Political Thought*. Athens: Foundation of the Greek Parliament and Foundation E. Venizelos, 171–192 (in Greek).

Psalidopoulos, M. & Mata, M. E. (eds.) (2002). *Economic Thought and Policy in Less Developed Europe: The Nineteenth Century*. London: Routledge.

Psalidopoulos, M. & Stassinopoulos, Y. (2009). A Liberal Economist and Economic Reform in Nineteenth-Century Greece: The Case of Ioannes Soutsos. *History of Political Economy*, 41 (3): 491–517.

Psalidopoulos, M. & Syrmaloglou, A. (2005). Economists in the Greek Parliament (1862–1910): The Men and Their Views on Fiscal and Monetary Policy, in M. M. Augello & M.E.L. Guidi (eds.), *Economists in Parliament in the Liberal Age: (1848–1920)*. Hampshire: Ashgate, 227–256.

Robbins, L. (1930). The Present Position of Economic Science. *Economica*, 28 (March): 14–24.

Schefold, B. (2010). Putting Development Economics into Historical Perspective: A View from Germany: An Interview with Bertram Schefold. *Revue de la regulation: Capitalisme, institutions, pouvoirs*, no. 7: Institutions, régulation et développement, part 2, 18 June: 1–15. Online.

Shionoya, Y. (1997). A Methodological Appraisal of Schmoller's Research Program, in Koslowski (1997): 57–78.

Shionoya, Y. (ed.) (2001). *The German Historical School: The Historical and Ethical Approach to Economics*. London: Routledge.

Soutsos, I.A. (1851). *Treatise on Production and Distribution of Wealth*. Athens: Koromilas (in Greek).

Soutsos, I.A. (1882–85). *Ploutology*, vols. 1–2, 2nd ed. Athens: Passaris (in Greek).

Stassinopoulos, Y. (2002). Economic Thought and Monetary Policy in Nineteenth-Century Greece, in Psalidopoulos & Mata (2002): 173–186.

Stefanidis, D.S. (1937). *Introduction to Applied Social Economics*. Thessaloniki: Author (in Greek).

Stefanidis, D.S. (1948–49). *Social Economics in Its Historical Evolution*, vols. 1–3. Athens: Author (in Greek).

Tamura, S. (2001). Gustav von Schmoller and Werner Sombart: A Contrast in the Historico-ethical Method and Social Policy, in Shionoya (2001): 105–119.

Varvaressos, K. (1937). The Problem of Economic Organisation. *Gazette of Greek Jurists*, 4 (20–21): 401–410 (in Greek).

Weber, M. (1949). *The Methodology of the Social Sciences*, ed. & trans. by E.A. Shils & H.A. Finch. Glencoe. IL: Free Press.

Zografos, I. (1876). An Essay on Money, in Zografos (1925), vol. 1: 1–88 (in Greek).

Zografos, I. (1878). On Tariffs and Taxation of Currant, in Zografos (1925), vol. 1: 175–230 (in Greek).

Zografos, I. (1925). *Public Finance Studies*, vol. 1–3, 2nd ed. Athens: Hestia (in Greek).

Zografos, I. (1929). *The New Trends in Theoretical Social Economics*. Athens: Greca (in Greek).

Zografos, I. (1934). *Is Economics Passing through a Crisis?* Athens: Zacharopoulos (in Greek).

Zolotas, X. (1926). *Griechenland auf dem Wege zur Industrialisierung*. Leipzig: Teubner.

Zolotas, X. (1929). *The Newer Tendencies of the Theoretical Social Economics*. Athens: Greca (in Greek).

9 A hundred years of German connection in Turkish economic thought

Historismus and otherwise

Eyüp Özveren

Historical background

As of the last quarter of the eighteenth century, the Ottoman Empire came under increasing pressure to adjust itself to the changing circumstances of the world system unfolding under the combined effect of the French and industrial revolutions. To remain as a multiethnic and multireligious large-scale empire, the Ottoman Empire had to transform itself into a modern state. The nineteenth century was the age of this prolonged quest for transformation. During the first three quarters of this century, the Ottoman Empire was placed under the influence of the British and French empires from which much of this exogenous thrust for change originated. However, continuous territorial dismemberment of the Ottoman Empire despite the ongoing process of modernization led to disillusionment. Within this context, the rise of Germany attracted the attention of Ottoman statesmen and offered them a convenient counterweight in international affairs as well as a new hope. As of the third quarter of nineteenth century, the Ottoman Empire voluntarily came under increasing German influence that culminated in the two historic visits of Kaiser Wilhelm II (1884 and 1898). The influx of German military personnel as well as economic projects such as the Baghdad Railway prepared the ground for a convergence of strategic interests (Ortaylı, 1983). It was no surprise that when the hour of the Great European War struck, the Ottoman Empire ended up on the German side. The two empires, together with their Austro-Hungarian ally, fought together and lost together.

This general convergence of historical trajectories helped generate a favorable climate for a parallel process of rapprochement in the realm of economic thought. There was already significant dissatisfaction with liberal economic thought and policy among influential Ottoman intellectuals before the penetration of German influence. This general discontent was to deliver a result within the domain of economic thought from within. The worldwide influential classical economics was thus confronted by what I have dubbed as naïve *Historismus alla turca* elsewhere (Özveren, 2002). If an interaction were to take place between the two parties, however, the Ottomans would benefit much from and could contribute little to the *Historismus* at large. In other words, the two were asymmetrically placed and hence disproportionate in theoretical rigor – hence the concomitant naïveté of the Ottoman *Historismus*. The latter is nevertheless important in two respects. First, no matter how naïve, the mere existence of an Ottoman *Historismus* helps to demonstrate further that *Historismus* at large was not a sheer German intellectual curiosity as already indicated by the presence of an English Historical School,[1] but prompted by the material circumstances of the time. Secondly, Ottoman *Historismus* prepared a favorable ground for a cross-fertilization that would take place in the following stage.

German influence penetrated to Turkish economic thought as late as the early twentieth century, and surprisingly, via an indirect route[2] – that is, Russian intermediation. Akyiğitzade Musa Bey is a critical link in this respect. He taught at the military academy and published two books that advocated trade protectionism, especially with respect to nascent industries, but also insisted on its transitional character, elaborating a case for the 'infant industry' argument (Çavdar, 1992: 131). He was originally from Kazan,[3] implying a different background in schooling or otherwise. It was in Russia that he must have first encountered the work of Friedrich List and *Historismus* (Berkes, 1972: 52–53). However, Musa Bey was not alone. There was also Alexander Israel Helphand (1867–1924), a Russian Jew and revolutionary brought up in Odessa, who obtained a doctorate degree in economics and finance in Basel (1891) with a thesis on recovery from the mishaps of work – a theme of considerable concern to German historical economists. It would be absurd to assume that Helphand was unacquainted with, and entirely uninfluenced by, either List or the followers of *Historismus*. He fled his country after the aborted revolution of 1905. Having developed ties with leading German Marxists during his long sojourns in Germany, he was forced to settle after 1910 in Istanbul, where he exercised considerable influence on some prominent Young Turks. He used the pen name of Parvus from 1912 to 1914. His book on the financial captivity of the Ottoman Empire in the hands of the great powers has been a popular source ever since its publication in 1914. Parvus's ideas resonated in Young Turk publications but especially in the journal *Türk Yurdu*. The concept of 'national economy' gained wide circulation. Based on this idea, Parvus insisted that indigenous economic development should start off with the peasantry (Sencer, 1977: 22, 22n) – a thesis disclosing his affinities with the Russian debates concerning the so-called Agrarian Question. In short, the penetration of German influence via the intermediary atmosphere of Russia served to uplift in quality the nascent Ottoman *Historismus*. As of then, it had become a formidable force to reckon with in the domains of scholarship, policy formulation and informed public opinion at large.

In the wake of World War I, while the Ottoman Empire was brought to the brink of physical destruction and actual dismemberment, in contrast, the intellectual hegemony of this approach was on the verge of completion. The best evidence for this can be found in the writings of Ziya Gökalp (1876–1924), the ideological father of modern Turkish nationalism. He and his colleagues (including Tekin Alp – that is, the Jewish convert Moiz Kohen, 1883–1961) were the advocates of the 'national economy' movement publishing in *Yeni Mecmua* (New Journal). Gökalp's article entitled 'Economic Patriotism' and dated May 9, 1918, summarized for the benefit of the reading public that the science of economics, a synonym for Manchester economics, was in fact the convenient cover for Britain's own version of 'national economy' (Çavdar, 1992: 165). He was the first to put the creation of large-scale industry as an objective for national economic policy. He was well aware of the socially transformative force of big industry *pace* List. Accusing the 'cosmopolitanism' – that is, universalism – of the economics taught in schools, he noted that thanks to the influence of economists like List and John Rae, economists of most nations had already parted ways with the liberal doctrine and now it was the turn of the Turkish economists (Toprak, 1982: 25). His colleague Tekin Alp, publishing in a different issue of the same journal, complained that economics taught at schools was restricted to the liberal school and its committed minds like Leroy Beaulieu and Charles Gide, and ignored economists such as List, Wagner, Schmoller and Philippovich as well as the rising tide of the 'national economy' under the impetus of the Great War (Çavdar, 1992: 176; Toprak, 1982: 25). The complaint was that whereas 'national economy' was being forced on the Ottoman state by policies necessitated by the dire circumstances, the ivory tower of academia withstood the temptation to engage fully with 'national economy' at a theoretical level. Tekin Alp remained an ardent advocate of List and referred to him as the 'economist Bismarck'. Once the 'national economy' perspective was accepted, however, there emerged more subtle divisions among the followers – for example, while Ahmet Muhittin accepted List's model of five stages, Gökalp endorsed Karl Wilhelm Bücher's three-stage scheme of development (Toprak, 1982: 30). This suffices to show that the Ottoman-Turkish awareness of German debates was not superficial.

Gökalp's blueprint for Turkish nationalism, *Türkçülüğün Esasları* (Principles of Turkism), came out in the year of the proclamation of the Turkish Republic. In the section entitled 'Economic Turkish Nationalism', the primacy of big industry and the urgent need for it were reemphasized. This could be attained only by trade protectionism as advocated by the doctrine of 'national economy' traced back to List and Rae. He appealed for the deployment of this doctrine by a ministry of economy as essential for the success of the new regime. Last but not least, he insisted that Turkish economists ought to start elaborating an appropriate theory and policy for their country by extensive stocktaking (Gökalp, 1963 [1923]: 122–23). Expressed shortly before his death, this manifesto for nationalism was also his last will. Gökalp was the head of the commission that met on a regular basis in Ankara during the War of Independence in order to shape an economic policy for the postwar regime. He represents a multidimensional transition between the old generation and the new of Ottoman-Turkish intellectuals, between the Empire and the Republic, between Istanbul and Ankara, as well as between the war-ridden 1910s and the obscure 1920s.

Postwar scene: An *Interregnum* interrupted?

The 1923–1929 period of the Republic witnessed numerous changes. Economic policy came ahead of economic thought because the first objective of governments was to achieve postwar reconstruction. The Treaty of Lausanne did not allow much fiddling with either the trade regime or monetary policy until the end of the 1920s. Because Germany was discredited with defeat, worried Turkish intellectuals looked for inspiration to John Maynard Keynes's *The Economic Consequences of the Peace* (1920), translated soon after its publication by the liberal member of the republican elite, Ali Fethi Okyar, who also served as prime minister. If Turkey were to be reintegrated with the international division of labor through trade according to the principle of comparative advantage, German-Turkish economic relations could not possibly play a significant role. In many ways, what Karl Polanyi called the 'Conservative Twenties' witnessed a search for restoration of the liberal order, the Turkish variant of which was a combination of liberal economic policy and reconstruction as the way to a peaceful reintegration with the world. This is a nutshell summary of also Keynes's vision manifest in his aforementioned book. In this sense, the 1920s remain an obscure decade as far as Turkish economic thought is concerned. This implied a drop also in German academic influence over economic thought, especially in the traditional Ottoman university, *Darülfünun* of Istanbul, where French-educated scholars made a comeback with their liberal creed. Once the delimiting provisions of the Treaty of Lausanne expired and the Great Depression hit the world, there was much more room for genuine policy improvisation backed by explorations in economic thought. However, this was a decade when the *Darülfünun* fell from grace with the new regime because it could not renew itself at a time of rapid social and cultural transformations. The center of gravity of intellectual debates and creativity started shifting to nonacademic platforms, such as journals and associations. We should remind ourselves here that behind this shift was a spatial relocation from Istanbul to Ankara. Ultimately, *Kadro*, a journal published in Ankara, was to campaign for university reform and prepared the basis for the transformation from earlier of the *Darülfünun* to the University of Istanbul in 1933.

Ankara-based *Kadro*, published between 1932 and 1935, was a highly influential journal that generated an intellectual movement. As its name implied, the cadres enlightened by the new journal were expected to shape the new regime's economic and social policy at a time of grave uncertainties in the international political and economic order. The journal was not academic per se, but it filled a vacuum with the high quality and the originality of its contents. The authors involved were of a higher academic quality than, and truly outperformed, many academics in the country. Şevket Süreyya Aydemir was the mentor, and his colleagues were Yakup Kadri Karaosmanoğlu, Vedat Nedim Tör, İsmail Hüsrev Tökin and Burhan Asaf Belge. Of these five names, Şevket Süreyya and İsmail Hüsrev had been to postrevolutionary Moscow in the early 1920s in order to pursue studies[4] in an exemplary party school, whereas Vedat Nedim and Burhan

Asaf had studied in postwar Germany. Vedat Nedim stayed in Berlin and did his PhD (1922) under the supervision of Werner Sombart. He obtained a doctorate in economics. His thesis was on how the Ottoman Empire became a subject of imperialism (Tekeli and İlkin, 2003: 78–80). Already friends with Vedat Nedim from high school, Burhan Asaf studied architecture in Munich and Karlsruhe and sociology at Kassel up until 1923 (Tekeli and İlkin, 2003: 95–96). In short, the *Kadro* members had been exposed directly or indirectly to a German influence. Disclaiming their once underground Marxist background, they adopted the task of crafting a revolutionary doctrine for the new Turkish regime. In their view, the Great Depression, by crippling the metropolitan economies and international trade, offered a golden opportunity for countries like Turkey to appropriate modern technology and to institute it within the context of a planned mixed economy. They envisaged *étatisme* in light of "Weberian and Sombartian theories of rationalization" (Özveren, 1996: 572) as an economic policy serving this end. They argued that one could overcome by such a policy the kind of underdevelopment fostered by the unequal exchange driven international division of labor, thereby prefiguring "post–Second World War dependency approaches" (Özveren, 2002: 141–42).

The *Kadro* authors were quite attentive to events and publications in Germany. In his article "Kreuger, Hitler, Goethe," written shortly before Hitler came to power, Vedat Nedim insisted that the unfolding crisis in Germany was the effect of a worldwide crisis and it would make little difference if either Hitler or the communists came to power insofar as they would remain helpless in the face of it (Tör, 1932b: 29). In a similar vein, a chronicle by Burhan Asaf published in the twelfth issue also referred to the chancellorship of von Schleicher accompanied by an analysis of his program with respect to the deepening crisis. That the economic problem was no longer one of distribution but generation of national income was emphasized (Belge, 1932, 12: 45–46).The fifth issue of *Kadro* came out with a brief note on Sombart's latest work that emphasized the need of Germany for a strong leader like Atatürk, Lenin and Mussolini (*Kadro* 1932, 5: 3–4). In the same issue, Vedat Nedim evaluated Sombart's *Die Zukunft des Kapitalismus* as a confirmation of the *Kadro* viewpoint, and announced that they would soon publish a letter from Sombart to their journal (Tör, 1932a: 37–38). This letter seems never to have arrived. In the sixth issue, an extensive interview with Hans Zehrer, associated with the journal *Die Tat*, was published and a parallelism between the *Kadro* and *Die Tat* was drawn. Much to the content of the *Kadro* authors, Zehrer identified the Turkish revolution as an example for the semicolonial and colonial countries (*Kadro* 1932, 6: 8). In 1933, Burhan Asaf published an article introducing Ernst Wagemann's *Was is Geld?* Burhan Asaf insisted that the *Kadro* had already expressed a desire for a proactive unorthodox monetary policy long before this book had appeared and this was mere affirmation of their monetary point of view (Belge, 1933b: 28–38). Vedat Nedim referred in the journal's pages to the German delegate, Herr Posse, whom he characterized as a self-conscious spokesman for the imperialist camp in the London Conference, who had given Turkey as an example for the industrializing agricultural countries (Tör, 1934: 15). Othmar Spann, noted for his commitment to the corporatist vision of state, also exerted an influence on Kadro's *Étatisme.* The deep interest of *Kadro* authors in German sources and events was abruptly terminated with the rise of Hitler to power. As of then, *Kadro* made no reference to German affairs and put a distance between its position and that of contemporary German authors referred to earlier. For example, Sombart's and Zehrer's rather dubious relations with Nazis must have made them suspect in the eyes of *Kadro* authors who had come from a Marxist background. They swiftly shifted focus from the exploration of a 'Third Way' to the more classical *Historismus.* An anonymous article leading the last issue of 1934–35 had a title revealing the *Historismus* influence at the origins of the *Kadro* perspective. The title translates as follows: "National Economy is an institutional economy" (*Kadro* 1934–35, 35–36: 3–4).

Kadro and Istanbul University

If capable economists chose contributing to the *Kadro* over seeking employment at the *Darülfünun*, this must have had a good reason. The journal was designed in part to fill the vacuum due to the academic indifference and inactivity of mostly Istanbul-based old-fashioned economists. However, *Kadro* authors did not content themselves with this but went ahead and launched a debate over how higher learning should be reformed. Their target was the inactive *Darülfünun.* The *Darülfünun* had by then lost much credit because of both its distanced attitude during the War of Independence and the devaluation of its diploma that resulted in a drop in public demand for enrolment at this practically monopolistic institution of higher learning. After Ankara replaced Istanbul as capital, the importance of the *Darülfünun* also declined significantly. Even after World War II, given the difficult circumstances of procurement of livelihood at a time when employment prospects were low, many chose to go to professional schools modeled after the German *Hochschule* or to the *Mülkiye* (relocated to Ankara to become the Faculty of Political Sciences of Ankara University), renowned for its preferential access to employment in government (Kazgan, 2009: 7–8).

The year before the university reform, Burhan Asaf wrote that the *Darülfünun* was left helplessly behind the times and needed a thorough restructuring (Belge, 1932, I, 8: 48). Criticisms of the *Darülfünun* and attention to the questions of higher learning reached an all-time high level in 1933. Şevket Süreyya published an article on what he dubbed 'Cavit Bey economics', and attacked liberal economics still in vogue among the academia, represented best by the finance minister of the Ottoman Empire, infamous for its financial bankruptcy. Economists of this breed were accused of resisting the new principle of state involvement in economic development. His utmost criticism was, however, academic: academics linked with this institution had proven themselves incapable of research and publication (Aydemir, 1933a: 7–9). He returned to the issues of 'Cavit Bey economics' and 'politics of the chair' in a subsequent piece. Aydemir identified İbrahim Fazıl (Pelin) as the epitome of the old-fashioned liberal economist shaped by French academic influence (Aydemir, 1933a: 11; 1933b: 15). Such 'economists of the chair' were responsible for the sorry state of economics among the academia. He was also the eldest of Turkish economists at the University of Istanbul. This made him the representative of a generation at odds with new ideas.[5]

In 1932, the government invited Professor Albert Malche, an expert in pedagogy of the University of Geneva, to prepare a report on university reform. Meanwhile, the government became excited enough to adopt a more drastic reform than what Malche proposed. It would be far-fetched to think that this outcome was the effect of *Kadro*. But it would be equally absurd to think that the *Kadro* had no influence over the shaping of public opinion concerning this matter. The *Kadro* columnist Burhan Asaf, who authored a retrospective look at this institution, welcomed the government decision (Belge, 1933a: 96). In a follow-up article, he expressed his desire that the new Istanbul University should renounce ivory tower academics and engage instead in the shaping of national policies together with the public (Belge, 1933c: 25–28).

To make the case for a thorough reform all the more pointed, the *Kadro* publishers summoned Dr. Muhlis Etem Ete of Istanbul University to contribute to their journal. Dr. Ete was a German-educated member of faculty who had been quite critical of the liberal establishment economics. He had studied at Leipzig and the Berlin Hochschule. In an article titled 'Economists of the Chair and the Science of Economics in Turkey' he observed that because of the inflexibility of the former structure of the *Darülfünun*, economics had been forced to develop outside of the academic milieu. Within the university, whatever existed of economics had to be liberated now from the confines of the Faculty of Law and be organized under a new independent Faculty of Economics. In addition to this organizational innovation, the content of economics taught ought to be revised in favor of the 'national economy' doctrine (Ete, 1933: 45–46). German-educated Dr. Ete was thus under the influence of List and his followers. As a matter of fact, he expressed his desire that the new Faculty of Economics should be emancipated from French influence and be shaped after the German model. A bifocal program in economics should aim at training both theorists and practitioners. This was all put into writing before the influx of German scholars. Even before *Kadro* was initiated, however, İsmail Hüsrev, of the founding team, had published a pamphlet (Tökin, 1931) on how economics should be taught. He was Soviet-educated, yet his proposals bore the mark of exemplary German practice.

German-speaking scholars at the Faculty of Economics

The University of Istanbul was inaugurated in October 1933. In the course of this transformation, a significant number of scholars were laid off while others were recruited. This process was facilitated by the rise to power of Nazis in Germany and their annexation of Austria (later in 1938), which paved the way to the dismissal and resignation of numerous scholars, who looked for employment opportunities elsewhere, including Istanbul. Atatürk was personally engaged in this recruitment process and corresponded with Albert Einstein, who sought his assistance in the employment of his German-speaking colleagues. The Turkish side was primarily interested in getting the most competent academics. Neither the political positions nor the ethnic origins of potential recruits were of any interest to the Turks. With this primarily educational motive in mind, they disliked any interference by third parties (Neumark, 2008b: 133). The Nazi government occasionally suggested providing 'better' scholars to displace these supposedly 'incompetent dissidents' as assistance to the Turkish government, whom it purportedly befriended (Scurla, 2008: 91). Such offers were turned down because the Turkish side feared that these candidates would, in fact, be incompetent. As for the nature of the employment contract, the Turkish government did not exploit to its own advantage the political misfortunes of the exiles. They were offered substantially better salaries than Turkish nationals. Exiles were expected to demonstrate a genuine effort to learn Turkish in the near future so as to both teach and publish in Turkish.

Because there was no independent Faculty (or Department) of Economics before the reform, few scholars were employed in this field, and even fewer dismissed. It was quite easy for German-speaking recruits to shape their new work environment according to their own preferences. Six recruits to the would-be Faculty of Economics were: (1) Wilhelm Röpke (1899–1966), a professor of political science at Marburg University, who was fired in 1933 because of his anti-Nazi stance as early as 1930. He was appointed as professor to one chair in economics. Having been unable to learn Turkish, he felt culturally alienated until he found a post at Geneva and left in 1937. He was retrospectively identified as one of the founders of the 'social market economy' doctrine. (2) Fritz Neumark (1900–1991), a professor at Frankfurt, was dismissed in 1933 because of Nazi anti-Semitism. He came to Istanbul with his family and was appointed to the second chair in economics. He mastered Turkish and eventually was noted for his highly esteemed 'Ottoman' Turkish.[6] Until İbrahim Fazıl's death, they shared sections of the course in fiscal economics (Neumark, 2008a: 83). In 1946, he was appointed as the head of the new Fiscal Institute, played an advisory role in the making of new legislation concerning taxes and stayed in Turkey until 1950, when he first returned to Germany as a visiting professor. (3) Gerhard Kessler (1883–1963), a professor of sociology at Leipzig University, had been involved in anti-Nazi politics and journalism and was forced to leave in 1933. He had given an oral examination to Neumark at Leipzig, where the latter defended a thesis on inflation; as such, they knew each other (Neumark, 2008a: 79). He stayed in Turkey until 1951. He contributed greatly to the development of the library of economic and social sciences. In 1946 he was active in setting up together with Orhan Tuna the first postwar official Turkish trade union. (4) Alexander Rüstow (1885–1963), a sociologist at Berlin Hochschule, left Germany in 1933 because the *Gestapo* was after him. At the University of Istanbul, he served as a professor of economic history. He could not master Turkish nor could he adapt himself culturally until 1949. Even so, he wrote his *Ortsbestimmung der Gegenwart* while in Istanbul. He was also active in anti-Nazi activities during the war. (5) Josef Dobretsberger (1903–1970) was a former Austrian cabinet minister and a professor at Graz University. He came in 1938 and stayed until 1941, when, feeling no longer secure in Turkey, he headed for Palestine. What prompted his departure was the appointment of Franz von Papen, whom he had already insulted in Vienna, as the Nazi ambassador to Ankara. Dobretsberger was hired to replace Röpke as the chair of general theory of economics and finance. (6) Alfred Isaac (1888–1956), a professor of management, fired from his post at Nurnberg because of anti-Semitic policies, arrived in 1937. He eventually acquired sufficient Turkish and assumed a leading role in setting up the management program (Hoss, 2008). The German faction thus constituted the more important group of the faculty members in economics, with relatively higher titles of academic rank.

There exist two important eyewitness accounts of the Faculty of Economics, one by Neumark (2008a), who stayed longest and played the most important role in shaping the program, and the other by the prominent Turkish economist Gülten Kazgan (2009), who became a student in the program shortly after World War II, at a time when Neumark was still teaching. She had thus been an eyewitness to the mature state of the program about a decade after its creation. Kazgan came to the University of Istanbul from the American College for Girls in Istanbul – in Kazgan's words, an 'exceptional' institution that far outperformed its well-known counterparts in the United States. Not only did Kazgan master English (and French) before coming to the university, but also she was capable of critical inquiry. Moreover, she had already been introduced to the influence of economics and social sciences (Kazgan, 2009: 4). This made her superior to her peers. She had much less to learn than they did. Kazgan evaluates this phase of her university life in light of her later academic experience at the University of Chicago in the 1950s. This retrospective evaluation, relying on an unrepresentative yardstick, leads to unfavorable conclusions. We nevertheless think Kazgan's observations concerning education and program are useful to contrast Neumark's remarks. Our following reassessment of the role of German refugees in the development of the Faculty of Economics is based on a critical reading of these two memoirs jointly.

Among the economists concerned, the majority was like Röpke and Rüstow – not to mention Kessler – who were deeply liberal in "heart and mind", as Neumark put it (Neumark, 2008a: 27). Probably it would be correct to add Neumark himself to this camp ideologically, even though he was open to Keynesian theoretical improvisations. There were, of course, differences of degree, as for example between Röpke, who ignored Keynes's impact after 1936 and remained a staunch liberal right to the end, suspicious of fiscal policy as indicating state socialism, and Neumark, who revised his position substantially on this issue (Neumark, 2008a: 78). There was also Kessler, a centrist under the influence of the German Historical School via his education under Wilhelm Stieda and Karl Bücher at Leipzig (Neumark, 2008a: 79). He was far more lenient towards social policy and state interventionism. Neumark speaks of him as the Prussian version of the Austrian Dobretsberger. Dobretsberger was a Catholic with strong leftist social and political leanings, a factor that contributed to his choice of research focus. The influence of Hans Kelsen, the philosopher and scholar of public law, together with that of Carl Menger and Eugen von Böhm-Bawerk of the Austrian School, had made an impression on him. It is no wonder that he applied with recommendation letters from Kelsen and Ludwig von Mises (Neumark, 2008a: 85–87). It would nevertheless be impossible to speak of a political difference of opinion among them that would impede their joint contribution to the reform process of the university. They were all, more or less, liberals, if one interprets liberalism loosely so as to imply more a political democratic than a die-hard economic stand. Ludwig von Mises's brother, Richard von Mises, a professor of mathematics and probability, was also a member of the community of exiles and refugees in Istanbul. Once he asked Neumark's opinion of his brother's reputation in economics. Neumark's reply reveals this clearly. He expressed that Ludwig von Mises was one of the last defenders of the classical liberal line identified with Ricardo, Say and Bastiat. Moreover, while Neumark acknowledged the importance of Mises's contributions to monetary theory, they differed sharply in opinions concerning both theory and its policy implications. Neumark found von Mises's views extreme and much at odds with the reality of the times.[7] In this sense, German-speaking economists in Istanbul knew where to draw the line between soft and strong versions of liberalism.

German refugees in Turkey: A mixed legacy?

From Neumark's account we infer two basic facts. First, all German-speaking scholars were academically competent and self-proven in their fields. Secondly, they benefited from their stay in Istanbul. For example, Röpke, who had the greatest cultural adjustment problems and left for Switzerland at the end, drafted several of his most important works during this stay. The same was true of Rüstow's three-volume magnum opus.[8] During their exile in Istanbul, these scholars had the time and the means to pursue important research and writing projects that would bear the fruits of international recognition. On the supply (of academics) side, employment in Istanbul had a positive balance sheet. On the demand side – that is, from the viewpoint of the Turkish authorities – the refugees gave a new impetus to the reform. Among the few native faculty members teaching economics prior to the arrival of exiles, there were the older Ömer Celal Sarç, who had done his PhD with Werner Sombart in Germany, and the younger Muhlis Etem Ete, whom we have seen earlier as well acquainted with the German system. In addition, there was Sabri Ülgener, the youngest of all, who knew German well thanks to his high school education at the Istanbul Boys' High School, and had read Sombart's but especially Max Weber's books (Neumark, 2008a: 125). Hence the refugees contributed to the speed of the reform, which would have taken place in any case. However, the availability of qualified and reputable German-speaking scholars gave the upper hand to the government in combating the reform-resistant faction of native academia not so much in economics but overall. In short, a positive overall balance applied to the demand side as well.

The mutually beneficial nature of the process should not obscure the fact that it was not the best of all possible worlds. First, there was the linguistic barrier. It made communication difficult and slow. Röpke and Neumark were lucky enough to have capable scholars like Sarç and Ete assigned to them as interpreters because of their German proficiency. Even so, there were times when even highly fluent German-educated translators like Ete felt incapable of translating, all the more so when students' comments or questions were concerned (Neumark, 2008a: 136). Another rare but extreme example is how Kessler's characterization of Marx was mistranslated so as to indicate that Marx was an enemy of the working class. Ülgener, then a student in the same class with a good knowledge of German, recounted how surprised he was to see that no one noticed this mistake, including his cousin and classmate Mehmet Ali Aybar, the future leader of the Workers' Party of Turkey! (Sayar, 1998: 53). In a similar vein, Kazgan remembers well that whereas a few like Neumark eventually mastered the language to lecture well enough, others continued to teach in German and be translated even after the war was over. For example, Isaac, though lecturing in Turkish, was so incapable of expressing himself that his assistant had to repeat virtually everything. Rüstow was another case in point. He lectured in German and was fortunate enough to be interpreted by Halit İlberer, a translator with a PhD. Even so, this impeded direct contact between the professor and students and, moreover, was a waste of class time. Kazgan recounts how, while Rüstow lectured in German, she would read another book in order to make use of her time, because she was already taught "Time is money!" in the American College (Kazgan, 2009: 11). Kazgan lists Kessler among the faculty from whom she benefited most because he spoke French well and taught his seminar courses in this third language. These seminars were mostly attended by students who had come from the prestigious Galatasaray Lycée, where the medium of instruction is French (Kazgan, 2009: 12).

The obligation to teach either by means of translation or in a foreign language made the subject matter appear oftentimes far less complex than it actually was. Consequently, topics of major importance were occasionally reduced to a caricature. This affected the quality of education negatively. When combined with the weakness of the educational background of students, this meant that German-speaking faculty had to teach much less than what they actually knew. Kazgan's remark about Rüstow is telling in this respect. Kazgan states that many years later she came to know that Rüstow was a reputable economist who had contributed to the conjuncture theory (Kazgan, 2009: 11). When virtually no mathematics was deployed and verbal description – in fact, dictation – remained the basic means of instruction, the lowest common denominator was inevitably rolled back to the very basics identified rightly or wrongly with the Historical School. In retrospect, Kazgan, among other things, being a historian of economic thought, associates the impression German scholars left on her with the broadly defined legacy of the German Historical School, including also a touch of its lesser

Austrian counterpart concerned with law. She adds that she and her peers could not understand properly either the German Historical School or the Austrian marginalists. She recounts how for a full semester, Neumark lectured on the concept of *Bedarf*, the meaning of which nobody conceived. When they finally realized that it was to do with 'needs', they fell short of linking this concept with price formation (Kazgan, 2009: 14).[9] While Neumark himself was no professed follower of the *Historismus*, his discussion of *Bedarfen* betrays the formative influence of his cultural and educational background on his teaching (Neumark, 1948: 101–27). After the war, when Sabri Ülgener of Istanbul University met Joseph Schumpeter at Harvard, they talked about the faculty at Istanbul. Schumpeter expressed dissatisfaction with the names Ülgener listed because he saw them as more or less under the influence of the German Historical School in general and, to a certain extent, of Sombart, whom he despised. Hence, Schumpeter also treated the German-speaking scholars at Istanbul as a bunch.[10] It is interesting to note that Schumpeter did not distinguish Neumark from the crowd. Neumark had replaced Schumpeter at Bonn in 1932. In 1938 he corresponded with Schumpeter in order to explore his employment prospects in the United States. Although Schumpeter responded most politely, he did not extend a helping hand (Neumark, 2008a: 177). When Neumark's account is interpreted together with the meaningful silence identified in Ülgener's memoirs of his meeting with Schumpeter, one might be compelled to think that the latter chose to stay away from assisting Neumark wholeheartedly.

The German-speaking faculty were obliged to teach not only much less than what they knew but also quite often topics different from what they were most competent in. For example, Röpke, assigned to the chair of economics, was obliged to teach economic geography according to his contract. After a while, he was allowed also to teach economic history and sociology (Neumark, 2008a: 82). Even making Röpke teach economic history at a program where the Turkish national Ömer Lütfü Barkan also served was also not the wisest decision. Kazgan remembers how Rüstow also had to teach economic geography, a course in which the numbers of certain kinds of economically useful animals in Turkey were covered time and again, so much so as to lead to a favorite joke among a generation of students who had survived a malaria-ridden wartime Turkey, the joke being the actual number of mosquitoes being asked as an exam question (Kazgan, 2009: 18). Last but not least, Neumark himself was originally contracted to teach (social) health economics and statistics. When he objected on the grounds that he was not qualified for the task, he was told that the contract was a pretext and what really mattered was whether he wished to teach higher-level courses to do with the science of economics, an argument to which he succumbed. Even so, he was forced to teach statistics for a few semesters; but again in this program there was also Ömer Celal Sarç, a most competent statistician in Neumark's words (Neumark, 2008a: 82–83). This misfit between qualifications and assignments implied a second-best use of available human resources.[11] As a result, the actual contribution of German-speaking scholars to higher learning remained considerably lower than what one might have expected.

There was one area where the German-speaking academics made a significant contribution, and that was the development of educational and research infrastructure and teaching material. The employment contract of these scholars included a clause according to which they were expected to write at least one textbook. A remarkable progress had been achieved in less than two decades by Germans as well as by Turkish nationals. The track record of this progress is only partially glimpsed in the bibliography of the second edition of Neumark's own book (1948). Works cited as in Turkish include contributions by Röpke (1937) and Dobretsberger (1938–39), but also translations of Gide (1937) and Truchy (1940–42). Neumark also enlists the works of Turkish colleagues, such as Pelin (1927–33), Baban (1944), Suvla (1945) and Kuyucak (1947). Along with the Germans came another novelty of the times – that is, the proper referencing of one's sources. German scholars also contributed numerous articles to the newly created faculty journal. The quality of the journal increased dramatically with original contributions. Last but not least, the creation of a specialized library under the guidance of Kessler was a most important accomplishment, with long-term formative influence on the minds of many future researchers. The contents of this library played a significant role in shaping the research orientation of the coming generation of Turkish scholars, at least until the 1960s. In this way, German influence perpetuated itself even after the departure of the refugees. Kazgan recounts how Kessler himself filled the library catalogue cards in his own handwriting. Years later, while she wrote her book on the history of economic thought, she used many of those original catalogue cards (Kazgan, 2009: 12).

Looking back in time, Kazgan singles out the strong presence of a sense of economic history as the most important effect of German-speaking scholars on the tradition now identified with the Faculty of Economics. Most distinguished scholars of this institution remained essentially history-friendly in their careers if not outright becoming economic and social historians, like Barkan, Ülgener, Halil Sahillioğlu and Sencer Divitçioğlu. Barkan must have had a major role in this, but so did the legacy of German scholarship with the Historical School in its formative background (Kazgan, 2009: 9). That this university has hosted the Institute for Social and Economic History all along testifies to the strength of history and social policy as the preferential fields of scholarly specialization, at least until the 1980s. Quite often, as far as their overall impact is concerned, the original contributions to social and economic history that originated from the Faculty of Economics outflanked those from the Department of History of the University of Istanbul.

Conclusion

German influence on Turkish economic thought was far more deep-rooted than the effect of German-speaking economists who found for themselves an island of refuge at the University of Istanbul. It is also not reducible to the effect of the German Historical School per se. In the minds of the people on the Ottoman-Turkish side, German influence meant automatically the same thing as that of *Historismus*, be that because either they wrongly simplified everything or they were most attuned to embrace the historical approach to development-related problems of the long term. As far as the other party and retrospectively involved third parties, such as historians of economic thought, are concerned, things looked different. Because German influence came to Turkey relatively late and stayed longer – that is, well into the 1940s – and by that time, *Historismus* was already experiencing a decline within its home-land as other approaches and diversity thereof tended to proliferate on the eve of Nazi rise to power, they rightly hesitate to attribute the greater part of the German influence in question to *Historismus* per se. Therefore, what seemed as *Historismus* from Turkey was already a much more diversified German influence from without, and *Historismus* looked like déjà vu to some of its carriers as well.

In a nutshell, German influence in general, but especially *Historismus* in particular, appeared relatively late in the nineteenth century but grew on a solid local tradition. It was in tune with the strong demands for economic development. Because development as a problem persisted, so did the German influence well into the 1930s. In its final phase, it was given a new rigor by the refugee economists, most of whom had already outgrown the teachings of the Historical School and at the least had adopted or elaborated an eclectic variant. They were put into the straightjacket of the German Historical School by serious misunderstanding and oversimplification on the part of their students and colleagues. Nevertheless, the seeds they cultivated had a lasting effect and inevitably bore the German imprint. The social policy emphasis of the Historical School was of a much smaller relevance in the case of Turkey, at least until the postwar period. It nevertheless also made a symbolic contribu-tion to labor legislation when the circumstances became ripe for it in the post-1945 era.

Caught in turmoil, the refugee scholars seemed unaware that they had German and German-inspired predecessors on this foreign soil. Prereform education at Istanbul University has been seen in the existing literature as more shaped by French mentality and influence. This may have been an effect of the fact that the German presence in the postreform transformation has been so strongly felt as to obscure the prereform level of German engagement at the *Darülfünun* at a time when economics was still taught under the Faculties of Law and Literature. However, records of the *Darülfünun* indicate that German scholars, such as Professor Flek and Professor Hoffmann, were hired at the Faculty of Law of this institution of higher learning as early as 1924 – that is, during the first decade of the Republic. They must have had an influence on the curriculum. Their scholarly profiles and role in shaping the content of economics taught remain yet to be researched. We should note here that there exists virtually no reference to them in the writings of their German successors. Being a further link in the chain of German influence, the refugee scholars were unaware of either the chain itself or its previous links.

Last but not least, the refugee scholars seem to have remained equally unaware of the Ankara-based *Kadro* economists, who had become a strong pole of attraction for debates over the future of economics and who were much more prone to direct identification with the legacy of the German Historical School. This is no surprise if we remind ourselves that they were transplanted to a foreign soil by an avalanche at a time when the concern with the day-to-day unfolding of world events forced upon them an unhistorically myopic focus. In spite of this, if they left behind a strong legacy of history-conscious economics, this betrays the inerasable formative effect of *Historismus* on their minds, regardless of whether they wished it. Even so, *Historismus* influence in Turkey worked at least as much through native scholars who volunteered to spread the message as through German refugees, who were often the involuntary bearers of this dissemination process by virtue of their own training and mind-sets.

Notes

1 There exists no evidence for any direct influence of the English Historical School on Ottoman-Turkish economists for the period under study.
2 This is somewhat paradoxical as one might have expected resident German personnel to play an important role. The convergence of Ottoman and German economic ideas and policy proposals suggests that informal channels of communication may have served to cultivate this accord. However, little evidence exists of such a process at work. Neither memoirs left behind nor published sources indicate such a connection. For example, we know that German field marshal Count Helmuth von Moltke had been in the Ottoman Empire from 1835 until 1839. This was when the Anglo-Ottoman Commercial Treaty of 1838 was signed and the Reform Edict of *Tanzimat* was proclaimed. From the nature of his undertakings and his deep interest in railways after his return to Germany, where he served as the chief of the general staff for 30 years, we understand that he must have been informed about Friedrich List's work (Berkes, 1978: 205–206).
3 Economic development under way in Kazan attracted much attention, including that of Max Weber, who felt compelled to qualify his position concerning the relationship between a religion and economic action: "Industrialization was not impeded by the Islam as the religion of individuals – the Tartars in the Russian Caucasus are often very 'modern' entrepreneurs – , but by the religiously determined structure of the Islamic *states*, their officialdom and their jurisprudence" (Weber, 1978: 1095).
4 Whereas Aydemir was compelled to terminate his studies after his second year, Tökin completed the three-year program and obtained a degree in economics that qualified him to become a lecturer (Tekeli and İlkin, 2003: 62, 109).
5 Pelin was characterized as a "Stone Age liberal" by Alexander Rüstow (Neumark, 2008a: 83). In this way he became an easy target for the *Kadro* authors as well as for the German-speaking economists. This treatment of Pelin is not completely fair. In his *İktisat*, a textbook published in 1933, he relied mainly on French sources and was mainly influenced by the French economist Charles Gide, to whom he referred time and again. Even so, he also referred to Gustav Schmoller on the historical statistics of Germany (Pelin, 1933, 2: 234). Especially his lengthy discussion of the debate over protectionism versus free trade gave due emphasis to the views of Friedrich List (and John Carey) and ultimately concluded, unsurprisingly by occasional recourse to Gide, that time was ripe for a synthesis in the grey tones rather than a full commitment to the extreme formulation of either cases – unbefitting for a "stone age liberal" (Pelin, 1933, 2: 77–95).

6 According to Kazgan, Neumark spoke Ottoman Turkish quite well after a while. Ottoman Turkish was largely used by the pretentious elderly elite able to deploy a sophisticated Persian and Arabic vocabulary (Kazgan, 2009: 14).

7 Neumark recounts an incident reported to him by Röpke. According to Röpke, before the war, the two had conversed on the prospects of war and exile. In that context, Mises had voiced his naïve belief in liberalism by posing a rhetorical question as to whether fascism and Hitlerism could have risen if only Cobden had been able to make his views fully accepted 100 years ago! Cobden was not only an ardent advocate of the Anti-Corn Law League and free-trade doctrine but also a fierce enemy of labor security and trade-union legislations (Neumark, 2008a: 97–98).

8 The same is true with Neumark, who had to teach history of economic thought, which he enjoyed most. Upon his return to Germany, he stood out among his peers as competent in this subfield. He admits that his 1975 article in the prestigious *Kyklos* grew out of the ideas that first occurred to him while at Istanbul University (Neumark, 2008a: 84).

9 Interestingly enough, the lengthy discussion of this concept also occupies an important place in Neumark's textbook, *Genel Ekonomi Teorisi* (General Economic Theory), written in Turkish, in which he maintains a distinction between the Turkish word for 'need' (*ihtiyaç*) and *Bedarf*, which he preserves in his text in the original German word. No Anglo-American or French textbook of the same period would have given equal weight to such an elaboration.

10 Ülgener mentions how excited Schumpeter was when he heard that the Italian economist Umberto Ricci had also been there. Schumpeter characterized him as a "great scholar" and then went on speaking about his connection as the last in the chain to the Walras-Pareto-Panteleoni lineage (Sayar, 1998: 98–99). German scholars had a certain cultural cohesion irrespective of their purely theoretical differences that impacted upon the design and priorities of the program at the Faculty of Economics, which unintentionally excluded the neoclassical-minded Ricci. Kazgan remembers being told by her seniors that Ricci had left because he could not get along well with the Germans. Because there was no one else to teach neoclassical economics voluntarily after Ricci, her generation was educated without seeing either a demand curve or a supply curve, not to mention the determination of the equilibrium price. When they were finally introduced to Keynesian economics in their final year, they could make no sense of it, because they were not familiar with neoclassical economics, which it presupposed and criticized (Kazgan, 2009: 13).

11 The same was true on the Turkish side as PhD-holding Sarç and Ete were assigned to Röpke and Neumark as translators. After a while, they themselves said that they could not continue as translators, as they had better things to do. Röpke and Neumark, still not being proficient in Turkish, had to teach their courses in either German or French or even in English, depending on the available translator (Neumark, 2008a: 134).

References

Aydemir, Ş. S. (1933a). Darülfünun, İnkılap Hassasiyeti ve Cavit Bey İktisatçılığı [*Darülfünun*, Sensitivity for the Revolution and the Economics of Cavit Bey]. *Kadro*, 14: 5–11.

Aydemir, Ş. S. (1933b). Don Kişotun Yeldeğirmenlerile Muharebesine, Kürsü Politikacılığına, ve Cavit Bey İktisatçılığına Dair [On Don Quixote's Battle with the Windmills, Politics of the Chair and the Economics of Cavit Bey]. *Kadro*, 17: 9–15.

Belge, B. A. (1932). Kronikler [Chronicles]. *Kadro*, 12: 45–46.

Belge, B. A. (1933a). Arkada Kalan Darülfünun'un Başına Gelenler [Whatever Has Happened to *Darülfünun* that Remained behind the Times]. *Kadro*, 18: 95–96.

Belge, B.A. (1933b). Para Tezimiz ve Prof. Wagemann [Our Monetary Thesis and Prof. Wagemann]. *Kadro*, 14: 28–38.

Belge, B.A. (1933c). Üniversitenin Manası [The Meaning of University]. *Kadro*, 20: 24–28.

Berkes, N. (1972). Ekonomik Tarih ile Teori Açısından Türkiye'de Ekonomik Düşünün Evrimi [The Evolution of Economic Thought in Turkey from the Viewpoint of Economic History and Theory], in F. Görün (ed.), *Türkiye'de Üniversitelerde Okutulan İktisat Üzerine* [On Economics Thought at the Universities in Turkey]. Ankara: Orta Doğu Teknik Üniversitesi, 39–55.

Berkes, N. (1978). *Türkiye'de Çağdaşlaşma* [Secularism in Turkey]. Istanbul: Doğu-Batı Yayınları.

Çavdar, T. (1992). *Türkiye'de Liberalizm (1860–1990)* [Liberalism in Turkey (1860–1990)]. Ankara: İmge.

Ete, M.E. (1933). Bizde Kürsü İktisatçıları ve İktisat İlmi [Economists of the Chair and the Science of Economics among Us]. *Kadro*, 23: 45–51.

Gökalp, Z. (1963) [1923]. *Türkçülüğün Esasları* [Principles of Turkism]. Istanbul: Varlık Yayınları.

Hoss, C. (2008). Sürgün Yolları: Scurla Raporu'nda Adı Geçen Mültecilerin ve Ailelerinin Sürgün Öyküsü [Roads to Exile: The Exile Story of Refugees and Their Families Whose Names Were Mentioned in the Scurla Report], in F. Şen (ed.), *Ayyıldız Altında Sürgün* [Exile under the Moon and the Crescent]. Istanbul: Günizi Yayıncılık, 143–247.

Kazgan, G. (2009). *Bir İktisatçının Tanıklıkları* [The Testimonies of an Economist]. Istanbul: Istanbul Bilgi Üniversitesi Yayınları.

Keynes, J.M. (1920). *Versay Sulhunun Netayic-I İktisadiyyesi [The Economic Consequences of the Peace*, transl. by A. F. Okyar]. Ankara: Matbuat ve İstihbarat Matbaası.

Neumark, F. (1948). *Genel Ekonomi Teorisi* [General Economic Theory]. Istanbul: Hak Kitabevi.

Neumark, F. (1975). Zyklen in der Geschichte ökonomischer Ideen. *Kyklos*, 28: 257–85.

Neumark, F. (2008a). *Boğaziçi'ne Sığınanlar: Türkiye'ye İltica Eden Alman Bilim, Siyaset ve Sanat Adamları (1933–1953)* [Refugees to Bosphorus: German Scientists, Politicians and Artists Who Sought Exile in Turkey (1933–1953)]. Istanbul: Neden.

Neumark, F. (2008b). Scurla Raporu Üzerine Eleştirel Notlar [Critical Notes on the Scurla Report], in F. Şen (ed.), *Ayyıldız Altında Sürgün* [Exile under the Moon and the Crescent]. Istanbul: Günizi Yayıncılık, 131–42.

Ortaylı, İ. (1983). *Osmanlı İmparatorluğunda Alman Nüfuzu* [German Influence on the Ottoman Empire]. Istanbul: Kaynak Yayınları.

Özveren, E. (1996). The Intellectual Legacy of the *Kadro* Movement in Retrospect. *METU Studies in Development*, 23, 4: 565–76.

Özveren, E. (2002). Ottoman Economic Thought and Economic Policy in Transition: Rethinking the Nineteenth Century, in M. Psalidopoulos and M. E. Mata (eds.), *Economic Thought and Policy in Less Developed Europe*. London: Routledge, 129–44.

Pelin, İ.F. (1933). *İktisat* [Economics]. Istanbul: Arkadaş Matbaası.

Sayar, A.G. (1998). *Bir İktisatçının Entellektüel Portresi: Sabri F. Ülgener* [The Intellectual Portrait of an Economist: Sabri F. Ülgener]. Istanbul: Eren.

Scurla, H. (2008). Alman Yüksekokul Hocalarının Türk Yüksekokullarındaki Faaliyetleri [The Activities of German Faculty in Turkish Schools of Higher Learning], in F. Şen (ed.), *Ayyıldız Altında Sürgün* [Exile under the Moon and the Crescent]. Istanbul: Günizi Yayıncılık, 47–119.

166 *Eyüp Özveren*

Sencer, M. (1977). Parvus'un Yaşam ve Kişilik Dialoğu [The Life and Identity Dialogue of Parvus] in P. Efendi (ed.), *Türkiye'nin Mali Tutsaklığı* [Financial Captivity of Turkey]. Istanbul: May Yayınları, 7–26.

Tekeli, İ. and Selim, İ. (2003). *Bir Cumhuriyet Öyküsü: Kadrocuları ve Kadro'yu Anlamak* [A Story to Do with Republic: Understanding the *Kadro* and Its Adherents]. Istanbul: Tarih Vakfı Yurt Yayınları.

Tökin, İ.H. (1931). *İktisat Nasıl Okutulmalı?* [How Should Economics Be Taught?]. Ankara: n.p.

Toprak, Z. (1982). *Türkiye'de "Milli İktisat" (1908–1918)* ['National Economy' in Turkey]. Ankara: Yurt Yayınları.

Tör, V.N. (1932a). (Kadro)yu Teyit Eden Bir Eser: *Die Zukunft des Kapitalismus* – Werner Sombart [A Work Confirming *Kadro*: *Die Zukunft des Kapitalismus* – Werner Sombart]. *Kadro*, 5: 37–38.

Tör, V.N. (1932b). Kreuger, Hitler, Goethe. *Kadro*, 4: 26–30.

Tör, V.N. (1934). İktisatta İstiklal [Independence in Economics]. *Kadro*, 22: 14–18.

Tör, V.N. (1934–35). Ulusal ökonomya kurumlu ekonomyadır [National Economy Is an Institutional Economy]. *Kadro*, 35–36: 3–4.

Weber, M. (1978). *Economy and Society*. Vol. 2. Berkeley: University of California Press.

10 Sweden and the historical school

Eight scholars going to Germany, 1874–1908

Benny Carlson

Introduction

During the period between the Franco-Prussian War and World War I, Sweden was under the influence of intellectual and political currents emanating from the German Empire. In Sweden, as in many other countries, this heritage was for a long time tucked out of view, since it had lost much of its splendour after the defeat of the "German model" in WWI.[1] As of lately, interest has begun to awaken and influences from the German Historical School (GHS) and its social gospel have been investigated from different angles, not least the impact on social scientists (Carlson, 1995, 2002; Wisselgren, 2000). That Bismarck's social reforms from the 1880s gave impetus to legislation in Sweden is generally agreed upon (see e.g. Edebalk, 2013).

The period when British classical doctrines dominated the scene "was hardly a glorious time for political economy in Sweden" (Sandelin et al., 2008: 63). The GHS ideas had emerged when Germany entered into the industrial "take-off" and German social scientists found classical British political economy less well suited to explain and manage economic and social developments on German soil. Sweden entered into a similar path as Germany, although one step behind. It is therefore not difficult to understand that GHS ideas for a while exerted attraction among Swedish intellectuals as an alternative to British doctrines. In the 1890s neoclassical ideas more or less took over the scene. However, GHS ideas on economic and social policy – socialism of the chair (*Kathedersozialismus*) – were still appealing. The Swedish environment was therefore receptive to GHS *methodological* ideas from the 1870s to the 1890s, but in the case of *policy* ideas Swedish soil was fertile up until WWI.

There was never a Swedish historical school of thought. To be able to trace the influence of the GHS in Sweden one should therefore focus on *individuals*. The most robust way to go about it is to focus on those who actually went to Germany to study under GHS economists. By doing so one can get a precise perception of how and by whom they were affected.

During a period of about 30 years, at least eight Swedes, who later on became prominent scholars or politicians, pursued studies under German historical economists. They appear (in order of year of study in Germany) in Table 10.1. Now, let us investigate these cases one by one.

Table 10.1 Swedes who studied under German economists

Name	Years	Universities	Teachers
Johan Leffler	1874–1876	Leipzig	Roscher
David Davidson	1879	Heidelberg	Knies
Pontus Fahlbeck	1884, 1888, 1890	Berlin, Göttingen, Marburg, Freiburg, Munich, Halle, Bonn, Leipzig	Conrad
Gustaf Steffen	1885–1887, 1900	Berlin, Munich	Wagner, Schmoller, Brentano
Knut Wicksell	1887–1889	Strassburg, Berlin	Knapp, Brentano, Wagner
Gustav Cassel	1898–1900	Tübingen, Berlin, Göttingen	Schönberg, Naumann, Schmoller, Wagner, Lexis, Cohn
Otto Järte	1904, 1906–1908	Munich, Berlin	Brentano, Sombart, Jastrow, Schmoller, Wagner
Nils Wohlin	1905–1906	Berlin	Wagner, Schäffle, Sering

Johan Leffler

Johan Leffler (1845–1912) is usually regarded as the first representative of the GHS in Sweden. He studied political economy and finance under Wilhelm Roscher in Leipzig (1874–1876) and took his PhD there. Back in Sweden he worked as a lecturer in political economy in Stockholm and was in 1886–1888 a member of the first chamber of the *Riksdag* (Hölcke, 1979: 428–430). In a portrait of Leffler it is stated that "the influence from socialism of the chair would characterize his work as teacher, author of textbooks and researcher in political economy" (Olofsson and Pålsson Syll, 1998: 528).

In 1881, Leffler published a textbook in economics in which he relied heavily upon representatives of the GHS, not least Adolph Wagner and Albert Schäffle. In the book he characterized the GHS:

> The historical-ethical (realist) school is characterized by its perception of economic natural laws as development laws and by the associated antipathy against "absolute solutions" of (or for all times and circumstances valid answers to) economic questions; furthermore by primarily using the inductive research method (conclusions from numerous historical and statistical observations), by firmly giving prominence to the organic character of the national economy; by stressing the justification of the social principle alongside the individual principle in the general economy – and by the mission of the state to positively intervene in the course of the national economy in the public interest; by strongly emphasizing the ethical element of economic

activity; and finally by the less distinct delimitation of political economy from other social sciences.

(Leffler, 1881: 126)

In 1885 Leffler introduced German socialism of the chair at a meeting with the Swedish Economic Association (founded in 1877).[2] He recalled the reaction of the older GHS (Roscher, Bruno Hildebrand, Karl Knies) against Adam Smith and David Ricardo and the formation of *Verein für Socialpolitik* in 1872. He gave a sympathetic but balanced view of the German ideas and underlined the influence these ideas had had outside Germany: "At present, there is hardly any people of culture, whose economic literature has not been more or less influenced by this new scientific and social policy trend" (Leffler, 1886: 151).

Leffler is not regarded as a very original economist but was nonetheless to "exert a certain influence over Swedish economic and social policy in the late 19th century" (Pålsson Syll, 2007: 193). He furthermore influenced the development of the economics discipline in Sweden as a board member and secretary of a foundation (*Lorénska stiftelsen*) which published writings in social science and funded young economists (Steffen, Wicksell, Cassel) going abroad to study. Wisselgren (2000: 117, 322) has mapped the networks around this foundation and designates Leffler as one of the most important links between German socialism of the chair and the debate on social policy in Sweden.

David Davidson

David Davidson (1854–1942) is one of the founders of modern economics in Sweden or at least a transitional figure between classical and neoclassical economics (Uhr, 1991: 46). He took his PhD in 1878 and was a professor at Uppsala University (1889–1919).

In 1879, Davidson got a scholarship from the law faculty in Uppsala and went to Heidelberg to follow the lectures of Karl Knies. After a few weeks he reported to a friend, "I am getting converted to his [Knies] teachings, but so far not completely." Davidson was looking for a topic for a thesis at the same time as he developed a very critical attitude: "I am starting to recognize that almost every statement within the existent political economy is to some extent false [. . .]. The only thing I would be capable of is a purely critical and negative investigation" (Carlson, 1995: 106).

Knies suggested a survey of labour value theories as a topic, whereupon Davidson started working on a thesis supposed to be entitled "Die Arbeit als Factor der Preisbildung". He read Karl Marx, Ferdinand Lassalle, Karl Rodbertus and – for the first time – David Ricardo (Carlson, 1995: 107–108).

Davidson followed Knies's lectures in practical economics, economic policy and finance and attended his seminar. He liked the seminar, but it was cancelled when Knies was elected to the Bavarian parliament. Davidson did not appreciate Knies's lectures as much as before: "His lectures are to a large extent very elementary" (Carlson, 1995: 109). At the end of the year, Davidson went back to Sweden.

In a portrait of his old teacher, Eli Heckscher (1951: 136) concluded that Davidson did not gain "any strong faith in his own scientific ability or even in the opportunities of his discipline" from Knies. This, however, does not mean that Knies did not influence Davidson. One can readily assume that the critical attitude towards economics, which was to be the hallmark of Davidson, had been fostered by his acquaintance with Knies.

The thesis on labour value theories soon turned into a thesis on rent. In it Davidson (1880: 104) stated that "the first thorough treatment of method within economics can be found in Knies". Heckscher notes that in this thesis another towering figure – Ricardo – had entered Davidson's world. In all subsequent portraits of Davidson (Ohlin, 1931: 335; Jacobsson, 1939: 9; Heckscher, 1951: 129, 146) his "spiritual relationship" with and lifelong admiration for Ricardo are mentioned. The irony of this is that Davidson in 1879, as a student of one of the leading proponents of the GHS, started reading Ricardo (who according to the Germans was the root of most evils within political economy) and subsequently became a follower of the classical British economists.

Did Davidson transmit any decisive influences from Germany to Sweden? Uhr (1975: 18) notes that Davidson's influence on economic policies was mainly felt in monetary and taxation matters. As far as monetary matters are concerned, Davidson was inspired by Knies but Knies's writings within this area showed "scarcely a trace of the Historian spirit" (Gide and Rist, 1937: 385). As far as tax matters are concerned, Davidson wrote an essay on indirect taxation during his time in Heidelberg. Ten years later he published a book on taxes in which he advocated progressive income taxation, an advocacy which led Uhr (2014: 149) to characterize the Swedish tax system as "an inheritance from Davidson". In this book Davidson referred to German tax laws, which he had studied during a trip in 1886, and to German economists like Cohn, Held, Knies, Nasse, Neumann, Schäffle and Wagner. However, he dismissed Wagner's social policy principle of taxation as "pure utopia" (1889: 149). Davidson was also, perhaps under influence from Rodbertus, "critical of pure economic liberalism in its general claim for free trade and free competition" (Heckscher, 1951: 147, 150). This critical attitude was reflected in Davidson's instalment lecture as professor of economics and fiscal law at Uppsala University in 1889, where he explicitly referred to the position of the GHS (1890: 295).

Pontus Fahlbeck

Pontus Fahlbeck (1850–1923) was a path-breaking social scientist. His contributions cover a range of disciplines. He was professor of history, political science and statistics (1889–1915) at Lund University and was a member of the *Riksdag* (1903–1911). He was politically conservative (constitutional matters) and socially radical (the labour question) and a predecessor of the radical right-wing movement which was formed in Sweden – inspired by German ideas – in the early twentieth century.

Fahlbeck himself in retrospect, according to historian Sten Carlsson (1953: 788), saw 1884 as a turning point in his scientific career: he turned from history to political science and political economy. It seems reasonable to connect this turning point with his four-month study trip to German universities in Berlin, Göttingen, Marburg, Freiburg and Munich of that year. Fahlbeck wrote a short report from his trip but did not mention any professors by name, only that they were active within history and law history. In the summer of 1888 he made a two-month trip to Berlin and Halle and in in the autumn of 1890 a three-week trip to Bonn, Leipzig, Halle and Berlin. His purpose this time was to get acquainted with teachings in political science. In Halle he visited the seminar in political science led by Johannes Conrad (Carlson, 2002: 82, 199–200).

In biographical sketches Fahlbeck is portrayed as heavily affected by German socialism of the chair (Carlsson, 1953: 791; Vallinder, 1992: 61); for a while in the 1890s he even planned to start a Swedish equivalent to *Verein für Sozialpolitik*. He explicitly sided with the GHS against the classical British and French economists in some of his writings in the 1880s and 1890s. In 1887 he wrote (p. 3) that the liberal economist had turned into stone and continued:

> The rebirth of political economy has happened in Germany and started about twenty years ago. Now this science is one among equals, a science which is growing and advancing. In its new shape, it has taken a new extra surname: the social policy school. This new school is already in control of all universities in Germany and Austria. It has advanced over the Alps and conquered the Italian universities; and even more, she has jumped across the Atlantic and is now thriving at all institutions of higher learning in the big Union. In other parts of Europe she has also been given a home. Only England, but even more France and most of all Sweden do not want to hear of the new doctrine. [. . .] In Sweden alone, the so-called political economists and leading men still believe in Adam Smith's doctrine as the revealed truth and still attempt to carry it out.

Ten years later, Fahlbeck launched an attack against the methods of the classical political economy, which to him represented scholastic thinking: "It is, like the disciplines of the Middle Ages, distinguished by many sophistries and abstract definitions and a kind of casuistry made out of deduction from hypothetical cases" (Fahlbeck, 1897: 32–33). The premises were false, and when one "started poke about in the foundation" the fancy building collapsed. A study of human economic activities had to be predominantly empirical because they were not given once and for all but must "be carefully studied for each period of time". Fahlbeck's hope was therefore that economic science would pull itself together and "as an historical-analytic and inductive science figure out the laws of economic life" (Fahlbeck, 1897: 33).

Fahlbeck over the years argued against socialism and liberalism, against internationalism and individualism. To him the nation was the basic unit in human life, an organism in which each individual had his role to play. Nations were competing with each other, but within nations individuals were to be protected from merciless competition. "To protect the weak against the strong was the first word of civilization and will remain so" (Fahlbeck, 1887: 7).

Fahlbeck consequently launched a program which can be characterized as socialism of the chair or even state socialism. In a book on "estates and classes" (1892: 174–176, 183, 187–189, 200–201) he assigned a series of tasks to the state. It must foster economic growth by nationalizing infrastructure, banks and major industries, by encouraging innovations and protecting infant industries. It must raise the intellectual and moral standard of the working class, mainly through education. It must legislate in German fashion about workers' protection and social insurance. Basically, Fahlbeck (1892: 174) espoused Wagner's law on the growth of the welfare state: "The way forward in all civilized societies runs slowly but irresistibly towards increased co-production trough state and municipality." Fahlbeck's program triggered a debate on state socialism within the Swedish Social Democratic Party (Tingsten, 1941: 183–184; Karlsson, 2001: 278–283).

However, after the turn of the century, Fahlbeck took "half a step back in his view of the expansion of the public sector" (Vallinder, 1992: 61). In a book on "the labour question" Fahlbeck (1910: 110) admitted that he had changed his mind: he had reached the conclusion that state production is in most cases less efficient than private production. He thus figured that the answer to the labour question lay with private companies. Workers should not be dependent upon selling their labour as a commodity on the market but rather get lifelong employment with protection in situations of sickness and old age. Consequently, the economy must be dominated by large and stable companies, by private trusts. One could perhaps say that he moved away from a German to an American (welfare capitalism) or Japanese (Zaibatsu) solution of the labour question. Nonetheless, Fahlbeck's admiration for Germany never waned. During WWI he was "wholeheartedly" behind Germany (Vallinder, 1992: 52).

Gustaf Steffen

Gustaf Steffen (1864–1929) transmitted many ideas from abroad and introduced sociology as an independent discipline in Sweden. He was a professor of political economy and sociology at the University of Gothenburg (1903–1929) and a member (Social Democrat) of the *Riksdag* (1911–1916). In biographical portraits of Steffen, influences from German socialists of the chair – Schmoller, Wagner, Schäffle – are most often mentioned (Lilliestam, 1960: 66; Thomasson, 1962: 285–286; Lönnroth, 2014: 155–156).

After his high school graduation in the spring of 1883, Steffen travelled to Aachen in Germany to study chemistry. In the spring of 1885 he moved on to Berlin to study at the Bergakademie. An interest in economic and social problems was brought to life by his observations of how affluence and poverty existed side by side in European cities. He started reading socialist literature – George, Marx, Engels, Bebel, Dühring, Fourier, Lassalle, Schäffle – and established contacts with German social democrats. During one week in the autumn of 1885 he attended Wagner's lectures every day and also one lecture by Schmoller.

As a radical socialist, Steffen was not in tune with socialists of the chair and certainly not with Bismarck. He ran the risk of being expelled from Germany and moved on to England in July 1887. He spent 10 years in England and was inspired by a plethora of -isms: anarchism, utopism, Darwinism, Fabianism, marginalism. His acquaintance with Fabians recalled his impressions of German socialism of the chair (Lilliestam, 1960: 30, 39–40, 44–51).

There was no "total recall", however. In a booklet on the labour question (Steffen, 1889) it is difficult to discern traits of socialism of the chair as far as political recommendations are concerned, and there are different opinions about the methodological approach in an extensive investigation of the wage system in England. Wicksell (1900) commended Steffen for not following the lead of the historical school but attempting to combine theory and history. Lilliestam (1960: 56–57), however, thinks this inductive investigation is influenced by the GHS.

Eventually, Steffen decided to embark upon an academic career. In the spring of 1900, he studied for Lujo Brentano in Munich and after that for Richard Ehrenberg (hardly a socialist of the chair) in Rostock, where he in 1902 took his PhD based on the investigation of the wage system in England. In his inaugural lecture as a professor (Steffen, 1903) he defined his discipline, referred to several German historical economists – Roscher, Conrad, Gustav von Schönberg, Wagner and Schmoller, "the perhaps sociologically most profound economist of our time" – and specified his area of research in terms of state, institutions and nation.

Steffen's positions up to WWI can be pinpointed from a series of seven volumes entitled "Social Studies" (1905–1912). In the second volume, Steffen (1905b: 35) praised Schmoller and Wagner for laying "a broad sociological base" for their research. In the third volume he dealt with "the State as bearer and guardian of culture", using Wagner's "excellent analysis" as springboard (1906a: 38–41). He wrote about "an immense volume of state activity" in the economy and pointed to successful state ownership of communications, banks and insurance companies and municipality ownership of local infrastructure (1906a: 57). Just as the conservative radicals, Steffen looked upon society as a kind of organism, where there is "an indissoluble community of life [. . .] between the whole and its different parts" (1906a: 89). When he dealt with taxation and social reforms, he poured superlatives over Wagner, "one of the most clearheaded, erudite and knowledgeable about all facets of society among modern economists" (1906a: 92–94). In the fourth volume (1906b), Steffen laid out his views about the Wagnerian social policy principle of taxation.

In Volume 7 Steffen declared himself as a socialist but not a radical socialist (1912: 42–43); he had already in the first volume used the term "national socialism" (1905a: 86). In Volume 7 (1912: 49–52, 59, 73) he argued for planned economy instead of extensive nationalization and for government to set minimum standards for wages, work conditions, social insurance, housing conditions and education. Minimum standards were to increase the efficiency of labour, and economic planning was to increase the use of the means of production. Social policy provided the means, and efficient national production was the overarching aim. He argued that modern social policy was a form of socialism. In Germany, even "the great enemy of socialists Bismarck had with the outlook of a brilliant statesman" entered into bold socialist experiments (Steffen, 1912: 77).

In another *magnum opus* about "world ages" (1918–1920), Steffen developed a theory according to which nations have to pass through a kind of human life cycle, a theory inspired by German historians (Lilliestam, 1960: 166–172). As is well known, Roscher was among those who had developed a theory of this kind.

In the *Riksdag* Steffen advanced several social policy propositions. However, his political career came to a halt in 1915, when he was expelled from the Social Democrats due to his activism on the German side in WWI.

In retrospect, Steffen is not regarded as one of the "great" Swedish economists. However, he introduced a plethora of ideas from abroad to a Swedish audience, his teaching was to a large extent based on German literature (Lönnroth, 2014; Sandelin, 2001), he introduced sociology as an academic discipline and he was a kind of genius behind the Swedish "people's home", preparing the ground for the shift within the Social Democratic Party from nationalization to economic planning in the 1930s.

Knut Wicksell

Knut Wicksell (1851–1926) is Sweden's foremost economist of all times, a professor of economics and financial law at Lund University (1901–1916). He was not at all affected by German historical ideas as far as methodology is concerned and only to a minor extent affected by socialism of the chair. However, alongside Steffen and Cassel he knew more about the German message than perhaps any other Swede.

Wicksell had pursued economic studies in England before going to Germany. He was of a "theoretical nature", and his acquaintance with classical and neo-classical economists had "inoculated" him against German historical influence.

In the autumn of 1887 and spring of 1888, Wicksell spent time in Strasbourg and followed Brentano's lectures on monetary systems and labour issues and Georg Friedrich Knapp's lectures on agricultural and other issues, in all about 110 lectures (Gårdlund, 1958: 107–108; Carlson, 1995: 131). Wicksell was moderately impressed and wrote in a letter to a friend,

> Both Brentano and Knapp seem to belong to the new German "historical school", and they scorn anything which is not based on special research into the situation of a shoepeg manufacturing industry in sixteenth-century

Saxony, or something of that sort. The generalizations and economic laws of the Englishmen are stuff and nonsense – "ach, die Leuten wussten ja gar nichts davon". [. . .] As far as more modern times are concerned, we must shrug our shoulders at all theories and definitions.

(Gårdlund, 1958: 108; Carlson, 1995: 130)

In March 1888, Wicksell left Strasbourg for Vienna, where he attended lectures by Carl Menger. He received Menger's pamphlet against Schmoller and concluded that the latter hardly came out on top. Having spent the summer in Sweden, Wicksell returned to Berlin in September. The following six months he attended about 25 lectures by Wagner and encountered the "middle way" message: the importance of choosing a middle way between liberalism and socialism and between induction and deduction. He thought Wagner was a good lecturer but dismissed the message as "extremely elementary" (Gårdlund, 1958: 109–114; Carlson, 1995: 133–134). In March 1889 he returned to Sweden. The most important event during his time in Germany seems to have been when he at the beginning of 1889 in a bookshop in Berlin found Böhm-Bawerk's *Positive Theorie des Kapitales*, a book which to him appeared as "a revelation" (Wicksell, 1914: 322).

In almost all biographical pictures of Wicksell one encounters a theoretical economist, inspired by classical economists like Malthus, Ricardo and Mill and neoclassical economists like Walras, Jevons, Menger and Böhm-Bawerk (Ohlin, 1926: 503, 509; Sommarin, 1931: 229, 267; Lindahl, 1953: 272, 306; Gårdlund, 1958: 108; 124; Uhr, 1960: 4, 30; Jonung, 2014). The same authors are also more or less agreed that Wicksell was no socialist of the chair but a left-wing, radical, egalitarian liberal.

There is, however, one item in Wicksell's repertoire which is heavily influenced by the Germans – that is by Wagner: tax policy. In *Finanztheoretische Untersuchungen* (1896) Wicksell referred to Wagner's *Finanzwissenschaft* frequently. Wicksell certainly wanted to drive the benefit principle far beyond what Wagner had imagined. No one should be forced to pay more in tax than is equivalent to the benefit he expects from the object of taxation on which he pays (see also Jonung, 2001: 39). This applies provided that there is justice in the existing distribution of property and income. If this is not the case, "then society has both the right and the duty to revise the existing property structure" (Wicksell, 1896: 144). Thus Wicksell adhered to Wagner's social principle of tax policy and acknowledged "the immense merit" Wagner deserved for his stand in stressing a task of the state which had received too little attention in the theory of public finance (Wicksell, 1896: 145).

Even though Wicksell was no champion of socialism, he noted that "the liberal school's dogma, that the public sector always produces more dearly and less well than the private sector, is confuted daily and incessantly by experience" (1905: 9–10). The state ran railways and managed forests successfully in many countries, and municipalities were beginning to run water, gas and electricity enterprises. Wicksell, however, never glorified the state as the Germans did. He outright disliked everything that smacked of "social kingdom", organism and nationalism.

Wicksell was a great theoretician, but he also exerted considerable political influence. Testimonials are not hard to find; to pick just a couple: Lindahl (1953: 267) observed that Wicksell "had a decisive influence on the evolution of political ideas in our country" and Jonung (2001: 13) states that Wicksell "exerted a radical influence on economic science as well as on economic policy and the public debate in Sweden."

Gustav Cassel

Gustav Cassel (1866–1945) was in the 1920s the world's most famous economist, rivalled only by Keynes (Carlson, 2009). He was a professor of political economy and public finance at Stockholm University (1904–1933) and achieved his fame as a monetary expert at international summits and during lecture tours across Europe. Around 1900, Cassel stood out as a radical liberal, influenced by German socialism of the chair and British Fabianism. After WWI, however, he turned into a right-wing liberal.

Cassel began his economic studies in earnest with a two-year sojourn in Germany from mid-1898 to mid-1900. He studied in turn under Gustav von Schönberg and Friedrich Neumann in Tübingen, Schmoller and Wagner in Berlin and Wilhelm Lexis and Gustav Cohn in Göttingen, and he established contact with Schäffle.

Cassel was not impressed by Schönberg and Neumann, the former not being able to "dig deeper into the theoretical context of things", the latter "only dealing with quasi-learned definitions" (Giöbel-Lilja, 1945: 135). These impressions spurred Cassel to lay his own theoretical foundation. He started working on an essay that eventually (1899) was to be published as "Grundriss einer elementaren Preislehre."

In the autumn of 1898, Cassel headed on to Berlin, where he attended lectures by Schmoller and Wagner. He was impressed by their "infinite knowledge" but soon discovered that especially Schmoller's theoretical footing was weak.

> However, I developed an enormous esteem for Wagner's research achievements. In particular his laying of the foundations of the social economy had a great influence on me inasmuch as it emerged as a vital task for economic science to clarify the economic basis of the legal system. In particular, private property could not be regarded as something given but must be founded on a sound socioeconomic justification, thus also being the object of rational limitation.
>
> (Cassel, 1940: 19)

During the spring of 1899, Cassel moved on to Göttingen. Once again his teachers, Lexis and Cohn, did not live up to his expectations.

Cassel's sojourn in Germany is yet another example of the irony of history. In an environment where theory was neglected he felt a calling to lay the foundation of a theoretical system which in 1918 culminated in a textbook, *Theoretische Sozialökonomie*. He did not turn into an economist in the spirit of German historicism but into a neoclassical designer of an equilibrium system in the spirit of Léon Walras.

In biographical sketches of Cassel his deductive leanings and lack of German historical influences are emphasized (Silverstolpe, 1944: 48; Mitchell, 1949: 201, 211; Landgren, 1968: 330). His own pupils have, however, pointed to his great interest in facts (Myrdal 1945: 4; Ohlin 1954; Lundberg 1967: 4). Cassel's perception of scientific work, stated in his textbook (1934: 19–20),[3] has some resemblance to Schmoller's famous metaphor about using induction and deduction alternately, just as using the left and right foot alternately when walking, but Cassel was leaning heavily on the deductive foot:

> Economic science [. . .] always requires cooperation between theory and observation, between deductive and inductive procedures. At an elementary stage theory must however be of major importance. [. . .] One must lay a foundation which is so solid that it must not be modified, no matter what changes and complications that may occur. The foundation of theoretical economics demands strict simplification in especially two respects. We must to begin with disregard changes in time and space.

Cassel's perception of economic and social policies was, however, coloured by German influences. His message in a book on social policy (1902) echoed from socialism of the chair. He renounced liberalism's atomistic view of society, formal view of freedom and faith in the blessings of free competition. He wanted to replace these axioms with "the highly organized society" which can use force to create greater real freedom and a policy of planning to steer development in desired directions. The overarching aim was to achieve maximum economic growth. The task of social policy was to develop the nation's labour force to the highest level of usefulness.

Cassel, in his ambition to find a middle way between left and right, between liberalism and socialism, between growth and distribution, displays many Wagnerian characteristics. In an exegesis, which seems to be an interpretation of Wagner's law, Cassel observes that the domain of the public economy tends to expand but finds it impossible to mark out any definite boundary (1906: 351–352). State and municipality, Cassel said, ought to own natural monopolies and natural resources – for example railways, forests, waterfalls, mines and quarries, water, gas and electricity works and tramways (1902: 100–103, 107–109). The state ought to establish, regulate and subsidize social insurance for the working class.

Cassel was in his own way a supporter of Wagnerian social taxation policy, but he did not speak so much of protecting the weaker as of developing the vigorous elements. In his eyes the important thing was "the great principle that the tax system must be arranged as is most beneficial for society, its prosperity and progress" (1906: 358). Taxes ought therefore to be taken primarily from unearned incomes and not from the result of productive labour.

Cassel's writings at the turn of the century – not least his book on social policy – greatly influenced Swedish opinion (see e.g. Y. Larsson, 1967: 195–196; J. Larsson, 1994: 85–88; Wisselgren, 2000: 230, 262). In retrospect, however, he is mainly remembered for his vigorous fight against socialism, economic planning and Keynesianism during the 1920s and 1930s (see Carlson, 1994).

Otto Järte

Otto Järte (1881–1961) had many strings on his bow. He was an official and politician, first on the left, and then on the right (conservative member of the *Riksdag* 1924–1932), contemplated as a successor to both the Social Democratic leader Hjalmar Branting and the conservative leader Arvid Lindman.

In his young days Järte planned to study political economy under Steffen and Wicksell, whom he regarded as socialists. Instead he enrolled in studies under Cassel in 1904. In 1905 he went off to Munich to study under Brentano, and in the autumn of 1905 he betook himself to Berlin to study under Werner Sombart, Ignaz Jastrow, Schmoller and Wagner (Anderson, 1965: 46, 50, 66, 71, 100–105). In 1908 Järte returned from Berlin, without a doctorate but steeped in German ideas.

Järte's biographer Ivar Anderson (1965: 110) considers that "Järte was a revisionist, influenced by the Bavarian liberal socialism of von Vollmar", and that he "shared the socialism of the chair view that work of social reform should be conducted under the direction of state power". Heckscher had reached a similar verdict: Järte imbibed admiration for "the basic conception of socialism of the chair, the need for social reform directed by the government" (*Otto Järte sjuttio år* 1951: 30–31).

These verdicts are probably coloured by Järte's subsequent development, for in his younger days he did not think much of the German "social kingdom", which he defined (1908b) as a military dictatorship, and its social policy, which he regarded as a swindle. He also declared that Marxism was "the only possible theoretical basis for the world movement of socialism" (1908a: 249).

Back in Sweden, Järte entered upon a career as public servant. He was soon assigned to conduct an investigation on unemployment, which marked the beginning of his career as a labour market specialist.

On the brink of WWI, Järte (1914: 22, 24, 28) was still critical of the German "social kingdom" and still adhered to Marxist ideas. However, when the war broke out, he argued for "a bold rallying alongside Germany"; he was consequently (like Steffen) kicked out of the Social Democrats (Anderson, 1965: 157). From now on he developed in a liberal-conservative direction, declaring that he had been taught liberal economics by Cassel and Heckscher. He became a leading figure in the Unemployment Commission and an architect behind the Swedish active labour market policy. In 1923 he joined the Conservative Party and soon took a seat in parliament. Later on he became an editorial writer for the major

Swedish conservative newspaper, *Svenska Dagbladet* (Anderson, 1965: 169, 185–186, 189, 196, 198).

Nils Wohlin

Nils Wohlin (1881–1948) has gone down in history as one of the Swedish farmers' movement's leading ideologues. He was a professor of statistics at Uppsala University (1916–1930), member of the *Riksdag* (1919–1942) (representing alternately the farmers' movement or the Conservative Party) and minister of commerce (1923–1924) and of finance (1928–1929).

A few years into the new century, Wohlin studied economics under Cassel, who advised him to attend Berlin University (Cassel, 1941: 375). Wohlin followed this advice and studied under Wagner, Schmoller and Max Sering in 1905–1906. In a letter to Heckscher, Wohlin declared that he found Schmoller's lectures masterly and that Sering's and Wagner's were of interest too (Carlson, 2002: 94).

Wohlin then continued his studies under Cassel and took his doctoral degree in economics in 1912. His biographer Birger Hagård (1976: 426) drew the conclusion that the period of study in Germany was crucial for Wohlin in many respects and that the socialists of the chair "exercised a deep and lasting influence". Schmoller affected Wohlin the most: "His negative view of Manchester liberalism and Marxism, which accompanied him during his whole life, was no doubt founded in the influence he suffered from von Schmoller and the younger historical school" (Hagård, 1976: 428). Wohlin's interest in agricultural issues was probably nurtured by the agrarian economist Sering. Wohlin himself eventually exclaimed, "We who have imbibed Prussian air in the lecture halls of the Berlin Academy do love it" (1918:11).

Wohlin (1919: 14) searched for a national middle way between international capitalism and socialism. He refused to accept the customary left-to-right ideological pattern, but placed conservatism at the centre between liberalism and socialism. He wanted to create a strong political centre based on the peasantry, which he saw as "an industrious middle class" (1918: 107); eventually the Agrarian Party was renamed the Centre Party.

Wohlin did not side with Germany during WWI. He came into sharp conflict with the German activists, who reeled off "imperialist vocabularies from their foreign textbooks" (1918: 19). He was a Swedish nationalist and advocated strict neutrality, and he attacked "our social philosophers of the German school" (Wohlin, 1918: 34).

Nor had Wohlin sympathy for a state socialist regime; it did not fit in with Swedish farmer class traditions. During WWI he warned that state socialism would spread from the German "central hotbed" (1918: 65). Social policy, however, was necessary to forestall socialism: "If nothing is done about the social question within the industry [. . .] development will probably inevitably [. . .] come to socialism" (Wohlin, 1919: 26). His general attitude towards social reforms was coloured by socialism of the chair: "The organised working class is indispensable for the nation's productive work and a strong social policy for raising its level is a necessity henceforth, as in the past" (Wohlin, 1918: 87–88). In his political deed he was nonetheless cautious, but during the Great Depression of the 1930s he demanded that social reforms be part of a conservative and national policy, and he pointed to the good example set by the former Imperial Germany. Having supported the "horse trade" agreement between Social Democrats and Agrarians in 1933, Wohlin returned to the Agrarian Party in the *Riksdag* (1935–1942).

How was Sweden influenced?

By focusing on a number of individuals, one gets a notion of the complexity of the spread of economic and social ideas. The effect on individuals exposed to a school of thought depends upon a host of factors: individual sources within the school, competing schools and the age, education, former exposure to ideas and ideological leanings of the individual.

In what ways were the eight Swedes influenced by GHS ideas? All of them were more or less affected in their choice of fields of research. Leffler, Fahlbeck and Steffen were influenced by the historical method. Most of the others were hardly inspired in a methodological sense. This is particularly evident in the case of economists. Davidson, Wicksell and Cassel reacted against the historical method and turned to more theoretical sources of inspiration, to classical and neoclassical economists. It is no small irony that while pursuing studies in Germany Davidson discovered Ricardo, Wicksell discovered Böhm-Bawerk and Cassel discovered Walras.

The policy message from the Germans and their *Verein für Sozialpolitik*, on the other hand, exerted a substantial influence upon all of the aforementioned actors, even though they had different ideological leanings. This influence can be seen in the way they analyzed and made recommendations about the role of the state in the national economy. Leffler and Fahlbeck were pioneers in this respect, Cassel's book on social policy from 1902 outlined a radical and coherent program along these lines of thought, Wicksell propagated the social principle of tax policy, and most of the others proposed different types of state intervention around the turn of the century.

Wagner was the German economist who exerted the most influence upon the Swedes. He was less devoted to the historical method than the others – he even sided with Menger against Schmoller in the *Methodenstreit* – at the same time as he propagated the most radical policy program; he was more of a state socialist than socialist of the chair.

The influence of the GHS in Sweden began in the late 1870s and evaporated at the end of WWI. When Germany lost the war, the German model was buried alongside its leading prophets, Schmoller and Wagner.

After WWI, Swedish economists were looking westwards for inspiration. Those who travelled to study abroad – Johan Åkerman, Bertil Ohlin, Gunnar Myrdal and Erik Lundberg – went to the United States. Over there some of them encountered German ideas in disguise. Many US scholars had studied in Germany and brought home the German methodological and political virus. This virus mutated in the new environment, and from the American historical school arose American institutionalism, which affected primarily Åkerman and Myrdal.

In the long run, even though it is impossible to follow these ideas step-by-step from the German "social kingdom" into the Swedish "people's home", there are some fascinating similarities between what prominent Swedes were exposed to in Germany, the ideas they themselves propagated and the basic traits of the Swedish welfare state model.

- Leffler was probably the most important early link between German socialism of the chair and the Swedish debate on social policy.
- Davidson had a significant impact on the construction of the Swedish progressive income tax system.
- Fahlbeck was an early proponent of state socialism in line with "Wagner's law".
- Steffen was a social democrat with an ambition to put economic planning before socialization.
- Wicksell advocated radical income equalization through social taxation policy.
- Cassel pioneered a radical, efficiency-oriented social policy.
- Järte was a driving force behind the active labour market policy.
- Wohlin was an ideologue promoting a political centre based upon the farmer class.

Several of these characteristics – progressive taxes, elements of state socialism, economic planning, income equalization, efficiency-oriented social policy, active labour market policy and farmers at the political centre (horse-trading with social democrats) – more or less capture the Swedish model launched in the 1930s.

Notes

1   By the "German model" I simply mean the national traits that have been discussed in terms of "social kingdom" and *Sonderweg*. The "de-Germanisation" of Swedish economics after WWI has been discussed by Sandelin (2001).
2   These ideas had previously been introduced at the first meeting of the association in 1877 by its secretary Johan Henrik Palme. See Henriksson (2001: 192).
3   In the 1932 English edition of this book, Cassel left out the introductory chapter with his methodological considerations.

References

Anderson, I. (1965). *Otto Järte – en man för sig*. Stockholm: Bonniers.

Carlson, B. (1994). *The State as a Monster: Gustav Cassel and Eli Heckscher on the Role and Growth of the State*. Lanham, NY: University Press of America.

Carlson, B. (1995). *De institutionalistiska idéernas spridning: Tyska historiska skolan, amerikansk institutionalism och svenska ekonomers utlandsstudier*. Stockholm: SNS.

Carlson, B. (2002). *Ouvertyr till folkhemmet: Wagnerska tongångar i förra sekelskiftets Sverige*. Lund: Nordic Academic Press.

Carlson, B. (2009). Who Was Most World-Famous – Cassel or Keynes? *The Economist* as Yardstick. *Journal of the History of Economic Thought*, 31 (4): 519–530.

Carlsson, S. (1953). Fahlbeck, Pontus Erland Andersson. *Svenskt Biografiskt Lexikon*, 14. Stockholm: Albert Bonnier.

Cassel, G. (1902). *Socialpolitik*. Stockholm: Hugo Gebers Förlag.

Cassel, G. (1906). Den offentliga hushållningens natur. *Ekonomisk Tidskrift*, 8 (7): 347–364.

Cassel, G. (1932/1967). *The Theory of Social Economy*. New York: Harcourt. Reprint by Augustus M. Kelley.

Cassel, G. (1934). *Teoretisk socialekonomi*. Stockholm: Kooperativa Förbundets Bokförlag.

Cassel, G. (1940–1941). *I förnuftets tjänst I–II: En ekonomisk självbiografi*. Stockholm: Bokförlaget Natur och Kultur.

Davidson, D. (1880). *Bidrag till jordränteteoriens historia*. Uppsala: Uppsala universitets årsskrift.

Davidson, D. (1889). *Om beskattningsnormen vid inkomstskatten*. Uppsala: Lundequistska.

Davidson, D. (1890). Om konkurrensens inskränkande och upphäfvande under fullständig näringsfrihet. *Ny Svensk Tidskrift*, 11: 295–308.

Edebalk, P.G. (2013). Järnkanslern Otto von Bismarck och de första socialförsäkringarna, in H. Swärd, P. G. Edebalk and E. Wadensjö (eds.), *Vägar till välfärd – idéer, inspiratörer, kontroverser, perspektiv*. Stockholm: Liber, 180–187.

Fahlbeck, P. (1887). *Den ekonomiska vetenskapen och näringsskyddet: Några ord för dagen*. Lund: Lindstedts Bokhandel.

Fahlbeck, P. (1892). *Stånd och klasser: En socialpolitisk öfverblick*. Lund: Collin & Zickerman.

Fahlbeck, P. (1897). Den nyare nationalekonomien. *Statsvetenskaplig Tidskrift*, 1 (1): 31–39.

Fahlbeck, P. (1910). *Arbetarefrågan: Villa och verklighet*. Stockholm: Norstedt & Söners Förlag.

Gårdlund, T. (1958). *The Life of Knut Wicksell*. Stockholm: Almqvist & Wiksell.

Gide, C. and Rist, C. (1937). *A History of Economic Doctrines*. Sydney: George G. Harrap.

Giöbel-Lilja, I. (1945). *Gustav Cassel: En livsskildring*. Stockholm: Natur och Kultur.

Hagård, B. (1976). *Nils Wohlin: Konservativ centerpolitiker*. Vadstena: Sahlströms Bokhandel.

Heckscher, E. F. (1951). David Davidson. *Ekonomisk Tidskrift*, 53 (3): 127–160.

Henriksson, R.G.H. (2001). The Swedish Economic Association from Its Foundation (1877) to the Turn of the Century, in M. M. Augello and M.E.L. Guidi (eds.), *The Spread of Political Economy and the Professionalisation of Economists: Economic Societies in Europe, America and Japan in the Nineteenth Century*. London: Routledge, 176–199.

Hölcke, O. (1979). Leffler, Johan Anders. *Svenskt Biografiskt Lexikon*, 22. Stockholm: Norstedts Tryckeri.

Jacobsson, P. (1939). David Davidson. *Ekonomisk Tidskrift*, 41 (1): 1–10.

Järte, O. (1908a). Karl Marx och socialismen. *Social Tidskrift* 8 (5–6): 197–201, 245–257.

Järte, O. (1908b). Preussiska kulturbilder I: Kejsarkulten. *Social-Demokraten*, 28 February.

Järte, O. (1914). *August Bebel som socialpolitiker*. Malmö: AB Framtidens Bokförlag.

Jonung, L. (2001). Inledning, in L. Jonung, T. Hedlund-Nyström and C. Jonung (eds.), *Att uppfostra det svenska folket: Knut Wicksell's opublicerade manuskript*. Stockholm: SNS, 13–57.

Jonung, L. (2014). Knut Wicksell, in C. Jonung and A.-C. Ståhlberg (eds.), *Svenska nationalekonomer under 400 år*. Stockholm: Dialogos, 120–137.

Karlsson, S. O. (2001). *Det intelligenta samhället: En omtolkning av socialdemokratins idéhistoria*. Stockholm: Carlssons Bokförlag.

Landgren, K-G. (1968). Cassel, Karl Gustav, in D. L. Sills and R. K. Merton (eds.), *International Encyclopedia of the Social Sciences*. New York: Macmillan, 330–331.

Larsson, J. (1994). *Hemmet vi ärvde: Om folkhemmet, identiteten och den gemensamma framtiden*. Stockholm: Arena.

Larsson, Y. (1967). *På marsch mot demokratin: Från hundragradig skala till allmän rösträtt (1900–1920)*. Stockholm: Monografier utgivna av Stockholms kommunalförvaltning.

Leffler, J. (1881). *Grundlinier till nationalekonomiken eller läran om folkens allmänna hushållning*. Stockholm: Norstedt & Söners Förlag.

Leffler, J. (1886). Katedersocialismen. *Nationalekonomiska föreningens förhandlingar*, 26 November 1885. Stockholm: Ivar Hæggströms Boktryckeri.

Lilliestam, Å. (1960). *Gustaf Steffen, samhällsteoretiker och idépolitiker*. Göteborg: Akademiförlaget-Gumperts.

Lindahl, E. (1953). Knut Wicksell 1851–1926, in J. Schumpeter, E. F. Heckscher, E. Lindahl and G. Myrdal (eds.), *Stora nationalekonomer*. Stockholm: Natur och Kultur, 267–309.

Lönnroth, J. (2014). Gustaf Steffen, in C. Jonung and A.-C. Ståhlberg (eds.), *Svenska nationalekonomer under 400 år*. Stockholm: Dialogos, 155–170.

Lundberg, E. (1967). Influence of Gustav Cassel on Economic Doctrine and Policy. *Skandinaviska Banken Quarterly Review*, 48 (1): 1–6.

Mitchell, W. C. (1949). *Lecture Notes on Types of Economic Theory*. New York: Augustus M. Kelley.

Myrdal, G. (1945). Gustav Cassel in Memoriam. *Ekonomisk Revy*, 2 (February): 3–13.

Ohlin, B. (1926). Knut Wicksell (1851–1926). *Economic Journal*, 36 (September): 503–512.

Ohlin, B. (1931). David Davidson. *Svenskt Biografiskt Lexikon*, 10. Stockholm: Albert Bonnier.

Ohlin, B. (1954). Porträtt av Gustav Cassel. *Stockholms-Tidningen*, 20 April.

Olofsson, J. and Pålsson Syll, L. (1998). Ekonomporträttet: Johan Leffler (1845–1912). *Ekonomisk Debatt*, 26 (7): 527–532.

Otto Järte sjuttio år; från vänner den 10 oktober (1951). Stockholm: Svenska Dagbladet.

Pålsson Syll, L. (2007). *De ekonomiska teoriernas historia*. Lund: Studentlitteratur.

Sandelin, B. (2001). The De-Germanization of Swedish Economics. *History of Political Economy*, 33 (3): 517–539.

Sandelin, B., Trautwein, H-M. and Wundrak, R. (2008). *Det ekonomiska tänkandets historia*. Stockholm: Förlag.

Silverstolpe, G. W. (1944). Karl Gustav Cassel. *Svenska Män och Kvinnor*. Stockholm. Bonnier.

Sommarin. E. (1931). Das Lebenswerk von Knut Wicksell. *Zeitschrift für Nationalökonomie*, 2 (2): 221–267.

Steffen, G. (1889). *Den industriella arbetarfrågan.* Studentföreningen Vredandis småskrifter 11. Stockholm.

Steffen, G. (1903). Om begreppet folkhushållning. *Ekonomisk Tidskrift,* 5: 1–15.

Steffen, G. (1905a). *Sociala studier: Försök till belysning av nutidens samhällsutveckling.* Booklet 1. Stockholm: Hugo Gebers.

Steffen, G. (1905b). *Sociala studier.* Booklet 2. Stockholm: Hugo Gebers.

Steffen, G. (1906a). *Sociala studier.* Booklet 3. Stockholm: Hugo Gebers.

Steffen, G. (1906b). *Sociala studier.* Booklet 4. Stockholm: Hugo Gebers.

Steffen, G. (1912). *Sociala studier.* Booklet 7. Stockholm: Hugo Gebers.

Thomasson, C-G. (1962). Gustaf Steffen: En säregen gestalt i svensk lärdomshistoria. *Statsvetenskaplig Tidskrift,* 65 (4): 279–307.

Tingsten, H. (1941). *Den svenska socialdemokratins idéutveckling I.* Stockholm: Tidens.

Uhr, C. G. (1960). *Economic Doctrines of Knut Wicksell.* Berkeley: University of California Press.

Uhr, C. G. (1975). *Economic Doctrines of David Davidson.* Uppsala: Almqvist & Wiksell.

Uhr, C. G. (1991). David Davidson: The Transition to Neoclassical Economics, in B. Sandelin, (ed.), *The History of Swedish Economic Thought.* London: Routledge, 76–121.

Uhr, C. G. (2014). David Davidson, in C. Jonung and A.-C. Ståhlberg (eds.), *Svenska nationalekonomer under 400 år.* Stockholm: Dialogos, 138–154.

Vallinder, T. (1992). Pontus Fahlbeck – en statsvetenskaplig klassiker, in G. Falkemark (ed.), *Statsvetarporträtt.* Stockholm: SNS, 51–70.

Wicksell, K. (1896). *Finanztheoretische Untersuchungen nebst Darstellung und Kritik des Steuerwesens Schwedens.* Jena: Gustav Fischer.

Wicksell, K. (1900). G F Steffen: Studier över lönesystemets historia i England. *Göteborgs Handels- och Sjöfartstidning,* 20 June.

Wicksell, K. (1905). *Socialiststaten och nutidssamhället.* Stockholm: Albert Bonniers.

Wicksell, K. (1914). Lexis och Böhm-Bawerk. *Ekonomisk Tidskrift,* 16 (11): 322–334.

Wisselgren, P. (2000). *Samhällets kartläggare: Lorénska stiftelsen, den sociala frågan och samhällsvetenskapens formering 1830–1920.* Stockholm: Brutus Östlings Bokförlag Symposion.

Wohlin, N. (1918). *Svensk ekonomi och politik: Några uppsatser från krigsåren 1914–1917.* Stockholm: Albert Bonniers.

Wohlin, N. (1919). *Den svenska konservatismens framtid: Föredrag inför nationella ungdomsförbundet i Stockholm den 10 mars 1919.* Stockholm: Hedberg & Björklund Tryckeribolag.

11 The influence of the German Historical School on economic theory and economic thought in Russia

Vladimir Avtonomov and Georgy Gloveli

Russian import of political economy and the reception of ideas of the old historical school

The German influence on Russian economic thought underwent several stages. As Schumpeter pointed out, in Germany the historical school constituted the third epoch in the development of German political economy. The first one was the epoch of cameralistics, the second corresponding to the English period of classical political economy and culminating in such works as those of von Thünen and Hermann (Schumpeter, 2003: 296). In Russia cameralistics was taught under Alexander I (1801–1825) and Nikolay I (1825–1855), at the same time as the classical ideas of Adam Smith and Jean-Baptiste Say were gaining popularity. In these periods the German influence on Russian economic thought was ambivalent. On the one hand, German professors were promoting classical political economy in Russia through universities, both German (especially Göttingen) and Russian (Moscow, Kharkov, Derpt [Tartu], and St. Petersburg). On the other hand, the Germans were spreading the tradition of cameralist sciences, which emphasized the role of state statistics.

Russia's first political economist and statistician was a Baltic German called Heinrich von Storch (1766–1835), the author of *Cours d' économie politique ou exposition des principes qui déterminent la prospérité des nations* (1815), who became known in Europe as the first-rank representative of "eclectic political economy" (Blanqui, 1837: 289). This tradition included the first courses of political economy, written by Russians back in the period of serfdom: *Notes on Political Economy* (1844) by Kharkov professor Timofey Stepanov (1795–1847), and *An Essay on National Wealth, or On the Origins of Political Economy* (1847) by Alexander Butovsky. The influence of these essays in Russia, however, was negligible, unlike that of the *Lehrbuch der politischen Ökonomie* (1826–1837) by Heidelberg professor Karl Rau, who also published the German translation of Storch's course (1819). Rau combined the approaches of the cameralists and the classical school, and divided political economy into *theoretical* (abstract universal theory of national economy) and *applied* (economical politics and financial science). His Russian students willingly accepted this division.

But during this era, which Alexander Herzen referred to as an amazing period of external political slavery and internal liberation, Russia's intellectual import contained not only political economy but also French utopian socialism (see Normano, 1945, ch. 3). The ideas of Saint-Simon, Fourier, Cabet and George Sand penetrated the educated Russian youth's living rooms and circles (including illegal ones). Slavophile philosophers had a different reaction to these contradictions: they advocated a conservative alternative to Western industrialization and pauperization by proclaiming communal ownership of land and village industrial teams (artels) the foundation of Russia's unique path of development. It is interesting that the Slavophiles draw heavily on such German authors as Friedrich List, who anticipated the historical school, and Freiherr August von Haxthausen. Haxthausen praised the Russian community and cottage industry in his 1847 book *Studien über die inneren Zustände, das Volksleben und insbesondere die ländlichen Einrichtungen Russlands*, written after a visit to Russia in 1843. Yuri Samarin, who was best educated in political economy among all the Slavophiles, quoted List's *National System of Political Economy* to justify diversity of national economic institutions. Samarin viewed socialism as an ideal of a lifestyle based on obshina (village community) and artel, but distorted by Western rationalism.

After Europe was hit by the revolutions of 1848, Russian Westernizers split into two camps. The first one accepted the ideas of the Manchester School. The other one remained faithful to Western utopian socialism or, as influential political emigrants Alexander Herzen and Nikolay Ogarev did, supported obshina and artel as the seeds of "Russian socialism".

With the Great Reforms came the debates between Russian supporters of liberal political economy and their socialist and Slavophile opponents. Large literary magazines, which published a mix of novels, poetry and critical essays with political and philosophical debates, played a special part in this battle. St. Petersburg's *Sovremennik* (The Contemporary), headed by Nikolay Chernyshevsky, was the most influential of all such magazines. Another St. Petersburg magazine, *Ekonomichesky ukazatel* (The Economic Indicator), became the Manchester School's platform, while Moscow's *Vestnik promyshlennosti* (The Messenger of Industry) voiced the position of the Slavophiles with their industrial protectionism.

The first person to enlighten the Russian public on "historical method in political economy" was Ivan Babst (1824–1881), a young historian and a professor of political economy at Kazan University. In yet another monthly magazine, *Russky Vestnik* (The Russian Messenger), he published in 1856 a lengthy review of Wilhelm Roscher's *System des Volkswirthschaft*. Soon afterwards he became famous for giving the public lecture "Upon Some Conditions Favoring the Multiplication of National Capital" and received an invitation to join Moscow University. In Moscow Babst headed the chair of political economy (1857–1874) and worked as the editor at *The Messenger of Industry* magazine and *The Shareholder* newspaper. In later years he also headed the Moscow Merchant Bank (from 1867). He published the translation of the first volume of Roscher's magnum opus (1860) and two books of his own (1860), which drew upon Rau and Roscher.

Babst, who became famous after calling on Russia to follow the West's "materialistic mindset", was not an original thinker. Interestingly, unlike Roscher, who supported governmental nonintervention, Babst defined historicism as a middle way between two extremes: classical liberalism and revolutionary socialism. Roscher refused to tackle the problem of economic inequality, while Babst relied on the peaceful way of positive legislation to help relieve poverty (Babst, 1856). He also advocated support for Russia's "adolescent" industry through moderate protectionism and the credit system.

New generations of Russian economists wanted to reach the level of European intellectual standards, but they realized the striking difference between Western roots of classical political economy and the Russian background of serfdom. They also realized that European industrialization had a darker side to it, its own controversies and conflicts. For that reason they were attracted both to the idea of economic evolution and to experimental economic forms in the West: industrial cooperatives, socialist communes, consumer associations and so on.

Alexander Korsak (1832–1874) was the first author to use the evolutionary approach to explain the economic divergence between Russia and the West, and the first to discuss potential forms of industrial progress other than the factory. Korsak was Babst's student at Kazan University, and followed Babst to Moscow, where he completed his master's thesis at Moscow University. Babst was known primarily for propagating the ideas of the historical school in Russia, but Korsak's work was an original Russian contribution to historical political economy, or the first Russian case of comparative studies.

Alexander Korsak: Russia's first comparative economist

Alexander Korsak defined his chief goal as verifying the idea that domestic (cottage) industry, usually combined with an agricultural lifestyle, was Russia's unique economic pattern that would allow it to avoid "the proletarian ulcer" (Korsak,1861). Korsak's historical method consisted of two parts: first, defining where the Russian cottage industry stood relative to stages of European industrial progress; second, explaining the divergent fates of industry in different nations.

Korsak was the first Russian author to explicitly formulate the stages of industrial progress: urban corporative craft – manufacture – factory. In doing so, first of all, he replaced the habitual notion of manufacture in the sense of processing industry by a logical and historical category of *manufacture* as a form of large-scale production relying on cooperation in specialized *handcraft*; he did that even earlier than Marx (see *Das Kapital*, volume 1, 1867). Second, Korsak was the one to introduce into Russian economic thought the category of *industrial revolution*, borrowing it from German chemist and social projector Marlo (real name Karl Georg Winkelblech, 1810–1865). Third, he described the *economy of scale* as the factory's primary advantage.

Korsak explained the uniqueness of Russian industry by the absence of the Western tradition of privileged labor: labor hidden behind city walls, specialized in skill, united in guilds and guaranteeing quality production. Russia's vast and monotonous territory, lack of a truly settled lifestyle and poor trade communication slowed down urban development. Cities were founded mostly for administrative and military purposes. They did not become, like they did in the West, self-governed communities and centers of a thriving middle class.

This is why Russian craft never took the form of urban workshops, never became the property of a separate social strata with its own pride and monopoly rights. Craft was scattered among the villagers, who did not form lasting teams, did not have any privileges and did not improve their skills through workshops. Korsak pointed out the distribution of *wholesale crafts*: all the population of a whole village, located near a high road, would take up one kind of craft (smithcraft, carriage-building, weaving, etc.). The village would produce cheap, simple goods that could be sold only at *remote* markets.

Western workshops, on the contrary, produced expensive quality goods. They were ousted when manufacture and the factory managed to produce cheap quality goods. The first manufactures, which struggled to produce *inexpensive* goods, appeared in countries that were conveniently located to import foreign raw materials and export goods (Italy and the Netherlands). They targeted mostly remote international markets of luxury goods (primarily thin cloth and silk). Later on, with royal support (especially in France and in German kingdoms), the number of luxury manufactures increased. At the same time, villagers developed a system of cottage production of most popular consumer goods from local materials. Since the cottage industry was the secondary activity of farmers, who worked on commission paid by entrepreneurs, it produced cheap goods. Therefore, the cottage industry was not a unique Russian feature.

Due to lack of craft skills among the general public, the tsardom of Muscovy used to assemble craftsmen in state-funded settlements, or invite foreigners to work at production facilities. Peter I attempted to transfer all of the Western industries of his time to the unprepared Russian soil. He popularized manufactures through monopolies and serfdom, measures that Korsak referred to as "misfortunate" (Korsak, 1861: 121). But in separate cases these measures stimulated the improvement of village cottage industry (as in the "cotton chintz" village of Ivanovo, Vladimir Principality).

During the industrial revolution the factory ousted old-fashioned craft, manufacture and cottage industry, albeit not everywhere. The factory had several advantages: it combined the labor of many workers, adults and children, around a *single* system of mechanisms, put into motion by a centralized driving force; it relied on technical progress based on chemistry and mechanics; and loan funds were readily available. The darker side was the miserable life of "masses deprived of capital," people who accumulated in cities.

Russia's undeveloped factory production, which failed to reach both cheapness and diversity of goods, left the cottage industries competitive, which were "negligible separately, but strong all together" (Korsak, 1861: 48). Thus, the peculiarity of forms of Russian industry reflects its economic backwardness, rooted in its geography and history. But Korsak was not too enthusiastic about the factory system with its "helpless" proletariat. He emphasized the *forced* nature of land expropriation in larger countries, such as England or Prussia, and provided data on multiple small-scale cottage industries in smaller countries, such as Switzerland and Sweden (Korsak, 1861: 183–185).

In his book, published in the year when serfdom was abolished, Korsak mentioned Russian *communal ownership* of land only once, in order to make fun of its "discoverer", August Von Haxthausen, who imagined that Russian village crafts were "associations reminiscent of Saint-Simonianism" (Korsak, 1861: 272–273). However, Korsak did not rule out the possibility of village industrial associations in the future.

Korsak's book left his contemporaries unimpressed, who were busy arguing about the obshina. In hindsight, it was highly praised by Mikhail Tugan-Baranovsky (Tugan-Baranovsky, 1899: 851). Russia's first professional economic historians, Iosif Kulisher and Mitrofan Dovnar-Zapolsky, both pointed out that Korsak had anticipated some of the conclusions of the younger German Historical School (GHS). But all these authors neglected Korsak's interesting conclusion on the connection between Russia's persistent cottage industry and peculiar form of agriculture.

Russia's cold continental climate made the schedule of field labor very tight. This prevented the village population from specializing *exclusively* in farming and from switching to the Western improved *alternate husbandry* system. This same factor forced farmers to look for additional employment and sources of income outside agriculture. They spent long periods of time (up to six or eight months), free from tending to their small land plots, producing cheap goods that competed with factory products.

This mixed, partly artisan, partly farming state of Russian laborers ("family form of industry") was named "the main issue of Russian life" (Ivaniukov, 1885: 26) by economists who were educated in the 1860s, and were influenced by the younger GHS in the 1870s.

Reception of the younger historical school's ideas

Ivan Babst's students at Moscow University, Alexander Chuprov (1842–1908) and Ivan Yanzhul (1846–1914), inherited his view of the historical method as the middle way between economic liberalism and revolutionary socialism. This view coincided with the creed announced in the 1870s by the younger GHS and *Verein für Socialpolitik*.

Chuprov and Yanzhul went to study at Leipzig University in 1872. They attended Roscher's courses on political economy and finance, and young Georg Knapp's course on the labor issue. From Knapp's lectures they learned about Schmoller and Brentano (Yanzhul, 1910: 79). It was just the time when young Lujo Brentano published his *Die Arbeitergilden der Gegenwart*, while in Eisenach Schmoller presided over the founding congress of *Verein für Socialpolitik*.

After Leipzig, Chuprov went on to study at Vienna University, where he attracted the attention of Lorenz von Stein (1815–1890), famous political scientist and author of the fundamental *Lehrbuch der Finanzwissenschaft*. Stein, who had been influenced by the older historical school, developed his own teaching on the government (Stein, 1865–1868), based on the idea of the state as the higher authority that sits above society and the class struggle, and aspires to help the poor classes.

Soon afterwards, in 1874, Chuprov received the chair of political economy at Moscow University. He quickly became Russia's most popular professor of political economy. He owed his popularity not only to his teaching skills but also to his activities as author of the Moscow daily *Russkie Vedomosti* (The Russian Reports)[1] and member of the Russian Special Higher Commission on Railways. The commission was assembled after the general public became outraged at massive misuse of funds during the construction of private railroads in the 1860s and 1870s, the period of Russian railroad-building fever. The commission developed a "Statute of Russian Railways" and acquired private railroads for state ownership.

Railway affairs provided ample material for Chuprov's master's (1875) and doctoral (1878) theses. He analyzed the peculiarities of production costs in the railroad industry, as well as the reasons for inevitable state regulation (natural monopoly; expropriation of private lands for construction; link to international relations and defense abilities). He skillfully used statistical data to support his conclusions.

Chuprov's friends, Yanzhul and Ivan Ivaniukov (1844–1912), also combined teaching with writing and governmental jobs. Yanzhul defended his master's (1874) and doctoral (1876) theses at Moscow University on the history of taxation and England's commercial policy, and became a professor of financial law. Yanzhul made annual visits to England in order to catch up on the latest economics literature. In late 1870s he wrote a detailed report on the English factory legislation as part of his work on the Moscow governor's commission evaluating the everyday life of factory workers. After that in 1881 Yanzhul put together a statistical report on the life of factory workers in Moscow Principality.

The highlight of Yanzhul's studies was the conclusion that it is the struggle of different class interests that defined financial institutions and trade policy of a certain historical period. When landlords dominated England's politics, they benefited from excise duties and limited trade. But factory owners were gaining more political weight, so indirect taxes and custom duties, which held back industrial development, started to diminish. Another point he stressed was that the free trade policy, which was beneficial for England as the leading industrial nation, could not be considered universally beneficial. Starting in the late 1870s, both in his articles and lectures Yanzhul promoted a shift to customs protectionism in Russia (introduction of protective tariffs), and advocated governmental regulation of factory workers' conditions of labor and life.

Yanzhul found a like-minded author in Adolf Wagner, whose *Grundlegung der politischen Ökonomie* and *Finanzwissenschaft* were published in Leipzig and

Heidelberg in the 1870s and 1880s. Yanzhul saw his own ideas reflected in Wagner's suggestions to use taxation as a tool for social reform, and in Wagner's division of financial history into two periods: a purely fiscal period, and a social and political one. The second period brought with it partial redistribution of national wealth and the introduction of progressive taxation on inheritance and capital.

Ivan Ivaniukov, unlike Chuprov or Yanzhul, graduated from St. Petersburg University. As a specialist in money and credit, Ivaniukov received an invitation to manage Bulgaria's finances after this land was liberated in the course of the Russo-Turkish War of 1877–1878. After that he taught at Petrovsky Agricultural Academy in Moscow; he defended his doctoral thesis, *Main Propositions of Economic Policy from Adam Smith till Present Time*, at Moscow University in 1881. In his thesis, Ivaniukov advocated the historical nature of property rights and the active role of the state in social reforms. He widely quoted the speech Schmoller had given at the Eisenach convention, and underlined that projects similar to those proposed by *Verein für Socialpolitik* could be applied in Russia. Thus, Ivaniukov manifested his affiliation with German "Kathedersozialisten", socialists of the chair.

In late 1860s Ivaniukov spent two years in the United States, where he worked as a hired hand at a farm to get acquainted with the life of local socialist communes. During the same period, Chuprov, accompanied by young scientist Nikolay Umov (1846–1915, first Russian physicist-theoretician), founded the short-lived Society for the Spread of Technical Knowledge among Peasants and Craftsmen.

Chuprov and Ivaniukov did not join the revolutionary populists (narodniki), but they stuck to their belief in Russian communal land ownership and family (cottage) industry. This belief brought them even closer to the younger historical school, which paid a lot of attention to history and statistics of European small-scale cottage industry in all of its various forms (*Hausfleiss, Hausgewerbe, Hausindustrie; industrie domestique, buissonniere*). At the same time, both Chuprov and Ivaniukov recognized the validity of the classical English deductive method, and both relied on the labor theory of value and on Marx's analysis of large-scale industry evolution. In his inaugural professorial speech at Moscow University, Chuprov underlined that each of the paradigms (English liberal political economy, historical school, Marxism) had a grain of truth in it. In his lectures on the history of political economy he emphasized that the historical school took the middle way between economic liberalism and revolutionary socialism. Ivaniukov expressed the same position in his textbook, symptomatically entitled *Political Economy as a Doctrine about the Process of Development of Economic Phenomena* (Ivaniukov, 1885).

Russian ministers of finance and Russian social policy makers

The historical school played a special part in shaping Russian political economy and social policy due to its influence on Russian financial science and finance law. Another factor was the role that professors of political economy and financial law played in rationalizing and implementing the reforms that brought Russia closer to European standards of tax, monetary and industrial systems. Among these reforms, three stand out in particular:

- Reformation of taxes and introduction of factory legislation by Nikolay Bunge, Russia's finance minister in 1882–1886;
- Movement towards customs protectionism, and development of first protective (1880s) and later prohibitive duties (1891);
- Finance Minister Witte's monetary reform that established a gold standard in Russia (1895–1898).

When he received a proposition to head the Finance Ministry, Bunge was working as the rector of Kiev University. Before that he had worked for many years as a professor of political economy, statistics and police law. Bunge gained his academic degrees for studies of trade legislation and credit even before the Great Reforms; in his writings of the 1850s through the 1870s he was repeatedly skeptical about "aprioristic conclusions" and "fatalistic doctrines" of the classical school. Bunge contrasted Adam Smith, who relied on ample historical material, with his followers from Ricardo and John Stuart Mill's school. He praised Henry Carey and especially Adolf Wagner for conceptual flexibility and for switching from "ideas of free industry" to protectionism. Although Bunge disapproved of Wagner's state socialism, he agreed with Wagner on the necessity of taking railroads into state possession, matching taxation with paying capacity of all social strata and providing the working class with public welfare (Bunge, 1895: 173–174).

Bunge became finance minister in the context of counterreforms following the assassination of Alexander II by revolutionary socialists. But Bunge's reforms can be viewed as a continuation of the Great Reforms: he cancelled capitation tax and introduced factory inspections. Bunge asked Ivan Yanzhul to take the post of factory inspector in Moscow Principality, which the latter accepted, hoping to use his knowledge of English factory legislation to develop a similar legal base in Russia.

In his senior years, Bunge published several of his works under the title *Essays on Political-Economic Literature* (1895). In this compilation Bunge pointed out "historical and statistical transformation of political economy" as the most pressing issue of the day. Bunge also revealed his sympathies regarding the *Methodenstreit*: in this argument between Schmoller and Menger, he supported Schmoller (Bunge, 1895: 173–174).

It is important that other Russian economists sympathetic to the historical school did not share this liking for Schmoller, among them Chuprov and Vladimir Levitsky (1854–1939), author of the only Russian monograph dedicated exclusively to *Methodenstreit* (Levitsky, 1890).

Sergey Witte, a famous Russian finance minister, wrote the only Russian book on Friedrich List (1889). Witte's monetary reform, together with the prohibitive tariff of 1891, shaped Russian industrial policy into something resembling List's "protecting the internal manufacturing power" (List, 1909: 247). Witte once again requested the services of Yanzhul and another follower of the new historical school and *Socialpolitik*, Ivaniukov.

Ivaniukov in 1898 received an invitation to join the Ministry of Finance, and later (1902) became a professor of economic history in the first Russian economic department at the St. Petersburg Polytechnic Institute, founded following Witte's initiative. Together with two other specialists in financial law, Ivaniukov helped Witte develop his *Lectures on National Economy and Lectures on State Economy*. The finance minister read these lectures in 1900–1902 to the tsar's brother, Grand Duce Mikhail Romanov (1878–1918), heir to the throne and member of the State Council. Later on Witte published the lectures, which reflected his admiration for Friedrich List and his concern about the success of Karl Marx's teaching in Russia. In terms of historicism, the most important fragment of the text is found under the header "Russia's Peculiar Sequence of Development of National Economy Stages":

> With the abolition of serfdom, we, bypassing the middle stages of economic development, bypassing the period of manufactures, go straight to production based on machines, relying on knowledge and experience of Western Europe.
>
> (Witte, 1997: 45)

Evolution of the GHS and evolution of Russian Marxist political economy

To our knowledge, nobody has ever studied parallel developments of the GHS and Russian Marxism in 1893–1904. It was a period when the GHS was switching from scrupulous historical-economic monographs to a striking demonstration of what synthesis can do. Karl Bücher proposed a generalized scheme of Western European economic evolution in his *Entstehung der Volkswirtschaft* (Bücher, 1893). This was the turning point, as Schumpeter called it, *from the "younger" to the "youngest" historical school*. Werner Sombart's provocative *Der moderne Kapitalismus* (1902) contained open polemics against Bücher's work, and Max Weber's *Die protestantische Ethik und der Geist des Kapitalismus* (1904), written in response to Sombart, signified the final turn to the new discourse.

It is generally considered that the term "capitalism" became widespread in the West after the appearance of Sombart's *magnum opus*. The heated debates about the "fate of capitalism in Russia" started in 1893. One side of the dispute was represented by Tugan-Baranovsky and other young "economic materialists," who followed Marxism as the doctrine of Russia's industrial and capitalist development. This development, they insisted, had to follow the *same stages* that Western Europe had gone through. The opposite side was the group of legal populists affiliated with such Russian journals as *Russkoye bogatstvo* and *Severnyj Vestnik* (The Russian Wealth and The Northern Messenger). They insisted that traditional Russian institutes – communal ownership of land and cottage industry – gave Russia a chance to go straight to socialism, bypassing the middle stages

– that is, European stages of manufacture and factory production. To denounce this idea, "neo-Marxists" interpreted Russian village crafts as scattered manufacture, a type of early capitalism.

But pretty soon many authors known as "neo-Marxists" (Struve, Bulgakov, Tugan-Baranovsky) started calling themselves "critical Marxists," as opposed to Ulyanov-Lenin and other orthodox Marxists, who argued for materialism in philosophy, and for revolutionary fight for dictatorship of the proletariat in politics. This change brought them nearer to the GHS. The "post-Marxist" evolution of all three authors demonstrates nearly all of the typical points of the historical school: emphasis on ethics, nonmaterial factors of social development, interdisciplinary studies and social reforms. We could mention Tugan-Baranovsky, who published an article entitled "Psychological Factors of Social Development" (1904), critical of Marxism for overestimating the role of economic interests and class struggle, and for neglecting the ideal motives of human behavior (Tugan-Baranovsky, 1905: 76).

Interestingly, a New York magazine, *New Journal*, published by Russian emigrants, identified Struve, Bulgakov and Tugan-Baranovsky as members of the Russian Historical School. It is also important that in their early period of "legal Marxism" they had been strongly influenced by the GHS.

In view of debates on the Russian cottage industry, an important issue was the classification of enterprises and *past and present industrial forms*, which had been the focus of attention of German economists, especially Bücher and Sombart. Bulgakov edited a collection of translations from German (*The History of Labour Related to the History of Some Forms of Industry*, 1897), which included Bücher's "Historic Development and Classification of Industrial Forms." The same collection of essays featured Knapp's "Slavery and Freedom in Agricultural Labor." Knapp's treaty *Grundherrschaft und Rittergut* (1897), describing the transformation of the German agrarian sector on the verge of the capitalist era, was the standard on which Bulgakov based his comparative study of capitalist agrarian evolution in Western European countries.

Disappointed in Marxism, Bulgakov wanted to develop a new "Christian political economy" (Bulgakov, 1906: 16). For that to succeed, it was vital, he added, to keep the "scientific empiricism of the historical school" (Bulgakov, 1903: 347).

Both Bücher and Sombart disregarded Russia's economic history, but as Struve and Tugan-Baranovsky were working on the history of Russian industry, they widely used Bücher's *Die Entstehung der Volkswirtschaft*[2] and Sombart's *Political Economy of the Industry*. Based on Tugan-Baranovsky's *Russian Factory*, Struve argued that the category of *decentralized commodity production* was a typical feature of Russia's economic evolution. Russia did not go through, as Bücher pointed out, the European stage of urban economy, when increasingly specialized craft would rely upon developed local markets. But Russia's huge territory, Struve wrote, provided enough space for trade capital, which would find remote markets for production of villagers' unspecialized craft. Russia did not have corporative craftsmanship, but it also didn't have corporative law obscuring the entrepreneurs' freedom. Struve considered this an advantage on the way to capitalism.

Struve edited the Russian translations of Gerhart von Schulze-Gävernitz's *Grossbetrieb* (1897) and *Volkswirtschaftliche Studien aus Russland* (1901). After five years of political emigration, Struve started teaching at St. Petersburg Polytechnic Institute, and his first course was "The Economy of the Industry," fashioned after Sombart's work.

In the Russian Empire, Bücher's *Die Entstehung der Volkswirtschaft* was reprinted more often than any other book by a Western economist. And Sombart wrote more works translated into Russian than any other economist: over 30 books!

On the contrary, Max Weber's *Die protestantische Ethik und der Geist des Kapitalismus* failed to attract public attention, and was not translated into Russian. Of all Weber's works, only *Die Börse* (1897) was translated into Russian; later, in Soviet times, parts of *Wirtschaftsgeschichte* (1923) got translated, too. Nevertheless, Weber influenced Bulgakov and Struve during the period they contributed to *Vekhi*'s collection of essays (1909). Bulgakov, with his ambition to take the economic morals beyond materialistic hedonism, was impressed by Weber's concept of birth of spirit of capitalism from the "worldly asceticism" of the Reformation. In his article entitled "National Economy and a Religious Person" (Bulgakov, 1911: 70–126), as well as in his later book *The Philosophy of Economy* (1912), Bulgakov proposed to deepen, historically and psychologically, the image of "the economic man." He lamented the absence of studies on Russian economic life similar to *Die protestantische Ethik und der Geist des Kapitalismus*. However, Bulgakov himself did not write a similar study either, barely noting that Russian capitalism was closely related to old belief (Bulgakov, 1911: 122).

During the *Vekhi* period, Struve rejected Bücher's "systematization of economic forms" and instead turned to Weber's methodology of "ideal types" (Struve, 1913: vii). He suggested a classification of three "ideal economic types," and three corresponding groups of categories in political economy:

1 Categories expressing economic relations of any economic actor with the outside world (main categories: need, subjective value, labor).
2 Categories expressing interrelations of economic agents (main category: price).
3 Categories expressing relations of social inequality (main category: capital).

Using this typology, Struve wanted to explain the transformation of political economy into a truly empirical science, based on historical phenomenology. Another thing he aimed to explain was the limits of state regulation of economic processes. The first task was inspired by Etienne Laspeyres and his brochure *Die Kathedersocialisten und die statistischen Congresse: Gedanken zur Begründung einer nationalökonomischen Statistik und einer statistischen*

Nationalökonomie (1875). The second one was based on the notion of "heterogony," coined by the famous German psychologist Wilhelm Wundt. Struve defined interrelations of economic agents expressed through prices as an irrational area of domination of heterogony of individual objectives (Struve, 1913: 38). This means that the outcomes of intentional human efforts are unavoidably different from the initial intent. The lessons of history, as Struve pointed out, teach that under very different forms of political, social and economic regimes, the price ("free price") resists regulation by the authorities ("dictated price"). Nevertheless, although full regulation of prices is impossible, "the area of rational price formation" is extended through railway tariffs, cartel agreements and regulation of salaries.

In his last decade of life, Tugan-Baranovsky became Russia's most respected theorist of cooperative movement and "ethical socialism." As a historian, he systematized the experience of capitalist development, *commune-building experiments*, utopian thought and cooperative unions (Tugan-Baranovsky, 1912, 1916). Tugan-Baranovsky's forecast regarding the socialist regime as a combination of state collectivism and free cooperatives reflected his idea that the economy combines spontaneous and irrational *genetic* processes with consciously directed *teleological* processes. The juxtaposition of *genetics* and *teleology* was borrowed from American positive sociologist Lester Ward (1841–1913).

We could also add that Bulgakov, Struve and Tugan-Baranovsky especially appreciated List's concept of "national association of productive forces" (Struve, 1894: 261; Bulgakov, 1914: 156). Struve and Tugan-Baranovsky joined the Science Academy's commission on Russia's natural productive forces founded in 1915. The peak of the commission's activities occurred after the October Revolution, without Tugan-Baranovsky, who had passed away, and without Struve, who had left the country.

Iosif Kulisher, Russian follower of the GHS, and comparison of stages of Russian and Western industrial evolution

The dispute between Marxists and populists reflected the industrial breakthrough that happened in the Russian Empire in the 1890s. The breakthrough was stimulated by active governmental interference ("the Witte system") and resulted in accumulation of proletariat in cities surrounding major factories. The economic boom and the "labor issue" stimulated growing interest in industrialization in European countries, especially England. In the 1890s and 1900s Russian publishers released nearly all of the best-known works on the history of English industry written by Western economic historians, such as Adolf Held (younger GHS), William Ashly, William Cunningham, Thorold Rogers, Arnold Toynbee and Frenchman Paul Mantoix. Schumpeter mentions all of these names (Schumpeter, 1954: 809, 821), but he disregards Russian authors.

Meanwhile, Iosif Kulisher (1878–1933), graduate of St. Petersburg University, came closer to writing a comprehensive economic history than perhaps anyone else did. In 1900–1903 Kulisher studied under Schmoller in Berlin and under Inama-Sternegg in Vienna. During these years he published several articles on the history of interest rates in *Jahrbücher für Nationalökonomie und Statistik*, and these articles later developed into a book entitled *Evolution of Return on Capital Due to Development of Industry and Trade in Western Europe* (two volumes, 1906 and 1908). In 1905 Kulisher became privatdocent at St. Petersburg University, where he read a special course on the economic history of the West. At the same time he worked at the Ministry of Trade and Industry (1905–1906) and the Ministry of Finance (from 1907). He wrote his own *Course of Political Economy* (1911), based on the idea of changeability of economic categories throughout history. But Kulisher's magnum opus was his *Lectures on the History of Economic Life in Western Europe* (eight reprints in Russia, 1909–1931; German translation in two volumes, published 1928–1929).

The title of one of Kulisher's articles, "Economic History as a Science, and Periods in Economic Development of Nations" (1908a), demonstrates how important he found the task of identifying major stages of economic evolution. Kulisher focused his attention on stages that Western European and Russian industry went through. He drew upon Bücher's scheme, and supported Marx's idea that the stage of manufactures was a period of its own, and that it preceded large-scale machine production. However, he made important amendments to both sets of periods.

To Bücher's scheme Kulisher added a stage of "world economy", while the stage of "national economy" he associated with the manufacturing period and industrial revolution taken together. Kulisher undertook the first detailed comparative historical analysis of manufactures in all major European countries, including Russia, and made the following conclusions (Kulisher, 1908b: 128–137, 198; Kulisher, 1931):

- Adolf Held was right to say that the first type of major capitalistic enterprise was not the centralized manufacture, as Marx thought, but the system of large-scale cottage industry.
- Manufactures featured extended working days, nearing the limit of human physical capacity, and mass exploitation of women's and children's labor long before the industrial revolution.
- The emergence of manufactures in Russia was more similar to, than different from, the same process in Europe. Peter the Great enforced manufacturing by giving privileges to foreigners and using forced labor. Kulisher showed that in European manufactures privileges for foreigners and reliance on forced labor were also quite common.
- State enforcement of manufactures in absolute monarchies resulted in booming industries in France, Prussia and Russia.

As he went on to analyze the period of industrial revolution, Kulisher emphasized the destruction of institutes that held back the economies within nation-states. Little by little, nations developed the institutes of free production and distribution, liberty of mobility and free choice of profession, and free contracts and commerce. These processes defined the historical period of movement towards laissez-faire, when absence of governmental interference and unions became considered "the natural state" of the economy.

Nevertheless, just like the GHS, Kulisher found natural the emergence of the new industrial period. This happened when the stock exchange and steam- and electricity-powered transport broke the borders of national economies and shaped a global economy. At the same time, factory legislation emerged, social insurance arrived and new institutes appeared: syndicates and trusts, trade unions and cooperatives (Kulisher, 2004: 457–458).

Kulisher rejected the methodological individualism of the marginal utility theory (Kulisher, 1908b: 387, 405). Nevertheless, in his concept of evolution of return on capital he used Marshall's category of *consumer surplus* (Kulisher, 1908b: 12). According to Kulisher, by the end of the nineteenth century the progress of transportation and the expansion of commodity exchanges brought the prices of many goods down significantly lower than what the consumers were actually ready to pay. At the same time, the increasing role of trade organizations, which defended the laborers' interests, was slowly diminishing the role of exploitation of technical labor in creating capitalist profit. The main source of profit, Kulisher argued, was the creative labor of inventors. Introduction of technical inventions allowed entrepreneurs to start mass production of goods and sell them at prices allowing for the customer's surplus to form (mass distribution), but profitable enough to create the entrepreneur's surplus (profit) (Kulisher, 1908b: 270–271).

After the October Revolution, as Kulisher worked as a professor at Petrograd/ Leningrad's universities, he included the economic history of Russia in his research, but in this area he was not a pioneer.

Nikolay Oganovsky, his criticism of the GHS and comparison of stages of agricultural revolutions in Russia and the West

In order to develop a university course of Russia's economic history, it was necessary to reconsider the evolutionary stages proposed by the GHS and Marxism. The first attempt was made by Mitrofan Dovnar-Zapolsky (1867–1934). He developed his *History of Russian National Economy* (1911) as a textbook for the course he read. After the October Revolution, he became one of the founders of Belarus University in Minsk.

But the author who went much further than Dovnar-Zapolsky in solving the tasks formulated earlier was Nikolay Oganovsky (1874–1938), who wrote *The Laws of the Agrarian Evolution* (three volumes, 1909–1914) and *Agriculture, Industry, and Market in the 20th Century* (1924).

Oganovsky was a statistician in zemstvos, an enthusiast of agricultural cooperation, a fruitful publicist and an activist of the People's Socialist Party. He was a member of the Constituent Assembly, broken up by Bolsheviks, but he made peace with the Communist government after the Civil War. He read the first course in economic geography at Moscow University (Oganovsky, 1922). Oganovsky held a high-ranking position in the People's Commissariat of Agriculture, but was arrested and exiled under the trial of the Labor Peasant Party (1930).

Oganovsky's ambition was to develop a concept explaining the *agricultural prerequisites* on which Western industrial superiority was based, and which conditioned Russia to be a country with *balanced growth* of agriculture, livestock farming and industry.

He harshly criticized both Bücher's and Marx's schemes for a single-factor approach and their inability to see the structural and institutional evolution of agrarian societies "behind the bright paint of the industry, which covered the Western economic life in the nineteenth century" (Oganovsky, 1911: 540).

Oganovsky based his theoretic structure on agricultural economy, which set the sequence of phases in the evolution of *European agriculture*: *extensive* mobile slash-and-burn farming; *extensive* three-field farming with fallowing on settled territory; and *intensive* multifield farming. Oganovsky took this system and expanded it: first, he connected agronomical aspects with geography and institutions; second, he connected the shift to intensive farming with escape from the Malthusian trap of overpopulation and beginning of steady industrial growth.

The three-field system, with its conservative regulation of the soil's fertility by fallowing, was the basis of European feudal system, with its serfdom. Fallowing alone was not enough to restore fertility, so lands became exhausted and forced peasants to expand farming lands by cutting pasture territory. This disturbed the balance between farming and livestock breeding. The amount of food barely increased, but a high mortality rate (wars, diseases, feudal conflicts) held back the growth of the population, and so did the limitations that being in serfdom placed on the size of serfs' families.

The liberation of serfs in Western Europe, Oganovsky argued, triggered the growth of the population. The Malthusian law of decreasing fertility of land was a distorted reflection of the fact that extensive farming had reached its limits. Abolishing fallowing and adopting a new structure of crops allowed farming to intensify: farmers now cultivated not only grains but also grass, root, legume and oil crops. However, since the evolution of farming depends not only on agronomical but also on institutional factors (landowning, inequality of social classes and strata), Europe's way to an intensive agriculture was paved with famines, agrarian uprisings and revolutions (1640, 1789, 1848).

Nevertheless, by the early twentieth century, intensive farming, supported by agricultural chemistry, spread all over Europe. During the nineteenth century, crop yield in Europe increased on average by 2 to 2.5 times (after almost 1,000 years of oscillating around the same level). Sharp peaks and falls in production, dependence on climate and fear of famines became a thing of the past (Oganovsky, 1909: 293). Complementary links developed between farming and livestock breeding, as well as between agriculture in general and urban industry. The system of multiple fields provided for year-round feeding of livestock (grass crops, turnip, beet pulp) and raw materials for the industry (beets and potatoes). Livestock, which ate a better diet, was now bred selectively, provided milk and meat to feed the growing industrial population in cities, and served as a source of additional organic fertilizer. The city, with its industrial enterprises, accepted excessive countryside population, and provided growing demand for agricultural production. In response, the city supplied improved agricultural machines, artificial fertilizers, warehousing and transport infrastructure, credit and so on. Oganovsky united all these processes under the heading "*sustainable development of productive forces*".

In the Russian Empire, nevertheless, these processes were active only in Western provinces: the rest of the country kept using the three-field system. This system was especially unproductive in the center of the country, with its marginal lands; it exhausted the fields and prompted the migration of peasants after the abolition of serfdom.

Oganovsky agreed that the three-field system had been so persistent in part because the obshinas imposed obligatory rotation of crops and strip farming on every member. But he also identified other factors that made it persistent: the pressure from the external market, and vast internal colonization. Trade capital found grain crops the most convenient commodity for export. Meanwhile, the geographic factor allowed extensive farming to constantly expand into new colonized territories: the Volga region, Novorossiya and the Crimea, Northern Caucasus, Siberia and the steppes (Oganovsky, 1911: 24–25). But giving over 90 percent of lands to grain crops (in Europe the share of grain crops was never higher than 70 percent) only increased the imbalance between farming and livestock breeding.

Oganovsky was certain, first of all, that progress required intensive agricultural technologies that would integrate livestock breeding and farming. Second, he believed that medium-sized and not large-scale enterprises were best for the agricultural economy. Third, he maintained that although technical *processing and exchange* (credit, distribution, purchase) of agricultural production obeyed the laws of industrial concentration, this concentration could be in cooperative, not *large-scale* capitalist, form (Oganovsky, 1909: 305).

According to Oganovsky's observations (just like according to Sergey Bulgakov's), large-scale commodity farming had been successful in Europe while it enjoyed the artificial support of the government. But as the parliamentary legislation in Western Europe grew more democratic, the positions of medium-sized farms grew stronger. Oganovsky considered farming cooperatives just as important as industrial syndicates.

Thus, the theory of agricultural evolution and the prerequisites for a shift towards a "two-sided" (agricultural and industrial market) type of development led Oganovsky to justify active cooperative and governmental regulation (Oganovsky, 1914: 16). He was close to Alexander Chayanov and other "new populists", who hoped the intelligentsia would help peasants to switch to intensive farming and cooperative organization. These economists also expected the government to take care of transport and warehousing infrastructure, as well as of international trade policy that would push the structure of export towards intensive crops and livestock.

Wrapping up our account, we could say that Iosif Kulisher was a direct *Russian* follower of the *German* Historical School, but Nikolay Oganovsky, who started out critical of the GHS, gradually became a major representative of the *Russian* historical movement in political economy. His concept of sustainable development of productive forces (Oganovsky, 1924: 10) can be considered an anticipation of Western discussions on self-sustained growth that began in the second half of the twentieth century.

Conclusion

Summing up the influence of the GHS on Russian economic thought, we would like to stress the following points:

- Reception of both the old and younger GHS gave new impulses to the eclecticism as a feature of Russian political economy. One of the reasons for its popularity consisted in the belief that the historical school offered the midway point between classical liberalism and revolutionary socialism.
- The GHS stimulated the beginning of Russian *comparative economic studies* and contributed to discovering structural and institutional peculiarities of Russian agriculture and industry (Korsak, Ivaniukov).
- After the emancipation of the serfs, joining the GHS was a chance for new generations of Russian economists to get access to established European science. The younger GHS and *Socialpolitik* advocated by its members corresponded to the Russian public mood, the widespread belief in progressive phased development and social reforms.
- The empiricism declared by the GHS corresponded to the Russian disposition towards *applied* political economy, but Russian economists (except Bunge) did not agree with Schmoller's antitheoretical extremism in the course of *Methodenstreit.*
- Discussion of productive forces and protectionist economic policy (List) became the main agenda of Russian industrial policy (especially under Bunge's and Witte's administrations).
- Theory of stages of economic development (Buecher, Sombart and others) played the major role in politically relevant discussion about capitalist development in Russia. The youngest GHS's ideas penetrated Russian Marxist and post-Marxist discourse (Struve, Tugan-Baranovsky, Bulgakov). Russian agrarian economist Oganovsky criticized Bücher's scheme and undertook a comparative analysis of structural prerequisites of "sustainable development of productive forces".
- Special interest was devoted to the period of manufactures and Russian follower of the GHS Kulisher undertook the first detailed comparative

historical analysis of manufactures in all major European countries, including Russia.

• Ethical problems (under the influence of Schmoller's school and the Weber-Sombart controversy on the "spirit of capitalism") permeated Russian economic discourse (Tugan-Baranovsky, Bulgakov).

Notes

1 "No other country in the world ever possessed a daily periodical of similar standing and level" (Normano, 1945: 69).
2 "When Bücher published his wonderful essays, it was a feast that the economic science had not seen in a long time," Struve wrote (1897: 192–193).

References

Babst, I. (1856). Historical Method in Political Economy. *The Russian Messenger*, no. 3, 94–143 (in Russian).

Blanqui, A. (1837). *Histoire de l'économie politique en Europe depuis les Anciens jusqu'à nos jours*. Vol. 2. Paris, Guillamin, Libraire-Editeur.

Bücher, K. (1893) *Die Entstehung der Volkswirtschaft. Sechs Vorträge*. Tübingen, Laupp.

Bulgakov, S. (Ed.). (1897). *The History of Labour Related to the History of Some Forms of Industry*. Translated from German. Saint Petersburg, V. A. Tikhanov (in Russian).

Bulgakov, S. (1903). *From Marxism to Idealism*. Saint Petersburg (in Russian).

Bulgakov, S. (1906). *A Short Essay of Political Economy*. Moscow (in Russian).

Bulgakov, S. (1911). *Two Cities: An Inquiry into the Nature of the Social Ideals*. Vol. 1. Moscow (in Russian).

Bulgakov, S. (1912). *The Philosophy of Economy*. Part 1. Moscow (in Russian).

Bulgakov, S. (1914). *History of Economical Teachings*. Moscow (in Russian).

Bunge, N. (1895). *Essays on Political-Economic Literature*. Moscow.

Ivaniukov, I. (1885). *Political Economy as a Doctrine about the Process of Development of Economic Phenomena*. Saint Petersburg, M. M. Stasyulevich (in Russian).

Knapp G. F. (1897). *Grundherrschaft und Rittergut*. Leipzig, Duncker & Humblot.

Korsak, A. (1861). *About the Forms of Industry in General and the Place of Domestic Production in Western Europe and in Russia*. Moscow, Grachev (in Russian).

Kulisher , I. (1908a). Economic History as a Science, and Periods in Economic Development of Nations. *Russkaya Mysl, 7*, 53–79.

Kulisher, I. (1908b). *Evolution of Return on Capital Due to Development of Industry and Trade in Western Europe*. Vol. 2. Saint Petersburg, A. G. Rozen (in Russian).

Kulisher, I. (1911). *A Course of Political Economy*. Saint-Petersburg, Prosveshenie (in Russian).

Kulisher, I. (1931). La Grande Industrie aux XVII et XVIII siècles. *Annales d'histoire économique et sociale*. 3e année. No. 9. P. 11–46.

Kulisher, I. (2004). *History of Economic Life in Western Europe*. Chelyabinsk, Sotsium (in Russian).

Laspeyres E. (1875). *Die Kathedersocialisten und die statistischen Congresse: Gedanken zur Begründung einer nationalökonomischen Statistik und einer statistischen Nationalökonomie*. Berlin: Habel.

Levitsky, V. (1890). *The Scopes and Methods of Science upon National Economy*. Yaroslavl. G.V. Falk's typolithography (in Russian).

List, F. (1909). *The National System of Political Economy.* Calcutta, Longmans, Green.

Marx, K. (1867). *Das Kapital, Kritik der politischen Oekonomie.* Vol. 1. Hamburg, Verlag von Otto Meisner.

Normano, J. (1945). *The Spirit of Russian Economics.* New York, John Day.

Oganovsky, N. (1909). *The Laws of the Agrarian Evolution. Vol. 1: The Theories of Capitalist Development.* Saratov, Sotrudnichestvo (in Russian).

Oganovsky, N. (1911). *The Laws of the Agrarian Evolution. Vol. 2: Essays on History of Land Relations in Russia.* Saratov, Sotrudnichestvo (in Russian).

Oganovsky, N. (1914). *The Laws of the Agrarian Evolution. Vol. 3: The Renewal of Agricultural Russia.* Moscow, Zadruga (in Russian).

Oganovsky, N. (1922). *Essays in Economic Geography Relative to World Economy.* Vol. 1. Moscow, Novaya derevnya (in Russian).

Oganovsky, N. (1924). *Agriculture, Industry, and Market in the 20th Century.* Moscow. V.S.N. Kh.'s edition. (in Russian).

Schulze-Gävernitz, G. von (1892). *Grossbetrieb Der Grossbetrieb: ein wirtschaftlicher und socialer Fortschritt. Eine Studie auf dem Gebiete der Baumwollindustrie.* Leipzig, Duncker & Humblot.

Schulze-Gävernitz, G. von (1899). *Volkswirtschaftliche Studien aus Russland.* Leipzig, Duncker und Humblot.

Schumpeter, J.A. (1954). *History of Economic Analysis* (published posthumously, ed. Elisabeth Boody Schumpeter). New York, Oxford University Press.

Schumpeter, J.A. (2003). *Ten Great Economists.* Taylor & Francis e-Library.

Sombart, W. (1902). *Der moderne Kapitalismus. Bd. 1. Die Genesis des Kapitalismus.* Leipzig, Duncker und Humblot.

Stein, L. von (1865–1868). *Die Verwaltungslehre.* 7 vols. Stuttgart, Cotta.

Struve, P. (1894). *The Critical Notes on a Question about Economic Development of Russia.* Saint Petersburg. I.N. Skorohodov's typography (in Russian).

Struve, P. (1913). *Economy and Price.* Vol. 1. Saint Petersburg, V. P. Riabushinskii (in Russian).

Tugan-Baranovsky, M. (1899). Economic Science: Russia. *Brockhaus and Efron Encyclopedic Dictionary.* Semi-Volume 55. P. 891–894. Saint Petersburg. Brockhaus i Efron (in Russian).

Tugan-Baranovsky, M. (1905). *Theoretic Foundations of Marxism.* Saint Petersburg, Mir Bozhiy (in Russian).

Tugan-Baranovsky, M. (1916). *Social Foundations of Cooperation.* Moscow. A.L. Shanyavsky's Moscow City Popular University. (in Russian).

Weber, M. (1904–1905). *Die protestantische Ethik und der Geist des Kapitalismus.* Archiv für Sozialwissenschaften und Sozialpolitik, Vol. 20, S. 1–54, 1904; Vol. 21, pp. 1–110.

Weber, M. (1924). *Gesammelte Aufsätze zur Sozial- und Wirtschaftsgeschichte.* Hrsg. von Marianne Weber. Tübingen, Mohr.

Witte, S. (1997). *Synopsis of Lectures on National and State Economy.* Moscow. Narodnoe khozyastvo. (in Russian).

Yanzhul, I. (1910). *Memoirs.* Saint Petersburg. Vol. 1. N.Ya. Stoykova's electrolithography (in Russian).

12 The evolution of the German Historical School in Bulgaria (1878–1944)

Nikolay Nenovsky and Pencho D. Penchev

The ideas of the German Historical School were disseminated in Bulgaria with some delay due to the general economic, social and ideological falling behind of Bulgaria compared to the developed western countries. In the different stages of their influence, they were commingled with ideas characteristic of different national traditions in economic thought (French and Russian) and/or with various other schools and trends, such as classical liberalism, quantitative monetarism and the Austrian School of economics. The economic, social and political development of Bulgaria during these years can be divided into two subperiods: (a) nation-building from 1878 to the outbreak of Balkan Wars and participation of Bulgaria in World War I (1912–1913 and 1915–1919), and (b) the postwar period from 1919 to the outbreak of World War II. At the end of this war a new government dominated by the communists was established in Bulgaria. These subperiods are a useful framework for understanding the evolution of the German Historical School in Bulgaria.

Building a national economy (1878–1912)

Historical and institutional context

Modern Bulgaria appeared on Europe's political map in 1878 as a result of the Russo-Turkish War (1877–1878) and the decisions of the Treaty of Berlin (1878). During the period between the liberation and the outbreak of the Balkan Wars (1878–1912) the Bulgarian economy was characterized by a large subsistence agriculture, with wheat being the key export product. The manufacturing industry was almost nonexistent in the Bulgarian Principality. The Treaty of Berlin predetermined Bulgaria's foreign trade positions compared to the developed Western European countries. By virtue of Article 8 the principality retained the validity of the "trade and maritime agreements, as well as all conventions and agreements signed between the foreign powers and the High Porte" (Kesyakov, 1926: 1–5). Most of those agreements were signed in 1861 and 1862 between the Ottoman Empire and all leading Western European powers. They stipulated that all foreign goods are subject to an 8% ad valorem duty when imported to the empire (Chakalov, 1928: 3). The provisions of the Treaty of Berlin limited the opportunities of the Bulgarian state to conduct independent foreign trade and economic policy.

At the very beginning of the independent national existence of Bulgaria the government did slowly but surely expand its control over various sectors of economy. This was due to the fact that the newly created Bulgarian Principality was an agricultural country with no domestic savings and as A. Gerschenkron observed, the state becomes the main instrument of industrialization. As envisaged by the constitution, initially there were six ministries and only one of them had economic functions – that is the ministry of finance. By the last amendment of the constitution in 1911 the number of the ministries rose to 10, five of which were charged with economic functions. Those were the ministries of finance; of agriculture and state property; of trade, industry and labour; of railways, posts and telegraphs; and of public buildings, roads and public works (Metodiev and Stoyanov, 1990: 35–35). In parallel, during the whole period there were continuous attempts to expand protectionism, and three acts on local industry encouragement were passed. In 1885 the state-owned railway operator was granted a monopoly on the country's rail transport, and in the same year coinage and note issuing were monopolised by the state; the posts and telegraphs also became a state monopoly; the underground natural resources became property of the state, as well as the largest coal mining company in the country, Mines of Pernik; and the Bulgarian Steamship Company was a mixed public-private enterprise. Apart from the Bulgarian National Bank (the central bank of the country), the public sector in banking was represented by the Postal Savings Bank, the Bulgarian Agricultural Bank established in 1903 and the Bulgarian Central Cooperative Bank established in 1910 (Avramov, 2007: 348–353).

While Bulgarian lands were under the Ottoman rule, the influence of the classical political economy was predominant among the Bulgarian intellectuals. Yet some of the main postulates of the German Historical School (protectionism, preference for domestic-made products, etc.) made their way into Bulgaria's general public. After the liberation of the country from Ottoman rule the role of historical analysis increased. It was a theoretical basis for the attempts of the Bulgarian elites to catch up with the developed economies. At the end of the nineteenth century there was a certain level of consensus among the politicians and economists of the country about the main features of the economic policy. In the programs of all Bulgarian political parties during this subperiod, there were demands for a state promotion of certain sectors of the economy, for government-funded building of roads and railways, for tariff protection and so forth (Nikolova and Sazdov, 1992). The *Bulgarian Economic Society* was founded in 1895 as a nonpartisan centre for debates, which included economists and politicians with different theoretical convictions. Among its main declared purposes were the encouragement of domestic industry and preference for local products instead of foreign. Even the Marxist theorists, who appeared in Bulgaria at the end of nineteenth century, supported the policy of encouraging the development of modern large-scale industry, which in turn would contribute to the emergence of modern agriculture with arguments that were elaborated by Fr. List (Blagoev, 1958 [1902]: 455).

Throughout their education, the Bulgarian economic and political elites adopted the *eclectic model* of liberal nationalism. After 1878 many Bulgarians studied in German universities. Thus a number of Bulgarians studied in Leipzig, where one of the lecturers was Karl Bücher. In Bücher's library, kept nowadays at Kyoto University, there are at least 15 Bulgarian doctoral dissertations written under his guidance or the guidance of his colleagues from Leipzig (Roscher, Ratzel, Brentano, Lamprecht, Stieda, Mayer, etc.) (Bücher, 1970). According to what V. Jordanov wrote in 1941, from 1879 to 1899, including all courses of study, more than 100 Bulgarian students received university education in Leipzig (based on Radonov, 1979: 313). For example in 1903–1904 73 Bulgarian students were enrolled in German universities, the largest group from the Balkan countries (Crowell, 1904: 594–595).

Initially, many Bulgarians studied in Russia, where the liberal principles were closely interrelated with the main postulates of the historical school (W. Roscher even spoke of a specific Russian-German historical tradition).[1] Of special significance were the prominent Russian economists I. Yanzhul and A. Chuprov (father), who taught a great number of renowned Bulgarian economists (G. Danailov being one of these). The influence of the Russian-German Historical School was manifested in the strong interest of Bulgarian economists in budget and public finance issues, and as a whole in practical problems and empirical and statistical studies.

Aspects of economic policy and economic thought

Among the main representatives of the Bulgarian economic thought after the liberation and until the end of the wars (1878–1919) were Grigor Nachovich (1845–1920), Ivan Evstatiev Geshov (1849–1924) and Georgi Danailov (1872–1939). They were responsible for some of the most important economic policy decisions during these years, and they illustrate that there was no dramatic contradiction between liberalism and the ideas of the German Historical School.

Grigor Nachovich was born in 1845. In 1860 he began his studies at *École supérieure de commerce de Paris*. Later on, he studied at the Sorbonne and at the College of France. There he read economic sciences, but could not complete his education. He graduated in Vienna. In France Nachovich fell under the influence of French liberalism, while in Vienna he made himself familiar with the achievements of the older German Historical School.

After the liberation of Bulgaria, Nachovich got actively involved with political life as a member of Parliament, minister of finance, minister of foreign affairs and religions, minister of interior, minister of trade and agriculture, minister of public buildings, agriculture and trade, and minister of public buildings, roads and communications (Tashev, 1999: 315–317).

In 1883 Nachovich published the brochure "Tobacco Industry in the Bulgarian Principality", and almost 20 years later he published his main economic study, entitled "Some Pages on Agriculture in Bulgaria and Abroad". His publications disclosed his broad theoretical knowledge in the fields of economics and economic history, philosophy, sociology, agronomy and so forth. Nachovich was among the few Bulgarian economists at the end of the nineteenth century who had a profound knowledge of the works of leading French, German and Russian authors.

Nachovich's views on private property rights, banks, credit and free economic initiative were typically liberal. According to him all measures for enforcement of property rights would eventually result in economic growth. Therefore, the legislature was obliged to ensure the inviolability of property rights against encroachment from the top, and the judicial system should guarantee inviolability against encroachment from the bottom. He was convinced that collective property hindered economic development, because the motivation for systematic efforts to increase production, improve agricultural equipment and so forth is lost. Nachovich's views on banks and credit were also liberal in nature. According to him, "the famous Scottish banks" were a model of independent credit institutions, which had benefitted and continued benefitting economic growth. Nachovich was aware that protectionism had a number of negative consequences (Nachovich, 1902: 52, 71).

The influence of the older German Historical School on Nachovich can be seen in several aspects. In his *Principles of Political Economy* Wilhelm Roscher declared that "By the science of National, or Political Economy, we understand the science which has to do with the laws of the development of a nation, or with its economic national life" (Roscher, 2008 [1854]: 55). Following this definition, Nachovich underwent a thorough study of all aspects of Bulgarian agriculture, without attempting to make universal implications for agriculture in general. However, once again following the principles of Roscher, who said that political economy has to answer the question "What is?", and also the question "What should be?", Nachovich not only described problems but also gave suggestions for improvements in agriculture. Among these are ideas about a new law on the improvement of agricultural education, adopting the new property law, promoting agricultural associations and abolishing usury (Nachovich, 1902: 244–246). According to Roscher the comparison between the economies of different countries and societies in certain periods is an important characteristic feature of the historical method of political economy (Roscher, 2008 [1854]: 66). This principle was widely applied by Nachovich, who compared Bulgarian agriculture and Bulgarian economic policy with those of Russia, France, the US, Italy, England and so forth. This makes his conclusions on the appropriate measures to encourage Bulgarian agriculture more adequate and justified. Nachovich broadly used arguments from economic history in order to illustrate or prove certain propositions. He adopted Roscher's theory of the main stages of economic development of mankind: historically people subsisted by hunting and fishing, and then they moved to the "status" of shepherds and nomads, and then to agriculture as the third step to civilization. He considered logically and argumentatively the appearance of private property in historical perspective, and defended the proposition that studying the economic history

of the advanced nations would bring benefits to the less developed
countries.

Nachovich was convinced of the capability of governments to improve the
fate of less developed countries and to introduce measures towards progress,
especially in agriculture. Among the main functions of the state, other than
protection of private property, he considered the encouragement of production,
attraction of foreign capitals, development of agricultural education, construction of railways, roads and granaries, drainage of wetlands, construction of
sewerage systems and flood control (Nachovich, 1902: 21–29, 97, 102, 187,
203–215).

Both in his scientific and theoretical works and in his activity as a politician,
Nachovich attempted to combine liberalism with governmental measures for
encouragement of the economy. In his position as finance minister in 1882–1883
Nachovich undertook the first steps towards the promotion of a domestic industry
and the implementation of an independent foreign trade policy (which was for-
bidden for Bulgaria under the terms of the Treaty of Berlin in 1878). On his
initiative, at the end of 1882 Parliament passed the first act by means of which,
although quite timidly, the state encouraged domestic industrial production.
According to this document Bulgarian goods would have to be preferred in
public procurement even when they were up to 15% more expensive than the
same foreign goods. At the end of December 1883 the first National Industrial
Development Act was passed (Yochev, n.d.: 72–73).

In 1883 again on the initiative of Nachovich the first independent Bulgarian
customs tariff was adopted. The tariff provided for higher duties imposed on
foreign goods imported to Bulgaria compared to those guaranteed by the Treaty
of Berlin (8% ad valorem) – the duties for certain goods reached 10%–12%
(Chakalov, 1928: 60). In addition, instead of imposing the same customs duty
rates on all goods, a specific duty was envisaged for the first time – that is there
was an attempt to protect domestic production through a system of high duties
on goods which were also produced domestically. That customs tariff, however,
concerned only the goods from countries which had not entered into trade agreements with the Ottoman Empire before signing the Treaty of Berlin, such as
Serbia and Romania. Thus, practically the importance of the customs tariff was
limited. Bulgaria had an economic structure similar to that of the other Balkan
countries, and therefore imports were mainly from the developed Central and
Western European countries. The economic views and political activity of Nachovich do not show any dramatic contradiction between liberalism and
historicism.

The tariffs and the legislative act for encouragement of domestic production
which were introduced on Nachovich's initiative are moderate in comparison
with similar tariff rates and measures in other countries. It should be noted,
however, that under the Treaty of Berlin Bulgaria was unable implement an
independent commercial policy, and that the potential of the state to encourage
local production in the first years after the liberation was almost nonexistent. In
this sense, although Nachovich should not be defined as a protectionist, he was

the first Bulgarian politician to introduce independent economic policy to encourage national economy.

Another leading policy maker was Ivan E. Geshov, born in 1849. In 1866 he enrolled at Owens College, where he spent three years and became one of the best students of William Stanley Jevons (Geshov, 1916: 32–33). According to Geshov himself he was particularly influenced by the social and cooperatives issues in Jevons's lectures. At the same time Geshov was strongly influenced by other British political economists, such as John Stuart Mill and Jeremy Bentham (Statelova, 1994: 8–13). He returned to Bulgaria in 1872. After 1878 Geshov took important administrative positions and got actively involved in political life. He was a governor of the Bulgarian National Bank (1883–1886), member of Parliament, minister of finance and from 1911 to 1913 prime minister and minister of foreign affairs of Bulgaria (Metodiev, 1987: 312–318).

The views of Geshov on different economic issues are presented in a series of papers, published in various journals. He demonstrated familiarity with the works of British classical political economy and French liberal economic thought. However, Geshov mentioned in his recollections that his views were formed mainly as a result of interaction of two broad theoretical conceptions: on the one hand the ideas of John Stuart Mill and Jevons (classicism and neoclassicism) and on the other the ideas of "some German public figures and economists, particularly in terms of state possession of such sources of National wealth as banks, railways, mines, and in relation to the broad government intervention in favor of the economic development of the country" (Geshov, 1916: 37).

In essence these concepts are not incompatible – what unites them is the concern about the social problems allegedly caused by industrialisation. Precisely for this reason Geshov was sceptical about the necessity of development of large-scale industry in Bulgaria. The economic conditions of post-liberation Bulgaria moved him to the understanding that the liberal principles would further need protectionism and government interference in order to encourage local crafts and agriculture. In his first scientific publications he stated that the principles of laissez-faire had become outdated and that statesmen and scientists unanimously questioned them. Two key arguments urged him to criticise economic liberalism. First, this was the clear sign coming from the developed European countries. According to him, the fact that the French, Germans and English paid more attention to state interference in the economy was a serious reason for Bulgarian politicians to introduce similar policies. The second argument was of local origin. Economic backwardness, lack of sufficient capital and private initiative weakness in Bulgaria required state support of the economy (Geshov, 1886: 122–123).

Geshov was the first Bulgarian economist and politician to develop and publish his views on how the Bulgarian state should encourage the economy. Among the key measures proposed by him were the implementation of protectionism and the adoption of a special law on industrial encouragement. In addition, Geshov urged the development of a set of measures to encourage agriculture and stock-breeding (Geshov, 1886: 127–131). He believed that private initiative was not capable of overcoming the problems faced by small craft producers, and therefore both central and local authorities were required "to undertake the community beneficial task to revive our crafts" (Geshov, 1899: 151).

According to him in certain cases the government had the right to impose restrictions on private property, personal freedom and business initiative. In this regard, he recommended legislative measures to limit the number of taverns in villages and even believed that the debts which peasants had incurred by buying alcoholic drinks should be declared uncollectable at court. He defended the need for legislative measures by which a part of the property of the peasants would become inalienable (Geshov, 1895: 410–414). Geshov sincerely believed in the benefits of some forms of collectivism in Bulgarian economy – he dedicated special studies to two forms of traditional collective associations – the proto-cooperatives of gardeners in Central Bulgaria and the so-called *zadruga* (a large family with common property) in Western Bulgaria (Geshov, 1899: 324–325, 66–93).

By his activity as minister of finance in the period 1894–1897 Geshov was able to implement his views on how the state should support the economy. On 20 December 1894, the National Assembly passed the Domestic Industry Promotion Act. Geshov was the author of all the main principles in this law (Grancharov, 1998: 151). The act decreed that all industrial enterprises established in certain branches 10 years after its adoption would be promoted for 15 years. The factories were granted certain tax exemptions and were entitled to duty-free import of raw materials and machines; a 35% reduction of the railway tariffs for transportation of raw materials, machines and ready-made products of the new enterprises was envisaged; and their production was preferred to that of foreign producers in the state or municipal procurement of supplies even where at equal quality the Bulgarian-made products were up to 15% more expensive (Yochev, n.d.: 158–159).

With the active involvement of Geshov in 1897 the Bulgarian government signed its first stand-alone trade agreement. It was signed with Austria-Hungary. The latter was the main trade partner of Bulgaria at the end of the nineteenth century, being the largest importer of industrial and other goods into the young principality (Ivanchov, 1896: 71–72). The most favoured nation clause was included in the agreement. The most important novelty was that new specific duties were introduced to replace the old 8% ad valorem duty for all goods. The highest duty of 25% was imposed on the import of ropes and rope products, and a duty of 20% was imposed on the import of sugar, sugar products, window glass and so forth. Increased protective duties were further envisaged for clothes, shoes and so forth. The low import duty of 8% was retained for machines, agricultural tools, wood and wooden products and so forth. The import duty for the goods not listed in the annex of the trade agreement was agreed at 14% (*State Gazette*, 1897). Just like Nachovich, Geshov cannot be defined as a protectionist. The tariffs imposed on his initiative were modest because Bulgaria had to negotiate them with powerful and influential countries because Geshov as a finance minister was not a supporter of the policy of self-sufficiency.

The most renowned Bulgarian professor at that time was Georgi Danailov (1872–1939). He studied in Moscow during 1891–1895 (with A. Chuprov, I. Yanzhul), and later in Vienna, Berlin and Munich (with G. Schmoller and L. Brentano; he maintained a particularly close relationship with W. Sombart, with whom he kept a correspondence and whose visit to Bulgaria he organized in 1932). We can identify three major achievements in Danailov's works. The first one comprises his studies in the area of economic and financial policy, where he clearly upholds the active interference of the state. The second encompasses his theoretical working papers and a number of microhistorical studies, where his sociological and institutional approach is clearly outlined. And third is the publication of his famous textbook on political economy (1906, 1933–1934), in which he made an appropriate educational synthesis of the major economic theories and approaches, basically of western and Russian scholars.

Especially interesting here is Danailov's position in the discussion on the choice between industry and agriculture as a leading sector for economic development. In his article on customs tariff reformation in 1900 Danailov explicitly asserted that the right time had come to develop large-scale industry in the country and protect it through customs duties tariffs. A great number of his arguments were the re-creation of the theories of prominent German scholars (List, Schmoller, Kautsky), of the German economic practice and to a degree of the American example of protectionism (Carey). Developing an industry is seen as a new natural phase of the Bulgarian economy.

> If you would like to know my view on this issue, even though I have not yet gotten to the core of the principles of the economic science, but I have scratched the surface, if someone were to ask me, "Would you like Bulgaria to become an industrial country?", I would in turn ask: "Would you like to become an educated and cultured man or would you rather stay with your elementary education you got in your birth town? – Would you care at all about your motherland Bulgaria being backward, sleepy, uncultured, and lifeless?" . . . Just like every person should seek to achieve perfection of mind; just as an individual country should seek to master ever higher culture, so every nation should strive to introduce industries because industry is a higher stage of economic culture than agriculture.
>
> (Danailov, 1900: 483)

Within the frame of practical decisions Danailov proposed the establishment of a customs union of the Balkan countries to fight ("defend ourselves" from) "the most formidable competitor of our industry – Austria-Hungary" (1900: 484). After the example of Prussia, he anticipated for Bulgaria central place within this union, due to the privileged position of the country in its relations with Turkey.

Of special interest is the presence of the German Historical School in Danailov's political economy textbook, from which several generations of Bulgarians have studied (first edition 1906; second edition 1933/1934). In his textbook

Danailov (1933/34) makes reference to authors of different and even opposite theoretical schools. Thus, in the first and economic part, priority is logically given to the German and Russian authors, while in the second priority is given to the classical school, the different syntheses (e.g. the synthesis of M. Tugan-Baranovsky) and the subjective Austrian School (Wieser, Böhm-Bawerk and to a lesser extent Menger). The author's historical method is always institutionally defined:

> The strictly historical method is not readily applicable in all cases; sometimes more valuable results could be achieved when the institutions are examined one by one from their embryonic forms down to their contemporary state while marking the political events of greater impact for the changes occurring to these institutions.
>
> (Danailov, 1933: 8)

On the whole the experience of Bulgaria during the period of nation-building (1879–1912), illustrated by the economic ideas and economic policy of Nachovich, Geshov and Danailov, shows that: (a) the ideas of the German Historical School are fully compatible with some of the tenets of liberalism and even with these of neoclassical economics, and (b) the economists and politicians in the peripheral economies of Europe purposefully were building an eclectic model in which various theoretical concepts are combined in order to provide conditions for a national catching-up process.

Postwar problems and developments

Economic and social environment

The Balkan Wars (1912–1913) and World War I (1914–1918) put a severe strain on the Bulgarian economy and finance. Inflation was soaring, and the national currency, the *lev*, devalued heavily, 26.65 times over an extended period of years (1912–1923).[2] Public finance was entirely upset, the banknotes in circulation increased around 14 times and coverage fell down to 3.2% of the gold banknotes and to 5.9% of the silver ones. The public debt and particularly the "flying debt" reached perilous amounts. Even before reparation payments began on 1 October 1923, foreign debt service reached 112 million gold francs or 16.3% of budget spending. Reparations under the Treaty of Neuilly were added to this debt, coming to 2,250 million gold francs at 5% annual interest over 37 years, plus occupation expenses, representing a quarter of the national wealth of the economy.

As in other European countries, financial stabilisation was conducted in the context of orthodox monetary ideology, which saw a stable currency and balanced public finances as the basis of economic development. With the Stabilisation Law (December 1928) the lev was finally and legally pegged to gold as the exchange rate of "92 levs per 1 gram of pure gold" was stipulated in Article 1. In further details, accounting also for the Bulgarian National Bank (BNB) commissions, the exchange rate of 139 levs per US dollar equalled 139 levs per 1.5 grams of gold (which is the gold content of the dollar). In 1928–1929, prices of agricultural products began falling sharply on the international markets, which worsened the revenues from Bulgarian exports, and in the commodity stock exchange markets in Varna and Burgas grain prices fell more than 50%. This threatened foreign reserves and respectively the servicing of the huge external debts. The price developments cancelled plans for liberalisation of foreign trade, and measures for trade and exchange controls were strengthened. Thus followed the 1928 Wine Export Promotion Act, the 1932 Grape Export Promotion Act and the 1935 Meat Export Promotion Act. In 1931 an Export Institute was set up (effectively starting to work in 1935), which was transformed into the Foreign Trade Institute in 1940. Earlier, in 1930 the food export agency was established and vested with monopoly powers to buy and trade cereals as a specific tool against deflation. Bulgaria continued to maintain the fixed exchange rate, and after the devaluation of the US dollar in 1933 the lev was fixed to the French franc. At the same time systematic exchange rate control, bilateral clearing agreements and compensational schemes were introduced; this way Bulgaria became the country most dependent on trade with Germany and became part of the German *Lebensraum* (Nenovsky et al., 2007).

Bulgaria's economic development could not be viewed in isolation from the political and social processes. In March 1920 the elections were won by the Bulgarian Agrarian People's Union, led by Alexander Stamboliyski, who was in office for three years (1920–1923) and made a systematic attempt to apply the main principles of agrarianism and overcome the country's isolation. On 9 June 1923 a coup d'état was staged (by the Military Union, led by Ivan Vulkov); Stamboliyski was killed and subsequently a government was formed led by the economist Professor Alexander Tsankov (as a representative of the newly established Democratic Alliance). As a reaction to this rightist overthrow, the September Uprising broke out (September 1923) sparked off by the ideas coming from the USSR of a new left revolutionary wave in Europe. The uprising was atrociously suppressed, and in 1924 Tsankov's government adopted a law on the protection of the state against terrorists and revolutionaries and the Bulgarian communist party was banned. The communists responded with the St. Nedelya Church bomb assault on 16 April 1925; 150 people were killed in the attack and the tsar survived by a mere chance. The Democratic Alliance was in power until 1931, with a more democratic faction forming within, led by the economist Andrei Lyapchev, who too formed a government in 1926. The economic upsurge was halted by the Great Crisis; the democratic parties forming the People's Bloc coalition (Alexander Malinov and Nikola Mushanov) won the elections. Subsequently, they were in power from 1931 to 1934. In 1932 Alexander Tsankov launched his People's Social Movement, much in the vein of the authoritarian regimes in Europe, Mussolini's above all. On 19 May 1934, a military coup was staged, which put an end to the short democratic period and marked the beginning of the autocratic reign of Tsar Boris (political parties, including Alexander Tsankov's party, were banned). Despite the desire for neutrality and the numerous political manoeu-vrings, Bulgaria was gradually drawn, economically, financially and politically, into the orbit of Germany and the rest of the revenge-seeking countries, and in March 1941 Prime Minister Bogdan Fillov signed in Vienna the country's accession to the Tripartite Pact.

New aspects of the economic policy and thinking

After the end of World War I Bulgarian economic thought entered a new stage. It was characterized by a wide variety of ideological currents and schools who have their supporters in the country – among them may be mentioned monetar-ists and quantitative economists (A. Hristoforov, S. Zagorov, O. Anderson, etc.), liberals (A. Lyapchev, S. Bochev, etc.), "Austrians" (S. Demostenov, N. Dolynsky, D. Mishaykov), Marxists and socialists (J. Nathan, P. Dzhidrov, S. Ganovsky, I. Stefanov, K. Grigorov) and others. The emigration of Russian economists and their settlement in Bulgaria had a positive influence on the development of Bulgarian economic thought (especially Demostenov, Dolinsky, Anderson and Kinkel). The increased state intervention in the economy resulted in increased demand for professionally trained economists, mostly in governmental economic institutions, but also in universities, chambers of commerce, banks and so forth. Especially needed were economists with financial, monetary and statistical knowledge.

In this environment, despite its gradual decline in Germany, the influence of the German Historical School in Bulgaria increased. Among the main reasons for this was the fact that Germany was Bulgaria's main trade partner, and that many of the students who had graduated in Germany before World War I after the end of the war already had successful careers in Bulgarian society. Moreover according to G. Markov's study (1979: 333) three quarters of Sofia University professors where with German education and specialization in Germany and after Slavtscheva-Reiber (2006: 169) Bulgaria ranked first in Europe in number of graduates of German schools and German-speaking pupils.

The basic principles of the historical approach, such as the increased focus on social issues, government intervention in the economy to overcome social contradictions, protectionism and the evolutionary approach to the analysis of economic and social phenomena, were widely accepted among the representa-tives of different schools of thought in Bulgaria. Theories of protectionism and autarchy were widely disseminated; the most interesting scholars were Georgi Svrakov (1901–1985) (student of Sombart) and Konstantin Bobchev (1894–1976), who in 1937 published a book entitled *Studies of the Theory of International Trade* (Bobchev, 1937).[3] Similarly to the Romanian economist Michail Manoi-lesco, Bobchev saw the need for constructing a new theory of international trade that would cover the practice of protectionism and the striving for industrialisa-tion of the Balkan countries. Bobchev's theory is a cross between Bertil Ohlin's ideas of international exchange and the theory of development of the forces of production (with a long history, starting with List).

Among the most prominent representatives of the German Historical School in Bulgaria during the postwar years were Alexander Tsankov (1879–1959), the main proponent of nationalism, and Ivan Kinkel (1883–1945), the author of the original theory of economic development.

Alexander Tsankov had an enormous impact on the economic policy and economic thought of Bulgaria. It was determined by two main factors. First, he held important positions in the executive and thus had a significant role in the political life of the country. Second, as a professor of political economy and rector of Sofia University with a huge number of publications, he had the opportunity to influence the formation of the Bulgarian economic elite.

Tsankov was born in 1879. He pursued law at Sofia University. Still in his student years, he was involved in the political life of the country as a member of the party of the so-called *broad socialists* (Social Democrats), whose ideas were based on Eduard Bernstein's works and his refutation of the Marxian predictions about the imminent demise of capitalism. Throughout his adult life as a scholar and politician he remained highly critical of capitalism. Tsankov adopted and implemented in his scientific works some of the basic theoretical postulates of Marx, but did not treat them as religious dogma.

In 1904, Tsankov went to Germany, where he studied political economy. His stay in Germany played a major part in the shaping of his theoretical and political views. In Munich he attended the lectures and seminars of L. Brentano, Georg von Meyer and Walter Lotts. Later on Tsankov moved to Breslau (1906), where Sombart taught, and then he followed his teacher to Berlin, and also attended the courses of Schmoller and Wagner. In Germany, under the supervision of Brentano, Tsankov began his first serious scientific pursuits. In Berlin, he began writing a doctorate entitled "Capital and Capitalistic Production Process in Böhm-Bawerk" under the guidance of Sombart. In his memoirs Tsankov writes of Sombart, "He had not the charming speech of Brentano for example, but he was speaking as a serious scientist who takes you over with the originality of his thought and with his flawless epic, smooth and logical presentation" (Tsankov, 2002: 34). Tsankov failed to complete and defend his doctoral dissertation because the Bulgarian Ministry of Education stopped his funding (Tsankov, 2002).

After he returned to Bulgaria in 1911 Tsankov became an associate professor of political economy at Sofia University, then participated in the work of the governmental apparatus for regulation and control of the Bulgarian economy during World War I, and in 1919 became rector of Sofia University (Naumov, 2004). His rapid academic career did not satisfy his ambitions, and he turned his attention towards a political career. After World War I the traditional democratic parties lost their credibility, and from 1920 to 1923, the country was ruled by the populist regime of BAPU (Bulgarian Agrarian People's Union). On 9 June 1923, this regime was overthrown by a military coup. The leaders of the coup appointed Tsankov as prime minister because he had no connections with the discredited prewar political parties. He remained in this position until the beginning of 1926. His premiership was marked by the actual state of civil war and severe repressions against left-wing opposition (communists). Tsankov initiated the implementation of a number of economic measures which reinforced governmental intervention and control over the economy. The main slogan of his government was the establishment of a strong state power. An expression of this slogan in the area of economic policy was the establishment of a foreign exchange control, the prohibition of the importation of goods that were not basic necessities, the increase of export duties on certain goods and the establishment of full governmental control over internal trade (Stoyanov and Tepavicharov, 1992: 92–172).

After being forced to resign as prime minister, Tsankov remained actively committed to political life – from 1926 to 1930 he was a chairperson of the National Assembly of Bulgaria, and minister of education from 1930 to 1931 (Metodiev, 1987). In 1932 he founded his own political party, which later on was called *People's Social Movement* and whose ideology was heavily influenced by Italian fascism and national socialism. After the military coup d'état of 1934, which laid the groundwork for royal dictatorship, all political parties in Bulgaria were banned. In the course of World War II Tsankov was a member of Parliament, and as such he was among the most prominent supporters and propagandists of national socialist ideas, especially in the social and economic spheres. However, he did not share the anti-Semitism of the Nazis and participated in the rescue of Bulgarian Jews in 1943 (Petrova, 2011). With the withdrawal of German troops from the Balkans, Tsankov emigrated from Bulgaria. The last years of his life he spent in Argentina, where he died in 1959.

His research activity was versatile – he published numerous papers, studies, treatises and a textbook on political economy and co-authored a study on the history of joint stock companies in Bulgaria and so forth. As a political activist Tsankov pronounced and issued a large number of keynote speeches and propaganda leaflets and participated in the preparation of political programs. During the last years of his life he wrote and published two volumes of memoirs. The thematic scope of his publications is wide. These include papers on current issues of the economic and foreign trade policy of Bulgaria, research in political economy, the significance and consequences of World War I, the financing of wars and the nature and impact of the Depression of the 1930s.

In his relatively early publications Tsankov attempted to made original contributions to the field of economic theory. In his study *The Capital and the Profit from It* (Tsankov, 1910) he analysed and criticised Adam Smith's and E. Böhm-Bawerk's views on the nature of capital. The tenets of the German Historical School were the main source of his criticism of the liberal views of Smith and Böhm-Bawerk. Tsankov believed that private capital is a historical and legal phenomenon, and that the main precondition for the origin of capital and the capitalist mode of production is the appearance of the exchange economy. As social capital he determines the capital of the state, which, he said, is the most perfect cultural unit (Tsankov, 1910). In his theoretical reasoning Tsankov widely used the concepts of Marx and other socialist writers, such as Rodbertus. Probably under the influence of Sombart, Tsankov combined socialist concepts with those of the German Historical School. According to Tsankov, "only as a means of obtaining larger and more values money becomes 'capital'" (Tsankov, 1910: 41). Marx's theory of exploitation of workers by capitalists was also adopted (Tsankov, 1910). The unpaid labour of the workers is the main source of the profits of capitalists. This, however, is not sufficient to explain profit. So Tsankov added that profit depends also on "market conditions, on the situation, and speculative ability of the capitalist entrepreneur" (Tsankov, 1915: 16).

In 1919 Tsankov gave a speech on the occasion of his election as the rector of Sofia University, which was published under the title *Money and Its Devaluation* (Tsankov, 1919). Here he gives his interpretation of the theory of Fr. G. Knapp for money as legal tender. Tsankov believes that from the definition of Knapp for legal tender can be concluded that the value of money is "something nominal, fictitious, invented by man, and established by the government." Unlike Knapp, Tsankov is convinced that the value of money is real: "the unit value of money is an objective measure of our revenues or, in general, of what we deserve as an economic unit" (Tsankov, 1919: 6). The Bulgarian author widely uses the theory of the Ukrainian economist Mikhail Tugan-Baranovsky on the trade cycle in the capitalist system. Tsankov accepts the assertion that in the boom phase the purchasing power of money decreases, while in depression it increases. There are two main reasons for the rotation of boom and bust periods. The first is the so-called capitalization of profits – that is the tendency for the capitalists to invest all their profits in ever expanding and increasing production, which results in overproduction. The second, and in some ways more important, reason for the trade cycle is the credit expansion of the banking system. Tsankov writes, "The investment of these new means in the capitalist production increases the latter and opens new and wide spaces, but the expanded individual companies further increase imbalances in the distribution of economic forces" (Tsankov, 1919: 72). After the exhaustion of available capital and the cessation of credit expansion, the economy goes into a state of depression (Tsankov, 1919).

In all of his studies Tsankov shows deep knowledge of basic economic theories and apparent preference for the principles of the German Historical School in their "original" or their Russian version. In the 1930s Tsankov made a turn to ideas that are close to fascism and national socialism. In fact, he considered these two doctrines a realization of the socialist ideals which he supported from his earliest years. In 1940 Tsankov writes that the outbreak of World War II is "grandiose revolutionary era, perhaps much more spectacular than English and French revolutions" (Tsankov, 1940: 571). The essence of that new revolution is in the destruction of capitalism. Tsankov is adamant: "As a new social order that comes, I think that it is the socialist system, socialism, not Marxism, not Bolshevism" (Tsankov, 1940: 571, 577). As an example of such a new socialist order Tsankov cites Nazi Germany and Fascist Italy. Tsankov developed similar ideas in 1942, when he observed that the economic system in the USSR could be defined as bureaucratic state capitalism, while a prototype of socialism is Germany. Key features of the socialist society, according to Tsankov, are: the introduction of four-year plans, the state protection of agricultural production, limitation of private interests and their alignment with public interests, distribution of wealth based on participation and merit, determination of profits by the state and so forth (Tsankov, 1942).

The scientific and ideological evolution of Tsankov to a large extent resembles that of one of his teachers – Werner Sombart. It began with social democracy and ended close to national socialism. In contrast to Sombart, however, the Bulgarian economist did not have interests in sociology, and actively participated in the political life of the country, where he made attempts to apply some of the principles of German historicism in practice.

Ivan Kinkel (1883–1945) was an interdisciplinary scientist, Russian by origin and education (Nenovsky, 2015). His versatile activities ranged from professorship in economic history, economics and history of economic thought at the University of Sofia (1921–1945) and the Free University of Sofia (1920–1945) to founder and first chairman of the Bulgarian Sociological Society (1931–1939) and founder of psychoanalysis in the country. He studied medicine in Berlin (1903–1905), graduated with a major in social philosophy from the University of Leipzig (1906–1908) and specialized in psychoanalysis in Zurich (1908–1911). Kinkel was convinced that only a diversity of views looking in one direction could produce the necessary scientific result. This shaped his interdisciplinary approach, which he himself would often refer to as an "eclectic method" of making a theory. According to Kinkel,

> If none of the old universal methods satisfies us today, could we at least construct a new monistic method in sociology? We must explicitly state that in principle, given sociology's contemporary state, this is not possible! Even if another sociological genius was to appear in our times of the stature of Kant or Marx wishing to construct a new synthetic method, the latter would still have to incorporate the self-contained principles of all individual methods constructed in sociology over the recent years, that is to say, this method would essentially be not a monistic, but an eclectic one.
>
> (Kinkel, 1931: 193)

In 1921, Kinkel published his fundamental study on economic development, its cyclic character and dynamic forces. According to Kinkel the main task, which the new theory has to solve, is to find out "what the economic progress and development of humankind is all about" (Kinkel, 1921: 285). The periodisation of economic and social history is examined on two analytical levels. The first, or fundamental level, is the level of the *three economic eras, the three cultural cycles* or the three "rungs of mankind's economic culture." It determines the long-term and civilization dynamics of the economy. The second and more specific level is the level of economic forms, which are four. The four economic forms are reproduced within every era or cultural cycle. It is extremely important to take into account the fact that economic forms reproduce themselves and develop, while never really repeating themselves, so that new and unknown patterns appear with each new cycle. Any form of determinism in Kinkel's model is instantly denied, making it very much consistent with contemporary theories of chaotic, nonlinear, complex and evolutionary forms of the development of nature and society.

According to Kinkel, the progress of economic or cultural periods is determined by the division of labour, as well as by the evolution of economic organizational forms within each period. Behind these two factors there are two other reasons: technological developments and population dynamics. The role of technology and of the quantitative and qualitative structure of population is often pointed out as instrumental in determining the character of a cultural period.

When one looks further into the dynamics of *the four economic forms*, in particular into the debatable issue of the recurrence of these forms in the three cultural economic eras, the presence of capitalism and state-planned economy in the Egyptian-Babylonian and the Ancient (Greek-Roman) periods appears to be particularly interesting. The outlook upholding the existence of capitalist relations in the ancient world is not new and was well-known to Kinkel from the works of E. Meyer, T. Mommsen, M. Weber, J. Kulisher and others. Kinkel defines *capitalism* as the existence of large income in kind or in money: a large-scale economy – that is a wide market, an amalgamation of a large human workforce, cooperation and above all exploitation of free and unfree human labour (Kinkel, 1921: 16–21, 122, 231, 289–292). Capitalism existed in all three cultural periods; however, it took different forms, which, in turn, became ever more complex as a result of the development and division of labour, the appearance of new branches of the economy and so forth. Each next form of capitalism not only integrated the basic features of the preceding one but also offered new and more sophisticated economic elements.

The fourth form of economy, or the *state-planned* one, which inevitably comes after the capitalist economy in each of the three civilization eras, follows the same rules of integrating the preceding elements and an accelerated and more complex development. Writing his book in the first years after World War I, Kinkel was aware of the trend of transition of contemporary western capitalism to this form of economy. According to Kinkel, a number of economic phenomena from the Bolshevik economy repeat the most primary forms of state economy from the previous cultural periods, such as the existence of state shops and food rationing, the destruction of money and the existence of state peasants, state employees and producers. This system is characterized by exploitation too, which, however, is mostly power-based and hinges on political instruments.

Similarly to the connection between the economic forms, there is a connection and continuity between *the three cultural eras*. Each new era carries the imprint of the preceding one, taking from it a number of key elements. This makes it possible for every new culture, instead of starting from scratch, to step on what has been already achieved, which in turn smooths the development at the beginning and gives better prospects for innovation of new economic practices at a later stage (Kinkel, 1921: 294–295). With time, each new culture, having repeated

past forms, heads forward to something unfamiliar until then. The new movement was the result of the appearance of technical means and a large-scale
process of division, differentiation and specialization of labour (Kinkel,
1921: 298–299).

Kinkel criticised the representatives of the German Historical School for their
choice of purely technical or organizational criteria for periodisation, such as
Karl Bücher's theory about the distance between production and consumption
of a good, and so forth. Special attention was given to Sombart's system's scheme,
which was admired by Kinkel. Sombart distinguished between four economic
orders, or systems, each of which consisting of three steps: individual, transitional
and social; but this theory of his was rejected because of the "theoretical mess"
(Kinkel, 1921: 29–32).

Concluding remarks

The German Historical School's main elements (organic and multicausal development, stage character and evolution, the role of moral and ethics, the empirical
and inductive method, etc.), which are broadly considered as a general theoretical
model for newly emerging and backward economies, suited well the interests of
the basic social groups and the intellectual views of the newly formed Bulgarian
elites. These postulates fitted perfectly the Bulgarian development public policy
agenda, the institutional framework and the need for professionalization. The
historical school was closely related with the theoretical models of economic
nationalism. In a sense, the dominance of the Marxian model after 1944 preserved
this trend to the extent the major principles of historical materialism were a
variety of the principle of historicism.

In Bulgaria the main dominating components of the historical school followed
its own evolution (old, young and youngest historical school) while also inter-
mingling with other major components of other theoretical schools. In terms of
methodology, the Bulgarian economic scholars did not differ essentially from
the representatives of the historical school; they shared the principles of empirical observation, inductivism and realism. Unlike them, they were much more
eclectic (even the Bulgarian "Austrians" actively use elements of German historicism) and less ambitious. Despite this, some of the Bulgarian economists sought
to construct theoretical models of their own. An example of this is Kinkel's
theory of development.

Notes

1   See Normano (1949) and Gloveli (2008, 2014).
2   See Nenovsky (2006, 2012) and Koszul (1932).
3   Konstantin Bobchev studied in Saint Petersburg (1913–1915), Sofia (1915–1919) and
    Germany (1922–1924) and defended his doctoral thesis on R. Leifmann's theory of
    marginal utility in Freiburg. Later, he specialised in Leipzig (1929) and in the period
    1934–1935 with the support of the Rockefeller Foundation, he spent some time in
    London (London School of Economics).

References

Avramov, R. (2007). *Communal Capitalism. Reflections on Bulgarian Economic Past*, Vol. 2. Sofia: Centre for Liberal Strategies (in Bulgarian).

Blagoev, D. (1958 [1902]). The Economic Development of Bulgaria. *Industry or Agriculture, Dimitar Blagoev: Essays*, Vol. 7, 415–667. Sofia (in Bulgarian).

Bobchev, K. (1937). *Studies of the Theory of International Trade*. Sofia (in Bulgarian).

Bücher, K. (1970). *Katalog der Karl Bücher Bibbliothek in der Wirtschaftswissenschaftlichen fakultät der Universität Kyoto*. Kyoto, University of Kyoto.

Chakalov, Y. (1928). *Reflections on History of Customs Regime in Bulgaria. Part II – From the Liberation of Bulgaria until 1888*. (in Bulgarian). Sofia, n.p.

Crowell, J. (1904). Students in German Universities, *Sciences*, 19 (484): 594–595.

Danailov, G. (1900). A Draft of a Customs Tariff in Relation to Our Trade Policy. *Journal of the Bulgarian Economic Society*, 4 (7): 465–490 (in Bulgarian).

Danailov, G. (1933/34). *Fundamentals of Political Economy*. Plovdiv, Hristo Danov (in Bulgarian).

Geshov, I. (1886). White-Collar Proletariat. *Periodical Journal of the Bulgarian Literary Society*, 19–20: 118–133 (in Bulgarian).

Geshov, I. (1895). Measures for Economic Development of Bulgaria. *Law Review*, 9: 409–416 (in Bulgarian).

Geshov, I. (1899). *Words and Deeds: Financial and Economic Studies*. Sofia, Iv. G. Govedarov and Cie (in Bulgarian).

Geshov, I. (1916). *Memories of Years of Struggles and Victories*. Sofia, Gutenberg (in Bulgarian).

Gloveli, G. (2008). *Historico-stadial and Evolutionary Conceptions in Russian Economic Though: A Century Perspective*. Moscow, Institute of Economics, Russian Academy of Sciences (in Russian).

Gloveli, G. (2014). *Receptions and Innovations of Historism in Russian Political Economy*. Moscow, RAS Institute of Economics (in Russian).

Grancharov, S. (1998). Reflections on Bulgarian Economic Thought (1878–1915). *Historical Review*, 3–4: 140–166 (in Bulgarian).

Ivanchov, T. (1896). Analytical Review of Bulgaria's Foreign Trade in 1895. *Journal of Bulgarian Economic Society*, 1 (2): 69–101 (in Bulgarian).

Kesyakov, B. (1926). *Contribution to the Diplomatic History of Bulgaria*. Sofia, n.p. (in Bulgarian).

Kinkel, I. (1921). *Attempt at Constructing a New Theory of Economic Development*. Annual of the University of Sofia, Faculty of Law, 17: 1–312 (in Bulgarian).

Kinkel, I. (1931). *Methods of Knowledge in Modern Sociology*. Annual of the University of Sofia, Faculty of Law, 26: 1–202 (in Bulgarian).

Koszul, J. (1932). *Les efforts de restauration financière de la Bulgarie (1922–1931)*. Paris, Félix Alcan.

Markov, G. (1979). Die Kulturexpansion des Dritten Reiches in Bulgarien: Wissenschaft, Hochschulbildung und verbreintung der deutschen Sprache (1934–1939). *Etudes Historiques*, 9: 329–347.

Metodiev, V. (ed.) (1987). *Bulgarian Public Institutions 1879–1986: Encyclopedia*. Sofia, Nauka i Izkustvo (in Bulgarian).

Metodiev, V. and Stoyanov, L. (1990). *Bulgarian Constitutions and Constitution Drafts*. Sofia, Petar Beron (in Bulgarian).

Nachovich, G. (1883). *Tobacco Industry in the Bulgarian Principality.* Sofia, n.p. (in Bulgarian).

Nachovich, G. (1902). *Some Pages on Agriculture in Bulgaria and Abroad.* Sofia, Iv. Daskalov (in Bulgarian).

Naumov, G. (2004). *Alexander Tsankov and Andrew Lyapchev in Politics and Government.* Sofia, Hersmes (in Bulgarian).

Nenovsky, N. (2006). *Exchange Rates and Inflation: France and Bulgaria in the Interwar Period and the Contribution of Albert Aftalion (1874–1956).* Sofia, Bulgarian National Bank.

Nenovsky, N. (2012). Theoretical Debates in Bulgaria during the Great Depression: Confronting Sombart, Marx and Keynes. Oeconomia, 2 (1): 67–101.

Nenovsky, N. (2015). Ivan Kinkel's (1883–1945) Theory of Economic Development. *European Journal of Economic Thought*, 22 (2): 272–299.

Nenovsky, N., Pavanelli, G. and Dimitrova, K. (2007). Exchange Rate Control in Italy and Bulgaria in the Interwar Period. History and Perspectives, in *The Experience of Exchange Rate Regimes in South-Eastern Europe in a Historical and Comparative Perspective.* Vienna, Oesterreichische Nationalbank, 80–117.

Nikolova, V. and Sazdov, D. (1992). *Programs, Program Documents and Statutes of the Bourgeois Parties in Bulgaria.* Sofia, Naika i Izkustvo (in Bulgarian).

Normano, J.F. (1949). *The Spirit of Russian Economics.* London, Dennis Dobson.

Petrova, D. (2011). *Alexander Tsankov and His Party (1932–1944).* Sofia, Diomira (in Bulgarian).

Radonov, Z. (1979). The Connections between Bulgarian and German Scholars and Museums (1878–1944), in *Bulgarian-German Relations and Connections, Research Studies and Materials.* Sofia, Bulgarian Academy of Sciences, 305–326 (in Bulgarian).

Roscher, W. (2008 [1854]). *Principles of Political Economy.* Radford, Wilder.

Slavtscheva-Reiber, A. (2006). *Geschichte, Entwicklung und Sprachwerbetatigkeit der deutschen Schulen in Bulgarien im Zeitraum 1900–1939.* Dissertation, University of Mannheim.

State Gazette, 1897, issue 71: 3–9 (in Bulgarian).

Statelova, E. (1994). *Ivan Evstratiev Geshov or the Hard Way towards Creating.* Sofia, Marin Drinov (in Bulgarian).

Stoyanov, V. and Tepavicharov, V. (1992). *The Political Alternative to Bulgaria (9 June 1923–4 January 1926).* St. Kliment Ohridski, University Publishing (in Bulgarian).

Tashev, T. (1999). *The Ministers of Bulgaria 1879–1999.* Sofia, Nauka I Izkustvo (in Bulgarian).

Tsankov, A. (1910). *The Capital and the Profit from It.* Sofia, State Publishing House (in Bulgarian).

Tsankov, A. (1915). *The Capital and the Profit from It.* Sofia, Royal Publishing House (in Bulgarian).

Tsankov, A. (1919). *Money and Its Devaluation.* Sofia, Slovo (in Bulgarian).

Tsankov, A. (1940). The New World Economic Order. *Journal of the Bulgarian Economic Society*, 39 (9): 561–601 (in Bulgarian).

Tsankov, A. (1942). *The Three Economic Systems: Capitalism, Communism and National Socialism.* Sofia, Poligraphia (in Bulgarian).

Tsankov, A. (2002). *My Time: Memoirs.* Sofia, Prozorets (in Bulgarian).

Yochev, E. (no date). *The Legislation in the Kingdom of Bulgaria (1879–1944).* Sofia, n.p. (in Bulgarian).

Concluding remarks

Harald Hagemann

Introduction

This volume on the dissemination of the ideas of the German Historical School (GHS) and its legacy in Europe is another indicator of a certain resurgence of interest which arises from an increased uneasiness about the development of modern mainstream economics aiming at imitating the sciences, although the validity of economic models is contingent on time and space. More than a decade ago Erik Grimmer-Solem and Roberto Romani (1999) challenged the appropriateness of the term "historical school". Heath Pearson (1999, 2002) went even further in fundamentally questioning the perceived view of the GHS as "not historical", "not German" and "not a School". However, even Schumpeter, who is quoted as a chief witness, dismisses the term only for the *older* GHS and confines "the concept, Historical School of Economics, to the age and to the group of Gustav von Schmoller" (Schumpeter, 1954: 507). Pearson's dismissal of the very idea of a GHS was heavily criticised by Bruce Caldwell (2001), who pointed out that there really *was* a GHS of economics.[1] Clearly, a lot depends on the issue of what constitutes a "school". In his considerations of a sociology of knowledge, Schumpeter (1954) had a rather strict definition of a genuine school when he states, with regard to the Ricardian school, that it had a master, a doctrine, a spirit of community, a core, zones of influence and borderlands. In this strict sense a GHS did not exist. There also never existed a German monopoly of the historical and ethical (or institutional) approach to economics. The process of diffusion of the ideas of the "GHS" also shows that they have multiple meanings adapted to the conditions and economic and social needs of the country of adaptation, as it has also been discussed in the introduction, by José Luís Cardoso and Michalis Psalidopoulos.

Nevertheless it remains a historical fact that the main representatives of the GHS, particularly in the period between the end of the French-German War in 1871 and the foundation of the *Verein für Sozialpolitik* in 1872 and World War I, were considered as a prominent group. This holds for contemporaries such as Richard T. Ely, who had obtained a PhD with Karl Knies at Heidelberg in 1878 and later founded the American Economic Association in 1885 and the Wisconsin School of Institutionalists, as well as for many economists in Italy, Japan or other countries. This holds until today, which is indicated not only by the contributions to this volume but also by Heath Pearson's more recent contribution on the GHS to *The New Palgrave* (Pearson, 2008), in which he has considerably moderated his earlier view.

German Historical Schools

The expression "historical school" designates a community of thought which has its foundations in *historism*, a movement arising in the eighteenth century in several European countries (less so in France) as a reaction to the dominance of science and reason ensuing from the age of enlightenment. It does not deny deductive reasoning but declares the historic singularity and relativity of all social actions against a purely axiomatic reasoning. In Germany the historical school of law founded by Friedrich Karl von Savigny (1779–1861), who objected to natural law with its idea of inalienable and universally valid basic rights of human beings in a famous controversy with Thibaut on the introduction of a civil code for Germany in 1814, can be conceived as the mother of all historical schools. Attempts to create a historical school have also been made in other areas as, for example, by Leopold von Ranke (1795–1886) and Johann Gustav Droysen (1808–1884) in history.[2]

In his classic study *The Foundations of Historism in German Economics*, Gottfried Eisermann (1956) has well argued that the conservative romanticist Adam Heinrich Müller (1779–1829) and, with some lag, the visionary prophet of a national economy Friedrich List (1789–1846) personify the double-sided nature of the first counter-movement against the entry of classical economic liberalism in Germany. Whereas Müller embodied the backward-looking feudal-conservative viewpoint and characteristically became a close associate of Metternich, List conceived the forward-looking perspective of the rising industrial bourgeoisie, one not equal to the leading British competitors at an early stage, and therefore developed the infant-industry theory and a stages theory of economic development emphasising productive powers and the specificity of national endowments, wants, cultures and conditions. It should be pointed out that List was not only a promoter of industrial development but also a liberal and democrat who emphasised that respect for human rights and civil liberties should accompany industrial development. His conception and sharp accentuation of the nation as the decisive economic unit, historically given, do not underlie any nationalism or chauvinism, as indicated by his advocating an economically united Europe.

Wilhelm Roscher (1817–1894), Bruno Hildebrand (1812–1878) and Karl Knies (1821–1898) are normally considered as the leading representatives of what has been termed the "older historical school". No doubt among them Roscher was the bellwether and the main founding father. His *Outline to Lectures on the State Economy in Accordance with the Historical Method* (Roscher, 1843), in which he transferred the approach of Savigny and the historical school of law and suggested an embracing historical and comparative study of economic systems to identify the stages of development and the laws of economic life, has to be considered as the programmatic basis of the older historical school on which Roscher later based his successful textbook *System of Economics*. In his *History of Economics in Germany*, Roscher (1874) gives the first systematic treatment of the development of the economy as well as the development of economic thought. His historical viewpoint does not exclude theoretical considerations, and Roscher bases his theoretical reflections for a greater part on the doctrines of British classical economics, however in an eclectic way and with emphasis on historical relativism. Nevertheless, it was more than "a historical sauce on a classical dish" (Wilbrandt, 1926: 97), and Roscher surely was closer to the ideas of the British classical economists than were Hildebrand and Knies.

Knies was the most eminent theorist of the three, in particular in the field of money and credit. In 1865 Knies succeeded Karl Heinrich Rau as the chair of economics at the University of Heidelberg, where he had a profound influence not only on Max Weber (who himself succeeded Knies in 1897) but also on Eugen von Böhm-Bawerk and Friedrich von Wieser, who had studied with Knies. Among Knies's many students who later became prominent economists were also several Americans, such as Richard T. Ely, John Bates Clark and Edwin R. A. Seligman. His early programmatic favouring of the historical method in *Political Economics from the Viewpoint of the Historical Method*, republished in a revised version three decades later (Knies, 1883), in which he opposed the existence of general economic laws (Knies, 1853: 235–249), Ricardos's abstract deductivism, and instead favoured the inductive method and historical relativism, remained Knies's only treatise in which he focussed on problems of method. In his opposition to the absolutism of theory and in his historical relativism Knies surely went further than Roscher. It is often argued that there exists a clear contrast between Knies's explicit favouring of the historical method and his theoretical contributions (see e.g. Schumpeter, 1954). However, from our point of view, this contradiction should not be exaggerated. In his analysis of money and credit the procedure is quite similar as in his "brilliant article" on the theory of value (Knies, 1855), which "had the great virtue of confronting his theory with historical data. Not until many decades later could one find a performance as impressive as his" (Chipman, 2005: 197, 204). Chipman's modern assessment corresponds with Schumpeter's statement: "Knies, it cannot be too often repeated, was primarily an economic theorist and, for the rest, an able general economist without any distinctive bent as to method" (Schumpeter, 1954: 539–540).

Knies had become a progressive liberal under the influence of his teacher and mentor, Bruno Hildebrand, at the University of Marburg since 1841. Both were standing up for the principles of the democratic revolution in 1848 and emigrated to Switzerland in the restoration period that followed. Knies became a schoolteacher in Schaffhausen, where he wrote his programmatical treatise, before returning to Germany as a professor at the University of Freiburg in liberal Baden in 1855. Hildebrand, who had become a member of the Paulskirchen parliament – that is the Frankfurt National Assembly – lost his professorship at Marburg.[3] In Switzerland he was appointed as a professor for state sciences at the University of Zurich and founded the Swiss Statistical Office in Berne. In

1861 Hildebrand returned to Germany as a professor at the University of Jena in Thuringia, where he also founded the first Statistical Office. A year before he became the founding editor of the *Jahrbücher für Nationalökonomie und Statistik*, which reflected the increasing significance of more sophisticated statistical methods for detailed empirical and historical research in economics, as also reflected in the work of Ernst Engel (1821–1896), who was the director of the Prussian Bureau of Statistics in Berlin from 1860 to 1882. In an important earlier attempt, Hildebrand's student Knies (1850) even had tried to establish statistics *as an independent discipline*. Hildebrand edited the *Jahrbücher für Nationalökonomie und Statistik* until his death in 1879, when he was succeeded by his son-in-law Johannes Conrad, who edited the journal until 1915. Conrad, who was also the mentor of many Americans at the University of Halle, was open-minded to theoretical contributions, as indicated by Böhm-Bawerk's (1886) two long essays in which he elaborated Menger's theory of value, allocation and exchange or Wicksell's article entitled "Interest and Wages" (1892), which formed the basis of his marginal theory of distribution. From all this we can conclude that the triumvirate Roscher, Hildebrand and Knies does not form a "school" in Schumpeter's sense.[4]

This changed with the historical and ethical approach of the "younger historical school", of which Gustav Schmoller (1838–1917) was the undisputed leader in Imperial Germany. Schmoller was also a main initiator of the foundation of the *Verein für Sozialpolitik*, the association of German-speaking economists, which officially was founded in 1873.[5] However, the first major conference on the "*soziale Frage*" (social question) had already taken place in July 1872 in Halle, where Schmoller was a professor until he moved to the newly established German university in Strassburg in the same year. From there he went in 1882 to the University of Berlin, where he stayed until his death in 1917. Although Schmoller took over chairmanship of the *Verein für Sozialpolitik* only in 1890 from Erwin Nasse, he had been the most influential member of this association from the beginning. The *Verein für Sozialpolitik* comprised the so-called *Kathedersozialisten* (socialists of the chair), who were opposing Marxism and socialist ideas on the one side and Manchester liberalism on the other side. The latter was represented in Germany by John Prince-Smith, a close follower of Bastiat, who was instrumental in founding the German Free Trade Union in 1847 and the Congress of German Economists in 1858. The ignorance of the poverty and social problems brought about by increasing industrialisation by many Congress members contributed to the foundation of the *Verein for Sozialpolitik*. In contrast to the members of the older historical school, and in particular Roscher, Schmoller broke with the classical tradition in economics. He was hostile to the abstract axiomatic-deductive method and instead favoured the inductive method. Schmoller emphasised the necessity to base economic reasoning on sufficient knowledge of historical facts and statistical material. He followed an ethical approach and advocated a paternalistic social policy – that is as a social conservative Schmoller believed in an improvement of the living conditions of working-class families through social reforms by the Prussian state. As the representative of the University of Berlin, Schmoller was a member of the Prussian Upper House from 1889 until his death. However, it took until 1900–1904 for Schmoller to publish his main work, the *Grundriss*, a compendium of economics which was published in two volumes comprising 1,400 pages and put together the material of his lectures over more than three decades. Schmoller's historical-ethical approach is also reflected in the structure of the book, which is hardly theoretical but more of a descriptive nature, full of microscopic details and value judgments. A synthesis of transforming the historical and statistical material into a coherent economic analysis does not exist. In fact Schmoller never really made a serious attempt in that direction.

By the time of the publication of the *Grundriss* the *Methodenstreit*, the dispute on method, had occupied German economists already for almost two decades. It was launched by Carl Menger's 1883–1884 attacks against historism and his insistence on theoretical analysis, and Schmoller's polemical reaction. The subsequent controversy on the appropriate method in economics and in the social sciences occupied German-speaking economists for more than two decades. Surprisingly, however, this dispute on method did not play a major role in the meetings of the *Verein für Sozialpolitik*.

This is completely different from the other famous controversy, the *Werturteilsstreit*, a fundamental debate about value judgments. This battle about norms and values in economics and the social sciences, which for good reasons can be termed a "second Methodenstreit" (Winkel, 1977: 155), raged until World War I. The question of whether economists or other social scientists should make normative judgments had been a hot issue at many meetings. The controversy fully broke out and escalated at the 1909 conference in Vienna. Eugen von Philippovich (1858–1917), the organizer, himself followed a middle course, theoretically and politically. As a professor at the University of Freiburg, where he was succeeded by Max Weber when he returned to Vienna in 1893, he made Menger's ideas known among a wider German audience. As a co-founder of the Party for Social Policy, member of the Austrian Upper House and leader of the Austrian Fabians, Philippovich was engaged in the fight for improving the living conditions of working-class families and had a certain impact on social legislation. In contrast to Schmoller and his followers, however, Philippovich was convinced that social reforms should be based on sound economic analysis. When Philippovich gave the opening keynote speech, entitled "The Essence of Economic Productivity and the Possibility of Its Measurement" at the Vienna meeting, it became the target of heavy attacks. In particular Werner Sombart (1863–1941) and Max Weber (1864–1920), besides Arthur Spiethoff, the outstanding "representatives" of the youngest historical school, managed to find value judgments even behind seemingly innocent concepts, like "productivity". Weber pointed out time and again that the preferences and prejudices of researchers should not be allowed to interfere with theoretical analysis, the collection of empirical data and its evaluation, as in his famous paper on "objectivity" in the social sciences (Weber, 1904). It was in particular the controversial style of Sombart, who in 1902 had published the first two volumes of his *Modern*

Capitalism for which he pretended to bridge the gap between the abstract-theo-
retical and the empirical-historical method,[6] who at the Vienna meeting questioned
whether economics had already reached the state of a science, which annoyed
Schmoller and other members of the older generation of the historical school,
such as Georg Friedrich Knapp (1842–1926), a close friend of Schmoller since
their common time in Strassburg. The debate on value judgments in German
economics continued and was unsettled when World War I broke out.

The catastrophe of the war and its aftermath had a deep impact on the humanities and the social sciences. This also strongly affected economics, which in
Germany traditionally had been embedded in wider state sciences. Moreover,
particularly the younger GHS had been strongly linked with the *Kaiserreich* –
that is Imperial Germany – which did not exist anymore after the war. Schmoller
and Adolph Wagner, who had been directly nominated by the king as a member
of the Prussian Upper House in 1910, both were closely linked to the old system
and died in 1917. So neither the old institutions nor their leading representatives
in economics did exist anymore. A further blow came with the hyperinflation in
the early 1920s, which caused Walter Eucken (1891–1950), who later became
the prominent founding father of Ordoliberalism or the Freiburg School, to break
with the GHS, in which as a student of Hermann Schumacher he himself had
been trained. It was just a matter of time before "the end of the historical-ethical
school" was proclaimed in a widely perceived essay. The author, Robert Wilbrandt
(1926), a professor at Tübingen and himself a former student of Schmoller and
Wagner, nevertheless was defending practical social policy against free-market
liberalism and reactionary nationalism.

While the GHS certainly had lost its dominant influence in the mid-1920s (the
historical-holistic strand later experienced a limited revival in the Nazi period),
a new centre of gravitation did not arise during the years of the Weimar Republic.
Thus Häuser (1994) rightly diagnoses a period of "ambiguity", with a pluralism
of theoretical and methodological approaches of varying quality.

Whereas remains of the historical school could be perceived in German economics until the 1950s, some aspects of their thought and of the German tradition
of state sciences have entered even into the writings of main opponents. Thus
Eucken's "regulating principles", such as monopoly controls or the correction
of negative external effects, require a strong state securing workable markets
and preserving the competitive order. Schumpeter, who was thoroughly Austrian
in his emphasis on theoretical analysis and "pure" economics, considering Walras
as the greatest of all economists, and thoroughly Weberian in his position to
keep out value judgments from economics, included not only economic history
and statistics in his work, as indicated by the subtitle of his monumental *Business Cycles* (1939). His concern for development and his belief in the unity of
social life and the inseparable relationship among its components time and again
stimulated him to transcend pure economic analysis in the direction of a more
broadly based economics. According to Streissler (1994) Schumpeter thereby
"grasped at the olive branch proffered by Max Weber" after the dispute on
method between Menger and Schmoller – namely "social economics as something

in between historical and purely theoretical economics" (p. 38). As Chaloupek points out in his contribution, Schumpeter took great care in doing justice to both parties in the dispute on method and deserves credit for providing the most convincing synthesis.

The dissemination of the German Historical School

It is a common theme in most of the contributions that the growing prestige of German universities is strongly linked to the political and economic rise of Germany after unification at the end of the French-German War in 1871 until 1914. Whereas the reputation of German universities and other scientific institutions was substantially higher in the sciences (as also indicated by many Nobel prizes in physics, medicine, biology and chemistry until the Nazi period), it also affected economics, although to a lesser degree. This is basically the period of Schmoller and the younger GHS. While in some countries, such as Belgium, German influences abruptly ended with the outbreak of World War I, in other countries, such as Greece or Turkey, there was a continuation or a slower decline. After the Nazi period and World War II German influences or scientific publications in German came to an end, and American influences started to dominate. This process of "de-Germanisation", which Benny Carlson (this volume), following Bo Sandelin, notes for Swedish economics after World War I, is a general one.

German academic influences in the late nineteenth and early twentieth centuries were not limited to European countries. Two particularly interesting cases are the United States and Japan. Due to Germany's academic pre-eminence in that period no less than 20 out of the group of the first 26 presidents of the American Economic Association had studied in Germany. This does not mean that all of them had been followers of the GHS, as indicated by the prominent case of Irving Fisher, who during his European studies in 1893–1894 preferred to attend the lectures by Frobenius in mathematics and Helmholtz in physics rather than the lectures by Schmoller and Wagner while in Berlin. There is also a certain similarity between the GHS and key elements of the leading representatives of American institutionalism, as exemplified by Thorstein Veblen's methodological dissent, Wesley C. Mitchell's statistical analysis of business cycles or John R. Commons's social reformism, although all these three economists were not trained in Germany.[7] In Japan the first nationwide economic society, the Association for the Study of Social Policy, was founded in 1896 according to the example of the *Verein für Sozialpolitik* in a period when Japan's model of modernization shifted from a British to a German orientation. The founding president, Noburo Kanai (1865–1933), a professor at Tokyo Imperial University, which became the centre for the dissemination of the ideas of the GHS in Japan, had studied in Germany from 1886 to 1889, mainly with Schmoller and Wagner at the University of Berlin. In the initial manifesto of 1899–1900 the extreme exercise of self-interest and uncontrolled free competition in a *laissez-faire* system were opposed, as were the revolutionary ideas of Marxism to solve the labour question. Social policy was seen as the task of the state, whose authority should not only protect workers but also achieve social harmony between capital and labour.[8] In November 1996 the Japanese Society for the History of Economic Thought held a kind of centennial conference on the GHS in Tokyo, which gave birth to the book edited by Shionoya (2001).[9]

In many of the contributions to the current volume, references to the work of Friedrich List are made. This is characteristic for catching-up economies, such as Italy, Spain, Greece, Turkey or Russia, or, as a Chinese colleague at a recent international conference stated, "For us, List is now more important than Marx." As Jean-Pierre Potier rightly states, "List's theories were not purely German". There are stronger French and American influences from a period when the economies of these two countries were the closest followers of the leading British economy. According to List free trade was a valuable ideal for competitors with some degree of equality in their stage of development. If this condition was not met, some form of protectionism aimed at the optimal development of national productive forces was necessary: the infant-industry argument. In the Paulskirchen parliament of 1848 the trade debate was one of the most important ones in which the followers of List, mainly from Southern Germany, finally got a majority for the levying of tariffs to protect the domestic economy, whereas the *Zollverein*, the Customs Union which had been established under Prussian leadership in 1834, initially favoured free trade ideas.[10]

As comes up in most contributions, the free trade versus protectionism debate was a controversy which took place in almost all countries. In contrast to an overly simplified view, often stated, that the members of the GHS were more interventionist and therefore tended to favour protectionism, the editors of this volume, José Luís Cardoso and Michalis Psalidopoulos, are rightly more cautious when they state in their introduction that this would be a misleading interpretation, and protectionism (in the sense of the cosmopolitan Friedrich List) "was not simply a departure from free trade. It was in line with liberal principles of governance and a tool to shape society by fostering its developmental potential", an argument attractive for all latecomers –that is economies which undergo a catching-up process – as for example made clear in the contribution by Jesús Astigarraga and Juan Zabalza.

In fact Bismarck's reorientation towards protective tariffs led to the greatest crisis of the *Verein für Sozialpolitik*, which even endangered its survival. The 1879 conference in Frankfurt, which took the tariff question as the central topic, was characterized by heavy controversies between free traders and protectionists. Main representatives of the opposing views were the chairman, Nasse, a committed liberal favouring free trade, and Schmoller. Whereas in his younger years he had strongly favoured a liberal trade policy and argued against protective tariffs, Schmoller now followed Bismarck in his reorientation of trade policy. Due to an unusually high attendance of industrialists and agricultural protectionists, the liberals lost the final vote in the general assembly.[11] It may have contributed to this outcome that Lujo Brentano (1840–1931), the most liberal and Anglophile member of the younger GHS and a charismatic speaker, could not attend the Frankfurt meeting for health reasons. Although he was a lifelong friend of Schmoller, Brentano strongly dissented from Schmoller's change of view on the trade question. He was deeply convinced that the industrialised German economy required free trade in order to supply cheap food for the workers, as in Britain after the final abolition of the corn laws, and to generate export markets for industrial goods.

Brentano had been a strong supporter of trade unions ever since he had made a long visit to Britain in 1868–1869 together with Ernst Engel. He was deeply convinced that the organized coalition of workers was the decisive means to solve the labour question, which became the central topic of his life. It was Brentano's Strassburg PhD student Heinrich Herkner (1863–1932) who wrote the classical book on the labour question (Herkner, 1894), which went into eight editions until 1922 and was translated into several European languages.[12] Brentano had also been in closer contact with Alfred Marshall over more than three decades, in particular on the social question and the labour movement. He was instrumental in publishing a German edition of Marshall's *Principles of Economics* in 1905, with a preface by Brentano, who was one of the few contemporary German professors who used Marshall's writings in his lectures.

The other notable exception from a widespread ignorance or only superficial reception was Adolph Wagner (1835–1917), Brentano's lifelong enemy and Schmoller's colleague in Berlin, who wrote a very favourable review of Marshall's *Principles*. He used this opportunity to publish in a leading international journal to strike at Schmoller and other members of the GHS in welcoming Marshall's work as a refined version of Ricardo's theory and pointing out that not all contemporary economists "approve of the patronizing and pretentious attitude towards English writers, and especially those of the classic school, which is taken by some of the extreme German representatives of the historical school" (Wagner, 1891: 319–320). Wagner probably was the best incarnation of a state socialist who reflected a characteristic German blend of social conservatism based on an organic concept of the state and the rejection of economic liberalism. Like Schmoller, he was a great admirer of Bismarck and believed in the implementation of distributive justice by the government. In contrast to Schmoller, he was steering a middle course between the GHS and a more theoretically oriented approach. Together with Lorenz von Stein (1815–1890) and Albert Schäffle (1831–1903), Wagner formed the "triumvirate" of German public finance (*Finanzwissenschaft*). Wagner today is mainly remembered for his historical "law of increasing expansion of public, and particularly state, activities" ("Wagner's law"). Wagner favoured progressive income taxation, taxes on wealth, inheritance, luxury and capital gains in his teachings and writings and executed a considerable influence on his students, including the foreign ones. This comes out very well in several of the contributions, particularly in those on Sweden and Spain. An important figure in that context was also Edwin R. A. Seligman, who had studied in Berlin and Heidelberg from 1879 to 1881, and later as a professor at Columbia University was a leading proponent of a progressive income tax.[13]

Less astonishing is that the GHS had a stronger impact on the development of *economic history* as an important subdiscipline, as comes out best in the contribution on Belgium, or Günther Chaloupek's discussion of the works of Karl-Theodor von Inama-Sternegg, Carl Grünberg and Karl Pribram, but also in the contribution on Turkey.

Overall, the comparative perspective followed in this volume shows a variety of approaches and differences in the diffusion and dissemination process. Language problems constituted a major barrier in some countries, such as Spain or Portugal, where the diffusion often took place via French or Italian translations, or later in Turkey even when the émigré economists were teaching there during the Nazi period. Several of the contributions focus on individuals as important carriers of the dissemination process. This sometimes has more the flavour of "German influences" than of a precise analysis of the diffusion, impact and legacy of the GHS. However, such a procedure is partly unavoidable and, moreover, can highlight important aspects. Vito Cusumano, for example, who not only is referred to by Vitantonio Gioia in his contribution on Italy but also figures prominently in Jean-Pierre Potier's contribution concerning his correspondence with Walras, attended the foundation conference of the *Verein für Sozialpolitik* in Eisenach. Two years later he published a book on the German school of economics on the social question, which caused the critical response entitled "Economic Germanism in Italy" by Francesco Ferrara, which initiated the debate on method in Italy. Seemingly, both sides were talking of a GHS, although it is not an easy task to precisely define what really constitutes a historical school. There even existed a historical school in England, where the social question in an industrialising economy came up first. So the historical approach was not an exclusively German phenomenon. It is clear that in the strict sense of Schumpeter an older GHS did not exist. As Streissler (1990) has shown, the contributions of German economists to utility theory in the nineteenth century had a strong influence on Carl Menger and the Austrian School and to a certain degree also on Alfred Marshall, an argument recently affirmed in greater detail by Chipman (2014), which elucidates that economics in Germany was not completely atheoretical. The cases of Brentano and Wagner show that even in the period of Schmoller and his followers – that is of the younger GHS – a certain variety existed. This falls together with the economic and political rise of Germany between 1871 and 1914, when the reputation of German academic institutions was at its international peak. At that time in Germany more than elsewhere historical arguments entered into economics. This had a certain influence on the next generation, where stronger historical elements can be traced in the works of the most outstanding representatives, such as Sombart, Spiethoff, Weber or even Schumpeter, but with a stronger bent, and in a different degree, for theoretical analysis.

Notes

1 For a critical assessment of Pearson's thesis, see also the convincing arguments by Knut Borchardt and Karl Häuser in Nau and Schefold (2002: 44–55).
2 For greater details see Rieter (2002).
3 For greater details on German economists in parliament in the liberal age, see Hagemann and Rösch (2005).
4 See Schumpeter (1954: 507, 808).
5 For the history of the *Verein*, see Hagemann (2001).
6 Schumpeter, who in his earlier review article of the third volume of Sombart's *Modern Capitalism* had recognized Sombart's right to call his work economic history and economic theory at the same time (Schumpeter 1927: 352), later appropriately considered Sombart's work as a "vision of the historical process that has an artistic quality and is drawn into the sphere of science by being nourished with historical fact and expressed by means of a primitive analysis", a work of "unsubstantial brilliance", based on "second-hand" material, in which Sombart "even out-Schmollered Schmoller" (Schumpeter, 1954: 816–818).
7 On the role and influence of the GHS in American economic thought, see Dorfman (1955), Herbst (1965), Schmalz (1998) and Bateman (2011).
8 For greater details see Morris-Suzuki (1990: 62–69) and Kumagai (2001).
9 See also Shionoya's own contributions (2005).
10 See Hagemann and Rösch (2005: 171).
11 For greater details see Hagemann (2001: 156–160).
12 Ironically after having become more conservative, Herkner later succeeded Schmoller in his chair at the University of Berlin (1910) and as chairman of the *Verein für Sozialpolitik* (1917–1930).
13 For a thorough investigation of the transfer of ideas in public finance from the German language area to the United States in the period 1865–1917, see the recent study by Schulz (2013).

References

Bateman, B. (2011). German influences in the making of American economics, 1885–1935, in H. D. Kurz, T. Nishizawa, and K. Tribe (eds.), *The Dissemination of Economic Ideas*. Cheltenham, UK: Edward Elgar, 108–124.

Böhm-Bawerk, E. von (1886). Grundzüge der Theorie des wirtschaftlichen Güterwerthes. *Jahrbücher für Nationalökonomie und Statistik*, 47: 1–82, 477–541.

Caldwell, B. (2001). There really *was* a German Historical School of economics. *History of Political Economy*, 33 (3): 649–654.

Chipman, J. S. (2005), Contributions of the older German schools to the development of utility theory, in C. Scheer (ed.), *Studien zur Entwicklung der ökonomischen Theorie. Vol. 20: Die Ältere Historische Schule: Wirtschaftstheoretische Beiträge und wirtschaftspolitische Vorstellungen*. Berlin: Duncker & Humblot, 157–259.

Chipman, J. S. (2014). *German Utility Theory: Analysis and Translations*. Abingdon: Routledge.

Dorfman, J. (1955). The role of the German Historical School in American economic thought. *American Economic Review*, Papers and Proceedings, 45: 17–28.

Eisermann, G. (1956). *Die Grundlagen des Historismus in der deutschen Nationalökonomie*. Stuttgart: Enke.

Grimmer-Solem, E. and Romani, R. (1999). The historical school, 1870–1900: A cross-national reassessment. *History of Economic Ideas*, 24: 267–299.

Hagemann, H. (2001). The Verein für Sozialpolitik from its foundation (1872) until World War I, in M. M. Augello and M.E.L. Guidi (eds.), *The Spread of Political Economy and the Professionalisation of Economists. Economic Societies in Europe, America and Japan in the Nineteenth Century*. London: Routledge, 152–175.

Hagemann, H. and Rösch, M. (2005). German economists in Parliament (1848–1918), in M. M. Augello and M.E.L. Guidi (eds.), *Economists in Parliament in the Liberal Age (1848–1920)*. Aldershot: Ashgate, 163–189.

Häuser, K. (1994), Das Ende der historischen Schule und die Ambiguität der deutschen Nationalökonomie in den zwanziger Jahren, in K. W. Nörr, B. Schefold and F. Tenbruck (eds.), *Geisteswissenschaften zwischen Kaiserreich und Republik*. Stuttgart: Franz Steiner, 47–74.

Herbst, J. (1965). *The German Historical School in American Scholarship: A Study in the Transfer of Culture*. Ithaca: Cornell University Press.

Herkner, H. (1894). *Die Arbeiterfrage: Eine Einführung*. Berlin: J. Guttentag.

Knies, K.G.A. (1850). *Die Statistik als selbständige Wissenschaft*. Kassel: J. Luckhardt.

Knies, K.G.A. (1853). *Die politische Oekonomie vom Standpunkt der geschichtlichen Methode*. Braunschweig: Schwetschke (2nd ed., 1883). *Die politische Oekonomie vom geschichtlichen Standpuncte*. Braunschweig: Schwetschke.

Knies, K.G.A. (1855). Die nationaloekonomische Lehre vom Werth. *Zeitschrift für die gesammte Staatswissenschaft*, 11: 421–475.

Kumagai, J. (2001). Orchestrating economic ideas: The formation and development of economic societies in modern Japan, in M. M. Augello and M.E.L. Guidi (eds.), *The Spread of Political Economy and the Professionalisation of Economists: Economic Societies in Europe, America and Japan in the Nineteenth Century*. London: Routledge, 200–215.

Marshall, A. (1890 [1905]). *Handbuch der Volkswirtschaftslehre (Principles of Economics)*. Trans. by H. Ephraim and A. Salz. Stuttgart: Cotta.

Morris-Suzuki, T. (1990). *A History of Japanese Economic Thought*. London: Routledge.

Nau, H.H. and Schefold, B. (2002). *The Historicity of Economics: Continuities and Discontinuities of Historical Thought in 19th- and 20th-Century Economics*. Berlin: Springer.

Pearson, H. (1999). Was there really a German historical school of economics? *History of Political Economy*, 31: 547–562.

Pearson, H. (2002). The German historical school of economics: What it was not, and what it was, in Nau and Schefold (eds.), 23–43.

Pearson, H. (2008). Historical school, German, in S. N. Durlauf and L. E. Blume (eds.), *The New Palgrave Dictionary of Economics*, 2nd ed. New York: Palgrave Macmillan.

Rieter, H. (2002). Historische Schulen, in O. Issing (ed.), *Geschichte der Nationalökonomie*. Munich: Franz Vahlen, 130–168.

Roscher, W. (1843). *Grundriss zu Vorlesungen über die Staatswirthschaft, nach geschichtlicher Methode*. Göttingen: Dieter.

Roscher, W. (1874). *Geschichte der National-Oekonomik in Deutschland*. Munich: R. Oldenbourg.

Schmalz, G. (1998). *Der Richtungsstreit in der früheren amerikanischen Wirtschaftslehre und der Einfluss der Deutschen Historischen Schule*. Marburg: Metropolis.

Schmoller, G. von (1900–1904). *Grundriss der Allgemeinen Volkswirtschaftslehre*, 2 vols. Munich: Duncker & Humblot.

Schulz, J.P. (2013). *Finanzwissenschaft im deutschsprachigen Raum und in den Vereinigten Staaten, 1865–1917*. Marburg: Metropolis.

Schumpeter, J.A. (1927). Sombarts Dritter Band. *Schmollers Jahrbuch*, 51: 349–369.

Schumpeter, J.A. (1939). *Business Cycles: A Theoretical, Historical and Statistical Analysis of the Capitalist Process.* 2 vols. New York: McGraw-Hill.

Schumpeter, J.A. (1954). *History of Economic Analysis.* New York: Oxford University Press; London: Allen & Unwin.

Shionoya, Y. (ed.) (2001). *The German Historical School: The Historical and Ethical Approach to Economics.* London: Routledge.

Shionoya, Y. (2005). *The Soul of the German Historical School: Methodological Essays on Schmoller, Weber and Schumpeter.* New York: Springer.

Sombart, W. (1902 [1987]). *Der moderne Kapitalismus: Historisch-systematische Darstellung des gesamteuropäischen Wirtschaftslebens von seinen Anfängen bis zur Gegenwart.* 3 vols. Munich: Deutscher Taschenbuch Verlag.

Streissler, E.W. (1990). The influence of German economics on the work of Menger and Marshall, in B.J. Caldwell (ed.), *Carl Menger and His Legacy on Economics.* Annual supplement to *History of Political Economy*, vol. 22. Durham: Duke University Press, 31–68.

Streissler, E.W. (1994). The influence of German and Austrian economics on Joseph A. Schumpeter, in Y. Shionoya and M. Perlman (eds.), *Schumpeter in the History of Ideas.* Ann Arbor: University of Michigan Press.

Wagner, A. (1891). Marshall's principles of economics. *Quarterly Journal of Economics*, 5 (3): 318–338.

Weber, M. (1904). Die "Objektivität" sozialwissenschaftlicher und sozialpolitischer Erkenntnis. *Archiv für Sozialwissenschaft und Sozialpolitik*, 19 (1): 22–87.

Wicksell, K. (1892). Kapitalzins und Arbeitslohn. *Jahrbücher für Nationalökonomie und Statistik*, 59: 552–574.

Wilbrandt, R. (1926). Das Ende der historisch-ethischen Schule. *Weltwirtschaftliches Archiv*, 24 (2): 73–108, 228–274.

Winkel, H. (1977). *Die deutsche Nationalökonomie im 19. Jahrhundert*, Darmstadt: Wissenschaftliche Buchgesellschaft.

Name index

For Product Safety Concerns and Information please contact our EU
representative GPSR@taylorandfrancis.com
Taylor & Francis Verlag GmbH, Kaufingerstraße 24, 80331 München, Germany

www.ingramcontent.com/pod-product-compliance
Ingram Content Group UK Ltd.
Pitfield, Milton Keynes, MK11 3LW, UK
UKHW021009180425
457613UK00019B/861

* 9 7 8 0 3 6 7 8 7 4 6 2 9 *